Natural Resource Management Reimagined

The systems ecology paradigm (SEP) incorporates humans as integral parts of ecosystems and emphasizes issues that have significant societal relevance such as grazing land, forestland, agricultural ecosystem management, biodiversity, and global change impacts. Accomplishing this societally relevant research requires cutting-edge basic and applied research. This book focuses on environmental and natural resource challenges confronting local to global societies for which the SEP methodology must be utilized for resolution. Key elements of SEP are a holistic perspective of ecological/social systems, systems thinking, and the ecosystem approach applied to real-world, complex environmental and natural resource problems. The SEP and ecosystem approaches force scientific emphasis to be placed on collaborations with social scientists and behavioral, learning, and marketing professionals. The SEP has given environmental scientists, decision makers, citizen stakeholders, and land and water managers a powerful set of tools to analyze, integrate knowledge, and propose adoption of solutions to important local to global problems.

ROBERT G. WOODMANSEE is Professor Emeritus and former Director of the Natural Resource Ecology Laboratory (NREL) at Colorado State University (CSU). He is also a former Program Director for Ecosystem Studies at the US National Science Foundation, and a founding member of the Long-Term Ecological Research (LTER) Program. His research interests are in biogeochemistry and landscape ecology, including spatial and temporal scaling in ecosystems.

JOHN C. MOORE is Professor in the Department of Ecosystem Science and Sustainability and Director of the NREL at Colorado State University. His research interests are in the fields of soil ecology, mathematical/theoretical ecology, and the application of the theory of complex adaptive systems to teaching and learning. His research on food web structure, function, and dynamics is positioned at the interfaces of community ecology, ecosystem ecology, and evolution linking species traits and adaptions to biogeochemical cycles.

DENNIS S. OJIMA is Professor in the Ecosystem Science and Sustainability Department and a senior research scientist in the NREL at Colorado State University. His research addresses climate change effects on ecosystems around the world. He was involved in the Millennium Ecosystem Assessment, the Intergovernmental Panel on Climate Change (IPCC), and in 2007 received the Nobel Peace Prize for his work on the latter.

LAURIE RICHARDS serves as a pre-award research administrator for approximately eighty-three research scientists and graduate students from both the NREL and Department of Ecosystem Science and Sustainability (ESS). She also acts as the publication editor and manager assisting NREL/ESS scientific staff with manuscript submission to many scientific journals.

ECOLOGY, BIODIVERSITY AND CONSERVATION

The world's biological diversity faces unprecedented threats. The urgent challenge facing the concerned biologist is to understand ecological processes well enough to maintain their functioning in the face of the pressures resulting from human population growth. Those concerned with the conservation of biodiversity and with restoration also need to be acquainted with the political, social, historical, economic and legal frameworks within which ecological and conservation practice must be developed. The new Ecology, Biodiversity, and Conservation series will present balanced, comprehensive, up-to-date, and critical reviews of selected topics within the sciences of ecology and conservation biology, both botanical and zoological, and both 'pure' and 'applied'. It is aimed at advanced final-year undergraduates, graduate students, researchers, and university teachers, as well as ecologists and conservationists in industry, government and the voluntary sectors. The series encompasses a wide range of approaches and scales (spatial, temporal, and taxonomic), including quantitative, theoretical, population, community, ecosystem, landscape, historical, experimental, behavioural and evolutionary studies. The emphasis is on science related to the real world of plants and animals rather than on purely theoretical abstractions and mathematical models. Books in this series will, wherever possible, consider issues from a broad perspective. Some books will challenge existing paradigms and present new ecological concepts, empirical or theoretical models, and testable hypotheses. Other books will explore new approaches and present syntheses on topics of ecological importance.

Ecology and Control of Introduced Plants
Judith H. Myers and Dawn Bazely

Invertebrate Conservation and Agricultural Ecosystems
T. R. New

Natural Resource Management Reimagined

Using the Systems Ecology Paradigm

Edited by

ROBERT G. WOODMANSEE
Colorado State University

JOHN C. MOORE
Colorado State University

DENNIS S. OJIMA
Colorado State University

LAURIE RICHARDS
Colorado State University

CAMBRIDGE
UNIVERSITY PRESS

CAMBRIDGE
UNIVERSITY PRESS

University Printing House, Cambridge CB2 8BS, United Kingdom

One Liberty Plaza, 20th Floor, New York, NY 10006, USA

477 Williamstown Road, Port Melbourne, VIC 3207, Australia

314–321, 3rd Floor, Plot 3, Splendor Forum, Jasola District Centre, New Delhi – 110025, India

79 Anson Road, #06–04/06, Singapore 079906

Cambridge University Press is part of the University of Cambridge.

It furthers the University's mission by disseminating knowledge in the pursuit of education, learning, and research at the highest international levels of excellence.

www.cambridge.org
Information on this title: www.cambridge.org/9781108497558

DOI: 10.1017/9781108655354

First published 2021

Printed in the United Kingdom by TJ Books Limited, Padstow Cornwall

A catalogue record for this publication is available from the British Library.

ISBN 978-1-108-49755-8 Hardback
ISBN 978-1-108-74013-5 Paperback

Contents

The plate section can be found between pp. 204 and 205.

Contributors

Authors

CAMERON ALDRIDGE, Natural Resource Ecology Laboratory and Department of Ecosystem Science and Sustainability, Colorado State University, Fort Collins, CO, United States.

DANIEL BINKLEY, Natural Resource Ecology Laboratory, Colorado State University, Fort Collins, CO, United States.

RANDALL B. BOONE, Natural Resource Ecology Laboratory and Department of Ecosystem Science and Sustainability, Colorado State University, Fort Collins, CO, United States.

INGRID BURKE, School of Forestry and Environmental Studies, Yale University, New Haven, CT, United States.

ELEANOR E. CAMPBELL, Earth Systems Research Center, University of New Hampshire, Durham, NH, United States.

DAVID C. COLEMAN, Odum School of Ecology, University of Georgia, Athens, GA, United States.

RICHARD CONANT, Natural Resource Ecology Laboratory and Department of Ecosystem Science and Sustainability, Colorado State University, Fort Collins, CO, United States.

MICHAEL B. COUGHENOUR, Natural Resource Ecology Laboratory, Colorado State University, Fort Collins, CO, United States.

STEPHEN J. DEL GROSSO, United States Department of Agriculture, Agricultural Research Service, Fort Collins, Colorado, United States.

JAMES K. DETLING, Natural Resource Ecology Laboratory and Department of Biology, Colorado State University, Fort Collins, CO, United States.

PAUL H. EVANGELISTA, Natural Resource Ecology Laboratory, Colorado State University, Fort Collins, CO, United States.

KATHLEEN GALVIN, Natural Resource Ecology Laboratory and Department of Anthropology, Colorado State University, Fort Collins, CO, United States.

WEI GAO, Natural Resource Ecology Laboratory and Department of Ecosystem Science and Sustainability, Colorado State University, Fort Collins, CO, United States.

MELANIE D. HARTMAN, Natural Resource Ecology Laboratory, Colorado State University, Fort Collins, CO, United States.

JACOB HAUTALUOMA, Department of Psychology, Colorado State University, Fort Collins, CO, United States.

N. T. HOBBS, Natural Resource Ecology Laboratory and Department of Ecosystem Science and Sustainability, Colorado State University, Fort Collins, CO, United States.

H. W. HUNT, Natural Resource Ecology Laboratory, Colorado State University, Fort Collins, CO, United States.

NICOLE E. KAPLAN, United States Department of Agriculture, Agricultural Research Service, Fort Collins, Colorado, United States.

SUNIL KUMAR, Animal and Plant Inspection Service, United States Department of Agriculture, Raleigh, NC, United States.

WILLIAM LAUENROTH, School of Forestry and Environmental Studies, Yale University, New Haven, CT, United States.

STACY LYNN, Natural Resource Ecology Laboratory, Colorado State University, Fort Collins, CO, United States.

JOHN C. MOORE, Natural Resource Ecology Laboratory and Department of Ecosystem Science and Sustainability, Colorado State University, Fort Collins, CO, United States.

GREGORY NEWMAN, Natural Resource Ecology Laboratory, Colorado State University, Fort Collins, CO, United States.

STEPHEN OGLE, Natural Resource Ecology Laboratory and Department of Ecosystem Science and Sustainability, Colorado State University, Fort Collins, CO, United States.

DENNIS S. OJIMA, Natural Resource Ecology Laboratory and Department of Ecosystem Science and Sustainability, Colorado State University, Fort Collins, CO, United States.

WILLIAM J. PARTON, Natural Resource Ecology Laboratory and Department of Ecosystem Science and Sustainability, Colorado State University, Fort Collins, CO, United States.

ELDOR A. PAUL, Natural Resource Ecology Laboratory and Department of Soil and Crop Science, Colorado State University, Fort Collins, CO, United States.

KEITH PAUSTIAN, Natural Resource Ecology Laboratory and Department of Soil and Crop Science, Colorado State University, Fort Collins, CO, United States.

ROBIN REID, Natural Resource Ecology Laboratory and Department of Ecosystem Science and Sustainability, Colorado State University, Fort Collins, CO, United States.

LAURIE RICHARDS, Natural Resource Ecology Laboratory, Colorado State University, Fort Collins, CO, United States.

MONIQUE E. ROCCA, Natural Resource Ecology Laboratory and Department of Ecosystem Science and Sustainability, Colorado State University, Fort Collins, CO, United States.

WILLIAM H. ROMME, Natural Resource Ecology Laboratory, Colorado State University, Fort Collins, CO, United States.

THOMAS ROSSWALL, Bellmansgatan 5, SE-118 20, Stockholm, Sweden.

MICHAEL G. RYAN, Natural Resource Ecology Laboratory, Colorado State University, Fort Collins, CO, United States.

DAVID S. SCHIMEL, Jet Propulsion Laboratory, California Institute of Technology, Pasadena, CA, United States.

THOMAS J. STOHLGREN, Natural Resource Ecology Laboratory, Colorado State University, Fort Collins, CO, United States.

DAVID M. SWIFT, Natural Resource Ecology Laboratory and Department of Ecosystem Science and Sustainability, Colorado State University, Fort Collins, CO, United States.

MATHEW WALLENSTEIN, Natural Resource Ecology Laboratory and Department of Soil and Crop Science, Colorado State University, Fort Collins, CO, United States.

CLARA J. WOODMANSEE, Consultant in Human Resources, State of Colorado, Denver, CO, United States.

KATHERINE S. WOODMANSEE, Consultant in Adult Learning and Education, Fort Collins, CO, United States.

ROBERT G. WOODMANSEE, Natural Resource Ecology Laboratory, Colorado State University, Fort Collins, CO, United States.

SARAH R. WOODMANSEE, Consultant in Rural Social Services, Oak Creek, CO, United States.

Preface

ROBERT G. WOODMANSEE, JOHN C.
MOORE, DENNIS S. OJIMA, AND LAURIE
RICHARDS

This book is dedicated to Dr. George M. Van Dyne, founder in 1967 and first Director of the Natural Resource Ecology Laboratory (NREL) and the Grassland Biome of the US International Biological Program. Dr. Van Dyne was editor of the book *The Ecosystem Concept in Natural Resource Management* (Van Dyne, 1969). The NREL and its network of collaborators throughout the world evolved to become one of the epicenters of development of ecosystem science and systems ecology. This book, *Natural Resource Management Reimagined: Using the Systems Ecology Paradigm*, commemorates more than 50 years of excellence in ecosystem science initiated by Van Dyne, one of the "fathers" of systems ecology.

The concept for this book evolved after co-editor Dr. Robert G. Woodmansee presented a paper, "The Rise of Ecosystem Ecology and its Applications to Environmental Challenges," at a symposium (Celebratory Symposium for ESA Century Anniversary) organized by Dr. Jill Baron at the European Ecology Federation annual meeting in Rome in September 2015. Dr. Woodmansee was approached by Dr. Michael Usher, series editor for the *Ecology, Biodiversity, and Conservation* series of books published by Cambridge University Press, about developing a book exploring ecosystem ecology based on the Rome presentation. Earlier co-editor Dr. John C. Moore had talked with Dominic Lewis of Cambridge University Press about developing a book celebrating the 50th anniversary of the NREL at Colorado State University. Woodmansee and Moore decided to combine these efforts.

Ecology (the study of the interactions of organisms and their environment) is a wonderful way to explain how the natural world works. But understanding the natural world is not enough as we face both current and future threats to our environments, natural resources, and societies. These threats require considerations of spatial scales ranging from nanometers to the globe, temporal scales of minutes to centuries or more, and institutional scales from households to multinational enterprises.

Scientific approaches and collaboration among many individuals, disciplines, and world views are critically needed to integrate vast amounts of knowledge in systematic ways and produce beneficial management options now and for the future. The editors of this book present the systems ecology paradigm (SEP) as *the right science and analytical approach at the right time* for resolving many of the Earth's natural resource, environmental, and societal challenges. The "go-to" SEP integrates mathematical simulation modeling, field and laboratory research, and transdisciplinary collaboration to accomplish its goals. SEP embodies two major components. First, the *systems ecology approach* is the holistic, systems perspective and methodology developed for the rigorous study of ecosystems. Second is the use of *ecosystem science*, the vast body of scientific knowledge much of which has been assembled using the "ecosystem approach" first envisioned in the book *The Ecosystem Concept in Natural Resource Management* (Van Dyne, 1969). SEP evolved at Colorado State University since the NREL's founding.

The editors all "grew up" professionally in the culture of the NREL. Robert G. Woodmansee began at the NREL as a graduate student in 1969 and became its third director from 1984 to 1992. He is a plant ecologist, range and soil scientist, ecosystem scientist, and systems ecologist. He was a member of the original USIBP Grassland Ecosystem Model (ELM) modeling team. He has practical ecosystem management experience having grown up on a farm in rural New Mexico and operating a farm/ranch in northern Colorado. John C. Moore joined NREL as a graduate student in 1982 and became its current director in 2006. John is a zoologist, soil ecologist, theoretical ecologist, and ecosystem scientist. Dennis S. Ojima became involved with the NREL as a graduate student in 1982 and was an interim director in 2005–6. He is a systems ecologist with training in plant ecology and soil science and a background of farming in rural California. Laurie Richards has proofread and edited the majority of publications, research proposals, and project reports generated by NREL staff over the past two decades.

As students of biology and ecology, each had learned about the natural world and how management might affect farmlands, ranches, and forests. Studying at Colorado State University in their PhD programs in systems ecology and ecosystem science, joining the NREL, and working on various derivatives of the ELM, all learned that knowledge and expertise about the natural world is essential but insufficient to explain ecosystem functioning, especially when humans are introduced as components of those systems. Their careers have been spent attempting to utilize systems thinking and the ecological knowledge base generated by researchers and practitioners around the world to explain how the world works. This book represents a benchmark in that quest and argues that the SEP is essential for understanding and resolving many critical real-world, complex environmental and natural resource challenges (sometimes called "wicked problems") facing societies around the world (e.g., changing climates; food and water security; loss of biodiversity; and pollution of our lands, air, and, waters).

Material presented in this book emphasizes the work of NREL scientists and their extensive network of national and international collaborators. The authors have attempted to recognize other ecosystem scientists and systems ecologists who have contributed to this science. They have not attempted to write a definitive review of all ecosystem science and systems ecology.

The general organizing principles of the application of SEP and steps involved in its application are presented throughout the book. Underpinning the fundamental philosophy of SEP is the belief that all members of society, both present and future, should have the right to conduct *activities* to meet their needs and all are entitled to live in a world that offers good health, well-being, dignity, and food and water security. Simultaneously, people are responsible for minimizing the known negative impacts of their activities. Science, policy making, management, and human behavior must be integrated to insure human and environmental needs are met.

The editors hope that non-ecosystem scientists, policy makers, land managers, science and academic administrators, enlightened community thought leaders, and students will take advantage of the 50 years of historical knowledge and philosophy of systems ecology depicted in here. Beyond gaining an historical overview of the evolution of a scientific discipline, systems ecology, the editors hope readers will gain knowledge of current groundbreaking research addressing critical real world, complex problems confronting the Earth's ecosystems and societies. All stakeholders with varying viewpoints will need to work collaboratively to resolve very complex societal and environmental problems.

Ecosystem science and systems ecology emerged as legitimate branches of science in the late 1960s when societies everywhere were beginning to recognize that our environment and natural resources were being threatened by human activities. Management practices in rangelands, forests, agricultural lands, wetlands, and waterways were inadequate to meet the challenges of deteriorating environments. Scientists recognized an immediate need to develop a knowledge base about how ecosystems function (dynamic interactions of processes), not just how they are physically structured (appear). Two decades were needed for this approach to develop and concluded with the acceptance that humans were integral components of ecosystems, not simply controllers and manipulators of lands and waters. Ecosystem science and systems ecology have flourished because of their fundamental contributions to our understanding of natural resources and the environment. Scientific knowledge about the structure and functioning of ecosystems, the services ecosystems provide to people, and the roles people play therein have become commonplace.

As ecosystem science matured, management options based on the systems approach began shifting solely from production of commodities to practices supporting sustainability, resilience, ecosystem services, biodiversity, and interconnections of ecosystems. Today's concepts of ecosystem management and related ideas such as sustainable agriculture, ecosystem health and restoration, consequences of and adaptation to climate change, and many other important challenges are a direct result of the systems thinking and methodology expressed in SEP. Emerging from the new knowledge about how ecosystems function and the application of the ecosystem approach is the realization among scientists, managers, policy makers, and key stakeholders that collaboration is needed and essential. SEP is meeting this need.

SEP incorporates human behavior as an integral part of ecosystems and emphasizes issues that have significant societal relevance such as management of grazing land, forestland, agricultural, and aquatic ecosystems. Application of the SEP is needed by societies to confront and resolve threats to global well-being.

Systems ecologists and ecosystem scientists know what challenges face Earth's environments and they know many of the solutions available to resolve them. Yet, scientific knowledge alone cannot implement change. Transfer of reliable scientific knowledge to people who manage our lands, waters, and other natural resources is essential. Land and water managers must become engaged in implementing solutions to major natural resource and environmental challenges because they are the people who ultimately determine what management practices are applied to the land and waters. Adoption of new concepts and technologies (best management practices) by managers of vast areas of lands and waters are needed to resolve many challenges (e.g., carbon sequestration, water quality and quantity in river basins, nitrogen loading in land and aquatic ecosystems, and soil loss in watersheds). Overcoming the barriers to adoption of best management practices is critically needed, and soon. Some barriers to adoption are clearly pragmatic such as economic constraints, cost of conversion, labor availability, age of manager or owner, and access to reliable knowledge. Other barriers are created by adherence to detrimental and dogmatic cultural norms and ideologies by landowners, managers, and policy makers. Overcoming detrimental barriers requires behavioral change in individuals and groups.

Behavioral, organizational, learning, and marketing professionals study behavioral change. Further application of SEP will require incorporating behavioral, organizational, learning, and marketing professionals as partners with systems ecologists. All are needed to implement the concept and technology of adoption and community-based social marketing to solve real world, complex management problems.

George Van Dyne's vision, shared by the editors of this volume, of inclusiveness and collaboration across disciplines, organizational status, and nationality makes it impossible to acknowledge all those individuals who made major contributions to the systems ecology paradigm and this book. You know who you are. Thank you!

Special thanks go to Dr. Michael Usher for his guidance and review of early drafts of chapters. Also, special acknowledgment is given to Sarah R. Woodmansee for patience, invaluable ideas and suggestions, support, and critical editing.

References

Van Dyne, G. (1969). *The Ecosystem Concept in Natural Resource Management*. New York: Academic Press.

1 · *The Systems Ecology Paradigm*

ROBERT G. WOODMANSEE,
JOHN C. MOORE, AND DENNIS S. OJIMA

> The problems of today cannot be solved by the level of thinking that caused them.
>
> Albert Einstein

1.1 Introduction

Addressing the challenges facing the Earth's ecosystems and societies will require innovative and powerful concepts and associated technologies to solve, mitigate, or adapt to the complex realities of the twenty-first century (Box 1.1; see Chapter 2). We use the term *ecosystem* as a blending of two words, *ecology* and *system*. Ecology, derived from the Greek *oikos* or *dwelling/house*, is the study of the interactions of organisms, including humans, with each other and their environment. System can be defined as a group of parts that operate together for a common purpose or function.[1] The term *ecosystem* must have a modifier (i.e., grazingland, forest, agricultural, urban, stream, patch, landscape, etc.), and must be defined in space and time to become a recognizable and definable "thing." The term can also be used to modify a noun as in ecosystem ecology, defined as the study of the biological, living (biotic), and physical, nonliving (abiotic) interactions within a geographic unit, with or without considering humans as parts of those systems. The definition is dependent on the problem or issue being addressed.

We argue in this book that the systems ecology paradigm (SEP) is an innovative concept that has proven enormously valuable in gaining an understanding of and suggesting resolutions for real-world environmental, natural resource, and societal challenges. SEP embodies two major components: (1) *SEP* (Van Dyne, 1969; Montague, 2018) which is the holistic, systems perspective (Systems Perspective, 2019) and

---

[1] "Introduction to Systems – A Primer," www2.nrel.colostate.edu/projects/LandCenter/Systems_Primer/index.htm. Click here for instructions using the "primer". Last accessed August 3, 2020.

Box 1.1 *Some changes occurring now in the real and complex world of interacting disturbances and uncertainties*

- Food security (production and distribution);
- Natural resource security (water, air, soil, primary and secondary productivity, and biodiversity);
- Demand for limited natural resources;
- Human population growth, migration, shifting demographics, and consequences;
- Changing climate and weather extremes;
- Changing atmospheric, soil, water, and biomass chemistry;
- Technology;
- Transportation infrastructure;
- Terrorism and war;
- Changing social and political structures and leadership.

---

methodology developed for the rigorous study of ecosystems, and (2) the use of *ecosystem science* which is the vast body of scientific knowledge much of which has been assembled using the "ecosystem approach" (Biodiversity A–Z, 2018; UNMEA, 2018). SEP employs the use of dynamic mathematical simulation models to integrate information and yield projections about future outcomes of ecosystem dynamics and is the application of ecosystem science using a systematic methodology based on facts and evidence (see Chapter 4). This book draws heavily on 50 years of contributions by scientists at the Natural Resource Ecology Laboratory (NREL, 2018) at Colorado State University and its world-wide network of collaborators to address the fundamental challenges shown in Box 1.1.

The major objectives of this book are to demonstrate how SEP has allowed ecosystem scientists and managers to gain fundamental under-standing of the structure and functioning of ecosystems (see Chapters 6, 8, and 9) and how that fundamental understanding has contributed to better management of, and policy making about, some ecosystems (see Chapter 7). This knowledge base has been gained using the integration of scientific discovery and the synthesis of concepts derived from the work of transdisciplinary teams of scientists who specialize in many different aspects of ecosystems. Given the current knowledge of the fundamental function-ing of ecosystems, scientists are able to forecast the role SEP must play to address both current and future challenges facing the Earth's ecosystems, natural resources, and human societies (see Chapters 2 and 13).

However, science alone is not enough (Abelson, 1993). If the science is to be relevant and make an impact on how we use and manage natural resources, it needs to be made available to land managers and policy makers in forms that they can use. They need to be persuaded to adopt new attitudes, concepts, and technologies that derive from the research. Environmental, natural resource, and social science researchers, as well as the outreach and extension communities, need to play a role in the dissemination of the results and predictions of scientific research. Without this, the science we do will not be able to benefit fully the physical, mental, economic, and environmental well-being of the communities and society we serve. Science alone cannot overcome the problems represented in Box 1.1. Only through clear communication of fact- and evidence-based knowledge, collaboration by stakeholders, cooperation among land managers and agencies, and trust can the barriers to needed innovations be overcome (see Chapter 13). Systems ecologists will need the help of sociologists, behavioral and organizational scientists, and marketing professionals to bridge the gap between science and meaningful, broad-scale application.

The raison d'être for SEP is simple. Society needs a *methodology* (systems ecology approach) and a *knowledge base* (ecosystem science) to solve critical and complex environmental and natural resource problems. We believe SEP is the right science at the right time – both now and in the future.

It is our hope that other scientists, policy makers, land managers, science and academic administrators, enlightened community thought leaders, and students who work collaboratively to solve very complex societal and environmental problems will take advantage of the 50 years of historical knowledge depicted in this book (see Chapter 10). Concepts and lessons learned about administrative and organizational characteristics that have allowed the NREL to survive and thrive for 50 years while many other peer organizations have floundered or failed are presented (see Chapter 12). We are confident that these observations can benefit other institutions attempting to establish or rejuvenate research organizations.

1.2 Evolution of the Systems Ecology Approach

The term "ecosystem" was first used by A. G. Tansley (1935) to define "a particular category of physical systems, consisting of organisms and inorganic components in a relatively stable equilibrium, open and of various sizes and kinds" (see Chapter 3). Tansley recognized humans as actors that influence the environment and he implied a reciprocal relationship between biophysical systems and people. E. P. Odum (Odum and Odum, 1963) expanded the concept to mean that the community of organisms interact with their physical environment by controlling the flows of energy and mass through the system's trophic structure, biodiversity, and process connections. Until recently, studies of "human-less" ecosystems have been the primary basis of our knowledge about the structure and functioning of ecosystems. Van Dyne (1969) organized a symposium, "The Ecosystem Concept in Natural Resource Management," in which he and other prominent ecologists further expanded the importance of the concept in rangeland, forest, wildlife, and watershed management and acknowledged that people are a part of "ecosystems." Chapter 3 in this volume provides an expanded discussion of the development of the ecosystem concept and the seminal role George Van Dyne played in the establishment of SEP (Coleman, 2010; see Chapters 3 and 12).

The SEP described herein is similar to the excellent presentations in the books *The Ecosystem Approach* (Waltner-Toews et al., 2008) and *Principles of Terrestrial Ecosystem Ecology* (Chapin et al., 2011). However, in this book we describe the evolution and application of the approach used by hundreds of researchers associated with the NREL for more than 50 years and what we see as its essential role in meeting future challenges. Our modern, holistic view of the "whole ecosystem" is partially captured in Figure 1.1.

This figure depicts people and communities interacting directly with the biophysical system within a geographically bounded unit (ECOSYSTEMS box). The ecosystem is influenced by external factors (white boxes outside the boundaries) and all of these external factors are subject to change. Within the ecosystem boundaries, people manage the biophysical system (land and water) for "ecosystem services" (products, ecological process regulation, and other human perceived "values") (Christensen et al., 1996; UNMEA, 2018). Examples of products (provisioning services) that people receive from the land and water are food, fiber, timber and other building materials, minerals for manufacturing, medicines, water, and wealth. Services (regulating services) provided include water and air cleansing, detoxification of harmful chemical compounds, erosion control, climate regulation, flood attenuation, habitat for desired animals, plants, and microorganisms, and nutrient and gene pool banking and supporting services including soil formation, nutrient recycling, and primary production. Among the "values" (cultural

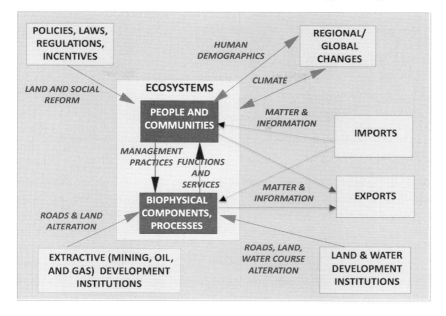

Figure 1.1 Ecosystems – the relationship of people and communities (societies) to the biophysical components and interactions (land, water, and air) in an ecosystem context. A black and white version of this figure will appear in some formats. For the color version, please refer to the plate section.

services) we receive are serenity, recreational enjoyment, spiritual renewal, and a sense or "spirit" of place. Both natural processes and management practices influence the chemistry and physical properties of the atmosphere, waters, and soils and climate interactions.

Biophysical attributes (biotic and abiotic) of ecosystems (land, water, and air) include a productive, potential capacity to retain and recycle nutrients, biodiversity, and other ecosystem services. All of these attributes are unique for each ecosystem in space and time. A universally optimistic goal for society is the management of desirable, resilient, and sustainable biophysical components to ensure access to the services necessary to support both people and communities, now and in the future (WCED, 1987; Pope Francis, 2015).

1.3 SEP and Ecosystem Science

The "systems approach" is a concept derived largely from the General Systems Theory (von Bertalanffy, 1968). It addresses problems in a logical

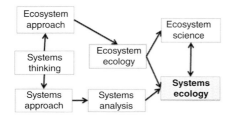

Figure 1.2 Relationship of the thought processes and concepts involved in SEP.

and disciplined manner, generally relying heavily on mathematical models to express interactions within systems. This approach has been adopted by many disciplines, such as organization and management science, engineering, computer science, physics, the military, and life sciences. Concepts underpinning the systems approach were further developed by Jay W. Forrester (1961, 1968) who laid the groundwork for much of the ecosystem modeling described in this book. We view SEP as the application of the systems approach to analysis of real and complex ecological, natural resources, as well as environmental and societal problems and challenges (Figure 1.2; Woodmansee, 1988; see Chapter 4).

The systems ecology approach can be viewed as the integration of "traditional" ecological, soils, and physical science research involving specific aspects of components, processes, and/or driving variables within ecosystems (ecosystem ecology), the philosophical scientific perspective incorporating holism and reductionism (systems thinking and the systems approach), and the rigorous methodology of systems analysis. The systems ecology approach is a perspective that recognizes people are components of ecosystems. It embraces rigorous thinking but not necessarily a dependence on mathematical modeling. Systems ecology has traditionally been associated with the mathematical modeling of ecosystems. Our perspective of systems ecology and the systems ecology approach extends from microscopic scales to patch or ecological sites, landscape, and regional- to global-scale ecosystems and focusing on their functioning (interactions within and among ecosystems). Ecosystem science is the body of knowledge about ecosystems and the methodologies and holistic perspectives developed for the rigorous study of ecosystems.

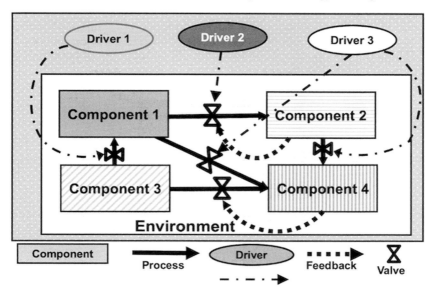

Figure 1.3 General systems notation showing components (boxes), processes (arrows and feedbacks as dashes and arrows), controls (valves), and driving variables (ovals). For a brief overview of systems terminology, see *Introduction to Systems: A Primer* (www2.nrel.colostate.edu/projects/LandCenter/Systems_Primer/index.htm). (Toggle between Outline for navigation and Notes for text. Be patient, the Adobe Presentation is slow to load.)

Systems thinking (Meadows, 2008), as applied to ecosystem science, is the process used to better understand how components that interact for a common purpose or function operate internally and influence one another within larger environmental and natural resource systems (Figure 1.3). Examples of systems thinking in nature include interactions among the atmosphere, water, soils, plants, animals, and people. The systems ecology approach, which relies heavily on systems thinking, is a set of accepted protocols for investigating phenomena, acquiring new knowledge, integrating previous knowledge, and synthesizing new concepts. All of these protocols are subject to a rigorous review of facts and evidence and are presented here in a more transparent and comprehensible language. An idealized process for applying these principles to complex, societally relevant, environmental problems is shown in Figure 1.4 (Woodmansee and Riebsame, 1993; see Chapters 4 and 10).

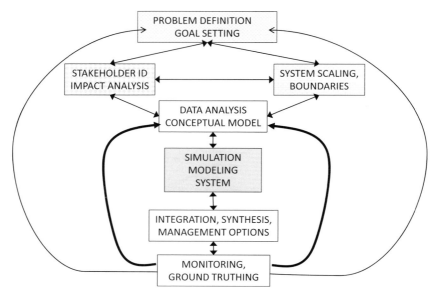

Figure 1.4 Steps in the system ecology approach used to collaboratively and systematically address important challenges facing society.

1.4 The Idealized Process

An idealized process for applying these principles to complex, societally relevant environmental problems is seen in Figure 1.4. (Woodmansee and Riebsame, 1993; see Chapters 4 and 10). The iterative steps in this process are:

- *Developing clear and unambiguous questions, problem definitions, and analysis goals.* This is the essential first step of the systems ecology approach. It is especially vital if an interdisciplinary team is analyzing the questions and problems. These definitions and goals are essential for team communications and later within stakeholder communities. Insufficient attention to this first step is often the "Achilles' heel" of the overall analysis.
- *Identifying key stakeholders who are influenced by these questions and problems.* Who will be affected by the analysis? The analysis team and stakeholders together perform impact analysis bringing in representatives of all sectors and disciplines necessary to analyze, understand, and solve the question/problems.
- *Developing clear descriptions of spatial, temporal, and institutional boundaries and scales* appropriate to the defined questions/problems by the analysis team and stakeholders (Rosswall et al., 1988; Woodmansee, 1988;

Figure 1.5 Some hierarchical dimensions that require specific attention when evaluating and managing ecological/social ecosystems.

Figure 1.5; see Chapters 2 and 6). The spatial, temporal, and institutional scaling concepts used in this book are discussed in Section 1.9.

- *The analysis team and stakeholders work collaboratively* to collect data from the warehouse of knowledge (ecosystem science) and analyze the defined questions/problems. The analysis team and stakeholders assemble and integrate data and information from any source necessary to support development of a conceptual model. The *shared conceptual model* of the system associated with the questions/problems identifies the processes and rates of processes, components, and driving variables that should or should not be included in the model. It is essential that every assumption regarding the elements to be included in the model be explicitly described.

- *Develop a mathematical simulation model – the heart of the SEP* based on the conceptual model(s) that represents the system of concern through time. Forrester (1968) suggested models should not be judged against some assumed perfection, instead they should be judged compared to other ways of describing a system of interest. Woodmansee (1978) expanded on this concept by suggesting simulation models with well-documented and transparent assumptions should be compared to mental models, word models, photographs, or drawings as tools for describing systems.

- *Conduct validation studies* of the simulation model comparing it to known reality (data sets and experience); if the initial analysis is inadequate and doesn't match reality, solve the problems, or answer the questions, assumptions made in the model formulation should be reexamined and/or *new research should be designed and conducted to address critical knowledge gaps.*

- *Reiterate the whole process*, if necessary, until the simulation model yields reasonable results and explains interactions within the modeled system that are poorly understood or unmeasurable.

- *Use models* to address the initial goals, generate scenarios, and make "predictions" about future conditions.
- *Monitor* (ground truth) the results of proposed solutions.
- *Adapt to new conditions if solutions are not working.*

The systems ecology approach is, above all, a declaration of a different mental paradigm that recognizes different human perspectives and their limitations. Just as any simulation, word, mental model, drawing, or sculpture is a product of the person or persons creating it, a scientific paradigm must prove useful to those using it. By providing a means of objectifying the thinking and communication processes involved in human/environmental interactions, the paradigm establishes movement toward objective reality. Acknowledgment of the human/environmental interface, often lacking in traditional ecology and the "natural sciences," is essential for cultures and societies to assess, plan, and implement proper management of the environment and natural resources for the betterment of societies across the globe.

1.5 Organizing Principles of the SEP

Emerging from the development of the systems ecology approach are some common principles that represent this paradigm.

- *Problems may have multiple causes.* It is important to recognize that complicated, societal problems are likely due to multiple causes and that uncertainty in the proposed solutions must be considered.
- *Precise definitions of problems.* Real-world environmental and societal problems require precise definition in space, time, and involved institutions, and likely require a multi-sector and multi-scale perspective.
- *Holistic, systems thinking perspective.* The whole is greater than the sum of its parts – but recognizing reductionism by using the scientific method is often necessary to fill in gaps of knowledge.
- *Co-production of knowledge with local collaborators and stakeholders.* Problems and issues associated with local people and communities are best addressed with the involvement and close cooperation with local stakeholders.
- *Teamwork.* Cooperation among senior and junior scientists, technicians, and support staff is necessary to address complicated and complex questions and/or problems. All must be committed to the cause.
- *Clear, honest, and effective communication.* This type of communication is essential between collaborators, stakeholders, managers, and decision makers for a successful systems ecology approach.

- *Interdisciplinary networks.* Real-world environmental and societal problems require working across traditional disciplinary boundaries (dismantling silos) to achieve understanding and solution.
- *Globalization of collaboration.* Many of the scientific breakthroughs in ecosystem science have been achieved through the collaboration of scientists throughout the world.
- *Focus on processes and controls.* Focusing on processes and their dynamics, rates of change of components, external driving forces, and internal feedbacks that control processes is essential.
- *Integration of research.* Modeling, field and laboratory studies, integration of data and information, and syntheses are fully interactive components of research and analysis (see Chapter 5 for supporting technologies).
- *Transparency and honesty.* Sharing and transparency of factual research results and conclusions, and model formulation and assumptions, are essential for both internal communication within teams and reporting to other scientists, managers, policy makers, and the public. It is especially important to identify and differentiate between ideology, beliefs, myths, fabrications, SWAG's,[2] and objective and verifiable reality.
- *The systems ecology approach is dynamic, iterative, and adaptive.*

1.6 Fundamental Philosophy

We accept that all of Earth's ecosystems are influenced by humans, either directly (as in agriculture, forestry, fisheries, natural areas, parks, cities, towns, or rural development areas) or indirectly (as in allowing "old growth" forest, grasslands, or aquatic systems to be "protected" from both natural and exotic events). Even polar regions and the deep ocean are now impacted by human-caused climate and chemical changes (IPCC, 2014). Likewise, all people and communities are influenced by the biophysical systems in which they reside. To be resilient and sustainable, these systems must apply thoughtful and prudent management practices to maintain ecological and socio-cultural integrity, even though the environments in which they exist are ever changing.

The fundamental philosophy underpinning this book is that all members of society, both present and future, should have the right to conduct *activities* (Figure 1.6) to meet their needs (*intended results*) for food

---

[2] Scientific wild ass guesses.

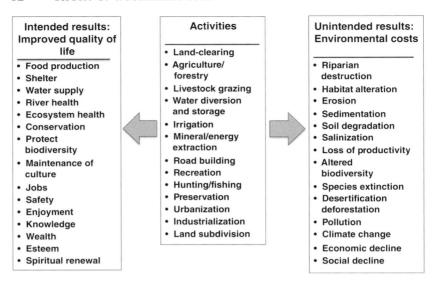

Intended results: Improved quality of life	Activities	Unintended results: Environmental costs
• Food production	• Land-clearing	• Riparian destruction
• Shelter	• Agriculture/ forestry	• Habitat alteration
• Water supply	• Livestock grazing	• Erosion
• River health	• Water diversion and storage	• Sedimentation
• Ecosystem health	• Irrigation	• Soil degradation
• Conservation	• Mineral/energy extraction	• Salinization
• Protect biodiversity	• Road building	• Loss of productivity
• Maintenance of culture	• Recreation	• Altered biodiversity
• Jobs	• Hunting/fishing	• Species extinction
• Safety	• Preservation	• Desertification deforestation
• Enjoyment	• Urbanization	• Pollution
• Knowledge	• Industrialization	• Climate change
• Wealth	• Land subdivision	• Economic decline
• Esteem		• Social decline
• Spiritual renewal		

Figure 1.6 Examples of human activities that lead to both intended and unintended consequences.

and water, shelter, safety, sense of belonging, self-esteem, and spirituality and to live in a world that offers good health, well-being, dignity, and safety. Simultaneously, people are responsible for minimizing the known negative impacts and formally analyzing and anticipating the *unintended consequences* of their activities (Lubchenco et al., 1991). Rarely are activities initiated for sinister or evil purposes, but rather the intention is most often to improve some aspect of the quality of life. All too often emphasis is placed on the positive aspects of intended consequences rather than the unintended consequences of the activity itself. Achieving positive outcomes without triggering unacceptable consequences requires a holistic and comprehensive knowledge of both ecological and social systems.

Pragmatically evaluating the positive and negative interactions of human activities and the biophysical realm requires a holistic, systems perspective of a particular problem as described in Section 1.4 (also see Chapter 10). These steps represent an iterative methodology intended to improve understanding and aid in decision making. Additionally, we must realize that cultural, economic, institutional, and political considerations form vital constraints on problem solving, for example ecosystem sustainability. This book is intended to demonstrate the integration of biophysical attributes (soils, climate, biodiversity, etc.) of ecosystems in addition to the social/cultural, political, and economic interactions within those systems. Our goal for this book is to describe the framework for this perspective.

1.7 Problems, Needs, and Institutions

Over the past five decades, ecosystem science and the systems ecology approach have emerged as a major pillar of science, policy, and management dialogue (see Chapter 7). The recognition of the explicit relationship between human and societal aspects of the environment with biophysical interactions has been integrated into our view of ecosystems. Further development of the interplay between the research community and managers will lead to a broader application of the approach, the discovery of solutions to critical social-environmental challenges, and development of management strategies for the future.

To increase our understanding of how to manage ecosystems, ensuring they fulfill human needs, requires several important concepts (Figure 1.7), some of which include: (1) integration of the best and current scientific and traditional knowledge of the interactions between physical, biological, social, and economic systems; (2) generation of new knowledge, some of which is at the intellectual frontier of science; and (3) integration of knowledge into efficacious management and policy decision-making processes. Science and traditional knowledge, rational management, and sound public policy must be interconnected and interactive for effective implementation of solutions to societal problems (Hautaluoma and Woodmansee, 1994; see Chapter 10). Figure 1.7 shows the relationship of one class of problems to societal needs and the institutional missions that provide research, traditional knowledge, and education (see Chapter 11).

Many other important problems fit the general model shown in Figure 1.7 (causes and consequences of global and regional climate change, the effects of biodiversity loss, energy development, managing wetlands for municipal water systems, effects of point source pollution, political changes, etc.). Also illustrated in Figure 1.7 is the ideal relationship of science with policy-making and management processes via the essential role of synthetic and original research. Synthetic research (data and literature mining) involves evaluating and integrating existing scientific and traditional knowledge bases and data into new concepts, allowing us to identify and better articulate what we know. It may be the most neglected activity in the environmental, natural resource, and

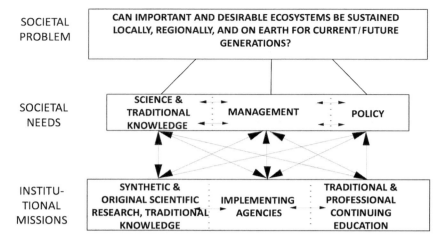

Figure 1.7 Ideal relationship of science and traditional knowledge, based on facts and evidence, management, and policy sectors to address societal problems, issues, and goals. In a perfect world, the arrows representing knowledge sharing between the science, management, and policy sectors would be transparent and interactive. To accomplish the ideal state, many research, outreach, and educational institutions must contribute reliable knowledge to policy makers and management agencies.

social sciences fields of study. Original research is critical for both filling real gaps and developing new frontiers of knowledge needed for the future (see Chapter 2). Original research entails the development of new knowledge and understanding through observation, monitoring, and experimentation. Both synthetic and original research is needed to advance intellectual frontiers in knowledge (Weathers et al., 2016).

1.8 Integrating Science, Management, and Policy

Communication of the best possible ecological and social/cultural knowledge requires new forms of traditional and professional continuing education utilizing modern technology, practical experience, good sense, and use of sound scientific research. We must remember that scientific understanding is essential, but that alone is insufficient for managing the types of ecosystems needed by society (Abelson, 1993) given that few people, including scientists, share the same view of the environment in which they live (Figure 1.8). Policy makers, many in the current management workforce, most of the public, and numerous scientists have little or no training in either the ecological or social/cultural sciences.

"WHAT YOU SEE DEPENDS ON WHERE YOU STAND"

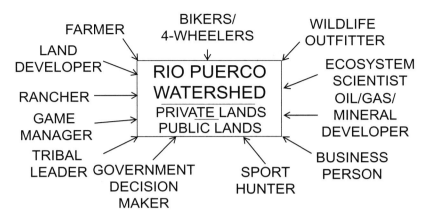

Figure 1.8 Some of the many viewpoints involved in analysis of an example watershed to answer the specific question "how can a watershed (the Rio Puerco Watershed in New Mexico) and its included landscapes be restored to healthy functioning following drastic disturbance?" The quote "What you see depends on where you stand" is variously attributed to Albert Einstein, C. S. Lewis (1955) in *The Magicians Nephew*, and many others. Figure modified from Riebsame and Woodmansee (1995).

Some of these groups may have received training in one or a few of these fields, but not all.

The traditional scientific approach or myth of analysis that demands "holding everything else constant" while the phenomenon of interest is evaluated is not only unrealistic, but unachievable. By itself, this approach is of little value for addressing problems in ecosystem resilience and sustainability. Scientific knowledge must become an integral part of the policy and management decision process (Christensen et al., 1996). Management and policy decisions are often based on intuition, myths, personal beliefs, ideology, ego, and/or value systems, some of which are not clearly rational or objective (Hautaluoma and Woodmansee, 1994). Similarly, policy approaches that are developed by bureaucrats not closely associated with the local people and ecosystems are seldom helpful. Management approaches that ignore scientific knowledge and attempt to adhere to vague policy and management approaches based on "that's the way Daddy and Granddaddy did it" are also inadequate. Therefore, scientists, managers, policy makers, and the public must find new ways to work together at the interface between the objectivity of science, the obligations of management and policy making, and the desires of society (Hautaluoma and Woodmansee, 1994; see Chapter 13).

Over the decades, ecosystem science has evolved from a research approach to a quantification of interactions, the flow of material and information, and processes of the exchange between biotic and environmental components of natural ecosystems to a scientific and systems approach. These processes also provide insights into possible solutions and management strategies for solving important societal challenges. The current challenges faced for adopting these approaches include societal adaptability, and resilience and sustainability in a nonstatic world. This book illustrates the continuing development and evolution of SEP. The paradigm is seen universally as a key perspective to view and resolve local-to-global environmental challenges, as well as part of the larger societal challenges facing the world today.

1.9 Space, Time, and Institution Scaling

Ecosystems operate across multiple scales of space, time, and institutions (Figure 1.5) including the microscopic levels of soil microbial processes associated with nitrogen transformations to macro scales of the earth system through modification of the carbon cycle brought about for economic gain. Often the reference scale used in ecosystem studies is guided more by the particular nature of the question being studied or the management issue being worked on.

The spatial, temporal, and institutional scales or hierarchies used by many ecosystem scientists throughout the world are referenced throughout this book. We assume many ecologists will recognize the hierarchies, but other readers including researchers from other fields, land managers, decision makers, and other stakeholders may not. We have learned through trial and error the importance of clearly defining the meaning of the different levels in the hierarchies. Also, much of the ecological/ social literature addresses local, regional, and global environmental challenges. But many these categories are often too vague to pragmatically address "on-the-ground" research and management challenges.

Definitions of scales at lower levels in spatial, temporal, and institutional dimensions are relatively easy and accepted by scientists (Figure 1.5). As spatial scales increase in size, timescales increase in length, and institutions increase in complexity, definitions become much more complicated, especially as interactions among dimensions come into play. For example, human activities have historically affected ecosystem processes at local scales; harvesting various plants or animals, using fires to modify habitats of food species, altering water flow to support human needs. However, the accumulated impact of human activities and the global influence of human activities on ecosystems around the globe has greatly altered ecosystem processes at a planetary scale. Human activities have altered the spatial distribution of ecosystems and the rate of ecosystem processes.

Biophysical functioning linking water and nutrient dynamics, primary and secondary production, decomposition, and energy flow to soil and climate properties across spatial scales are examined in detail in Chapter 6. Temporal scales are referenced in progression throughout the chapter. As interactive components of ecosystems, humans and their social and institutional structures and institutions will be introduced in Chapters 2, 7, 9, and 13 by analyzing their relationship to landscapes and larger geographic areas. Obtaining a clear definition of the problems or questions of scientific focus is critical and they must be independently defined, at each level of space, time, and institutional scale.

1.9.1 Spatial Hierarchy

Levels of the spatial hierarchy are used in this book simply to help analyze and hopefully resolve one or a set of scientific and management problems. The levels are intended to be pragmatic rather than theoretical. However, Woodmansee (1990) stated, "It is important to remember that nature is not a grand hierarchy of systems at various levels of organization; rather, nature simply is." Details of studies using this hierarchical approach are discussed throughout this book. The spatial levels are used also to disaggregate the goals in Boxes 2.1–2.3 in Chapter 2 into manageable pieces (McKenzie-Mohr, 2011).

1.9.1.1 Organism (Populations)

The basic unit in the biophysical realm of an ecosystem is a living organism. Here we focus on a plant in a subplot as the fundamental unit (Woodmansee, 1990). The subplot concept is *one autotrophic plant or autotrophic cell in its supporting soil matrix and climate environment* (Figure 1.9). With few exceptions, all life starts with photosynthesis operating in a single plant, algal cell, or a few photosynthetic bacteria. Gross primary production (GPP) of a single plant is the total organic matter synthesized following photosynthesis. Environmental factors, such

Photosynthesis
(CO_2)

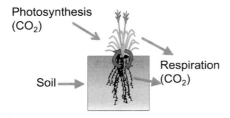

Respiration
(CO_2)

Soil →

Figure 1.9 Plant (organism) in an ideal soil matrix.

as water, temperature, and nutrients, control GPP. Net primary production (NPP) is the amount of plant organic matter left after carbon is lost as CO_2 from plant respiration needed to support plant metabolism. Following photosynthesis and the synthesis of organic compounds, those compounds are circulated and recirculated within the plant to meet the metabolic needs of stems, roots, leaves, and flowering parts. Plants shed dead and dying parts that become debris (dead roots and litter) and "food" for microorganisms in the immediate vicinity of the plant. Some plant parts and cells may be eaten by herbivores and transported away from the subplot. Chapter 6 discusses many of these concepts. A plethora of mathematical models has been produced that simulates these dynamics (see Chapter 4).

A cautionary note: while a single plant, animal, or microorganism is relatively easy to define, the soil environment of an organism is not. In plant communities, root systems of different plants intermingle and overlap as do soil fauna and microorganism populations. Therefore, we can conceptualize a plant in its soil environment and we can position a physical sampling device to enclose a single plant aboveground but in nature we cannot be certain we are sampling one organism in its environment.

1.9.1.2 Ecological Site as an Ecosystem (or Plot or Patch or Stand)
The concept of a land-based ecological site is based on an idealized plant community and an interrelated, recognizable soil type or polypedon (see Figures 1.10 and 1.11). The plant community and its soil body are defined in space by plant community boundaries and soil type (Anderson et al., 1983; Woodmansee, 1990). The plant community is made up of groupings of individual plants whose root systems can be intermingled in the soil milieu within the site.

Natural disturbances such as fires, floods, pests, and diseases, in addition to human land-use activities (e.g., fences, crop type, grazing and

Figure 1.10 An ecological site within a landscape. A black and white version of this figure will appear in some formats. For the color version, please refer to the plate section. Photo by R. G. Woodmansee

forest management, and management infrastructure) can dramatically alter the definition of an ecological site. Management practices affect all ecological sites within landscapes, yet each site will respond differently to each activity (e.g., modern precision agriculture, range and forest management). Governance and policies effect ecological sites mostly through their impacts on landscapes.

A vast amount of knowledge generated about this level of the ecological hierarchy over the past five decades is largely due to the application of the systems ecology approach. Contributions to ecosystem science at the ecological site scale include (see Chapter 6 and 8 for more details):

- Definition of spatial, temporal, and institutional boundaries;
- Site scale C, N, P, S, and H_2O processes and budgets;
- Functional group diversity needed to accomplish necessary biophysical processes and ecosystem services;
- Effects of disturbances such as climate change, nitrogen loading from atmosphere, fertilizers, fire, and drought;

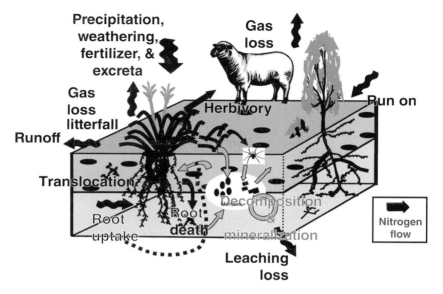

Figure 1.11 Nitrogen cycle in an ecological site that illustrates structural components and important processes (arrows). Concepts appropriate to this scale in the ecological hierarchy are soil organic matter dynamics; nitrogen and carbon evolution and sequestration; microbial/soil fauna interactions, belowground food webs, root production and death, decomposition, mineralization, soil and litter C, N, P, and S interactions, soil aggregate formation and function, and interactions of C, N, P cycles and relationships within soils. Additionally, C, N, and P budgets and processes, nutrient exchanges and transport, and plant and microbe competition have connected these belowground and aboveground linkages.

- Relationship of primary production from plant community and herbivore grazing and food selection/diets;
- Effect of grazers on primary production within plant communities and how plants compensate for disruption by herbivores;
- Plant diversity, succession, and state-and-transition models;
- Biotic community biodiversity;
- Belowground ecological processes and biodiversity occurring at the cm^3, mm^3, and nm^3 scales within the soil of an ecological site (see Figure 1.11);
- Ecosystem services;
  - Supporting services (primary production, nutrient cycling, decomposition, and soil formation);
  - Provisioning services (food, raw materials, and water).

1.9.1.3 Landscapes as Ecosystems

Simply put, a landscape can be viewed by an observer standing on high ground (Figure 1.12) where there is no unique definition of landscape. Problems define landscapes. The systems ecology approach calls for a clear problem statement followed by a precise boundary setting in space, time, and institutional situation. Landscapes are composed of interacting ecological sites (defined below) that interact with other landscapes to make regions, small or large, depending on the problem being addressed.

Most human activities that directly deal with land use occur at the landscape scale in the ecological hierarchy. Small watersheds, farming, ranching, forest management, urban development, and outdoor recreation activities such as hunting, skiing, and hiking occur at landscape scales. Management decisions are typically applied to landscapes.

Figure 1.12 Example of a landscape ecosystem that illustrates many ecological sites. A sagebrush community is in the foreground, an aspen forest is adjacent, with a subalpine forest positioned behind, and alpine tundra on the horizon. Each may be a distinct ecological site, yet many different ecological sites are intermixed. A black and white version of this figure will appear in some formats. For the color version, please refer to the plate section. Photo by R. G. Woodmansee

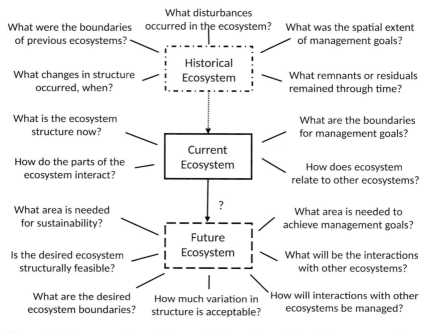

Figure 1.13 Representations of the spatial dimensions of historical, current, and future ecosystems, and questions that need to be addressed to better understand past, present, and future ecosystem functions.

As with the ecological site scale, a vast amount of knowledge has been generated about this level of the ecological hierarchy during the past five decades. Much of the knowledge referenced in this book has been and can continue to be used to answer practical questions about the management of ecosystems (see Chapter 7).

Landscape-scale research has generally embraced two landscape concepts. For practical research purposes, geographic barriers, institutional or political boundaries, or human community development and management boundaries can be used to define landscapes spatially. The definition of a landscape must also include a period of concern since landscapes can change over time. Figures 1.13 and 1.14 are especially pertinent at the landscape scale (see discussion in Section 2.3). Inherent in this concept are the notions of natural range of variability, historical range of variability, and ecosystem legacies (Jogiste et al., 2017; Wohl, 2017).

One concept of a landscape is a geographic area composed of ecological sites that are connected by material that flows from one

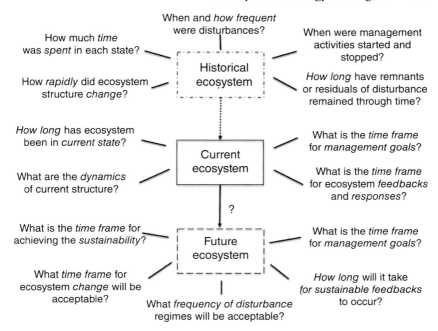

Figure 1.14 Representations of the temporal dimensions of historical, current, and future ecosystems and questions that need to be addressed to better understand past, present, and future ecosystem functions.

ecological site to another or through information controls among the sites within the landscape, for example one site provides potential cover for a herbivore who will choose to graze or drink water nearby (Woodmansee, 1990). Ecological sites in landscapes can be linked by water (interflow, run-on/runoff, erosion/sedimentation), wind (erosion/sedimentation), animals including humans (food selection, removal, disposal, and redistribution; urination; and defecation), animal influence on plant community distribution and diversity, and animal influence on CH_4, NH_3, and N_2O production (see Chapter 6). Common aggregations of ecological sites within this concept of landscapes are catenas or hill slopes, watering locations, and fence corners in grazinglands. Humans can dramatically influence all of these interactions.

Another concept of a landscape emphasizes the pattern of ecological sites within a defined area and the influence of that pattern on habitat use by animals and humans (Risser 1990). The ecological sites composed of plant communities, indigenous and mobile animals (including humans), and microorganisms, function to provide necessary ecosystem services for those included. Important concepts within this view of landscapes are plant and animal biodiversity, migration patterns and corridors, and use of landscapes by people. People and mobile vertebrates and invertebrates use whole landscapes, not just ecological sites therein.

Ecosystem services are often defined as those that provide support, provision, regulation, and cultural benefits, which are properly applied to the landscape and ecological site scales in the ecological hierarchy (Figure 1.5). For example, water capture, retention, and release from upland ecological sites are a critical set of processes that determine water availability in downslope ecological sites.

Landscapes and the ecological sites therein are the scales at which land, water, and atmospheric interactions are expressed (see Chapter 8). The generation of atmospheric and water-borne chemicals, particulates, and sediments occur at landscape scales from ecological site-scale processes (see below); urban, industrial, or transportation point sources; or volcanoes, wildfires, and war. Those substances are then mixed in the atmosphere and flowing waters and are then deposited in ecological sites and surface waters within landscapes. Some substances are transported away to other landscapes, regions, and continents within the Earth. The interactions of ecological site processes within landscapes are complicated and interdependent.

Migrations, invasions, and extirpation of plants, animals, microorganisms and diseases as influenced by changing climates, nitrogen loading from the atmosphere or surface waters, or humans as vectors of transport, are issues central to landscape-scale ecosystems as well as ecosystems above and below in the ecological hierarchy. This set of issues is very complex and requires careful application of SEP for understanding.

1.9.1.4 Small Regions as Ecosystems (Including Watersheds within Basins)

Small regions, including small watersheds, are ecosystems containing landscapes that are linked ecologically by: (1) animal migrations, (2) atmospheric chemicals, (3) wind-borne debris such as dust from one landscape causing early snow melt in another, (4) stream and river basin water transport, (5) N redistribution, (6) smog and haze, and (7) people, for example from fertilizer use, transport of invasive species, and diseases. Species distributions, abundance, and movements affected by climate change, habitat fragmentation, land-use modifications, and issues from plant biodiversity, animals, and soil organisms, often require analysis at specific regional scales of resolution.

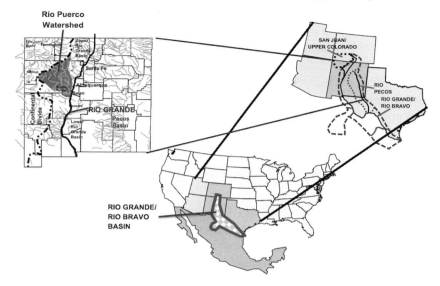

Figure 1.15 Representation of watershed (small region), regions, and subcontinental-scale ecosystems. The Rio Puerco watershed is in New Mexico, USA. Headwaters of the Rio Grande/Rio Bravo Basin are in the USA and Mexico. A black and white version of this figure will appear in some formats. For the color version, please refer to the plate section.

Smaller regions such as small river basins, agricultural districts, grazing-lands, forestlands, and administrative units (e.g., counties, community or public lands, and water agencies) are the *hierarchal level where individuals can become stakeholders involved in community decision making* rather than leaving all the decision making to representatives. This level in the ecological hierarchy is where education, outreach, and engagement can include real, recognizable examples for learners. *Stakeholder participation is a profoundly important concept for the application of the systems ecology approach going forward into the twenty-first century.*

1.9.1.5 Regions as Ecosystems (Large River Basins and Nations)

Precisely defining the spatial, temporal, and institutional boundaries of a region in relation to specific environmental and natural resource problems is crucial and demands the strict application of SEP. Some large nations at subcontinental scales have subregions that are best defined by physiography and climate, for example Canada, the United States, Mexico, Russia, Brazil, and China (Figure 1.15). Other subcontinental regions (e.g., Western and Central Europe, East Africa) have subregions that must include in their definition the nations contained therein. An essential role of the systems ecology approach in defining problems at regional and national scales is to ensure the physical, political, and administrative boundaries of the system associated with the problem are clearly defined and the hierarchy levels above (continents) and below (landscapes or subregions) are properly considered (O'Neill 1988). This is a daunting but necessary task that is often ignored.

As with small regions, regions can be linked ecologically by: (1) animal migrations,)2) atmospheric chemicals,)3) wind-borne debris such as dust from one landscape causing early snow melt in another, (4) river basin water transport, (5) N redistribution, (6) smog and haze, and (7) people, for example from fertilizer use, transport of invasive species, and diseases. Species distributions, abundance, and movements affected by climate change, habitat fragmentation, land-use modifications, and issues from plant biodiversity, animals, and soil organisms, often require analysis at specific regional scales of resolution.

1.9.1.6 Continents (and Islands) as Ecosystems

Defining continental-scale ecosystems is relatively easy at short timescale, that is, less than millions of years. Continents are influenced by other continents by ocean and atmospheric circulation and chemistry. Internally, continents are physically influenced by physiography, and climate, weather, and vegetation patterns. Land use, urbanization, and industrialization can also influence these patterns in conjunction with the political governance and policies that make up the geographic scale below the continent (regions, nations, or states). Analyzing these system dynamics is the essence of the systems ecology approach. Empirical studies alone cannot address these complicated dynamics.

Atmospheric accumulation, transport, and deposition of chemicals and particles as described below in Section 1.9.1.7 are especially important at the continental scale. Examples of problems that are uniquely continental include: acid rain; nitrogen loading of lands, rivers, and lakes; ozone depletion; and smog and haze; and are all results of atmospheric interactions that differentially impact locations and ecosystems within continents.

Continental-scale issues include: (1) exchanges of chemicals, particulates, dust, and sediments with in the atmosphere and large rivers; (2) changing climates and extreme weather events due to land-use changes, industrialization, and urbanization; and (3) alterations of hydrologic cycles, erosion, and sedimentation caused by large-scale water management projects. Further complicating the analysis is the profound influence of the expansion of land, water, and air transportation systems. Manufactured goods, food, fertilizers, fossil fuels, and species are massively redistributed within continents. The interactions of these transported items on ecosystem functioning are poorly understood.

1.9.1.7 The Earth as an Ecosystem

The atmosphere stands apart as critically important when evaluating environmental challenges that are uniquely global. The atmosphere is the integrator of gases such as CO_2, CH_4, O_3, N_2O, NO_xs, NH_3, and SO_2 and their chemical reactions. These gases are derived from ecological sites via natural ecosystem processes; human–influenced processes resulting from industrial and agricultural activity; lightning; volcanoes; wildfires; and fossil fuel burning. The atmosphere integrates countless ecological sites and other sources at the Earth's surface. A major challenge for terrestrial ecosystem science is the adequate integration of these gas exchanges throughout the ecological hierarchy represented in Figure 1.5.

We certainly recognize that the oceans of the earth have a tremendous influence on the atmosphere and subsequently on terrestrial ecosystems. However, the focus of this book is based on the scientific research associated with the NREL and its many collaborators, with an emphasis on terrestrial ecosystems throughout the world.

The atmosphere is the receptor, distributor, and depositor of important bioactive ions such as NH_4^+, NO_3^-, SO_4^{-2}, PO_4^{-3}. As with atmospheric gases, these ions are derived from ecological sites via natural and human-caused processes, such as lightning, volcanoes, wildfires, and point sources of industrial and agricultural activity, and fossil fuel burning. The ions are carried in the atmosphere and deposited as wet and dry deposition on ecological sites where they are either incorporated into the biota and soils or redistributed by water or wind within the landscapes and watersheds. The challenge facing ecosystem science is describing the origin, redistribution, and impacts of increased concentrations of these bioactive ions.

Nonbioactive particulate material such as dust from deserts, agricultural practices, urbanization, and industrial by-products that are carried in the atmosphere and redistributed over the Earth's surface are becoming recognized as important. They influence atmospheric haze and have been shown to influence the timing and rate of snowmelt.

The impacts of global climate change and their influence on atmospheric circulation and the distribution of warming/cooling patterns, precipitation patterns, and types and frequencies of extreme weather events are all critical for understanding how ecosystems function at all levels in the hierarchy shown in Figure 1.5. These are the climate drivers of ecosystem functioning.

1.9.2 Temporal Hierarchy Used in This Book

The time dimension requires differentiation between events such as floods, fires, tornados, and hurricanes; phenomena represented by yearly time periods, for example insect outbreaks, short-term droughts, and toxic chemical spills; disturbances requiring decades for expression or recovery, for example forest fires, hurricanes, degradation of arable lands, climate change, and their extension into centuries and millennia (Figure 1.5).

All the challenges recognized in this chapter have critical time dimensions: historical ecosystem legacies, current states, and critically all have future states (Figures 1.13 and 1.14). Each has important timescales ranging from single events to millennia or longer.

Accomplishing the goals of analysis and synthesis requires rigorous description of the current state of specific ecological systems, their history, the nature of proposed or continuing stresses, and the nature of both current and proposed management systems. Indeed, the specific questions and problems will dictate how the systems are bounded and characterized. The geographic (spatial) and time (temporal) dimensions of the ecosystem must reference specific problems and questions; for example, will biological invasions be expressed at the regional, landscape, or ecological site scales over periods of seasons, years, decades or centuries?

Figures 1.13 and 1.14 represent a concept of past, current, and future ecosystems and types of information needed for thorough analysis. As an ecosystem changes through time, its spatial expression may also change with respect to its biological, physical, economic, and social and political attributes and drivers. Important attributes must be described and quantified where possible with careful attention given to how each attribute relates to others.

Obviously, the amount of information needed to complete the analysis shown in Figures 1.13 and 1.14 is enormous and is simply not available for many ecosystems (Jogiste et al., 2017; Wohl, 2017). However, we must make assumptions about these attributes, either consciously or unconsciously. *Assumptions about important but poorly understood attributes are an essential part of science, management, and indeed daily living, but they must be clearly stated.* Fortunately, technologies such as geographic information systems, remote sensing, advanced mapping systems, and data-mining methods are rapidly developing and will help quantify previous assumption-rich attributes such as disturbance history or management activity that might have altered successional or development trajectories (see Chapter 6). Clear descriptions of the historical, current, and future desired attributes of ecological systems are essential for evaluating issues of changing climates, food security, water security, soil security, population growth, shifting demographics, and the resilience and sustainability of any ecosystem.

Some historical and current ecosystems are well understood, yet some are not. We can utilize SEP to draw upon knowledge from historical and current ecosystems to forecast likely events and trajectories for future ecosystems and prepare to adapt to the changing states. Alternatively, we can ignore forecasts and hope we are able to respond when needed.

1.9.3 Institutional Dimensions: Challenges

Figure 1.5 depicts the interactions between institutional hierarchies and space and time dimensions. The institutional hierarchies represented in Figure 1.5 are social organizations, such as households, clans, communities, towns, and cities. Social organizations may also include religious organizations and nongovernmental organizations (NGOs) with varying arrangements for governance. Businesses range from small family- or household-operated enterprises to multinational, multienterprise entities with powerful boards of directors. Professional organizations range from labor unions and coalitions of labor groups, to industry advocates for fossil fuels or renewable energy, to chemical and other trade organizations, to banking and manufacturing associations, to agriculture and timber groups. Scientists, academicians, universities, and school systems have hierarchies as do most governments that have "agencies" that are arranged in hierarchies or bureaucracies. Depending on the problem, issue, or question being addressed, consideration of any or many of these hierarchies may be critical for analysis and resolution.

Elected or appointed representatives conduct governance and policy making in larger regions. Smaller regions such as river basins, agricultural districts, grazinglands, forestlands, and administrative units (e.g., counties, community or public lands, and water agencies) are *the hierarchal level where individuals can become stakeholders involved in community decision making* rather than leaving all the decision making to the representatives. This level in the ecological hierarchy is where education can include real, recognizable examples for learners. *Stakeholder participation is a profoundly important concept for the application of the systems ecology approach going forward into the twenty-first century.*

All levels in the spatial, temporal, and institutional hierarchies are dynamic, further adding to the complexities of the challenges discussed in Chapter 2. The following book chapters describe the development and contributions to knowledge in these areas. Chapter 13 describes examples of specific research and actions needed in selected areas to better understand and manage ecosystems for sustainability.

1.10 What's in This Book: The Roadmap

The contents of this book are listed in Table 1.1.

Table 1.1 *Summary of* Natural Resource Management Reimagined: Using the Systems Ecology Paradigm

Chapter	Title	Description
1	The Systems Ecology Paradigm	Definitions underpinning holistic systems ecology philosophy are presented and uniqueness of the systems ecology paradigm is described.
2	Environmental and Natural Resource Challenges in the Twenty-First Century	With the Earth and its inhabitants facing myriad environmental and social challenges, many of which are life altering and some life-threatening, ecosystem science and the systems ecology paradigm focuses on real-world, complex problems at many scales from local to global.
3	Evolution of Ecosystem Science to Advance Science and Society in the Twenty-First Century	What is ecosystem ecology, what has it contributed in the past, and what are its prospects are for the future: a historical perspective.
4	Five Decades of Modeling Supporting the Systems Ecology Paradigm	The maturing of general systems theory and mathematical modeling through the evolution of collaborative research programs is the foundation of the SEP at the NREL. These programs have evolved into internationally recognized standards in systems ecology.
5	Advances in Technology Supporting the Systems Ecology Paradigm	From the age of the CDC 6400 mainframe computer, desktop calculators, and crude chemical analytical procedures to climate models

Table 1.1 (*cont.*)

Chapter	Title	Description
		run on supercomputers, satellite observations of global vegetation patterns, computer imaging, and smartphone technology allowing nearly instant global collaboration, technology has allowed the development of the SEP.
6	Emergence of Cross–Scale Structural and Functional Processes in Ecosystem Science	Integration of ecological site or patch, landscape, and regional scale hydrologic cycles, biogeochemistry, and plant, animal, and microbial interactions (food webs) has been a hallmark of research and discovery associated with the NREL and its collaborators. The knowledge gained from this integration is the basis for how ecosystems function and how they are structured.
7	Evolution of the Systems Ecology Paradigm in Managing Ecosystems	The knowledge gained from Foundations of Ecosystem Functioning using the SEP has profoundly influenced the policies affecting management of ecosystems. Crop agriculture, grazingland, and forest ecosystem management has dramatically changed based significantly on research contributions using the SEP.
8	Land/Atmosphere/Water Interactions	Based on fundamental knowledge of the functioning of ecosystems and their management, knowledge about the interactions of croplands, grazinglands, and forests with surface waters and the atmosphere is emerging. NREL scientists and collaborators are at the forefront of research on greenhouse gas dynamics and nutrient exchanges between terrestrial ecosystems and the atmosphere. Knowledge from this research is vital for mitigation of and adaptation to changing climate and chemical environments.
9	Humans in Ecosystems	Beginning in the mid-1980s, NREL scientists and collaborators transcended a significant disciplinary barrier – they *(cont.)*

Table 1.1 (*cont.*)

Chapter	Title	Description
		merged ecosystem science with social science. Prior to that time ecosystem science was considered an ecological or biophysical discipline and social science was considered too "fuzzy" to be a "real" science. With that disciplinary barrier broken, NREL scientists and collaborators have fashioned important new knowledge about the interactions between people and their environment. People are now viewed as components of ecosystems.
10	A Systems Ecology Approach for Community-Based Decision Making: The Structured Analysis Methodology (SAM)	The protocol for managing ecosystems described herein is a formal application of the ecosystem approach. The Structured Analysis Methodology (SAM), a science-based process, was developed to help communities of stakeholders evaluate and solve specific landscape to small regional (such as watershed management, wildlife ranges, municipalities, counties) environmental and natural resource problems.
11	Environmental Literacy: The Systems Ecology Paradigm	The NREL has a long and impressive history of supporting graduate and postgraduate training. Many staff members also have supported graduate and undergraduate teaching and advised in many academic departments and programs at Colorado State University (CSU). Some staff members have moved to academic departments but retained affiliation with the NREL. Recently, the NREL has successfully established a new academic program, the Department of Ecosystem Science and Sustainability. In addition to university academic programs, a much greater emphasis has been placed developing public K-12 environmental education and educational outreach and engagement programs within the

Table 1.1 (*cont.*)

Chapter	Title	Description
		broader CSU community and with the public outside the university community. These extended programs are developing rapidly and are becoming models for implementation nationally and internationally.
12	Organizational and Administrative Challenges and Innovations	The NREL has remained an internationally recognized center of excellence in ecosystem science over five decades. The Lab has evolved as a model of enduring administrative excellence based on sound management principles; strong leadership; supportive university administrations; creative, innovative, and entrepreneurial scientists; and dedicated, loyal support staff.
13	Where to From Here? Unraveling Wicked Problems	The world is facing daunting challenges such as changing climates, exponential population growth, demands for social and economic equity, food security, water scarcity, species loss, soil security, political chaos, and much more. Our look into the future will focus on a few specific challenges that can immediately be addressed by systems ecologists and their international networks of collaborators. The need for scientific knowledge and methodologies capable of dealing with interacting and complex environmental, social, and economic problems is imperative.

References

Abelson, P. H. (1993). Science, technology, and national goals. *Science*, 259, 743.

Anderson, D. W., Heil, R. D., Cole, C. V., and Deutsch, P. C. (1983). *Identification and Characterization of Ecosystems at Different Integrative Levels*. Athens, GA, Special Publication, University of Georgia, Agriculture Experiment Stations.

Biodiversity, A–Z. (2018). UN Environment World Conservation Monitoring Centre. www.biodiversitya-z.org/content/ecosystem-approach (accessed July 23, 2018).

34 · **Robert G. Woodmansee et al.**

Chapin, F. S., Chapin, M. C., Matson, P. A., and Vitousek, P. (2011). *Principles of Terrestrial Ecosystem Ecology*. New York: Springer.

Christensen, N. L., Bartuska, A. M., Brown, J. H., et al. (1996). The report of the Ecological Society of America committee on the scientific basis for ecosystem management. *Ecological Applications*, 6(3), 665–91.

Coleman, D. C. (2010). *Big Ecology: The Emergence of Ecosystem Science*. Oakland, CA: University of California Press.

Forrester, J. W. (1961). *Industrial Dynamics*. Cambridge, MA: MIT Press.

(1968). *Principles of Systems*. Cambridge, MA: Wright–Allen Press.

Hautaluoma, J. E., and Woodmansee, R. G. (1994). New roles in ecological research and policy making. *Ecology International Bulletin*, 21, 1–10.

IPCC. (2014). *Climate Change 2014: Synthesis Report*. Contribution of Working Groups I, II and III to the Fifth Assessment Report of the Intergovernmental Panel on Climate Change, ed. Core Writing Team, R. K. Pachauri, and L. A. Meyer. Geneva, Switzerland: IPCC.

Jogiste, K., Korjus, H., Stanturf, J. A., et al. (2017). Hemiboreal forest: natural disturbances and the importance of ecosystem legacies to management. *Ecosphere*, 8(2), e01706. https://doi.org/10.1002/ecs2.1706 (accessed June 18, 2018).

Lewis, C. S. (1955). *The Magician's Nephew*. New York: Harper Collins Children''s Books.

Lubchenco, J., Olson, A. M., and Brubaker, L. B., et al. (1991). The Sustainable Biosphere Initiative: an ecological research agenda – a report from the Ecological Society of America. *Ecology*, 72(2), 371–412.

McKenzie-Mohr, D. (2011). *Fostering Sustainable Behavior: An Introduction to Community-Based Social Marketing*. Gabriola Island, BC: New Society Publishers.

Meadows, D. H. (2008). *Thinking in Systems: A Primer*. White River Junction, VT: Chelsea Green Publishing.

Montague, C. L. (2018). Systems ecology. *Oxford Bibliographies*. www.oxfordbibliographies.com/view/document/obo-9780199830060/obo-9780199830060-0078.xml (accessed July 8, 2018).

NREL. (2018). Natural Resource Ecology Laboratory at Colorado State University. www.nrel.colostate.edu (accessed June 13, 2018).

Odum, E. P., and Odum, H. T. (1963). *Fundamentals of Ecology*, 2nd ed. Philadelphia and London: W. B. Saunders.

O'Neill, R. V. (1988). Hierarchy theory and global change. In *Scales and Global Change: Spatial and Temporal Variability in Biospheric and Geospheric Processes*, ed. T. Rosswall, R. G. Woodmansee, and P. G. Risser. SCOPE Series 38, Hoboken, NJ, John Wiley and Sons: 29–45.

Pope Francis. (2015). *Laudato Si': Encyclical Letter on Care for Our Common Home*. http://w2.vatican.va/content/francesco/en/encyclicals/documents/papa-fran cesco_20150524_enciclica-laudato-si.html (accessed June 13, 2018).

Riebsame, W. E., and Woodmansee, R. G. (1995). Mapping common ground on public rangelands. In *Let the People Judge*, ed. J. Echeverria and R. B. Eby. Washington, DC: Island Press, 69–81.

Risser, P. G. (1990). Landscape pattern and its effects on energy and nutrient distribution. In *Changing Landscapes: An Ecological Perspective*, ed. I. S. Zonneveld and R. R. T. Forman. New York: Springer, 45–56.

Rosswall, T., Woodmansee, R. G., and Risser, P. G., ed. (1988). *Scales and Global Change: Spatial and Temporal Variability in Biospheric and Geospheric Processes* (SCOPE Report 35). Published on behalf of the Scientific Committee on Problems of the Environment (SCOPE) of the International Council of Scientific Unions (ICSU). New York: John Wiley.

Systems Perspective. (2019). *Systems Thinking*. Wikipedia. https://en.wikipedia.org/wiki/Systems_thinking (accessed January 8, 2019).

Tansley, A. G. (1935). The use and abuse of vegetational concepts and terms. *Ecology*, 16, 284–307.

UNMEA. (2018). United Nations Millennium Ecosystem Assessment. United Nations. www.millenniumassessment.org/en/index.html (accessed June 13, 2018).

Van Dyne, G. (1969). *The Ecosystem Concept in Natural Resource Management*. New York: Academic Press.

Von Bertalanffy, L. (1968). *General Systems Theory: Foundations, Development, Applications*. George Braziller: New York.

Waltner-Toews, D., Kay J. J., and Lister, N.-M. E., eds. (2008). *The Ecosystem Approach: Complexity, Uncertainty, and Managing for Sustainability*. New York: Columbia University Press.

WCED. (1987). *Our Common Future: Report of the World Commission on Environment and Development*, ed. G. H. Brundtland. Oxford: Oxford University Press.

Weathers, K. C., Groffman, P. M., Van Dolah, E., et al. (2016). Frontiers in ecosystem ecology from a community perspective: the future is boundless and bright. *Ecosystems*, 19, 753.

Wohl, E. (2017). Historical range of variability. *Oxford Bibliographies*. www.oxfordbibliographies.com/view/document/obo-9780199363445/obo-9780199363445-0001.xml (accessed June 18, 2018).

Woodmansee, R. G. (1978). Critique and analyses of the grassland ecosystem model ELM. In *Grassland Simulation Model*, ed. G. S. Innis. New York: Springer-Verlag.

(1988). Ecosystem processes and global change. In *Scales and Global Change: Spatial and Temporal Variability in Biospheric and Geospheric Processes* (SCOPE Report 35), ed. T. Rosswall, R. G. Woodmansee, and P. G. Risser. Published on behalf of the Scientific Committee on Problems of the Environment (SCOPE) of the International Council of Scientific Unions (ICSU). New York: John Wiley.

(1990). Biogeochemical cycles and ecological hierarchies. In *Changing Landscapes: An Ecological Perspective*, ed. I. S. Zonneveld and R. R. T. Forman. New York: Springer, 57–71.

Woodmansee, R. G., and Riebsame, W. E. (1993). *Evaluating the Effects of Climate Change on Grasslands*. Proceedings of the XVII International Grassland Congress, Palmerston North, New Zealand, Hamilton, New Zealand, Lincoln, New Zealand, Rockhampton, Australia, Palmerston North, New Zealand, The New Zealand Grassland Association.

2 · *Environmental and Natural Resource Challenges in the Twenty-First Century*

DENNIS S. OJIMA AND ROBERT G. WOODMANSEE

> There's no use talking about a problem unless you talk about the solution.
> Betty Williams (Nobel Peace Prize winner, 1976)

2.1 Introduction

The Earth and its inhabitants are facing complex environmental social, and management challenges and problems that are and will continue to be life-altering and life-threatening. Identifying and categorizing these challenges has been the subject of many prestigious national and international working groups. Summaries of the products of three of these working groups: the UN Sustainable Development Goals (UNSDG, 2015), Future Earth (2015), and the Global Land Project (GLP, 2005), are shown in Boxes 2.1–2.3.

The systems ecology paradigm (SEP) described in this book focuses on real-world, complex, or so-called wicked problems, embedded within many of the goals shown in Boxes 2.1 and 2.2 with the intent of finding solutions. Borrowing from Betty William's quote above, this chapter addresses *problems* using concepts and procedures in the systems ecology approach. Chapter 13 addresses *solutions*.

The goals of the agendas shown in Boxes 2.1–2.3 and others are laudable but are too broad to evaluate and resolve empirically or with modeling. Thus, we select a limited subset that will benefit from ecosystem science and the systems ecology approach as defined in Chapter 1 (actionable systems ecology). For example, the UNSDGs 2, 12, 13, 15, and 17 (see Box 2.1) readily lend themselves to the application of this approach. We select these examples because attempting meaningful analysis, integration, research, and synthesis of specific ecological, social, economic, and governance problems across all Sustainable Development

Box 2.1 *Challenges addressed in the United Nations Sustainable Development Goals (UNSDG, 2015)*

Goal 1: End poverty in all its forms everywhere

Goal 2: End hunger, achieve food security and improved nutrition, and promote sustainable agriculture

Goal 3: Ensure healthy lives and promote well-being for all

Goal 4: Ensure inclusive and quality education for all, and promote lifelong learning

Goal 5: Achieve gender equality and empower all women and girls

Goal 6: Ensure access to water and sanitation for all

Goal 7: Ensure access to affordable, reliable, sustainable, and modern energy for all

Goal 8: Promote inclusive and sustainable economic growth, suitable employment for all

Goal 9: Build resilient infrastructure, promote sustainable industrialization, and foster innovation

Goal 10: Reduce inequality within and among countries

Goal 11: Create inclusive, safe, resilient, and sustainable urban environments

Goal 12: Ensure sustainable consumption and production patterns

Goal 13: Take urgent action to combat climate change and its impacts

Goal 14: Conserve and sustainably use oceans, seas, and marine resources

Goal 15: Sustainably manage forests, combat desertification, halt and reverse land degradation, and end biodiversity loss

Goal 16: Promote just, peaceful, and inclusive societies

Goal 17: Revitalize the global partnership for sustainable development

Goals (SDGs), Future Earth, or the GLP goals is beyond the capabilities of any single research organization such as the Natural Resource Ecology Laboratory. Local-to-global collaboration among research organizations and individual scientist, managers, decision makers, and other stakeholders (National Research Council, 2010) is required to more effectively attain these goals.

The Resilience Alliance is a notable international collaborative effort that addresses issues similar to those shown in Boxes 2.1–2.3 (Resilience

Box 2.2 *Future Earth (2015) addresses eight key challenges to global sustainability*

Challenge 1: Deliver water, energy, and food for all, and manage the synergies and trade-offs among them by understanding how these interactions are shaped by environmental, economic, social, and political changes.

Challenge 2: Decarbonize socioeconomic systems to stabilize the climate by promoting the technological, economic, social, political, and behavioral changes enabling transformations, while building knowledge about the impacts of climate change and adaptation responses for people and ecosystems.

Challenge 3: Safeguard the terrestrial, freshwater, and marine natural assets underpinning human well-being by understanding relationships between biodiversity, ecosystem functioning, and services, and developing effective valuation and governance approaches.

Challenge 4: Build healthy, resilient, and productive cities by identifying and shaping innovations that combine improved urban and societal environments with declining resource footprints and providing efficient services and infrastructures that are robust to disasters.

Challenge 5: Promote sustainable rural futures to feed rising and more affluent populations amid changes in biodiversity, resources, and climate by analyzing alternative land uses, food systems, and ecosystem options, and identifying institutional and governance needs.

Challenge 6: Improve human health by elucidating and finding responses to the complex interactions among environmental change, pollution, pathogens, and disease vectors, ecosystem services, and people's livelihoods, nutrition and well-being.

Challenge 7: Encourage sustainable consumption and production patterns that are equitable by understanding the social and environmental impacts from the consumption of all resources, opportunities for decoupling resource use from growth in well-being, and options for sustainable development pathways and related changes in human behavior.

Challenge 8: Increase social resilience to future threats by building adaptive governance systems, developing early warning of global and connected thresholds and risks, and testing effective, accountable, and transparent institutions that promote transformations to sustainability.

Box 2.3 *Objectives and research themes of the joint International Geosphere/ Biosphere Program and the International Human Dimensions Programme on Global Environmental Change (IHDP) science plan and implementation strategy*

GLP has three objectives that determine the research framework:

1. Identify the agents, structures, and nature of change in coupled human-environment systems on land, and quantify their effects on the coupled system;
2. Assess how the provision of ecosystem services is affected by the changes in (1) above; and
3. Identify the character and dynamics of vulnerable and sustainable coupled human–environment systems to interacting perturbations, including climate change.

These objectives yielded three specific themes and identified key issues within each theme:

Theme 1: The dynamics of land system change.
   Issue 1.1: How do globalization and population change affect regional and local land-use decisions and practices?
   Issue 1.2: How do changes in land management decisions and practices affect biogeochemistry, biodiversity, biophysical properties, and disturbance regimes of terrestrial and freshwater ecosystems?
   Issue 1.3: How do the atmospheric, biogeochemical, and biophysical dimensions of global change affect ecosystem structure and function?
Theme 2: The consequences of land system change.
   Issue 2.1: What are the critical feedbacks to the coupled Earth System from ecosystem changes?
   Issue 2.2: How do changes in ecosystem structure and functioning affect the delivery of ecosystem services?
   Issue 2.3: How are ecosystem services linked to human well-being?
   Issue 2.4: How do people respond at various scales and in different contexts to changes in ecosystem service provision?
Theme 3: Integrating analysis and modeling for land sustainability.
   Issue 3.1: What are the critical pathways of change in land systems?
   Issue 3.2: How do the vulnerability and resilience of land systems to hazards and disturbances vary in response to changes in human-environment interactions?
   Issue 3.3: Which institutions enhance decision making and governance for the sustainability of land systems?

Walker and Salt, 2006; Alliance, 2018). The following statement is taken from the Alliance website:

Translating resilience concepts into practice is a rapidly evolving field of research and a key objective of projects and programs seeking sustainable transformations. The Resilience Alliance has been at the forefront of developing tools and approaches for assessing and managing resilience in a wide variety of social-ecological systems. Key elements of resilience in practice include:

- Describing and developing a conceptual model of the social–ecological system
- Understanding system dynamics including alternate regimes and thresholds
- Identifying interactions across scales including structural influences of larger systems and novelty emerging from smaller sub-systems
- Mapping governance networks and exploring adaptive governance options
- Active adaptation, resilience-based stewardship & transformation.

Weathers and colleagues (Weathers et al., 2016) elegantly described research, methodology, data, and leadership needs *within* the ecosystem ecology research community to better address the challenges and opportunities posed by environmental and socioecological pressures and concerns. Their findings yielded three major themes: "frontiers," "capacity building," and "barriers to implementation."

The "frontiers" theme was further divided into: (1) focusing on the drivers of ecosystem change, (2) new understanding of ecosystem process and function, (3) evaluating human dimensions of ecosystem ecology, and (4) new approaches to problem solving and applied research with a focus on enhancing relevance to human welfare.

"Capacity building" emphasizes the need to embrace the holistic, systems approach while recognizing the need for and tension between the reductionist approach to ecology. The need for managing "big" data sets, advancing technologies, collaboration, and network building are also addressed. Training is another area of emphasis in capacity building.

Several "barriers to research" were identified by Weathers et al. (2016). These included the need for theoretical thinking, new training models, cultural differences within the scientific community (silos), attitudes about collaboration, and rewards, if any, for collaboration and networking.

The GLP of the International Geosphere/Biosphere Program (IGBP) and International Human Dimensions Programme on Global Environmental Change (IHDP) (GLP, 2005) provided an analysis of needs to "measure, model and understand the coupled human-environmental system" (Box 2.3). The GLP identified major scientific challenges including overcoming disciplinary fragmentation, issues of scale, case study comparisons, using the past to inform the future, and synthesizing insights in dynamic models. The report focuses on three major and associated issues and questions.

The conclusions about the challenges facing the ecosystem ecology and human dimensions of research communities, drawn by GLP (2005) and Weathers et al. (2016) are especially gratifying to the NREL and their network of collaborators given their past (Baron and Galvin, 1990) and continued (this book) leadership in these areas. While the Weathers et al. (2016) focus was on the ecosystem ecology community, the focus of the NREL ensures the SEP is available, understandable, and used by managers, policy makers, and citizens; aspirations closely aligned with the GLP.

Our goals in this chapter are to address twenty-first-century challenges through the lens of the SEP. We use ecological hierarchies, space, time, and institutional scales (Figure 2.1) as concepts and tools to help disaggregate the broad goals shown in Boxes 2.1–2.3, breaking them into comprehendible and researchable topics. Our focus is on science that leads to actions that support environmental, natural resource, and socio/ecological decision making, management, and solutions (see Chapter 13).

Bringing the power of the SEP to bear on future challenges requires a continual "upgrade" of our tools within systems sciences, ecosystem science, and social science to develop long-lasting adaptive strategies to manage ecosystems (Ojima and Corell, 2009). We must also integrate social, organizational, behavioral, learning, and marketing sciences into the realm of systems ecology. The integration of these perspectives is essential for societies around the Earth to make wise policy and management decisions.

2.2 Challenge Selection

What are the big questions, problems, and challenges we see coming in the next several decades and beyond? As a means of organizing challenges into definable and workable constructs, we attempt to link the challenges to geographic levels in a simple spatial hierarchy shown as the "Space" dimension (Figure 2.1) (O'Neill, 1988; Woodmansee, 1990). The concept of the spatially defined hierarchy used in this book is not theoretical; it is pragmatic. The levels within the hierarchy are defined by specific problems of concern and focus on definable ecosystem structure and ecological, hydrologic, atmospheric, and human-mediated processes and

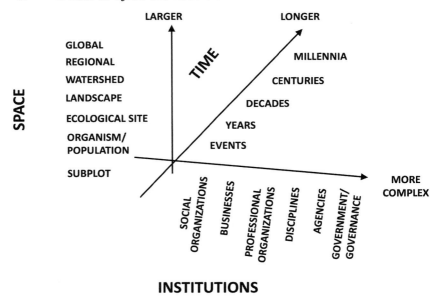

Figure 2.1 Important "scales" that need consideration in decision making. Some hierarchical dimensions require specific attention when evaluating and managing ecological/social ecosystems.

transfers of matter and information (see Chapter 1). At smaller levels in the spatial hierarchy, we seek relative homogeneity, for example any 1 m^2 plot in a 1 ha ecological site is statistically similar to any other m^2. At larger scales, yet still seeking relative homogeneity, we might differentiate between shortgrass steppes, mid-grass prairie, and tallgrass prairie within the North American Grasslands. These distinctions all depend on the problem being addressed. In this chapter, we focus on examples of research and analysis needed within each hierarchical level to address some of the challenges identified in Boxes 2.1–2.3. We also list problems at specific spatial scales while recognizing that many problems at larger scales require an integration of information from smaller scales, while many problems at small scales need the context of larger scales (O'Neill, 1988).

Additionally, we recognize that each level within the spatial hierarchy interacts with levels in the temporal and the institutional dimensions (Figure 2.1). Spatial, temporal, and institutional scales are discussed in Section 1.9. We identify challenges that the SEP can help comprehend, analyze, and resolve by following the protocol suggested in Section 1.3 and further elaborated in Chapter 10.

2.2.1 General Challenges

Against the backdrop of the UN SDGs, Future Earth, Frontiers in Ecosystem Ecology, Resilience Alliance, and the IGBP GLP (GLP, 2005), our focus is on challenges that involve terrestrial ecosystems (including people) as they relate to topics such as: (1) food, water, and soil security; (2) ecosystem services, including biodiversity; (3) habitat alterations; and (4) animal, microorganism, and plant migrations. Some of the environmental and social challenges derived from Boxes 2.1–2.3 needing the SEP to resolve them are listed in Table 2.1, which focuses on general issues where more knowledge and experience are needed. Each issue listed in column 1 needs to be disaggregated into tractable pieces (McKenzie-Mohr, 2011), researched, analyzed, and then reassembled (integrated) into coherent systems using the systems ecology approach. Tables similar to Table 2.1 can be constructed (but not here) of temporal and institutional hierarchies to help define problems and goals (see Chapters 1 and 10).

While the focus of this book is on terrestrial ecosystems and their included freshwater components, the SEP described herein is equally applicable to marine systems. With few exceptions, the issues suggested in Tables 2.1–2.7 apply to both terrestrial and marine ecosystems (see SDG 14, Box 2.1).

2.2.2 Critical Research Areas within Spatial Scales

Tables 2.2–2.7 give specific examples of research areas within each spatial hierarchical level (Figure 2.1) that are critical for analysis, research, and problem solving if society is to move toward a more adaptive, resilient, and sustainable future. As with Table 2.1, the information in Tables 2.2–2.7 is not intended to be definitive, but rather to stimulate focus, discussion, and debate about what research is really needed to answer important questions and resolve problems. Each item in these tables must be examined to determine if it can be further divided (divisible) into specific "subsets" that have recognizable analysis pathways and tractable solutions or end-states (McKenzie-Mohr, 2011; see Section 1.5 and Chapter 10). Each of the last columns in Tables 2.2–2.7 is intended to be a reminder to ask, "How much research is enough?" or "Do we already know enough to better manage our existing ecosystems within acceptable ranges of variability?" (Wohl, 2017). A major challenge facing systems ecologists in the digital age is the unintended consequence that much of the knowledge and hard literature established prior to the digital age is inaccessible, with the exception of minimal availability in libraries,

Table 2.1 *Example issues (column 1) extracted from Boxes 2.1–2.3 for which ecosystem science and the SEP can provide meaningful future analysis direction and contribute to solutions*

General issues	**Organism**/ populations	Ecological site	Landscapes	**Small regions**/ watersheds	Regions/ nations	Continent	*Globe*
Changes in global nitrogen cycles	X	X	X	X	X	X	X
Changes in global carbon cycle	X	X	X	X	X	X	X
Climate changes	X	X	X	X	X	X	X
Changes in ecosystem management and land use	X	X	X	X	X		
Consequences of human population growth			X	X	X		
Consequences of shifting human demographics			X	X			
Relationships between structure (including biodiversity) and functioning of biophysical systems (diversity of processes)	X	X	X				

Relationships between structure and functioning of biophysical systems and ecosystem services	X	X		X		
Influence of people on healthy functioning ecosystem processes			X	X		
Food security	X	X	X			
Water security	X	X	X	X		
Soil security		X	X			
Invasive species	X	X	X	X	X	
Integrating social, behavioral, and ecosystem sciences			X	X	X	
Defining resilience and sustainability of ecosystems		X	X	X		
Governance, policy, and management	X	X	X	X	X	X
Ecosystem science literacy and education	X	X	X	X	X	X

(cont.)

Table 2.1 (*cont.*)

General issues	Organism/populations	Ecological site	Landscapes	Small regions/watersheds	Regions/nations	Continent	Globe
Development of decision support systems	X	X	X	X	X	X	X
Co-development of knowledge/actionable science		X	X	X	X	X	
Global/local networking/information sharing				X	X	X	X
Sustainable development			X	X	X		

Many of those future contributions will be based on extensive existing knowledge. Columns 2–7 are spatial scales at which the systems ecology approach can make direct contributions. Similar tables can be developed for temporal and intuitional hierarchies.

Table 2.2 *Challenges stated in Boxes 2.1–2.3 that require the SEP for solution at the organism level of resolution*

Challenge	Critical new knowledge	Critical long-term research and monitoring	Specific gap filling	Sufficient knowledge available now to apply BMPs
Interactions of climate change, habitat fragmentation, and species introductions with organisms within ecological sites	X	X		
Animal, plant, microorganism, and disease adaptability and resilience in changing environments	X	X		
Interactions of habitat alteration and land modification with specific organisms and populations		X	X	X
Interactions of key species with provisioning services, e.g., new foods, crops, genetic resources	X			
Interactions of key species with regulating services, e.g., carbon sequestration, climate regulation, water and air purification	X	X		
Interactions of key species with supporting services, e.g., nutrient cycling, primary production, and soil formation		X	X	X

(cont.)

Table 2.2 (*cont.*)

Challenge	Critical new knowledge	Critical long-term research and monitoring	Specific gap filling	Sufficient knowledge available now to apply BMPs
Interactions of key species with cultural services, e.g., arts, cultural norms and values, and recreational experiences				X
Ecosystem science literacy and education				X
Governance, policy, and management	X			X

Columns 2–4 indicate the general type of information necessary to meet the challenge. Column 2 indicates that new frontiers in research and understanding are needed. Column 3 highlights the type of research that requires long-term measurements for verification of forecasts, adaptive strategies, and modeling results. Column 4 indicates where new research findings are essential to add important value to existing knowledge. Column 5 indicates where sufficient information exists to apply BMPs to help meet the challenge.

or ignored because it is difficult to retrieve. "One of the problems of this electronic age is that almost everything published prior to the digital age, in printed format, is forgotten" (Michael Usher, personal communication; see Section 11.4). Access to pre-2000 scientific journals has improved, but access to book chapters dealing with actionable science is often difficult. During the development and evolution of ecosystem science and systems ecology, many of the seminal papers were published as chapters in books because they were based on concepts, ideas, and models drawn from integration and synthesis of previous research and experience, not original data and data analysis. Scientific journal reviewers were loath to accept papers that were not data driven. Many of these ideas first appeared in proposals to the National Science Foundation (NSF). At that time, the NSF and their review panels were receptive to bold, new ideas; thus, the birth of a new science.

Column 5 in Tables 2.2–2.7 indicate that some aspects of the challenge can be sufficiently addressed with knowledge developed over the past century, yet other aspects are outside the current knowledge base and require further research. For example, as seen in row 3 of Table 2.2, we know how to manage native species and populations in vast areas of drylands across the globe, yet this knowledge is seldom used. However, if exotic species are introduced, additional research will be required.

2.3 Spatial Hierarchy: Disaggregating Complex (Wicked) Problems

We use levels of the spatial hierarchy (see Section 1.9) simply to help us evaluate and resolve one or a set of real-world, complex problems challenging the sustainability of the Earth's ecosystems. Here we introduce the concept as a means to disaggregate the goals in Boxes 2.1–2.3 into manageable pieces. (McKenzie-Mohr, 2011).

2.3.1 Organisms (Plant and Populations)

Vast amounts of knowledge exist about individual organisms and populations. A plethora of research and mathematical models has been produced that simulates these dynamics (see Chapter 4). However, accessing, integrating, and synthesizing that knowledge as it relates to global changes remains elusive. Table 2.2 indicates examples of knowledge needs at the organism level of resolution.

2.3.2 Ecological Site Scale (or Plot or Patch or Stand)

Research accomplishments at the ecological site scale described in Chapter 1 have laid the foundation for fundamental understanding of the structure and functioning of ecosystems, development of many modern best management practices (BMPs) (see Chapter 7), and for tackling future environmental challenges. For practical management purposes, ecosystem functioning at the ecological site scale has been analyzed and described. Based on the current ecosystem knowledge warehouse, the current state of simulation modeling, success of management practices derived from application of the systems ecology approach, and experience of many ecosystem scientists and managers, we can confidently say *we know how to manage grassland, shrubland, and forest ecosystems*. Some of the remaining challenges are listed in Table 2.3.

Table 2.3 *Challenges embedded in topics in Boxes 2.1–2.3 needing the SEP for solution at the ecological site level of resolution*

Challenge	Critical new knowledge	Critical long-term research and monitoring	Specific gap filling	Sufficient knowledge available now to apply BMPs
Greenhouse gas sources and sinks in agricultural, grazinglands, and forests		X	X	X
Bioactive nitrogen sources, transformations, and sinks		X	X	X
Particulate, dust, other chemical (including fertilizers) sources, sinks, and impacts	X	X		
Interaction of organisms within ecological sites resulting from climate change, habitat alteration, and land modification	X			
Interaction of ecological sites within landscapes	X	X		
Animal, plant, and disease affinities and avoidance in changing environments	X			
Effects of interacting changing climate, bioactive nitrogen loading, habitat alteration, and land modification on specific ecological sites	X			

Table 2.3 (*cont.*)

Challenge	Critical new knowledge	Critical long-term research and monitoring	Specific gap filling	Sufficient knowledge available now to apply BMPs
Provisioning services – food, crops, fiber, water				X
Provisioning services – genetic resources, medicinal resources, energy, etc.	X			
Regulating services – carbon sequestration, climate regulation, water and air purification, etc.	X	X		
Supporting services – nutrient cycling, primary production, soil formation, etc.			X	X
Cultural services – arts, cultural norms and values, recreational experiences, etc.	X			
Hydrologic cycle, erosion, and sedimentation				X
Transportation infrastructure (roads, trains, oil, gas, pipelines) network impacts	X			
Ecosystem science literacy and education			X	X

(*cont.*)

Table 2.3 (*cont.*)

Challenge	Critical new knowledge	Critical long-term research and monitoring	Specific gap filling	Sufficient knowledge available now to apply BMPs
Governance, policy, and management	X	X		

Columns 2–4 indicate the general type of information necessary to meet the challenge. Column 2 indicates new frontiers in research and understanding are needed. Column 3 highlights the type of research that requires long-term measurements for verification of forecasts, adaptive strategies, and modeling results. Column 4 indicates where new research findings are essential to add important value to existing knowledge. Column 5 indicates where sufficient information exists to apply BMPs to help meet the challenge.

One of the leading challenges is disseminating existing, actionable knowledge to land managers, policy makers, and the citizenry, and then convincing them to adopt the BMPs for the benefit of themselves and others (see Chapter 13). Table 2.3 reflects the view that future challenges will be best met by using the systems ecology approach and the existing warehouse of ecosystem knowledge to address problems at landscape and higher levels in the ecological hierarchy.

2.3.3 Landscapes as Ecosystems

Knowledge referenced in this book has been and can continue to be used to answer practical questions about the management of landscape ecosystems, for example farms, ranches, forest and rangeland administrative units, parks, and protected areas. Ecosystem science has provided a basic understanding of the physical and biological factors of climate, topography, geologic substrate, soil patterns, vegetation communities, and associated biota that directly influence the functioning of landscapes under relatively static environmental conditions. An explicit example of the use of this knowledge is found in Hoffmann et al. (2014) who summarized the contributions of livestock species and breeds to ecosystem services.

The challenge for society and ecosystem science is to identify and resolve critical unknowns at the landscape level that will address current complex and complicated (wicked) problems and help anticipate the yet unknown problems identified in Table 2.4. Changing climate, human infrastructure, cultural norms, physical infrastructure, microeconomics, land modification, and habitat fragmentation have profound, direct effects on landscapes, but their interactions are not as well understood (Mitchell et al., 2014). The current lack of understanding of the *interactions* of ecological sites, changing climate and carbon and nutrient dynamics, hydrologic cycles, economics, and societal influences within our landscape-scale ecosystems is a major challenge as we move further into the twenty-first century (see Table 2.4).

Landscapes are the scale of ecosystems at which management practices by individuals, households, or groups responsible for specific lands are put in place. These management actions may or may not be influenced by agencies and policies mandated by representatives from outside the local community. External (regional, state, national) governing policies can strongly influence landscape management. However, local actions by land managers must be implemented to successfully manage landscapes and hopefully adopt BMPs to meet broader societal needs and ensure ecosystem health, resilience, and sustainability. A major research, education, and engagement challenge is convincing managers to adopt these practices.

2.3.4 Small Regions and Watersheds as Ecosystems

Watersheds, agricultural districts, community grazinglands, forestland administrative units, and civil administrative units (e.g., counties, community or public lands, and water management agencies) are small regions that are the *hierarchal level where individuals can become stakeholders involved in community decision making* as described in Chapter 1 (Table 2.5). Small regions are often strongly influenced by economics that in turn can be influenced by changing climate, technology, political leadership, and human demographics. New methods of education, outreach, and engagement are needed at this level of the ecological hierarcy because stakeholder participation, collaboration, co-production of knowledge, and community-based decision making is profoundly important for applying the systems ecology approach to management of ecosystems (Ojima and Corell, 2009; Weichselgartner and Kasperson, 2010; Tabara and Chabay, 2013; Moser, 2016a; Moser, 2016b).

Much has yet to be learned about the blending of ecosystem and social sciences (including political science), and the development of decision

Table 2.4 *Challenges stated in Boxes 2.1–2.3 needing the SEP for solution at the landscape level of resolution*

Challenge	Critical new knowledge	Critical long-term research and monitoring	Specific gap filling	Sufficient knowledge available now to apply BMPs
Greenhouse gas sources and sinks in agricultural grazinglands and forests		X	X	X
Bioactive nitrogen sources, transformations, and sinks			X	X
Particulate, dust, other chemical (including fertilizers) sources, sinks, and impacts		X	X	
Interaction of landscapes within regions	X			
Human population growth, demographics	X			
Animal, plant, and disease migrations, redistributions, and biodiversity	X	X	X	
Effects of climate change, habitat fragmentation, and land modification	X	X		
Provisioning services, e.g., new food, crops, fiber, and genetic resources			X	X

Table 2.4 (*cont.*)

Challenge	Critical new knowledge	Critical long-term research and monitoring	Specific gap filling	Sufficient knowledge available now to apply BMPs
Regulating services, e.g., carbon sequestration, climate regulation, and water and air purification		X	X	
Supporting services, e.g., nutrient cycling, primary production, and soil formation			X	X
Cultural services, e.g., arts, cultural norms and values, and recreational experiences				X
Social organization, cultural norms	X	X		
Integrating social, behavioral, and ecosystem sciences	X			
Hydrologic cycle, erosion, and sedimentation		X	X	X
Transportation (roads, trains, oil, gas, pipelines) network impacts	X			
Transportation access	X			
Macro and microeconomic impacts on ecosystem processes and services		X	X	

(*cont.*)

Table 2.4 (*cont.*)

Challenge	Critical new knowledge	Critical long-term research and monitoring	Specific gap filling	Sufficient knowledge available now to apply BMPs
Development of decision support systems	X			
Co-development of knowledge/ actionable science	X			
Ecosystem science literacy and education	X		X	
Governance, policy, and management	X	X		X

Columns 2–4 indicate the general type of information necessary to meet the challenge. Column 2 indicates the new frontiers in research and understanding that are needed. Column 3 highlights the type of research that requires long-term measurements for verification of forecasts, adaptive strategies, and modeling results. Column 4 indicates where new research findings are essential to add important value to existing knowledge. Column 5 indicates where sufficient information exists to apply BMPs to help meet the challenge.

support systems and collaborative decision making (see Chapter 10) to insure beneficial outcomes for community resiliency and sustainability (Table 2.5).

2.3.5 Regions Including Nations As Ecosystems

Elected or appointed representatives, lawyers, and well-organized lobby-ists and organizations conduct governance and policy making in larger regions (Table 2.6). Regions are often strongly influenced by economics and political persuasion that in turn are influenced by changing societal norms and human demographics. Science is often downplayed if not completely ignored when decisions are made about the efficacy of management actions that influence regional ecosystems. Ecosystem

Table 2.5 *Challenges stated in Boxes 2.1–2.3 that need the SEP for solution at the small region/watershed ecosystem levels of resolution*

Challenge	Critical new knowledge	Critical long-term research and monitoring	Specific gap filling	Sufficient knowledge available now to apply BMPs
Greenhouse gas sources and sinks in agricultural grazinglands and forests	X	X	X	
Bioactive nitrogen loading and distribution in the atmosphere and surface waters	X	X	X	
Particulate, dust, other chemical sources, and sinks	X		X	
Climate change impacts	X	X	X	
Human population growth and demographics	X			
Animal, plant, disease migrations and redistributions, and biodiversity	X	X		
Habitat fragmentation and land modification	X	X	X	
Transportation (e.g., roads, trains, oil, gas, and pipelines) network impacts	X		X	
Transportation access				X
Social organization and cultural norms	X	X		
Integrating social, behavioral, and ecosystem sciences	X			

(*cont.*)

Table 2.5 (*cont.*)

Challenge	Critical new knowledge	Critical long-term research and monitoring	Specific gap filling	Sufficient knowledge available now to apply BMPs
Macro and microeconomic impacts on ecosystem processes and services	X			
Development of decision support systems	X			
Co-development of knowledge/ actionable science	X			
Ecosystem science literacy and education	X		X	X
Governance, policy, and management	X			
Networking/ information/data sharing	X			

Columns 2–4 indicate the general type of information necessary to meet the challenge. Column 2 indicates the new frontiers in research and understanding that are needed. Column 3 highlights the type of research that requires long-term measurements for verification of forecasts, adaptive strategies, and modeling results. Column 4 indicates where new research findings are essential to add important value to existing knowledge. Column 5 indicates where sufficient information exists to apply BMPs to help meet the challenge.

scientists and systems ecologists must find ways into the decision-making processes at this level of the ecological hierarchy to ensure consideration of the biological and physical health, safety, and well-being of ecosystems and societies. Table 2.6 indicates some of the research challenges facing systems ecologists when attempting to inform decision making at regional and national levels.

Table 2.6 *Challenges stated in Boxes 2.1–2.3 that need the SEP for solution at the regional and national levels of resolution*

Challenge	Critical new knowledge	Critical long-term research and monitoring	Specific gap filling	Sufficient knowledge available now to apply BMPs
Greenhouse gas sources and sinks in agricultural grazinglands and forests		X	X	
Bioactive nitrogen loading and distribution in the atmosphere and surface waters	X		X	
Particulate, dust, other chemical sources, and sinks	X	X		
Interaction of nations and regions within continents, e.g., cooperation, wars.			X	X
Climate change impacts	X	X		
Human population growth and demographics	X			
Animal, plant, disease migrations and redistributions, and biodiversity	X	X		
Habitat fragmentation and land modification	X	X	X	
Transportation (e.g., roads, trains, oil, gas, and pipelines) network impacts	X		X	

(cont.)

Table 2.6 (cont.)

Challenge	Critical new knowledge	Critical long-term research and monitoring	Specific gap filling	Sufficient knowledge available now to apply BMPs
Transportation access				X
Social organization and cultural norms	X	X		
Integrating social, behavioral, and ecosystem sciences	X			
Macroeconomic impacts on ecosystem processes and services	X			
Development of decision support systems	X			
Co-development of knowledge/ actionable science	X			
Ecosystem science literacy and education			X	X
Governance, policy, and management	X			
Regional and national networking/ information/data sharing	X			

Columns 2–4 indicate the general type of information necessary to meet the challenge. Column 2 indicates the new frontiers in research and understanding that are needed. Column 3 highlights the type of research that requires long-term measurements for verification of forecasts, adaptive strategies, and modeling results. Column 4 indicates where new research findings are essential to add important value to existing knowledge. Column 5 indicates where sufficient information exists to apply BMPs to help meet the challenge.

2.3.6 Continents (and Islands) As Ecosystems

Describing the physical, ecological, economic, and political interactions of regions and nations within continents (see Chapter 1) is one of the major challenges facing ecosystem science today (see Table 2.7). At these large scales, biological and physical interactions tend to be overshadowed by political and economic interests. Yet, the future health, safety, and well-being of the Earth's ecosystems and societies is and will be dependent on the success of ecosystem scientists in influencing policy making and economic decisions at the highest levels of civil society.

Land uses, industrialization, urbanization, and transportation systems are driven by population growth, economics of food and natural resources, availability of markets, aspirations of wealth, health, safety, and education, good or bad governance, wars, and ecologically sound or unsound policies within the regional ecosystems that make up the continent (Table 2.7). All these interactions can have a profound effect on the ecosystems throughout the ecological hierarchy (Figure 2.1). Analysis of continental-scale questions requires the systems ecology approach to precisely define the problems of concern, systematically evaluate them, and then focus on the potential solutions as described above.

2.3.7 The Earth As an Ecosystem

Table 2.8 shows some of the challenges facing society that require the systems ecology approach for resolution at the Earth level. The impacts of global climate change and their influence on atmospheric circulation, and the distribution of warming/cooling patterns, precipitation patterns, and types and frequencies of extreme weather events are all critical for understanding how ecosystems function at all levels in the hierarchy (Figure 2.1). These are the climate drivers of ecosystem functioning.

Transportation and communication systems are dramatically influencing the interactions of the Earth's ecosystems. Food, fertilizers, plants, animals, microorganisms, fossil fuels, building materials, and minerals are exchanged globally and are facilitated by modern, nearly instant communication systems. Ecosystem science and the systems ecology approach are needed to fully understand the impacts of these redistribution pathways on the environment, natural resources, and society.

Powerful arguments can be made that future healthy economies throughout the world will be underpinned by healthy ecosystem

Table 2.7 *Challenges stated in Boxes 2.1–2.3 that need the SEP for solution at the continental level of resolution*

Challenge	Critical new knowledge	Critical long-term research and monitoring	Specific gap filling	Sufficient knowledge available now to apply BMPs
Greenhouse gas sources and sinks in agricultural grazinglands and forests		X		
Bioactive nitrogen loading and distribution in the atmosphere and surface waters	X	X	X	
Particulate, dust, other chemical sources, and sinks	X			
Interaction of nations and regions within continents	X			
Integrating social, behavioral, and ecosystem sciences	X			
Ecosystem science literacy and education	X	X		
International networking/ information/data sharing	X			
Governance, policy, and management			X	X

Columns 2–4 indicate the general type of information necessary to meet the challenge. Column 2 indicates the new frontiers in research and understanding that are needed. Column 3 highlights the types of research that require long-term measurements for verification of forecasts, adaptive strategies, and modeling results. Column 4 indicates where new research findings are essential to add important value to existing knowledge. Column 5 indicates where sufficient information exists to apply BMPs to help meet the challenge.

Table 2.8. *Challenges embedded in the topics stated in Boxes 2.1–2.3 needing the SEP for solution at the whole Earth level of resolution*

Challenge	Critical new knowledge	Critical long-term research and monitoring	Specific gap filling	Sufficient knowledge available now to apply BMPs
Greenhouse gas sources and sinks in agricultural grazinglands and forests		X	X	
Bioactive nitrogen loading and distribution in the atmosphere and surface waters	X		X	
Particulate, dust, and other chemical sources and sinks	X		X	
Integrating social, behavioral, and ecosystem sciences	X			
Governance, policy, and management	X			
International networking/ information/data sharing	X			

Columns 2–4 indicate the general type of information necessary to meet the challenge. Column 2 indicates the new frontiers in research and understanding that are needed. Column 3 highlights the type of research that requires long-term measurements for verification of forecasts, adaptive strategies, and modeling results. Column 4 indicates where new research findings are essential to add important value to existing knowledge. Column 5 indicates where sufficient information exists to apply BMPs to help meet the challenge.

functioning and ecosystem services. Governments, financial institutions, and trade and marketing organizations will need to be constantly reminded that ecosystem science and its knowledge is available and must be considered in intelligent financial, economic, and policy decision making.

Sound international agreements, policies, and good, transparent, and accountable governance will be required for implementing strategies to meet future environmental and social challenges facing the Earth. *Ecosystem science must "have a seat at the table" when these critical strategies are developed (e.g., Future Earth, World Bank, SDGs).*

All of these global-scale issues are scientifically challenging, require strict application of systems analysis (the systems ecology approach) and massive data sets, are computationally difficult, and demand significant scientific and institutional collaboration across the globe – the globalization of collaboration.

References

Baron, J. S., and Galvin, K. A. (1990). Future directions of ecosystem science. *BioScience*, 40(9), 640–2.

Future Earth (2015). *Future Earth 2025 Vision.* www.futureearth.org/sites/default/files/future-earth_10-year-vision_web.pdf (accessed June 18, 2018).

Global Land Project (GLP) (2005). Science Plan and Implementation Strategy IGBP Report No. 53/IHDP Report No. 19. IGBP Secretariat, Stockholm. 64pp. www.igbp.net/download/18.1b8ae20512db692f2a680006384/1376383121392/report_53-GLP.pdf.

Hoffmann, I., From, T., and Boerma, D. (2014). Ecosystem services provided by livestock species and breeds, with special consideration to the small-scale livestock keepers and pastoralists. Background Study Paper No. 66 Rev. 1. Commission on Genetic Resources for Food and Agriculture. Food and Agriculture Organization of the United Nations (FAO). Rome. www.fao.org/3/a-at598e.pdf; see also www.fao.org/3/a-i6482e.pdf.

McKenzie-Mohr, D. (2011). *Fostering Sustainable Behavior: An Introduction to Community-Based Social Marketing.* Gabriola Island, BC: New Society Publishers.

Mitchell, M., Griffith, R., Ryan, P., et al. (2014). Applying resilience thinking to natural resource management through a "planning-by-doing" framework. *Society and Natural Resources*, 27, 299–314.

Moser, S. (2016a). Editorial overview – Transformations and co-design: Co-designing research projects on social transformations to sustainability. *Current Opinion in Environmental Sustainability*, 20, v–viii.

(2016b). Can science on transformation transform science? Lessons from co-design. *Current Opinion in Environmental Sustainability*, 20, 106–15; http://dx.doi.org/10.1016/j.cosust.2016.10.007.

National Research Council. (2010). *Toward Sustainable Agricultural Systems in the 21st Century*. Washington, DC: The National Academies Press.

Ojima, D. S., and Corell, R. W. (2009). Managing grassland ecosystems under global environmental change: Developing strategies to meet challenges and opportunities of global change. In *Farming with Grass: Achieving Sustainable Mixed Agricultural Landscape*, ed. A. J. Franzluebbers. Ankeny, IA: Soil and Water Conservation Society, 146–55.

O'Neill, R. V. (1988). Hierarchy theory and global change. In *Scales and Global Change: Spatial and Temporal Variability in Biospheric and Geospheric Processes*, ed. T. Rosswall, R. G. Woodmansee, and P. G. Risser. SCOPE Series 38. Hoboken, NJ: John Wiley and Sons, 29–45.

Resilience Alliance (2018). *Resilience Alliance*. www.resalliance.org (accessed June 18, 2018).

Tabara, J., and Chabay, I. (2013). Coupling human information and knowledge systems with social–ecological systems change: Reframing research, education, and policy for sustainability. *Environmental Science and Policy*, 28, 71–81.

UN Sustainable Development Goals (UNSDG) (2015). *Sustainable Development Goals: 17 Goals to Transform Our World*. www.un.org/sustainabledevelopment/sustainable-development-goals/# (accessed June 18, 2018).

Walker, B., and Salt, D. (2006). *Resilience Thinking: Sustaining Ecosystems and People in a Changing World*. Washington, DC: Island Press.

Weathers, K. C., Groffman, P. M., Van Dolah, E., et al. (2016). Frontiers in ecosystem ecology from a community perspective: The future is boundless and bright. *Ecosystems*, 19, 753. https://doi.org/10.1007/s10021–016–9967–0.

Weichselgartner, J., and Kasperson, R. (2010). Barriers in the science-policy-practice interface: Toward a knowledge-action-system in global environmental change research. *Global Environmental Change*, 20(2), 266–77.

Wohl, E. (2017). Historical range of variability. *Oxford Bibliographies*. www.oxfordbibliographies.com/view/document/obo-9780199363445/obo-9780199363445–0001.xml (accessed June 18, 2018).

Woodmansee, R. G. (1990). Biogeochemical cycles and ecological hierarchies. In *Changing Landscapes: An Ecological Perspective*, ed. I. S. Zonneveld and R. R. T. Forman. New York: Springer, 57–71.

3 · *Evolution of Ecosystem Science to Advance Science and Society in the Twenty-First Century*

DAVID C. COLEMAN, ELDOR A. PAUL,
STACY LYNN, AND THOMAS ROSSWALL

3.1 Introduction

There has been considerable debate over the last few decades about what ecosystem ecology and ecosystem science constitute: what have they contributed in the past, and what are their prospects for the future (Baron and Galvin, 1990; Weathers et al., 2016)? In this chapter we trace the origin of the ecosystem science concept and its evolution over time as a guiding principle for sustainable development and its future direction with some considerations from the perspective of four ecosystem ecologists. Numerous other aspects of ecosystem science are covered elsewhere in this volume.

An ecosystem is a community of living organisms and its interactions with the physical environment as linked through energy and nutrient flows combined with atmospheric, hydrologic, and organic and mineral soil components. Although the actual word "ecosystem" was not coined until the 1930s (Tansley, 1935), there is a rich scientific history relative to its components (Coleman et al., 2018).

Early in human history, hunter-gatherers recognized the rich diversity of plants and animals in the unique combination of cool-subtropical or warm-temperate environments, available water, and often dark-colored soils with relatively high organic matter contents. Such fertile environments most often occurred in river valleys and flood plains. It could be said that humans had an early understanding of their ecosystems. Ecosystems were manipulated with grazing and burning but were not intensively worked until the start of agriculture, approximately 12,000 years ago. However, the major effect man was having on the landscape was not highlighted until Marsh (1864) wrote about *Man and Nature*, a treatise on physical geography and human interactions. In the twentieth century, scientific attention was given to the study of how humans affected ecosystems, documented in several notable volumes (e.g., Thomas, 1956; Turner et al., 1990; Lambin and Geist, 2006).

Ecosystem science concepts trace back to van Helmont (1579–1642) when he placed a 2.3 kg willow tree into a pot with 90.8 kg of soil. After five years of growth, with rainwater as the sole irrigation source, the tree weighed 76 kg; however, the soil had lost only 57 g. Based on that era's background of knowledge, Van Helmont concluded that water was the principal component of vegetation (Brady, 1984). In 1754, Joseph Black described carbon dioxide as the gas critical to photosynthesis and decomposition. It is now recognized as a greenhouse gas. In 1776, Leeuwenhoek, a Dutch lens grinder, recognized what he called animal-cules in the presence of decaying plant vegetation with the use of a primitive microscope, thus credited as the first sighting of microorganisms (Waksman, 1932; Paul and Clark, 1989).

In 1804, De Saussure suggested that plants improve air by utilizing CO_2 and giving off O_2 (Miller and Gardiner, 1998), and that they obtain N from soil, thus utilizing C, N, and O in plant growth. Boussingault (1802–77) is credited with the development of the concept of mineral nutrition, further promulgated by Liebig in his 1849 mineral theory of plant nutrition (Brock, 1997). The Swedish botanist Carolus Linnaeus (1707–78), responsible for our present system of organism classification, classified garden soils as *Humus daedalea* and field soils as *Humus rualis*. He possibly foretold the difficulties in microbial classification before the advent of the molecular age when he placed all organisms that had previously been viewed microscopically by Leeuwenhoek under the designation "Chaos" (Feller, 1997).

Rothamsted scientists Lawes and Gilbert (1851) described their study of the sources of N in vegetation and the movement of plant residues into soil organic matter (Warkentin, 2006) in disagreement with Liebig regarding the relevance of N_2 fixation relative to plant growth. Warington (1883), credited as the first to describe nitrification, stated, "The soil beneath our feet has been universally regarded as, in some mysterious sense, the mother of us all." At that time, Darwin's work on earthworms (Darwin, 1837) and Pasteur's work on the role of micro-organisms, a third life form in addition to plants and animals (Waksman, 1932), was recognized as was the specific role of fungi in decomposition (Warington, 1883). Warington also realized that the first mineral-N-decomposition product was ammonia. The microbial nature of the denitrification process in the return of N to the atmosphere was established by Guyen and Dupetit in 1886, thus completing the N cycle (Waksman, 1932). However, it remained for Winogradsky in 1891 to identify the organisms involved in the inorganic transformation of N, and to initially identify some of the organisms and processes involved in N and C cycling through the air, plants, and soil (Waksman, 1932), within what we now call ecosystems.

Darwin can be considered the first author to publish a book on ecosystem studies that covered biota, soil structure, and soil movement-perturbation (Darwin, 1881). Thus, his work joins Müller's (1884) publication on the role of vegetation and soil fauna on the formation of soil horizons in different forest soils (Feller, 1997; Feller et al., 2003, 2006). Wilde (1946) quotes Dokuchaev as making a statement that is still very relevant today: "The eternal genetic relationships that exist between the forces of the environment and physical matter, living and nonliving domains, plants and animals and man, his habits, and even his psychology – these relationships comprise the very nucleus of natural science."

Other forerunners of the ecosystem concept include Alexander von Humboldt (1845–52), who considered the interconnected nature of the physical world in his classic treatise, *Cosmos* (Wulf, 2015). Ernst Haeckel (1879) considered the entirety of biological interactions and coined the term "ecology." For more information on these nineteenth-century ecological pioneers, see Golley (1993).

Möbius (1877) described the interacting organisms living together in a habitat (biotope) as biocoenosis. The related concept, (biogeocenosis), which was a logical development of the work of Dokuchaev and other Russians, was introduced by Sukachev in 1940 (Mirkin, 1987). This concept developed the relationships between living (biotic) and nonliving (abiotic) components of nature. Another Russian scientist, Vernadsky (1926, reprinted 1986), established in *The Biosphere* the importance of biogeochemical cycles within biogeocenosis. It was an early explanation of life as a geological force that can change major characteristics of the Earth as a system. Vernadsky (1944, 1986) concluded that the living components of biogeocoenosis include autotrophic organisms (photosynthetic green plants and chemosynthetic microorganisms). The heterotrophic organisms included animals, fungi, and bacteria. Archaea are also now included given their ability to use a wide array of energy sources in acidic, basic, saline, and hot environments (Woese and Wheelis, 1990; Bardgett, 2005), and the viruses said to equal the bacterial-like forms in numbers and importance in ecosystem functioning due to their ability to transfer genes and affect mortality (Reavy et al., 2014). Additional components of the biogeocoenosis included the atmosphere, solar energy, soils, water, and mineral resources (Odum and Odum, 1953). Vernadsky (1986) stated that each biogeocoenosis maintained uniformity and structure as well as the energy exchanges between them.

Vernadsky's writings, which were anticipated by LeRoy (1928), also apply to the planet Earth concepts often promulgated in the Gaia hypothesis (Lovelock, 1972). The hypothesis states that organisms interact with their inorganic surroundings on Earth to form a synergistic, self-regulating, complex system that helps to maintain and perpetuate the conditions for life on the planet.

Plant and animal ecology, the study of the distribution and abundance of plants and animals, the effects of environmental factors, and the interactions among and between plants and other organisms, had a strong beginning in the early twentieth century (Weaver, 1968). The emphasis on plant succession–climax led to the concept of ecosystems as we define it today. Tansley (1935) first defined the major ideas of ecosystem science, which are formalized in the implicit concepts noted above. This was then expanded by Eugene and Howard Odum (1953: 9) as follows: "An ecosystem is a community of living organisms in conjunction with the nonliving components of their environment (things like air, water, and mineral soil), interacting as a system. These biotic and abiotic components are regarded as linked together through nutrient cycles and energy flows." Hutchinson (1957), Macfadyen (1963), and Margalef (1997) expanded the concept to include biogeochemical cycling and ultimately an ecosystem approach.

3.2 The Development of Interdisciplinary Research Programs

By the early 1960s there was a growing, worldwide interest in conducting measures of ecosystem productivity. As noted by Macfadyen (1963), "the relative importance of different species in a community can be compared more simply on the basis of their contribution to the energy flow of the community than in terms of biomass. The population that exploits the greatest quantity of stored energy contributes the most to the rapid liberation of nutrient substances. These will ultimately find their way back to the plants and thus contribute to a rise in energy intake for the community as a whole."

The global biological community resolved to measure ecosystem energetics and nutrient dynamics worldwide as part of the International Biological Programme (IBP) launched by the International Council of Scientific Unions (ICSU), renamed as the International Council for Science in 1964 (Worthington, 1975). The IBP followed the success of the ICSU International Geophysical Year (IGY). In 1962, three major topics were proposed by C. H. Waddington, president of the International Union of Biological Sciences, one of which was entitled "Man and ecology: The ways in which Man may modify the natural environment so that it can produce what he needs with the highest efficiency on a long-term basis" (Worthington, 1975). The IBP eventually consisted of seven sections, one of which specifically considered the productivity of terrestrial communities (Greenaway, 1996). For IBP historical details, see Coleman (2010).

The United States was slow to become involved in the program due to differences of opinion among senior biologists, some of whom believed that little would be gained from the proposed new studies. Only with strong support from nonecologists, such as Roger Revelle, an oceanographer from the Scripps Institution of Oceanography, was a major new Analysis of Ecosystems Program established by the US National Science Foundation (NSF) in 1967. The many threads of activity are covered by Coleman (2010). Under the aegis of this US NSF program, eight major biome programs for studying ecosystem function were funded. These included the Grasslands Biome, Eastern Deciduous Forest, Desert, Coniferous Forest, Alpine, and Tundra Biomes (Golley, 1993; Aronova et al., 2010; Coleman, 2010). Beginning in 1967, the U.S. grassland biome at Colorado State University and other Great Plains universities were complemented by those in Canada (Coupland, 1979), the Czech Republic (Ülehlova, 1979), France, Poland (Petrusewicz, 1967; Petrusewicz and Macfadyen, 1970), the UK, Russia, and Japan (Numata, 1975), under the general theme that included research on the production and overall energy flow of the world's grassland areas. The purpose was to make ecologically sound recommendations for use of the world's native and managed grassland areas (Coupland, 1979; Breymeyer and van Dyne, 1980).

A wide range of state variable and process-study measurements were taken at the network sites (Coleman, 2010). The world's literature on the microflora of grassland was summarized (Clark and Paul, 1970) and techniques were developed for the quantification and ^{14}C analysis of grassland and microbial biomass (Warembourg et al., 1979; Parkinson and Paul, 1982) and their products (Shields et al., 1973). Information was synthesized from national and international meetings in the US, Canada, Belgium, the UK, India, and France on ecosystem processes, consumers, decomposers, nutrient cycling, and primary productivity (Table 3.1) with an emphasis on the integration of concepts (Petrusewicz, 1967; Misra and Gopal, 1968; Phillipson, 1970; Duvigneaud, 1971; Bowen, 1972; Breymeyer and Van Dyne, 1980; Bliss et al., 1981).

We could say that the five-year US IBP typified an "r selected" organism: rapid growth and turnover, with cutbacks beginning only four years later. The US Long-Term Ecological Research (LTER) program was established in 1980, and continued to develop over many decades, with no termination date specified (Callahan, 1984). The program recognizes the importance of long-term studies. The International Long-Term Ecological Research (ILTER) (Vanderbilt and Gaiser, 2017), which consists of four subunits, influences many areas across the globe (www.ilter.network/?q=content/networks-and-regions), such as the European network and the East Pacific Regional Network (Kim et al., 2018).

Mathematical modeling of ecosystem dynamics was a hallmark of the biome programs. The US Grassland Director George Van Dyne (1969) insisted on the centrality of this aspect in the program, with postdoctoral researchers embedded in several network sites (Innis et al., 1980). This led to the development of simulation models, including: (1) the Century-DayCent Model (Parton et al., 1987, 1998), (2) detrital food webs (Hunt et al., 1987), and (3) the Phoenix model of the dynamics of carbon and nitrogen in grassland soils (McGill et al., 1981), SO_2 dynamics in grasslands, and land surface and atmospheric processes (Coughenour et al., 1980, 1993), followed by later work, such as developing an understanding of biogeochemical cycles and biodiversity as key drivers of ecosystem services (Moore and de Ruiter, 2012; Wall, 2012).

The biome programs encouraged visits by international scientists to work with colleagues on site. The Grassland Project (NREL) included collaborations with colleagues from Canada, Iceland, Poland, Sweden, South Africa, Nigeria, Australia, and the UK. The International Tundra Biome, one of the most successful biome studies, held a month-long synthesis workshop (Bowen, 1972) with participation by scientists from over 20 countries. The 1972 Grassland-Tundra International Synthesis Meeting that emphasized the extensive collaboration across the two biomes was followed by an additional synthesis meeting in Fairbanks,

Table 3.1 *Major scientific discoveries that stemmed from the IBP Biome studies*

1. The importance of belowground processes (roots, soil microorganisms. soil organic matter, soil fauna, and mycorrhiza) in terrestrial ecosystems. This involved both carbon and nutrient flows, which in some sites comprised up to 75% of the total production and turnover per year. (Phillipson, 1970; Anderson et al., 1978; Clark and Rosswall, 1981; Coleman et al., 1983; Weintraub and Schimel, 2003).

2. The development of tracer research for carbon and nitrogen cycling for ecosystem studies (Dahlman and Kucera, 1968; Paul and van Veen, 1978; Andrén et al., 1990; Coleman and Fry, 1991).

3. Roles of canopy and underground processes in nutrient cycling, including N-fixation. (Rodin and Bazilevich, 1967; Paul, 1978; Rychnovska, 1979; Breymeyer and Van Dyne, 1980; Fitter, 2005; Moore and de Ruiter, 2012). There are additional examples from several biomes, with many studies carried out post-IBP (e.g., Nadkarni et al., 2002; Lowman et al., 2009).

4. The stream continuum concept developed out of several watershed-level studies, originating in collaborative studies in the coniferous and deciduous forest biomes (Triska et al., 1982; Wallace, 1988). Corollary of this: "nutrient spiraling," comparing paths of uptake and release of key nutrients, such as N and P in streams (Webster et al., 1992).

5. Microbial and faunal processes are of paramount importance in ecosystem function (Petrusewicz, 1967; Petersen and Luxton, 1982). Some of the biomes, e.g., grassland and desert, began with studies of "microbiology and decomposition," which later morphed into "decomposition and nutrient cycling" (Clark and Paul, 1970; Ülehlova, 1979; Anderson and Domsch, 1980; Coleman et al., 1980; Hunt et al., 1987).

6. The absolute necessity to conduct *whole-system* experiments to better understand mechanisms occurring in nutrient cycling and overall ecosystem resilience (Bormann and Likens, 1967; Van Dyne, 1969; Coupland, 1979; Burke et al., 1989; Baron and Galvin, 1990).

7. Ecosystems are active all year round. Phenomena such as root growth, microbial turnover, etc., are pulsatile and very dynamic outside of the commonly considered "growing season." Examples of this were found in all of the biomes (Coleman et al., 1980).

8. Across-discipline understanding and synthesis, as well as modeling, are required for concept development and off-site projection. (Innis et al., 1980; McGill et al., 1981; Parton et al., 1987).

9. The importance of long-term site analysis and multi-site comparisons. Many of the US sites became members of the US NSF LTER Program and are now part of the NEON site network (Paul et al., 1997; Pace and Groffman, 1998).

10. The role of aboveground fauna in biological feedbacks and nutrient cycling (Kitazawa, 1971; Dyer and Bokhari, 1976; Webb, 1977; Breymeyer, 1980; Zlotin and Khodashova, 1980; Whitford, 2000).

11. The significance of anthropogenic management (Andrén et al., 1990; Cheeke et al., 2013).

12. The importance in ecosystems biogeochemistry and global change of nanometer to megameter analysis to global scales (Burke et al., 1998; Hinckley et al., 2014).

Alaska to discuss soil organisms and decomposition in tundra (Holding et al., 1974). In the case of the latter, data on negative correlations between Oribatid mites and standing crops of fungal hyphae in several Arctic tundra sites were an important early finding of trophic interactions and possible significant impacts on nutrient fluxes (nitrogen and phosphorus) in these nutrient-limited sites (Whittaker, 1974). The international collaboration included noted scientists in N and P nutrient cycling (Clark et al., 1980; Coleman et al., 1983).

Due to large time lags in the submission of papers for publication in refereed scientific journals, reviewers criticized the lack of major syntheses at the end of 1975 (Mitchell et al., 1976; Golley, 1993; Coleman, 2010). Although the short-term consensus of some of the scientific establishment was that the biome programs were of questionable strength (Mitchell et al., 1976), the programs led to the establishment of numerous major ecosystem research centers including: (1) The Ecosystem Center, Woods Hole, Massachusetts; (2) The Institute of Ecology, later Odum School of Ecology, University of Georgia, Athens, Georgia; (3) the Natural Resource Ecology Laboratory (NREL), Colorado State University, Fort Collins, Colorado; and (4) the Forest Sciences Department at Oregon State University. Appendix 3.1 provides a breaf history of post-IBP research at one of these centers, the NREL. Numerous international ecosystem research groups developed from collaborations that began in the IBP era including: (1) The Institute of Ecology, Warsaw, Poland (Petrusewicz, 1967); (2) the Swedish Abisko Research Station's Tundra Biome Program (Sonesson, 1980); (3) the Coniferous Forest ecosystem study based at several Swedish universities (Persson, 1980), (4) the Ecosystem Research Group at Banaras Hindu University, India (Singh, 1968); and (5) the Institute of Geography, Soviet Academy of Sciences, Moscow (Rodin and Bazilevich, 1967). A number of other sites that have been developed on the IBP model include: (1) DOE-Oak Ridge, University of Georgia, Athens; (2) University of Washington; (3) Arizona desert sites; (4) Harvard Forest; and (5) the Land-Margin Ecosystem Research sites, all of which have added a terrestrial-to-aquatic ecosystem linkage, such as the Georgia and Florida Coastal Ecosystem projects. The addition of several Arctic and Antarctic LTER sites has increased the international reach of these large, interdisciplinary ecosystem projects. For a list of others, see Coleman (2010).

The final report from the US National Committee for the IBP included the recommendation: "Since man is an integral component of most ecosystems, new programs of research should be developed to increase understanding of the biological and social responses of human populations to environmental stresses" (National Academy of Sciences (NAS), 1974). The IBP was thus followed by the UNESCO Man and the Biosphere Program, which was launched in 1971 (Greenaway, 1996), with an emphasis on the interaction between ecosystems and the human population.

In 1969, ICSU established a Scientific Committee on Problems of the Environment (SCOPE) to identify and undertake analyses of emerging environmental issues that are caused by or impact humans and the environment. The first report was prepared as an input to the UN Conference of the Human Environment held in Stockholm in 1972. An early initiative was to address how humans were influencing major biogeochemical cycles, initially carbon, nitrogen, phosphorus, and sulfur (Cowling, 1977; Bolin et al., 1979).

3.3 The Paradigm Shift to Social-Ecological Systems

An ecosystem approach to management can be considered as a merger of considerations from: (1) ecosystem science as developed by Tansley, Odum, and other scientists; (2) the study of biogeochemical cycles (Vernadsky, Gaia); and (3) human influence on ecosystems (from G. P. Marsh to the Anthropocene). An ecosystem approach is defined by the Convention on Biological Diversity (CBD) as "a strategy for the integrated management of land, water, and living resources that promotes conservation and sustainable use in an equitable way" (CBD, 2000).

The findings of the biome programs across decadal time spans (Table 3.1) include a number of patterns and processes, some of which were anticipated by such foresighted scientists as Vernadsky. These findings include: (1) the role of eukaryotes (fungi and fauna) and prokaryotes (archaea and bacteria) in driving biogeochemical cycling at all levels of resolution, ranging from landscapes to the biosphere (Moore and de Ruiter, 2012; Hinckley et al., 2014), including the dominance of belowground processes, for example mycorrhiza and non-mycorrhizal fungi and faunal roles in detrital food webs (Petersen and Luxton, 1982) in most terrestrial ecosystems; (2) the use of tracers to measure root production and turnover (Dahlman and Kucera, 1968; Singh and Coleman, 1974; Warembourg and Paul, 1977); and (3) the marked impacts of episodic weather events, often outside of the usually defined "growing season" (Coleman, 2010). These biome studies fostered the collaboration between microbiologists, botanists, zoologists, and hydrologists. The later focus on biogeochemical cycles and global change processes made it necessary for ecosystem scientists to work with climatologists, chemists, etc. These collaborations were promoted at the international level through the IGBP (1986–2015; Steffen et al., 2004; Canadell et al., 2007).

The notion of soils being "central organizing principles" (embodying the long-term "corporate memory" of soil organic matter) of terrestrial ecosystems (Coleman et al., 1998) has been noted frequently in monographs and textbooks (Pace and Groffman, 1998; Fitter, 2005; Moore and de Ruiter, 2012; Paul, 2015). Thus, our concepts of global-level biogeochemical processes have transcended the earlier concepts inherent in the Gaia hypothesis. Within the framework of the IGBP, Crutzen and Stoermer (2000) suggested a new subdivision of geological time, "to emphasize the central role of mankind in geology and ecology by suggesting use of the term 'Anthropocene' for the current geological epoch" (Table 3.2).

Table 3.2 *National and international programs that affect ecosystem research*

1845–present	Long-term agricultural and forestry experimental stations
1957–1958	IGY International Geophysical Year (ICSU)
1964–1974	IBP International Biological Program (ICSU)
1969–present	Scientific Committee on Problems of the Environment (ICSU) (SCOPE) project on biogeochemical cycles
1972–present	MAB Man and the Biosphere Program (UNESCO)
1980–present	LTER and ILTER Long-Term Ecological Research and International Long-Term Ecological Research
1980–present	World Climate Research Program
1987–2015	International Geosphere-Biosphere Program (IGBP)
1991–2014	DIVERSITAS International Program for Biodiversity
1996–2016	International Human Dimension Programme on Global Environmemental Change (IHDP)
1998–2028	US National Ecological Observatory Network (NEON)
2001–2012	Earth System Science Partnership (ESSP)
2005	Millennium Ecosystem Assessment (MA)
2012–present	Intergovernmental Science Policy Platform on Biodiversity and Ecosystem Services (IPBES)
2013–present	Research for Global Sustainability Future Earth
2015–2030	UN Transforming Our World: The 2030 Agenda for Sustainable Development with the 17 Sustainable Development Goals (SDGs)
2018	Merger of International Council for Science and the International Social Science Council (ICSU-ISSC)

The current debate on the Anthropocene (Lewis and Maslin, 2015) as a subdivision of geological time (Crutzen and Stoermer, 2000) indicates that we have moved outside the possibility for the Earth system to self-regulate primarily through man-induced changes of the global biogeochemical cycles. To understand land-cover and land-use changes important for the functioning of the Earth system, and how such changes affect terrestrial ecosystems, social scientists needed to become involved. The IGBP launched several projects addressing this crucial issue (Lambin and Geist, 2006). With the experience from these studies, it became obvious that close collaboration between natural and social sciences were also necessary in other domains of global change research, which led to the establishment of the Earth System Science Partnership (ESSP, 2002–12; Ignaciuk et al., 2012). However, it was challenging to integrate disciplines of both natural and social sciences (Mooney et al., 2013).

The concept of ecosystem services (Costanza et al., 1997; Daily, 1997; Wall, 2012) is now firmly established on a global basis as highlighted by the Millennium Ecosystem Assessment (MA, 2005), which grouped the services provided by ecosystems into: (1) provisioning services (food, freshwater, wood, and fiber), (2) regulating services (climate, flood, and disease regulation, water purification), (3) supporting services (nutrient cycling, soil formation, primary production), and (4) cultural services (aesthetic, spiritual, educational, and recreational) (MA, 2005). The MA made an attempt to quantify human influence on ecosystem services and to put monetary values on various ecosystem services (de Groot et al., 2012). It was also important as the foundation for an assessment framework through the Intergovernmental Science Policy Platform on Biodiversity and Ecosystems Services (IPBES). Costanza et al. (2017) called for ecosystem services to be at the core of a needed fundamental change in economic theory and practice to address not only the environmental, but also the economic and social components of sustainable development. The ecosystem approach is thus now part of global policy considerations, for example the CBD, and are crucial for the achievement of most of the Sustainable Development Goals (ICSU-ISSC, 2015).

The MA, carried out in support of five international conventions and societies in many countries, recognized the need for working with rather than against nature to produce the services that societies depend on. Thus, the link between science and policy has been strengthened and the importance of an ecosystem approach recognized. The inclusion of cultural-ecosystem services highlights the need to also engage the humanities (Diaz et al., 2018). Planetary boundaries (Rockström et al., 2009) define a safe operating space for humanity based on the intrinsic biophysical processes that regulate the stability of the Earth system (Steffen et al., 2015).

With the establishment of the UN SDGs in 2015, the international science community was challenged to provide the insights necessary to make development pathways sustainable. It was not an easy task to link the global change research community with the scientists working on these development issues due to the differences in their points of departure (Bizikova et al., 2007). Future Earth was launched in 2015 to advance global sustainability science, build capacity in this rapidly expanding area of research, and provide an international research agenda to guide natural and social scientists across the globe (Bondre 2015; Rockström, 2016).

One of the highlights of strong ecosystem projects is that they involve a diversity of scientific thought and disciplines, often with international ties. The development of such a cadre of highly skilled and interactive scientists with strong ecosystem viewpoints and long-term benefit required planning and commitment (Wall, 2004, 2012). Ecosystem science has played a significant role in the integration of ecology, agronomy, forestry, and biogeochemistry, both as a science and in response to societal questions. While natural systems continue to be a good source of basic information for understanding ecosystem structure and function, most of the globe is now affected by anthropogenic effects that require a comprehensive approach, including an understanding of the social drivers of land-use and land-cover change (Lambin et al., 2001). Ecosystem science has progressed over the past 50 years, transitioning from a focus on international collaboration within different biomes to an underpinning of the Earth functioning as a system evidenced by the development of the IGBP and other programs and as an important driver and regulator of climate change processes. It is necessary that policy makers and scientists from many disciplines work together to develop policies for linked social-ecological systems, predict consequences of such policies, and evaluate outcomes (Carpenter et al., 2009).

The definition of ecosystems used in this chapter (Odum and Odum, 1953; CBD, 2000) involves the interaction of biotic communities with their environment. According to that definition, ecosystems have been present on the Earth for approximately four billion years, populated by the human race only during the last few million years. The written understanding of natural science essentially started 300 years ago with major breakthroughs during the late nineteenth century. Understanding how the individual components interact in nature is so complex that it requires involvement with more than one discipline. Thus, the ecosystem approach was born with a number of names. It was also recognized that due to nature's variability, both spatially and temporally, most studies needed to be carried out on well-organized, long-term research sites (Hinckley et al., 2014). This approach is now recognized as a natural organizational approach in a large number of applications, including agriculture, forestry, and range management, as well as in natural systems (Sage, 1995; Richerson et al., 2001).

The onset of agriculture involved oral traditions for crops and animals, and a concentration of human settlements that were often unsustainable due to the overuse of soil resources, pollution (such as salt accumulation due to misuse of irrigation water), and even climate changes that occurred after the last ice age. Currently, only a very small portion of the world is unaffected by man's activities, thus necessitating the study of socioeconomics as a significant part of ecosystem research to maintain sustainable ecosystems (Wall, 2012).

It is essential to engage physical, biological, and social scientists from many disciplines, as well as stakeholders, in both framing research questions and engaging in socially important outcomes. Scientists must in many cases step down from their ivory towers and engage with society. We need basic research to understand the components of ecosystems, interdisciplinary research to understand complex problems (e.g., DeFries and Nagendra, 2017), and transdisciplinary research to interact with society (Lang et al., 2012). We must be able to build on a wide range of knowledge that requires interdisciplinary and transdisciplinary research (Klein, 2008). Numerous opportunities are available for using an ecosystem approach to implement an agenda, such as Agenda 2030, which highlights the importance of ecosystem services for the SDGs, and elucidating the interactions among the 17 SDGs (Griggs et al., 2017). All are required if we are to meet the challenges involved in providing food security (Food and Agricultural Organization [FAO], 1983) and adjusting and ameliorating the challenges of climate change.

Fortunately, numerous opportunities have become available for achieving the aforementioned goals. Satellite observations are much more definitive and accessible at ever finer scales. Data management is now more accessible to many more investigators. Modeling is progressing rapidly, with increased capacity for handling large data sets and incorporating actual data. The large number of new investigators in countries such as China should integrate known knowledge into new questions relative to their own social needs. The revolution in biology attributable to the use of molecular techniques is transitioning from merely using new approaches to determine the basis of current knowledge to asking important questions related to diversity and function of the biota. The importance of the integration of the social, economic, physical, and biological sciences is now better recognized as shown by the merger of the ICSU and the ISSC. Thus, the readers of this volume are challenged to move on to greater heights in science, technology and socioeconomic advances. The ecosystem approach is a natural, organizing opportunity for required research, teaching, and social outreach with expectations for significant advancement in all aspects of this important field.

Appendix 3.1 Brief History of the NREL after the IBP

Early post-IBP successful research projects accomplished the following

1. F. E. Clark established long-term ^{15}N plots which are still of interpretive use today (Clark, 1977).
2. Bob Woodmansee, Jerry Dodd, Bill Lauenroth (postdoc at that time), and Mike Coughenour measured the season-long effects of sulfur dioxide on mixed-grass prairie from the US Environmental Protection Agency (EPA) (Lauenroth and Preston, 1984).
3. Dave Coleman, Pat Reid, Don Klein, and Vern Cole measured belowground processes including microbes, fauna, roots, and nutrient cycling studied in gnotobiotic microcosms. The major findings of this research concluded that trophic interactions by microbivorous fauna (protists, nematodes, and microarthropods) led to significantly enhanced nutrient return to soils, followed by enhanced plant growth (Coleman et al., 1983; Ingham et al., 1985).
4. The need for simulation modeling expertise encouraged Bill Hunt to rejoin NREL. Eager graduate students included Ted Elliott who worked on soils, and Russ Ingham who worked on microbivorous nematodes and their effects on N and P cycling in soils.
5. Mel Dyer and Unab Bokhari (1976) led a successful project on the effects of herbivory on plant respiration and biochemical changes in leaves induced by herbivores. This scientifically successful project was funded for several years.

6. Bob Woodmansee developed an NSF-funded study on the topic of nitrogen cycling in rangelands, which was centered on the fates of organic and inorganic N from urine and dung patches. That project was the impetus of Dave Schimel's outstanding scientific career (Woodmansee, 1978).

7. Modeling continued apace on several projects in the NREL, including the research by William J. Parton, Ted Elliott, and Dennis S. Ojima. Of special note is the development of the Century Model, one of the more widely used and cited soil organic matter models across the globe. (Parton et al., 1987, 1998).

8. By the early 1980s, Jim Ellis and Dave Swift (1988) bridged the disciplines of ecosystem studies and anthropology with several funded grants used to perform research on the nomadic herdsmen of the Turkana region in northern Kenya. This work gained both them and their students, such as Layne Coppock, significant international renown. This research continues today.

9. Bob Woodmansee, Bill Lauenroth, and colleagues obtained funding in 1981 for Long-Term Ecological Research (LTER) studies at the Pawnee Site, which was later renamed the "Shortgrass Steppe" Project (Lauenroth and Laycock, 1989).

10. Jim Detling, Layne Coppock, Mel Dyer, and postdoctoral fellow Russ Ingham, conducted one of the longer-running studies on the Pawnee site. They researched prairie dogs as keystone creatures in the shortgrass and mixed-grass steppe, and included experimental enclosures and exclosures at Wind Cave National Park (Coppock et al., 1980).

11. Vern Cole, Dave Coleman, Gary Peterson, and others successfuly initiated the Great Plains Project with NSF and United States Department of Agriculture funding to study the effects of tillage agriculture soil fertility.

12. Social sciences work was well recognized, most notably Kathy Galvin's work in Africa.

Since the establishment of the NREL in 1967, the directors successfully increased the funding and development of various programs. James Gibson served as director between 1974 and 1984 and again in the late 1980s and early 1990s. This led to the development of the NREL's current facilities in the Natural and Environmental Sciences Building. Robert G. Woodmansee served as director in the 1980s, and was able to offer some NREL Research Scientists half-time academic appointments, providing some much-needed stability. From 1993 to 2005, Diana Wall served as director. She provided positions for several new staff and post-doctoral fellows. She has had a very successful career in Antarctic research and sustainable ecosystem services. The current director, John C. Moore, has led the lab since 2006. He was successful in developing further ties with the academic side of Colorado State University, including the development of the Department of Ecosystem Science and Sustainability. The department currently has an undergraduate student body of 400, an MS program, and a faculty of 20, all in close association with NREL. John has initiated the pursuit of more broad-based grants, funded by the US Department of Education and National Science Foundation, for further outreach in environmental education. Faculty joint appointments between NREL/Ecosystem Science and Sustainability and other CSU colleges and departments continue to maintain a successful graduate program; a group where camaraderie promotes the exchange of ideas and syntheses.

The wide range of past and current research projects at the NREL covers many program areas that are vastly important locally, nationally, and internationally. As noted above, NREL scientists have also played an active role in shaping the international research agenda.

References

Anderson, J. F., and Domsch, K. H. (1980). Quantities of plant nutrients in the microbial biomass of selected soils. *Soil Science*, 130, 211–16.

Anderson, R. V., Elliott, E. T., McClellan, J. F., et al. (1978). Trophic interactions in soils as they affect energy flow and nutrient dynamics III: Biotic interactions of bacteria, amoebae and nematodes. *Microbial Ecology*, 4, 361–71.

Andrén, O., Lindberg, T., Paustian, K., and Rosswall, T., eds. (1990). *Ecology of Arable Land: Organisms, Carbon and Nitrogen Cycling*. Ecological Bulletin, 40. Copenhagen: Munksgaard International, 85–126.

Aronova, E., Baker, K. S., and Oreskes, N. (2010). Big science and big data in biology: From the IGY through the IBP to the LTER, 1957–present. *Historical Studies in the Natural Sciences*, 40, 183–224.

Bardgett, R. (2005). *The Biology of Soil: A Community and Ecosystem Approach*. Oxford: Oxford University Press.

Baron, J., and Galvin, K. A. (1990). Future directions of ecosystem science. *BioScience*, 40, 640–2.

Bizikova, L., Robinson, J., and Cohen, S. (2007). Linking climate change and sustainable development at the local level. *Climate Policy*, 7, 271–7.

Bliss, L. C., Heal, O. W., and Moore, J. J., eds. (1981). *Tundra Ecosystems: A Comparative Analysis*. IBP Publication No. 25. Cambridge: Cambridge University Press.

Bolin, B., Degens, E. T., Kempe, S., and Ketner, P., ed. (1979). *The Global Carbon Cycle. SCOPE Report* 13, Chichester, New York, Brisbane, Toronto: John Wiley and Sons.

Bondre, N. (2015). Towards Future Earth. *Global Change Newsletter*, 84, 32–5.

Bormann, F. H., and Likens, G. E. (1967). Nutrient Cycling. *Science*, 155, 424–9.

Bowen, S., ed. (1972). *Proceedings 1972 Tundra Biome Symposium*. US IBP Tundra Biome Report, July 1972. Hanover, NH: USA-CRREL.

Brady, N. C. (1984). *The Nature and Properties of Soils*, 9th edn. New York: Macmillan Publishing.

Breymeyer, A. I. (1980). Trophic structure and relationships. In *Grasslands, System Analysis and Man*, ed. A. I. Breymeyer and G. M. Van Dyne. Cambridge: Cambridge University Press, 799–819.

Breymeyer, A. I., and Van Dyne, G. M. (1980). *Grasslands, System Analysis and Man*. Cambridge: Cambridge University Press.

Brock, W. H. (1997). *Justus von Liebig: The Chemical Gatekeeper*. Cambridge: Cambridge University Press.

Burke, I. C., Lauenroth, W. K., and Wesman, C. A. (1998). *Progress in Understanding Biogeochemical Cycles at Regional to Global Scales! Successes, Limitations, and Frontiers in Ecosystem Science*. New York: Springer Verlag, 165–94.

Burke, I. C., Yonkers, C. M., Parton, W. J., Cole, C. V., and Schimel, D. S. (1989). Texture, climate, and cultivation effects on soil organic matter content in U.S. grassland soils. *Soil Science Society of America Journal*, 53, 800–5.

Callahan, J. T. (1984). Long-term ecological research. *BioScience*, 34, 363–7.

Canadell, J. G., Pataki, D. E., and Pitelka, L. F., eds. (2007). *Terrestrial Ecosystems in a Changing World*. New York: Springer Verlag.

Carpenter, S. R., Mooney, H. A., Agard, J., et al. (2009). Science for managing ecosystem services: Beyond the Millennium Ecosystem Assessment. *Proceedings of the National Academy of Sciences of the United States of America*, 106 (5), 1305–12.

Cheeke, T. E., Coleman, D. C., and Wall, D. H., eds. (2013). *Microbial Ecology of Sustainable Agroecosystems*. Boca Raton, FL: CRC Press.

Clark, F. E. (1977). Internal cycling of ^{15}N in shortgrass prairie. *Ecology*, 58, 1322–33.

Clark, F. E., and Paul, E. A. (1970). The microflora of grassland. *Advances in Agronomy*, 22, 375–435.

Clark, F. E., Cole, C. V., and Bowman, R. A. (1980). Nutrient cycling. In *Grassland System Analysis and Man, International Biological Programme 19*, ed. A. I. Breymeyer and G. M. Van Dyne. Cambridge: Cambridge University Press, 659–712.

Clark, F. E., and Rosswall, T., ed. (1981). *Terrestrial Nitrogen Cycles: Processes, Ecosystem, Strategies and Management Impacts*. Ecological Bulletin, 33. Stockholm: Swedish Natural Science Research Council.

Coleman, D. C. (2010). *Big Ecology: The Emergence of Ecosystem Science*. Berkeley: University of California Press.

Coleman, D. C., Callaham, M., and Crossley, D. A. (2018). *Fundamentals of Soil Ecology*, 3rd edn. San Diego: Elsevier.

Coleman, D. C., and Fry, B., ed. (1991). *Carbon Isotope Techniques in Plant, Soil, and Aquatic Biology*. San Diego: Academic Press.

Coleman, D. C., Hendrix, P. F., and Odum, E. P. (1998). Ecosystem health: An overview. In *Soil Chemistry and Ecosystem Health*, ed. P. H. Wang. Special Publication No. 52. Madison, WI: Soil Science Society of America, 1–20.

Coleman, D. C., Reid, C. P. P., and Cole, C. V. (1983). Biological strategies of nutrient cycling in soil systems. *Advances in Ecological Research*, 13, 1–55.

Coleman, D. C., Sasson, A., Breymeyer, A. I., et al. (1980). Decomposers subsystem. In *Grasslands, System Analysis and Man*, ed. A. I. Breymeyer and G. M. Van Dyne. Cambridge: Cambridge University Press, 609–55.

Convention on Biological Diversity (CBD) (2000). *CBD Convention of the Parties (COP) 5th meeting*, Decision V/6.

Coppock, D. L., Detling, J. K., and Dyer, M. I. (1980). *Interactions among Bison, Prairie Dogs, and Vegetation in Wind Cave National Park*. Final report to National Park Service, Wind Cave National Park, Hot Springs, S.D.

Costanza, R., d'Arge, R., de Groot, R., et al. (1997). The value of the world's ecosystem services and natural capital. *Nature*, 387, 253–60.

Costanza, R., de Groot, R., Braat, L., et al. (2017). Twenty years of ecosystem services: How far have we come and how far do we still need to go? *Ecosystem Services*, 28, 1–16.

Coughenour, M. B., Kittel, T. G. F., Pielke, R. A., and Eastman, J. (1993). *Grassland/Atmosphere Response to Changing Climate: Coupling Regional and Local Scales*. Final Report to US Deptartment of Energy, DOE/ER 60932-3.

Coughenour, M. B., Parton, W. J., Lauenroth, W. K., Dodd. J. L., and Woodmansee, R. G. (1980). Simulation of a grassland sulfur-cycle. *Ecological Modeling*, 9, 179–213.

Coupland, R. T. (1979). *Grassland Ecosystems of the World*. Cambridge: Cambridge University Press.

Cowling, D. W. (1977). *Nitrogen, Phosphorus and Sulphur: Global Cycles (SCOPE Report 7)*, ed. B. H. Svensson and R. Söderlund. Ecological Bulletin, 22. Stockholm: Swedish Natural Science Research Council.

Crutzen, P. J., and Stoermer, E. F. (2000). The "Anthropocene." *Global Change Newsletter*, 41, 17–18.

Dahlman, R., and Kucera, C. (1968). Tagging native grassland vegetation with carbon-14. *Ecology*, 49, 1199–203.

Daily, G. C. (1997). *Nature's Services: Societal Dependence on Natural Ecosystems*. Washington, DC: Island Press.

Darwin, C. (1837). On the formation of mold. *Transactions Geological Society of London*, 5, 505.

   (1881). *The Formation of Vegetable Mold through the Action of Worms with Observations of Their Habits*, ed. J. Murray. London: Wallace Clowes and Sons.

DeFries, R., and Nagendra, H. (2017). Ecosystem management as a wicked problem. *Science*, 356, 265–70.

De Groot, R., Brander, L., van der Ploeg, S., et al. (2012). Global estimates of the value of ecosystems and their services in monetary units. *Ecosystem Services*, 1, 50–61.

Diaz, S., Pasenal, U., Stenseke, M., et al. (2018). Assessing nature's contributions to people. *Science*, 359, 270–3.

Duvigneaud, P., ed. (1971). *Productivity of Forest Ecosystems: Proceedings of the Brussels Symposium*. Paris: Unesco.

Dyer, M. I., and Bokhari, U. G. (1976). Plant–animal interactions: Studies of the effects of grasshopper grazing on blue grama grass. *Ecology*, 57, 762–72.

Ellis, J. E., and Swift, D. M. (1988). Stability of African pastoral ecosystems: Alternate paradigms and implications for development. *Journal of Range Management*, 41, 450–9.

Feller, C. L. (1997). The concept of humus in the past three centuries. In *History of Soil Science*, ed. D. H. Yaalon and S. Berkowicz. Advances in Geoecology 29. Reiskirchen, Germany: Catena Verlag GMBH, 15–46.

Feller, C., Blanchart, E., and Yaalon, D. H. (2006). Some major scientists (Palissy, Buffon, Thaer, Darwin and Muller) have described profiles in soil and developed soil survey techniques before 1883. In *Footprints in the Soil: People and Ideas in Soil History*, ed. B. P. Warkentin. Amsterdam: Elsevier, 85–105.

Feller, C. L., Thuriès, L. J.-M., Manlay, R. J., Robin, P., and Frossard, E. (2003). The principles of rational agriculture by Albrecht Daniel Thaer (1752–1828): An approach to the sustainability of cropping systems at the beginning of the 19th century. *Journal of Plant Nutrition and Soil Science*, 166, 687–98.

Fitter, A. (2005). Darkness visible: Reflections on underground ecology. *Journal of Ecology*, http://doi.1111/j.1365–2745.2005.00990.x.

Food and Agricultural Organization (FAO). (1983). *World Food Security: A Reappraisal of the Concepts and Approaches*. Director General's Report. Rome: FAO.

Golley, F. B. (1993). *History of the Ecosystem Concept in Ecology: More than the Sum of Its Parts*. New Haven,CT: Yale University Press.

Greenaway, F. (1996). *Science International: A History of the International Council of Scientific Unions*. Cambridge: Cambridge University Press.

Griggs, D. J., Nilsson, M., Stevance, A., McCollum, M., eds. (2017). *A Guide to SDG Interactions: From Science to Implementation*. Paris: International Council for Science (ICSU).

Haeckel, E. (1879). Über Entwicklungsgang und Aufgabe der Zoologie. In *Gesammelte Populaere Vortraege aus dem Gebiete der Entwicklungslehre*. Zweites Heft. Bonn: Verlag Emil Strauss.

Hinckley, E. S., Wieder, W., Fierer, N., and Paul, E. A. (2014). Digging into the soil beneath our feet: Bridging knowledge across scales in the age of global change. *EOS, Transactions, American Geophysical Union*, 95(11), 95–7.

Holding, A. J., Heal, O. W., MacLean, S. F., and Flanagan, P. W., eds. (1974). *Soil Organisms and Decomposition in Tundra*. Stockholm: Tundra Biome Steering Committee, 227–47.

Hunt. H. W., Coleman, D. C., Ingham, E. R., et al. (1987). The detrital food web in a short grass prairie. *Biology and Fertility of Soils*, 3, 57–68.

Hutchinson, G. E. (1957). *A Treatise on Limnology*. Vol. 1. New York: Wiley.

Ignaciuk, I., Rice, M., Bogardi, J., et al. (2012). Responding to complex societal challenges: A decade of Earth System Science Partnership (ESSP) interdisciplinary research. *Current Opinion in Environmental Sustainability*, 4, 147–58.

Ingham, R. E., Trofymow, J. A., Ingham, E. R., and Coleman, D. C. (1985). Interactions of bacteria, fungi, and their nematode grazers: Effects on nutrient cycling and plant growth. *Ecological Monographs*, 55, 119–40.

Innis, G. S., Noy-Meir, I., Godron, M., and Van Dyne, G. M. (1980). Total ecosystem simulation models. In *Grasslands, System Analysis and Man*, ed.

A. I. Breymeyer and G. M. Van Dyne. Cambridge: Cambridge University Press, 759–98.

International Council of Scientific Unions (ICSU-ISSC). (2015). *Review of the Sustainable Development Goals: The Science Perspective*. Paris: International Council for Science (ICSU).

Kim, E.-S., Trisurat, Y., Muraoka, H., et al. (2018). The International Long-Term Ecological Research–East Asia–Pacific Regional Network (ILTER-EAP): History, development, and perspectives. *Ecological Research*, 33, 19–34.

Kitazawa, Y. (1971). Biological regionality of the soil fauna and its function in forest ecosystem types. In *Productivity of Forest Ecosystems*, ed. P. Duvigneaud. Paris: Unesco, 485–98.

Klein, J. T. (2008). Evaluation of interdisciplinary and transdisciplinary research: A literature review. *American Journal of Preventative Medicine*, 35(28), S116–S123.

Lambin, E. F., and Geist, H. J., eds. (2006). *Land-Use and Land-Cover Change*. Berlin: Springer Verlag.

Lambin, E. F., Turner, B. L., Geist, H. J., et al. (2001). The causes of land-use and land-cover change: Moving beyond the myths. *Global Environmental Change*, 11, 261–9.

Lang, D. J., Wiek, A., Bergmann, M., et al. (2012). Transdisciplinary research in sustainability science: Practice, principles, and challenges. *Sustainability Science*, 7 (Suppl. 1), 25–43, https://doi.org/10.1007/s11625–011–0149-x.

Lauenroth, W. K., and Laycock, W.A. (1989). *Secondary Succession and the Evaluation of Rangeland Condition*. Boulder, CO: Westview Press.

Lauenroth, W. K., and Preston, E. M., ed. (1984). *The Effects of SO$_2$ on a Grassland: A Case Study in the Northern Great Plains of the United States*. Ecological Studies, 45. New York: Springer Verlag.

Lawes J. B., and Gilbert, J. H. (1851). Agricultural chemistry especially in relation to the mineral theory of Baron Liebig. *Journal of the Royal Agricultural Society of London*, 12(1). London: R. Clowes and Sons.

LeRoy, E. (1928). *Les origines humaines et l'évolution de l'intelligence, III: La noosphère et l'hominisation*. Paris: Boivin.

Lewis, S. L., and Maslin, M. (2015). Defining the Anthropocene. *Nature*, 519, 171–80.

Lovelock, J. E. (1972). Gaia as seen through the atmosphere. *Atmospheric Environment*, 6, 579–80.

Lowman, M., D'Avanzo, C., and Brewer, C. (2009). A national ecological network for research and education. *Science*, 323, 1172–3.

Macfadyen, A. (1963). *Animal Ecology: Aims and Methods*. London: Pitman.

Margalef, R. (1997). *Our Biosphere*. Oldendorf, Germany: Ecology Institute.

Marsh, G. P. (1864). *Man and Nature, or Physical Geography as Modified by Human Action*. Facsimile of first edition, ed. David Lowenthal. Seattle: University of Washington Press.

McGill, W. B., Hunt, H. W., Woodmansee, R., and Ruess, J. O. (1981). PHOENIX, a model of the dynamics of carbon and nitrogen in grassland soils. In *Terrestrial Nitrogen Cycles: Processes, Ecosystem Strategies, and Management Impacts*, ed. F. E. Clark and T. Rosswall. Ecological Bulletin, 33. Stockholm: Swedish Natural Science Research Council, 40–115.

Millennium Ecosystem Assessment (MA). (2005). *Ecosystems and Human Well-being: Synthesis.* Washington, DC: Island Press.

Miller, R. W., and Gardiner, D. T. (1998). *Soils in Our Environment.* Upper Saddle River, NJ: Prentice Hall.

Mirkin, B. M. (1987). Paradigm change and vegetation classification in Soviet phytocoenology. *Vegetatio*, 68, 131–8.

Misra, R., and Gopal, B., eds. (1968). *Proceedings of the Symposium on Recent Advances in Tropical Ecology, Part II.* Varanasi, India: International Society for Tropical Ecology.

Mitchell, R., Mayer, R. A., and Downhower, J. (1976). Evaluation of 3 Biome Programs. *Science*, 192, 859–65.

Möbius, K. (1877). *Die Auster und die Austernwirtschaft.* Berlin: Verlag von Wiegandt, Hemple & Parey. (English translation: *The Oyster and Oyster Farming.*) *U.S. Commission Fish and Fisheries Report*, 1880, 683–751.

Mooney, H. A., Duraiappah, A., and Larigauderie, A. (2013). Towards future Earth: Evolution or revolution? *Proceedings of the National Academy of Sciences (PNAS)*, 110, 3665–72.

Moore, J. C., and de Ruiter, P. C. (2012). *Energy Food Webs: An Analysis of Real and Model Ecosystems.* Oxford: Oxford University Press.

Müller, P. E. (1884). Studier over Skovjord, som Bidrag til Skovdyrkningens Teori: Om Muld og Mor i Egeskove og paa Heder. *Tidskrift for Skovbrug*, 7, 1.

Nadkarni, N., Schaefer, D., Matelson, T. J., and Solano, R. (2002). Comparison of arboreal and terrestrial soil characteristics in a lower montane forest, Monteverde, Costa Rica. *Pedobiologia*, 46, 24–33.

National Academy of Sciences (NAS). (1974). *U.S. Participation in the International Biological Program.* Report No. 6. Washington, DC: NAS.

Numata, M., ed. (1975). *Ecological Studies in Japanese Grasslands, with Special Reference to the IBP Area.* Tokyo: University Tokyo Press.

Odum, E. P., and Odum, H. T. (1953). *Fundamentals of Ecology.* Philadelphia: Saunders.

Pace, M. L, and Groffman, P. A., eds. (1998). *Successes, Limitations and Frontiers in Ecosystem Science.* New York: Springer.

Parkinson, D., and Paul, E. A. (1982). Microbial biomass. In *Methods of Soil Analysis, Part 2 – Chemical and Microbiological Properties*, 2nd edn., ed. A. L. Page, R. H. Miller, and D. R. Keeney. Agronomy Monograph 9. Madison, WI: American Society of Agronomy, 821–30.

Parton, W. J., Hartman, M., Ojima, D., and Schimel, S. (1998). DAYCENT and its land surface sub model: Description and testing. *Global and Planetary Change*, 19, 32–48.

Parton, W. J., Schimel, D. S., Cole, C. V., and Ojima, D. S. (1987). Analysis of factors controlling soil organic matter levels in Great Plains grasslands. *Soil Science Society of America Journal*, 51, 1173–9.

Paul, E. A. (1978). Contribution of nitrogen fixation to ecosystem functioning and nitrogen fluxes on a global basis. In *Environmental Role of Nitrogen-Fixing Blue-Green Algae and Asymbiotic Bacteria*, ed. V. Granhall. Ecological Bulletin, 26. Stockholm: Swedish Natural Science Research Council, 282–93.

(2015). *Soil Microbiology, Ecology and Biochemistry*, 4th edn. San Diego, CA: Elsevier, Academic Press.

Paul, E. A., and Clark, F. E. (1989). *Soil Microbiology and Biochemistry*. San Diego, CA: Elsevier, Academic Press.

Paul, E. A., Follett, R. F., Leavitt, W., et al. (1997). Radiocarbon dating for determination of soil organic matter pool sizes and fluxes. *Soil Science Society of America Journal*, 61, 1058–67.

Paul, E. A., and van Veen, J. A. (1978). The use of tracers to determine the dynamic nature of organic matter. *Proceedings of the 11th International Congress of Soil Science*, Edmonton, Canada, June, 1978. Vol. 3, 61–102.

Persson, T., ed. (1980). *Structure and Function of Northern Coniferous Forests: An Ecosystem Study*. Ecological Bulletins, 32. Stockholm: Swedish Natural Science Research Council.

Petersen, H., and Luxton, M. (1982). A comparative analysis of soil fauna populations and their role in decomposition processes. *Oikos*, 39, 287–388.

Petrusewicz, K., ed. (1967). *Secondary Productivity of Terrestrial Ecosystems (Principles and Methods)*. Warsaw and Krakow: Panstwowe Wydawnictwo Naukowe, Polish Academy of Sciences.

Petrusewicz, K., and Macfadyen, A. (1970). *Productivity of Terrestrial Animals: Principles and Methods*, IBP Handbook No. 13, ed. F. A. Davis. Oxford and Edinburgh: Blackwell Scientific Publications.

Phillipson, J., ed. (1970). Methods of Study in Soil Ecology: Proceedings of the Symposium Organized by Unesco and the International Biological Programme (Paris, France, November, 1967). Paris: Unesco.

Reavy, B., Swanson, M. M., and Taliansky, M. (2014). Viruses in soil. In *Interactions in Soil Promoting Plant Growth*, ed. J. Dighton and J. Krumins. New York: Springer Science and Business, 163–80.

Richerson, R. B., Boyd, R., and Bettinger, R. L. (2001). Was agriculture impossible during the Pleistocene but mandatory during the Holocene? A climate change hypothesis. *American Antiquity*, 66, 387–411.

Rockström, J. (2016). Future Earth. *Science*, 351, 319.

Rockström, J., Steffen, W., Noone, K., et al. (2009). A safe operating space for humanity. *Nature*, 461, 472–5.

Rodin, L. E., and Bazilevich, N. (1967). *Production and Mineral Cycling in Terrestrial Vegetation*. English edn. (Transl. Scripta Technica Ltd., ed. Fogg, G. E.) London: Oliver & Boyd.

Rychnovska, M. (1979). Ecosystem synthesis of meadow energy flow. In *Grassland Ecosystems of the World*, ed. R. T. Coupland. Cambridge: Cambridge University Press, 165–79.

Sage, R. F. (1995). Was low atmospheric CO_2 during the Pleistocene a limiting factor for the origin of agriculture? *Global Change Biology*, 1, 93–106.

Shields, J. A., Paul, E. A., Lowe, W. E., and Parkinson, D. (1973). Turnover of microbial tissue in soil under field conditions. *Soil Biology and Biochemistry*, 5, 753–64.

Singh, J. S. (1968). Net aboveground community productivity in the grasslands at Varanasi. In *Proceedings of Symposium on Recent Advances in Tropical Ecology*, ed. R. Misra. Varanasi, India: International Society for Tropical Ecology, 631–54.

Singh, J. S., and Coleman, D. C. (1974). Distribution of photo-assimilated carbon-14 in the root system of a shortgrass prairie. *Journal of Ecology*, 62, 389–95.

Sonesson, M., ed. (1980). *Ecology of a Subarctic Mire*. Ecological Bulletin, 30. Stockholm: Swedish Natural Science Research Council.

Steffen, W., Richardson, K., Rockström, J., et al. (2015). Planetary boundaries: Guiding human development on a changing planet. *Science*, http://doi:10.1126/science.1259855.

Steffen, W., Sanderson, R. A., Tyson, P. D., et al., ed. (2004). *Global Change and the Earth System*. Heidelberg: Springer Verlag.

Tansley, A. (1935). The use and abuse of vegetational concepts and terms. *Ecology*, 16, 284–307.

Thomas, W. L., Jr., ed. (1956). *Man's Role in Changing the Face of the Earth*. Chicago: University of Chicago Press.

Triska, F. J., Sedell, J. R., and Gregory, S. V. (1982). Coniferous forest streams. In *Analysis of Coniferous Forest Ecosystems in the Western United States*, ed. R. L. Edmonds. Stroudsburg, PA: Hutchinson Ross, 292–332.

Turner, B. L. II, Clark, W. C., Kates, R. W., et al., ed. (1990). *The Earth as Transformed by Human Action: Global and Regional Changes in the Biosphere over the Past 300 Years*. Cambridge: Cambridge University Press.

Ülehlova, B. (1979). Microorganisms in meadows. In *Grassland Ecosystems of the World*, ed. R. T. Coupland. Cambridge: Cambridge University Press.

Vanderbilt, K., and Gaiser, E. (2017). The International Long Term Ecological Research Network: A platform for collaboration. *Ecosphere*, 8(2), e01697.

Van Dyne, G. M., ed. (1969). *The Ecosystem Concept in Natural Resource Management*. New York: Academic Press.

Vernadsky, V. I. (1944). Problems of biogeochemistry, II: The fundamental matter–energy difference between the living and the inert bodies of the biosphere. *Transactions of the Connecticut Academy of Arts and Sciences*, 35, 483–512.

(1986). *The Biosphere*. New York: Copernicus, Springer-Verlag. Originally published 1926 in Russian.

Von Humboldt, A. (1845–52). *Cosmos: A Sketch of the Physical Description of the Universe*, trans. Elizabeth J. L. Sabine. Vols. 1–3. London: Longman, Brown, Green and Longmans, and John Murray.

Waksman, S. A. (1932). *Principles of Soil Microbiology*. Baltimore: Williams and Wilkins.

Wall, D. H., ed. (2004). *Sustaining Diversity and Ecosystem Services in Soils and Sediments*. Washington, DC: Island Press.

ed. (2012). *Soil Ecology and Ecosystem Services*. Oxford: Oxford University Press.

Wallace, J. B. (1988). Aquatic invertebrate research. In *Forest Hydrology and Ecology at Coweeta*, ed. W. T. Swank and D. A. Crossley, Jr. Ecological Studies, 66. New York: Springer, 257–68.

Warembourg, F. R., and Paul, E. A. (1977). Seasonal transfers of assimilated ^{14}C in grassland: Plant production and turnover, soil and plant respiration. *Soil Biology and Biochemistry*, 9, 295–301.

Warembourg, F. R., Paul, E. A., Randell, R. L., and More, R. B. (1979). Model of assimilated carbon distribution in grassland. *Oecologia Plantarum*, 14, 1–12.

Warington, R. (1883). *Changes Which Nitrogenous Matter Undergo within the Soil*. London: Harrington and Sons.

Warkentin, B. P., ed. (2006). *Footprints in the Soil*. Amsterdam: Elsevier.

Weathers, K. C., Groffman, P. M., and Van Dolah, E., et al. (2016). Frontiers in ecosystem ecology from a community perspective: The future is boundless and bright. *Ecosystems*, 19, 753–70.

Weaver, J. E. (1968). *Prairie Plants and Their Environment: A Fifty-Year Study in the Midwest*. Lincoln: University of Nebraska Press.

Webb, D. P. (1977). Regulation of deciduous forest litter decomposition by soil arthropod feces. In *The Role of Arthropods in Forest Ecosystems*, ed. W. J. Mattson. New York: Springer, 57–69.

Webster, J. R., Golladay, S. W., Benfield, E. F., et al. (1992). Catchment disturbance and stream response: An overview of stream research at Coweeta Hydrologic Laboratory. In *River Conservation and Management*, eds. P. Boon, G. Petts, and P. L. Calow. Chichester: Wiley, 232–53.

Weintraub, M. N., and Schimel, J. (2003). Interactions between carbon and nitrogen mineralization and soil organic matter chemistry in Arctic tundra soils. *Ecosystems*, 6, 120–43.

Whitford, W. G. (2000). Keystone arthropods as webmasters in desert ecosystems. In *Invertebrates as Webmasters in Ecosystems*, ed. D. C. Coleman and P. F. Hendrix. Wallingford: CAB International, 25–41.

Whittaker, J. B. (1974). Interactions between fauna and microflora at tundra sites. In *Soil Organisms and Decomposition in Tundra*, ed. A. J. Holding. Stockholm: Tundra Biome Steering Committee, 183–96.

Wilde, S. A. (1946). *Forest Soils and Forest Growth*. Waltham, MA: Chronica Botanica.

Woese, C. R., and Wheelis, M. L. (1990). Towards a natural system of organisms: Proposal for the domains Archaea, Bacteria, and Eucarya. *Proceedings of the National Academy of Sciences of the United States of America*, 87, 4576–9.

Woodmansee, R. G. (1978). Additions and losses of nitrogen in grassland ecosystems. *BioScience*, 28, 448–53.

Worthington, E. B., ed. (1975). *The Evolution of IBP*. Cambridge: Cambridge University Press.

Wulf, A. (2015). *The Invention of Nature: Alexander von Humboldt's New World*. New York: Alfred A. Knopf.

Zlotin, R. I., and Khodashova, K. (1980). *The Role of Animals in Biological Cycling of Forest-Steppe Ecosystems*. Stroudsburg, PA: Dowden, Hutchinson & Ross.

4 · Five Decades of Modeling Supporting the Systems Ecology Paradigm

WILLIAM J. PARTON, STEPHEN J. DEL
GROSSO, ELEANOR E. CAMPBELL,
MELANIE D. HARTMAN, N. T. HOBBS,
JOHN C. MOORE, DAVID M. SWIFT,
DAVID S. SCHIMEL, DENNIS S. OJIMA,
MICHAEL B. COUGHENOUR,
RANDALL B. BOONE,
KEITH PAUSTIAN, H. W. HUNT, AND
ROBERT G. WOODMANSEE

4.1 Introduction

Interest in ecosystem models began in the 1960s as a means to help quantify natural processes and to assess the human impacts on them (e.g., Bormann and Likens, 1967; see Chapter 6). Development of ecosystem models was part of the International Biological Program (IBP). The IBP program initiated extensive field observations for Grassland, Deciduous and Coniferous Forests, Desert, and Tundra biomes in many countries around the world. A major goal of the IBP program was to explore connections between nutrient cycling and biology and how human activity alters biogeochemical processes. The IBP program coordinated extensive field observations for almost all processes (e.g., species–level plant growth, soil carbon (C) and nitrogen (N) cycling, insect and mammal predation) and included a major effort to develop ecosystem models using the IBP field observations. The US IBP Deciduous Forest, Coniferous Forest, and Tundra programs had similar efforts to develop ecosystem models to represent the dynamics for the respective biomes. The IBP models developed during the 1968 to 1978 time period are not currently used; however, much was learned regarding model development from these initial efforts and submodels from these initial ecosystem models are included in current models.

The use and development of ecosystem models and the system ecology approach (see Chapter 1) have been key parts of the research conducted at the Natural Resource Ecology Laboratory (NREL) at Colorado State University from the 1960s to the present time. A detailed description of the systems ecology approach is presented in Chapter 10 and Figure 1.4, and includes a precise description of the problem or challenge being addressed, the primary goals of the research or assessment project, identification of stakeholders who would use the research results, clear definition of the spatial, temporal, and where appropriate institutional scales involved. Simultaneously, conceptual models of the emerging system are formulated followed by development of mathematical ecosystem models and testing of the results from the models using field and laboratory data sets. Most of the major research projects included a mixture of ecological model development, field and laboratory research, and the use of ecological models to understand how ecosystems operate and to help design field and laboratory experiments for improving our understanding about ecosystem dynamics. In this chapter we summarize the development and application of ecosystem models at Colorado State University with an emphasis on those developed at NREL because this lab has been a leader in ecosystem modeling and the authors have led many of the important efforts. We trace how model complexity, extent of validation and application, interactions between modeling and measurement projects, usefulness of model outputs, and other factors have evolved through time. The chapter will present information about model development during four different time periods: (1) the IBP years (1968–1978), (2) post-IBP NSF-funded NREL projects (1980s), (3) the 1990s, and (4) 2000 to the present. We will provide a brief description of the models developed during each time period, the linking of the models to field and laboratory research efforts, and the use of these models to enhance scientific understanding about ecosystem dynamics and provide information about the best ways to manage various ecosystems. We show that ecosystem models were primarily used to enhance scientific understanding during the 1970–1990 time period, while ecosystem models are currently being used to determine the impact of different management practices, influence national policy decisions, and project the impact of future climatic changes. We close by prioritizing future research efforts needed to reduce uncertainties and better address contemporary issues.

4.2 IBP Model Development Period (1968–1978)

4.2.1 ELM Model Development

NREL received substantial funding to manage the US IBP Grassland program. One of the major efforts was to develop the ELM (not an acronym) grassland model (Innis, 1978). Detailed biological field observations from five grassland sites (annual, short grass, tall grass, mixed grass, and the Palouse region) was used to develop and test the ELM model. The primary goal of the ELM modeling effort was to develop a grassland ecosystem model capable of simulating the impacts of grazing and climate on grassland ecosystem dynamics. The major goals of the ELM and other IBP biome models include: (1) showing that complex ecosystem models can be developed, (2) using the models as a research tools to determine how ecosystems work, (3) using the models to determine which types of observational data sets are needed, and (4) using the models to simulate the impacts of management practices (e.g., grazing intensity and forest management) on ecosystem dynamics. Similar types of data were collected at all of the Grassland IBP research sites which included nutrient cycling, plant production, soil water and temperature, and information about mammalian and insect consumers. The extensive data sets collected at these sites were used to develop and test the ELM model with the goal of having the model work effectively at all of the research sites. The ELM model was conceived by a team of scientists with diverse backgrounds (mathematics, meteorology, soil C and nutrient cycling, plant production, animal and plant production, and statistics). Subsequent model development was challenging since biologists had little experience in this area (most modeling at that time was performed by physicists and mathematicians). There were no modeling journals, so biologists had to learn on the job, and computational efficiency was very poor. These limitations, along with a desire to represent all processes in a complex manner (e.g., subroutines were included for daily soil water and temperature fluxes, multispecies plant production, multispecies insect and mammal biomass consumption, and soil C, N, and phosphorus (P) cycling) compromised practical application of the model to address land management questions.

The ELM model was more complex than current grassland ecosystem models because it represented all the detailed processes at a daily time step (Figure 4.1). The plant production model within ELM was also more complex because it included a phenological component with eight different phenological phases and up to ten different competing plant species. The mammalian consumer model simulated animal energetics,

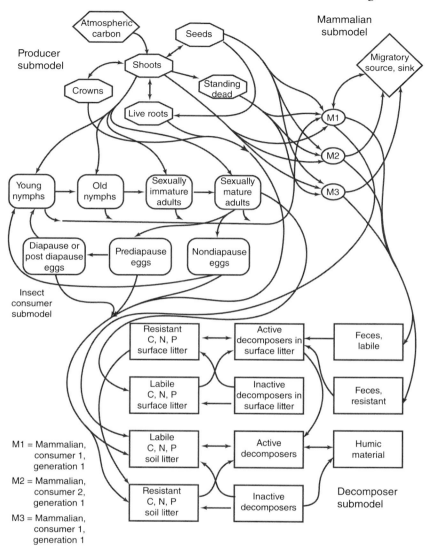

Figure 4.1 Flow diagram for the ELM grassland model.

population dynamics, and consumption of grass biomass from up to ten species and ten generations. The insect consumer submodel simulated the complex population dynamics for different insect consumers and consumption of live and dead plant biomass. The soil C, N, and P submodels represented the ecosystem dynamics of four different soil layers, while the soil water and temperature model simulated daily changes in soil water and temperature in 15 cm layers down to a depth of 2 meters. We are not aware of any currently used grassland models with this level of complexity. The primary data sets from the IBP grassland biome used for model development included aboveground plant production for different plant functional groups, consumption of live plant biomass from insect and mammalian consumers, soil C, N and P measurements as a function of soil depth, and daily soil water and temperature by depth. One of the primary goals of the model was to determine the impact of animal and insect grazing on grassland ecosystem dynamics and project the optimal way to graze grassland ecosystems. Unfortunately, the ELM model was only used to investigate the impact of grazing by cattle and insects for several sites (Parton and Risser, 1979, 1980; Capinera et al., 1983). The ELM model is not currently being used; however, ELM soil C, N, P, and soil water and temperature submodels were used in grassland ecosystem models developed at NREL during 1980s and 1990s (Hunt and Parton, 1986; Parton et al., 1987; Parton et al., 1988).

4.2.2 Energy Flow in Bird Communities

One of the earliest attempts to develop simulation models with direct, substantial application to real-world issues was the model developed by John Wiens and George Innis (Wiens and Innis, 1974). They developed a bird population bioenergetics model that estimated population density changes, biomass changes, and bioenergetics demands of bird populations. The development of this model was driven by an interest in being able to estimate the impact of bird populations on oceanic fish populations and on fish hatchery losses. Specifically, they used the model to estimate the number of mosquito fish (*Gambusia affinis*) that a western grebe (*Aechmophorus occidentalis*) would be expected to consume foraging on ponds in a fish hatchery raising these fish. Such information is important to managers of the hatchery in determining whether they have a grebe (or kingfisher) problem or not.

4.3 Post–IBP Grassland Model Development and Research

After 1978 the NSF funding for IBP was transferred to the Ecosystem Studies program at NSF which then became one of the major sources for funding of ecosystem modeling and research at NREL. Scientists at

NREL during the 1980s were organized around five major research groups which focused on different ecosystem components. All of these groups included detailed ecosystem modeling as part of their research programs. The strong link between biological field studies and ecological modeling was demonstrated by the grassland model developed by Parton et al. (1978). The model was developed to represent detailed observations of aboveground plant growth, soil water dynamics, and root growth from root growth windows. Detailed growing season time series of root growth for juvenile, suberized, and nonsuberized roots were measured along with soil water status as a function of depth. The model is much less detailed than the ELM model since it only simulated ecosystem-level plant production (i.e., intraspecies competition was not represented), root growth, and soil water dynamics. The root growth submodel was recently incorporated into to the DayCent ecosystem model which was first developed in the late 1990s.

The five major research groups at NREL in the 1980s included: (1) the Belowground Project, (2) the Atmosphere Biosphere Interactions and Trace Gas projects, (3) the Great Plains Agricultural project, (4) the South Turkana Ecosystem Project, and (5) the Animal Energetics Project. All of these projects included substantial field and laboratory experiments, development of ecological models, and using the models to help design field experiments and improve our understanding about how ecosystems operate. The Belowground Project focused on studying soil C and nutrient dynamics in grasslands and evaluating the impact of different soil organisms on soil C and nutrient dynamics (Coleman et al., 1983). The Atmosphere/Biosphere Interaction Project looked at the interactions between the atmosphere and biosphere with a focus on the impact of grasslands on C, water, trace gas (CH_4, N_2O, NO_x) dynamics (Nitrogen Cycling project; R. G. Woodmansee, unpublished data, 1978, funded NSF proposal; Schimel et al., 1985, 1991; Mosier et al., 1991; Parton et al., 1995) and SO_2 dynamics in grasslands (see Chapter 8) and plant and ecosystem responses to increasing CO_2 and climate change (see Chapter 8). The Great Plains Project evaluated the impacts of dryland agriculture in the Great Plains on plant production, soil C, N, and P dynamics. The South Turkana Ecosystem Project (STEP) studied the ways that semi-nomadic pastoralists in northwest Kenya interacted with savanna and grassland ecosystems (Coughenour et al., 1985; Ellis and Swift, 1988; see Chapter 9). The Animal Energetics Project investigated the impact of vegetation on animal energetics and developed models of population dynamics for elk, deer, and antelope

(Hobbs et al., 1981; see Section 4.3.5). Another important model developed during the 1980s was the radionuclide PathWays model which simulated the transport of radionuclides from atomic bomb testing in Nevada during the 1960s (Kirchner et al., 1983).

4.3.1 Century Model Development

One of the major research efforts from the Great Plains and Atmosphere Biosphere projects was the development of the Century model (Parton et al., 1987, 1988). The initial goal of the Century model was to simulate the impact of agricultural management practices in the Great Plains on crop yields and soil C and nutrient dynamics. The model was also designed to represent the impacts of rangeland management practices on ecosystem dynamics for Great Plains grasslands. The Century model uses a monthly time step to simulate crop production and live biomass, soil water dynamics, soil C dynamics, and soil nutrient (N, P, and S) cycling for native grasslands and agricultural fields (Figure 4.2). The model uses simplified representation of the soil water dynamics and soil C and nutrients cycling submodels derived from the ELM grassland

CENTURY MODEL

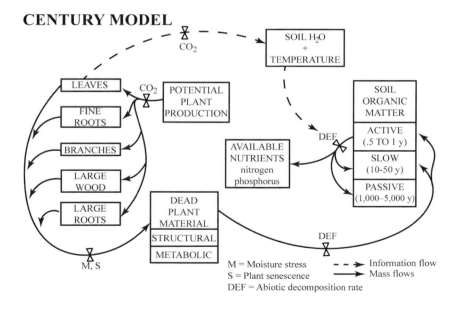

Figure 4.2 Simplified flow diagram for the Century ecosystem model.

model. Key assumptions in the model are that soil organic matter dynamics can be represented using three soil organic matter pools (microbe, slow, and passive soil organic matter [SOM]), that flows of organic N, P, and S are driven by the soil C flows, that the C to element (N, P, and S) ratios are different for each SOM pool and change as function of soil mineral N, P, and S levels, and that soil nutrient availability is the primary factor that controls plant production. The model was developed using observed process-level soil C and nutrient cycling data from crop production and grasslands studies at research sites connected to the Great Plains Agricultural and Atmosphere Biosphere Interactions projects and was then tested using observed Natural Resources Conservation Service (NRCS) regional data sets from the Great Plains region. One of the major parts of this research was the analysis of extensive regional NRCS observations of soil C and N from native grassland and cropped fields in the Great Plains and observations of grassland plant production in the Great Plains (Sala et al., 1988; Burke et al., 1989). During the 1980s there were very few regional data sets (climatic, plant production, soil C and N, biophysical) available to test the ability of models to simulate regional patterns in plant production and soil C and N levels. Results showed that the Century model could simulate observed changes in soil C and nutrient mineralization rates associated with cultivation of grassland soils (rapid decline in soil C and nutrient availability for 30 years), regional patterns of soil C and N (highest soil C in the Northeastern Great Plains), and regional patterns of observed grassland plant production in the Great Plains (decreasing plant production with decreasing annual precipitation) using the simplified representation of the ecosystem process. The initial focus of the Century modeling effort was to look at ecosystem dynamics during the 50- to 100-year time period following cultivation of grasslands in the Great Plains. The Century model has been successfully used to simulate the impact agricultural management practices on crop yields and soil carbon and nitrogen dynamics for numerous long-term agricultural sites around the world (Paustian et al., 1992; Parton and Rasmussen, 1994; Smith et al., 1997). The model results and long-term agricultural management data sets show that the major controls on soil carbon storage are the lignin content of plant material and amount of carbon added to the soil (positively correlated to both variables). More recently the Century model (Parton et al., 2005) has been successfully applied to simulate the long-term (10,000- to million-year time periods) dynamics of plant production, soil nutrients (N and P), and soil C for tropical forests in Hawaii.

4.3.2 PHOENIX Model

The NREL Belowground Project focused on studying the impacts of soil organisms on soil nutrient cycling and C dynamics. The major models developed as part of this project include: (1) PHOENIX model (McGill et al., 1981), (2) BAHUDE (Bachelet et al., 1989, (3) GEM model (Hunt et al., 1991; Chen et al., 1996), and (4) the Food Web model (Hunt et al., 1987). The Belowground project included extensive field laboratory experiments which evaluated the impact of soil organisms on soil nutrient cycling, plant production, and soil organic matter dynamics. The first model developed as part of the project was the PHOENIX model (Figure 4.3) which included a detailed representation of soil C dynamics, soil nutrient dynamics, soil water dynamics, and plant production. The model simulated the dynamics of soil bacteria and fungi and the impacts of soil bacteria, actinomycetes, and fungi on soil nutrient cycling and soil C flows. The PHOENIX model included a more detailed representation of the soil nutrient cycling and soil organic matter dynamics than used in the ELM Grassland model. It was incorporated into a new version of the ELM model on a project that examined the effects of SO_2 on grassland ecosystems in Montana (Coughenour 1981; see Chapter 8). Bachelet et al. (1989) developed the BAHUDE model which used an improved version of the PHOENIX model (improved plant production and soil water and temperature submodels) to simulate the impact of nematode, grasshopper, and cattle grazing on grassland dynamics. Model results showed that belowground nematode grazing had a bigger impact on plant production than aboveground cattle and grasshopper grazing (Bachelet et al., 1989). Hunt et al. (1991) made major changes to the PHOENIX model and developed the GEM model which includes a much more detailed representation of photosynthesis and plant growth, and a more detailed representation of belowground food web. The GEM model was used to simulate the impacts of climate change at the Central Plains Experimental Range (CPER) grassland site in northeastern Colorado and found that increasing temperatures reduced photosynthesis during the middle of the growing season, increased the length of the growing season, and had little impact on annual plant production. Elevated CO_2 levels resulted in increased plant production and soil C levels.

4.3.3 The Food Web Model

One of the major goals of the Belowground Project was to determine the role of soil fauna on soil nutrient mineralization. The project used a

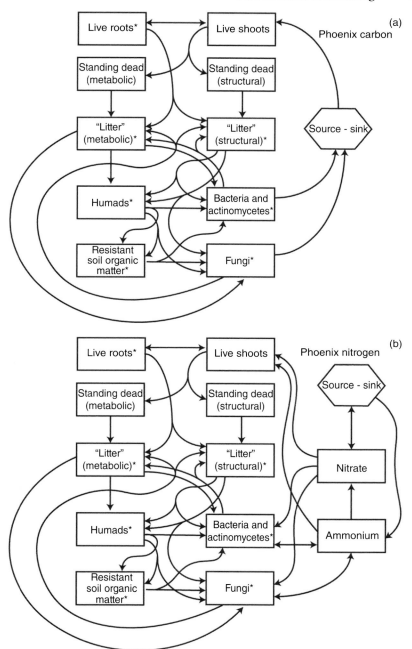

Figure 4.3 Flow diagram for the PHOENIX biogeochemical model.

variety of field and laboratory experiments to determine the impact of soil fauna on nutrient mineralization. The data collected by the project and ideas about how soil food webs work were used to develop a series of complex food webs for the CPER grassland site. The initial food web model simulated carbon and nitrogen dynamics at steady state within a grassland rhizosphere that included plant roots, labile and resistant detritus, and inorganic nitrogen as basal resources, and functional groups of microbes, protozoa, and invertebrates. The model used a simple mass-balance approach to account for the steady state biomass of species that were present, and the fate of C and N as a result of the trophic interactions within the food web. A second iteration of the model used traditional ODDs (overview, design concepts, and details) to simulate the dynamics of the functional groups, C, and N. This approach formalized a community-ecosystem framework for studying food webs that included the theoretical approaches advanced by community ecologists with the energetic biogeochemical approaches used by ecosystem ecologists (Moore et al., 1988). Melding the two iterations developed a means to estimate the elements of the Jacobian matrix using empirical data and the C and N fluxes (Moore et al., 1993; de Ruiter et al., 1995). These concepts are summarized in *Energetic Food Webs: An Analysis of Real and Model Ecosystems* (Moore and de Ruiter, 2012), published by Oxford University Press in their series on Ecology and Evolution.

Soil food webs are complex networks that are typically described with plant roots, litter, and soil organic matter as the basal resources and functional groupings of microbes and invertebrates as consumers. Functional groups are groups of species that share food sources, feeding modes, life history traits, and habitats (Hunt et al., 1987; Moore et al., 1988). The model revealed a pattern of dominant flows of energy akin to patterns that emerged from the South Turkana Ecosystem Project (Coughenour et al., 1985). Within the soil food web are subassemblages of functional groups that form dominate pathways of material flow, also known as "energy channels," that originate from roots and detritus consumed by different functional groups of consumers and linked by a suite of predatory functional groups. The detritus channel can be further subdivided into a channel based on fungi and their consumers and a channel based on bacteria and their consumers.

Moore et al. (1988) used the concept of the "energy channel" based on the trophic interactions and biogeochemical flow (C and N) among species, to address the May's paradox (May, 1973) that demonstrated using randomly constructed webs that diversity does not necessarily beget stability. May (1973) posited that if species were arranged into "blocks" of interacting species rather than as random assemblages, great diversity could ensue. Energy channels represented a ubiquitous niche-based form of blocking or compartmentalizing within food webs, a result that was supported by later work (Rooney et al., 2006). Consistent with theory, the stability of soil webs is dependent on this underlying structure of channels and on the relative dominance of activity within the channels (Moore et al., 2003, 2004).

4.3.4 SAVANNA Model and South Turkana Ecosystem Project

The South Turkana Ecosystem Project, described in more detail in Chapter 9, featured ecosystem modeling as a primary effort. The project began in the early 1980s, and model development was carried out through the early 1990s (Coughenour 1992, 1993). The model that was developed came to be known as SAVANNA (see Figure 4.4).

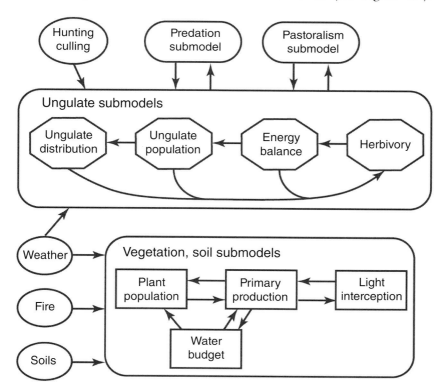

Figure 4.4 SAVANNA ecosystem model flow diagram.

The model is described in Chapter 7. Key features of this model were its representation of: vegetation productivity and its responses to highly variable rainfall with recurrent drought; use of these vegetation resources by pastoral livestock; and responses of the livestock to the highly variable vegetation resources. SAVANNA simulates plant production, soil water dynamics, grazing offtake, and livestock and wildlife abundances, conditions, and productivities. The model simulates direct competition among the three vegetation life-forms and the numbers and amounts of biomass of shrubs and trees in different size classes. It uses a weekly time step to represent important seasonal variations while making it computationally feasible to simulate landscape dynamics for 50- to 100-year time periods.

It was critical in this ecosystem for the model to represent spatial as well as temporal variations in forage resources. A key element of pastoralism in this region is the movement of livestock in response to changing distributions of grazing and browsing resources (Chapter 9). Therefore, the model needed to be spatially explicit, and represent the dynamic distributions of vegetation biomass across a very heterogeneous landscape. It then needed to represent distributions of livestock in response to grazing and browsing resources. Consequently, SAVANNA was developed as one of the first fully spatially explicit ecosystem models in that it simulates grid-cells across the landscape simultaneously. The model is spatially explicit at the landscape level but spatially inexplicit at the patch level. Each grid-cell simulates a patch that includes herbaceous plants, shrubs, and trees. The model dynamically simulates the fraction of each grid-cell with herbaceous plants, shrubs, and trees as well as runoff and run-on areas within grid-cells. The results are scaled up to the landscape level by adding up the fractions of each patch type (herbaceous grasses, shrubs, and trees) for all of the grid-cells.

After the South Turkana Ecosystem Project, the SAVANNA model was further developed and was widely used to assess the impact of human activities, fire, wildlife grazing, and cattle grazing on savanna ecosystems around the world. Applications include: evaluation of the effects of wildlife and livestock, altered rainfall, improved veterinary care, permitting or restricting livestock grazing in key portions of the Conservation Areas, renovation of nonfunctional water sources, human population growth, and changes in the amount of cultivation within the Conservation Areas. The model was extensively used to evaluate the ecosystem impacts of wildlife, human activities, and livestock grazing in other parts of Africa (e.g., Boone et al., 2002, 2004, 2007; Hilbers et al.,

2015; Fullman et al., 2017). It was used to determine the impact of elk on vegetation dynamics in Rocky Mountain National Park (Peinetti et al., 2001; Weisberg and Coughenour, 2003), the impact of wild horses on the Pryor Mountain Wild Horse range (Coughenour, 2000), and to determine the impacts of fire and grazing on savanna systems in Australia (Liedloff et al., 2001). SAVANNA was used to assess population dynamics of elk and bison, and fire impacts on ecosystem dynamics in Yellowstone National Park (Coughenour and Singer, 1996; Plumb et al., 2009). Applications to National Parks are described further in Chapter 7.

The interactive roles of humans on ecosystem dynamics has been a key component of the South Turkana project and SAVANNA modeling. Lesorogol and Boone (2016) and Boone et al. (2011) present excellent descriptions of how ecosystem models have been used to study linked human–natural system for pastoral systems in Africa. Ecosystem modeling was used to develop a basic understanding of the linkages between the dynamics of semi-arid East African pastoral systems and pastoral house-hold decision-making and resource utilization strategies. Although this modeling was developed during the South Turkana Ecosystem Project, it remained to be seen if those models could be applied in a practical fashion to the problems facing pastoral societies in East Africa. Two projects funded by the global Livestock Collaborative Research Support Project of USAID permitted us to address some of these issues: the Integrated Management and Assessment (IMAS) project and the Integrated Assessment of Pastoral–Wildlife Interactions in East Africa: Implication for People, Policy, Conservation and Development in East Africa (POLEYC) project. The objective of these projects was to help pastoralists, land managers, and other stakeholders in East African pastoral systems to balance food security, wildlife conservation, and ecosystem integrity, given the often-conflicting interactions between pastoralism and wildlife conservation in these regions. Ecosystem modeling was to be used as a decision-making tool toward that end.

On the IMAS and POLECY projects there were two principle study areas: the Kajiado District in southern Kenya, including Amboseli National Park, and the Ngorongoro Conservation Area (NCA) in north-ern Tanzania, which is adjacent to Serengeti National Park. Both of these areas have real or potential conflicts between pastoral land use and wildlife conservation. In these projects the SAVANNA Modeling System was used to address questions of concern in the two study areas, principally questions regarding conflicts between pastoralists and wildlife.

4.3.5 Ruminant Energy and Nitrogen Balance Model and Animal Energetics Project

The interest in determining the carrying capacity of Rocky Mountain National Park for elk led us to develop a simulation model of forage intake and resultant nutritional state for wintering elk in the park. We were interested both in the effects of different numbers of elk on the vegetation and on the nutritional state of the animals themselves during winter. Both of these effects are important in making a management decision about carrying capacity. We had data on the digestibility and nitrogen content of elk diets in the winter ranges of the Park (Hobbs et al., 1981).

To address this issue in the park, we developed a generalized model of ruminant energy and nitrogen balance (Swift, 1983). This model is driven by data on diet digestibility and N content. It estimates daily energy (kcal) and nitrogen requirements, voluntary intake (forage removal), rates of digestion and of passage of undigested forage from the rumen, partitioning of digested energy and N to maintenance growth and fattening, changes (positive or negative) in lean body mass and adipose reserves, and returns of energy and N to the ecosystem in urine and feces. The model has proven useful in evaluating carrying capacity, and in conjunction with a diet selection submodel (Ellis et al., 1976) has been used in ecosystem model applications. Some components of the model have been extracted and used within the DayCent modeling system.

4.3.6 The PATHWAY Model

In the early 1980s residents in the area near the Nevada Test Site (NTS), a nuclear weapons testing facility, became concerned about a possible relationship between the incidence of cancers in humans and the exposure to radioactive fallout from the NTS. While data on deposition of radioactive species from weapons tests were available, no pertinent contemporary data existed that directly measured doses received by humans or estimated them indirectly by monitoring doses that could have been received through consumption of agricultural products exposed to radioactive fallout. Thus, it became necessary to develop a simulation model of the movement of radionuclides through the local agricultural systems, into crops and into humans through their consumption to estimate doses received by the human population (Kirchner et al.,

1983). This model, named PATHWAY, used the existing data on radioactive fallout deposited on agricultural systems to simulate uptake and storage of radionuclides by crop plants and their concentration in harvested products. An additional, simpler models then used PATHWAY model outputs and information on the dietary habits of local residents to estimate total doses of radionuclides ingested. Because the results from PATHWAY were used as part of a litigation process, great care was taken to analyze the uncertainty or likely error in the model's predictions. The importance of this effort from a modeling viewpoint was that it dealt with a very important human health issue with no other reasonable way to retrospectively estimate doses received. This represented a huge step in moving simulation models from constructs of theoretical interest to tools that make informed judgments about important human issues.

4.4 NREL 1990s Model Development

Most of the model development work during the 1980s focused on process-based ecosystem models using site-level field observations and laboratory generated ecological data. The major goal of these models was to determine how ecosystems function. Funding for model development was greatly enhanced during the 1990s because of the concern regarding the impact of global change on ecosystem dynamics and the potential for ecosystem C fluxes and trace gases (CH_4 and N_2O) to alter the climate of the earth. The National Science Foundation (NSF), Department of Energy (DOE), National Aeronautics and Space Administration (NASA), and other agencies provided substantial funding to develop and test ecosystem models that could be used at the regional to global scales. NASA and US EPA funding for the NREL Atmosphere/ Biosphere program resulted in the development of the global version of the Century model which was capable of simulating ecosystem dynamics for most of the major biomes (grassland, savanna, forests, tundra, and agroecosystems) (Schimel et al., 1996, 1997b). This enhanced funding also supported the development of global data sets for climatic and ecosystem variables (plant production, nutrient cycling, soil water, tree biomass, and soil C and N) which were used to help parameterize and test the new global ecosystem models.

The Vegetation-Ecosystem Modeling and Analysis Project (VEMAP) (1995) Ecosystem model comparison effort was one of the major large-scale ecosystem modeling efforts during the 1990s. NSF, DOE, Electric

Power Research Institute, and EPA funded the BIO-BGC, Century, TEM, DOLY, and MAPS modeling teams to assess the impacts of potential climatic changes on ecosystems in the US. This included a major effort to collect regional data sets (e.g., climatic data, remote sensing Normalized Difference Vegetation Index, plant production, soil C) which could be used to calibrate and test the different ecosystem models (Kittel et al., 1996). Funding was available to help improve the different models, compare model results, and predict the potential impacts of climatic changes on plant production, nutrient cycling, water fluxes, and net carbon exchange in the US. Numerous papers were published which compared the response of the different ecosystem models to potential climatic changes (VEMAP et al., 1995; Schimel et al., 1996, 1997a, 1997b, 2000; Pan et al., 1998). In general, all of the models were able to simulate the observed regional patterns for soil C, tree biomass, and plant production; however, the predicted changes in these variables with climatic change were quite different. The differences in the model predictions resulted from the fact that some of the models did not consider the impact of soil nutrients on plant production, and uncertainty regarding the impact of elevated CO_2 levels on plant production. Many of the climatic, biophysical and ecological data sets collected as part of the VEMAP program are still being used to test current global ecosystem models. The VEMAP model comparison effort highlighted the importance of including soil nutrient (N and P) constraints on plant production and the necessity of simulating soil nutrient dynamics in global ecosystem models.

During the 1990s a number of ecosystem models were developed at the NREL to evaluate the impact of climate and land-use changes (see Chapter 8). During this time, numerous models were developed by other research groups nationally and internationally to assess climate change impacts ecosystems. A number of model intercomparison efforts were conducted during this period to determine how well the various models simulated ecosystem dynamics. Smith et al. (1997) reported on a model comparison project where observed agricultural soil C and N and plant production data sets from long-term agricultural experiments were used to test the ability of soil C and nutrient cycling models (ROTHC, Century, NCSOIL, CANDY, DNDC, and DAISY) to simulate the changes in plant production and soil C levels for different agricultural practices (see Smith et al., 1997 for a description of the models). Observed long-term soil C and plant production data sets from ten different sites around the world were used in this effort. The results showed that most of the models did a good job of simulating the changes in soil C levels resulting from the different management practices. There were substantial differences in the ability of models to predict soil C dynamics at the site level and the comparison showed that there was no particular model which did the best job of simulating soil C and plant production dynamics. As part of the Potsdam NPP Model Inter-comparison project, Cramer et al. (1999) reported on a global model comparison where observed global plant production data sets were used to test the ability of global ecosystem models to simulate global patterns in plant production. The models represented three major categories: satellite-based models that use data from the NOAA/AVHRR sensor as their major input stream (CASA, GLO-PEM, SDBM, SIB2, and TURC), models that simulate C fluxes using a prescribed vegetation structure (BIOME-BGC, CARAIB 2.1, CENTURY 4.0, FBM 2.2, HRBM 3.0, KGBM, PLAI 0.2, SILVAN 2.2, and TEM 4.0), and models that simulate both vegetation structure and C fluxes (BIOME3, DOLY, and HYBRID 3.0). A major part of this effort included a synthesis effort of existing plant production data sets which were then used to derived 0.5×0.5 degree global maps of plant production (see Cramer et al., 1999 for a description of the models). The regional patterns in plant production were well represented by most of the models. Major differences in simulated plant production were related to differences in the way that soil nutrient was represented in the models. Models that did not consider soil nutrient constraints on plant production tended to overestimate plant production for humid ecosystems (forest and tropical systems).

The models developed at NREL were used extensively to project the impacts of climate change, elevated CO_2 levels, and different management practices on grasslands, savannas, and agroecosystems during the 1990s (Ojima et al., 1994; Parton et al., 1994, 1995; Hall et al., 1995; Xiao et al., 1995; Gilmanov et al., 1997). The Century and GRASS-CSOM models were primarily used to investigate the impact of climate change and elevated CO_2 levels for grasslands and savannas sites around the world. The GRASS-CSOM model included more detailed plant ecophysiology than Century (Coughenour and Chen, 1997) and was used at fewer sites. As part of this effort, observed grassland plant production from these sites was used to calibrate and test the Century and GRASS-CSOM model's predictions of soil C levels and grassland plant production (Parton et al., 1996). The Century model was used to determine the impact of grazing practices and fire frequency on ecosystem dynamics. The results showed that grazing levels from light to moderate generally have a positive impact on plant production, while heavy grazing reduced plant production and soil C levels. The results from our extensive field and Century modeling work at the Konza tall grass prairie show that a fire frequency of three to five years is necessary to maintain high plant production. Annual fires greatly enhance N losses from the system, however N inputs from soil N-fixation are enhanced as a result of frequent fires. The model results suggest that elevated atmospheric CO_2 levels enhance grassland plant production as a result of increased photosynthesis rates and reduced plant transpiration rates. Decreasing precipitation and increasing temperature causes plant production and soil C levels to decrease.

The Century model was used extensively to evaluate the impacts of different agricultural management practices on agroecosystems (Paustian et al., 1992; Parton and Rasmussen, 1994; Metherell et al., 1995; Probert et al., 1995; Kelly et al., 1997; Smith et al., 1997). The ability of the Century model to simulate long-term changes in soil C, nutrient cycling, and plant production was tested using observations from long-term agricultural experimental sites around the world (the US, Europe, and Australia). The results showed that adding N in the organic form results in much higher soil C and N stabilization compared to inorganic N additions. The field data and model results showed that soil C levels increase with increasing C inputs and are higher for organic matter additions that have high lignin content.

4.5 NREL Modeling from 2000 to the Present

Ecosystem modeling work at NREL during the 1990s was focused on improving existing ecosystem models and using site-level observational data sets to calibrate and test model performance. The models were used to simulate the impacts of different management practices on soil C dynamics and plant production and to determine the impacts of climate changes on regional and global scales with a primary focus on C dynamics. Since 2000 there have been three major modeling activities: (1) development of the DayCent ecosystem model which simulates most biogenic trace gas fluxes (CO_2, N_2O, NO_x, and CH_4) for all of the major biomes; (2) extensive use of ecosystem models to evaluate the impacts of different management practices (e.g., biofuel feedstock production, agricultural cultivation and fertilizer practices, management of wild life) and climatic changes at the site, regional, and global scales; and (3) use of advanced statistical techniques (Bayesian statistics and model selection techniques) to parameterize, provide model error assessments, and test ecosystem models.

4.5.1 DayCent Model Development and Application

At the end of the 1990s and the beginning of 2000 it became clear that N_2O and CH_4 emissions from agriculture are important sources of greenhouse gases (GHGs) and that there was a need to evaluate the net GHG emissions for different land management practices. Addition of fertilizer to agricultural fields could cause increased plant production and soil C inputs; however, fertilizer additions greatly enhance soil N_2O fluxes and often reduce soil CH_4 oxidation. This is important since N_2O is about 300 times more effective than CO_2 as a GHG and CH_4 is about 35 times more effective than CO_2. The DayCent model (daily version of the Century model) was developed at the end of the 1990s (Parton et al., 1998, 2001; Del Grosso et al., 2000a, 2000b) to simulate net GHG fluxes from agricultural systems and has been expanded to represent full GHG fluxes from most of the natural and managed ecosystems in the world (grasslands, forest, savanna, tundra, and agricultural systems). This daily time step version of Century was needed to simulate soil CH_4 and N_2O fluxes because N_2O and CH_4 fluxes vary substantially on a daily basis with large pulses of N_2O and CH_4 often occurring when the soil is anaerobic. For example, about half of the annual total N_2O fluxes for agricultural fields in some northern systems can occur during the one- to two-week snow melt time period (e.g., Wagner-Riddle et al., 2008, 2017) and CH_4 fluxes spike when rice paddy soils are flooded (e.g., Sun et al., 2016) or in response to rainfall events after paddies are drained (Kim et al., 2016).

The DayCent model (Figure 4.5) simulates daily soil N_2O fluxes from nitrification and denitrification, CH_4 production from anaerobic soils and consumption in dryland soils, and soil NOx and N_2 fluxes associated with nitrification and denitrification. The model includes a detailed description of soil water and temperature dynamics (0 to ~2 meters) since soil water and temperature are major factors controlling N_2O and CH_4 fluxes. The DayCent model has a more detailed representation of plant production for agricultural and natural systems than Century and includes the impact plant phenology on plant growth, crop yields, and plant C allocation. The model simulates soil C dynamics and nutrient mineralization (N, P, S, and K) with revised versions of the Century soil C and nutrient dynamics submodels. The plant production, soil water

DAYCENT MODEL

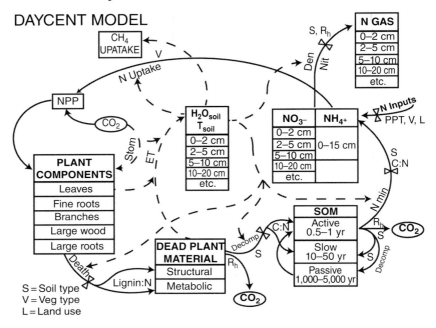

Figure 4.5 DayCent ecosystem model flow diagram.

and temperature, soil C, and soil nutrient submodels have been extensively tested using observed data sets from natural and managed ecosystems.

The DayCent model has been utilized to simulate soil C dynamics, crop yields, soil nutrient dynamics, and trace gas fluxes from all of the major crops and crop rotations (corn, wheat, barley, soybeans, sorghum, sugarcane, alfalfa) using observational data sets from sites all around the world (the US, Australia, China, Brazil, Argentina, Germany, the UK, Canada) (Frolking et al., 1998; Del Grosso et al., 2010; Fitton et al., 2014; Scheer et al., 2014; Grant et al., 2016). The results show that the model can simulate ecosystem dynamics for all of these cropping systems reasonably well and typically represents the observed impacts of different management practices on changes in soil C and N levels, crop yields, and trace gas fluxes. The model correctly simulates the observed increases in crop yields and soil N_2O fluxes with increasing soil fertilizer, the impact of cultivation on soil C levels and trace gas fluxes, the potential to reduce soil N_2O fluxes using slow release fertilizer, the potential to increase soil C levels using reduced soil tillage, and the increases in soil C levels associated with the addition of compost and other organic matter amendments. Recently the DayCent model has been successfully used to simulate daily net ecosystem exchange (NEE) and actual evapotranspiration (AET) for grasslands (annual, short grass steppe, and tall grass prairie), and forests (coniferous and deciduous) using AmeriFlux eddy covariance data sets (Malone et al., ; Savage et al.,).

4.5.2 Use of NREL Models for Environmental Decision Making

One of the primary goals of most NREL modeling efforts was to use models to help make decisions on how to best manage ecosystems (see Chapter 7). The models developed from the 1970s to the early 1990s were primarily used to enhance our scientific understanding about how ecosystems operate. Extensive testing and validation of our models using comprehensive site and regional data sets from the 1990s to the present time has greatly enhanced confidence in the model projections and allowed us to use our ecosystem models to project the impacts of management practices on ecosystem dynamics and reduce the negative impacts of anthropogenic activity on the environment. The use of NREL models to aide in the environmental decision-making process has been quite extensive and includes: (1) the use of models to manage agroecosystem and reduce GHG fluxes at the site, regional, and global scales; (2) the use of DayCent to determine the impacts of biofuel feedstock production on the environment; and (3) use of models to simulate the impact of native consumers on grassland, savanna, and forest ecosystems.

4.5.2.1 DayCent Biofuel Life Cycle Analyses

The DayCent model has been extensively used to evaluate the impacts of growing annual and perennial biofuel crops on the environment at the site and regional scales. Currently, about 40 percent of harvested corn grain in the US is used to produce ethanol. Davis et al. (2012) used DayCent to simulate the environmental impacts of growing switchgrass and miscanthus on the land currently used to grow corn grain for ethanol production. The DayCent model was set up to simulate the growth of switchgrass (with and without fertilizer additions) and miscanthus (without fertilizer) for the US corn belt at the county level along with the growth of corn and soybeans. Key results from this study showed that if the land currently used for corn ethanol production were converted to switchgrass and miscanthus more ethanol could be produced. The results also showed that net GHG emissions could be reduced by 30 percent or more by growing switchgrass and miscanthus instead of corn and that nitrate leaching to the Gulf of Mexico could be reduced by 15–22 percent. The reduction in GHG fluxes came from net C storage in the soil and lower N_2O emissions associated with growing switchgrass and miscanthus compared to annual cropping.

Hudiburg et al. (2016) performed a similar type of analysis using DayCent to investigate the impact of growing perennial biofuels (switchgrass and miscanthus) for the 32 Billion US Renewable Fuel Standard. The DayCent model was used to simulate crop yield, biomass production of switchgrass and miscanthus, soil C changes, and net GHG fluxes for different management practices and alternative fractions of land in perennial vs. corn biofuel production. The DayCent model results combined with an economic model showed that 2022 US GHG emissions from the transportation sector could be reduced 7 percent by growing perennial biofuel crops due to gasoline displacement and soil C storage from perennial grass feedstocks. The reduction in US GHG emissions could be about 12 percent if a cellulose biofuel credit was included. This study demonstrates how results from ecosystem models can be combined with economic models to determine the optimal management practices which include economic and environmental factors.

4.5.2.2 Land Management Scenarios Using DayCent

DayCent has been extensively used to investigate how crop rotations and management practices interact to control GHG fluxes from agricultural systems (Del Grosso et al., 2012, 2016; Migliorati et al., 2015; Bista et al., 2016). Parton et al. (2015) used DayCent to simulate the historical (1860 to 2000) changes in plant production and GHG fluxes for all of the counties in the Great Plains. Crop yield data from the United States Department of Agriculture (USDA) Agricultural Census and National Agricultural Statistics Service were used to calibrate the model to simulate historical changes in crop yields and rotations. The results showed that from 1900 to 1940 crop yields were low and that most of the GHG fluxes occurred because of soil carbon losses associated plowout of grassland in the Great Plains. The dominant GHG fluxes in the Great Plains currently come from CH_4 emissions from cattle and soil N_2O fluxes associated with N fertilizer applied to dryland and irrigated agriculture. Model results suggest that the use of best management practices (slow release fertilizer, no-tillage cultivation, and CH_4 inhibitors for cattle) in the Great Plains could reduce net GHG fluxes by up to a

100 percent, depending on the adaptation rate for these practices, without reducing crop yields.

The DayCent model was used to investigate the potential to reduce net GHG fluxes from major nonrice crop (corn, wheat, and soybeans) production at the global scale. The results showed that the combined use of nitrification inhibitors and no-till cultivation could result in a 50 percent reduction in net GHG fluxes and increased crop yields (7 percent). DayCent was, and continues to be, applied to estimate soil GHG fluxes for the US National GHG Inventory (EPA, 2017), to compare the impacts of conventional vs. improved land management strategies for decision support tools (e.g., COMET-FARM) and perform life-cycle assessments (Adler et al., 2017). Availability of multi-site, standardized data sets with comprehensive model driver and testing data (e.g., GRACEnet) (Del Grosso et al., 2013) has facilitated model evaluation and improvement. Current research needs include software to generate model input files and funding to conduct rigorous model comparisons.

4.5.2.3 Agent-Based and Coupled Systems Modeling

Boone et al. (2011) have successfully linked agent-based models with ecosystem models. Agent-based modeling uses a bottom-up approach to discovery, treating individuals as the basic units of decision making that determine, in this case, changes in populations. Agents may include animals, people, automobiles, cities, or others, and they interact with each other and their environments based on rules (Billari et al., 2006; Boone and Galvin, 2014). In contrast to inductive or deductive approaches to hypothesis formation, here the method is termed abduction, where rules are hypothesized that would allow population-level patterns to grow through interactions between individuals (e.g., Griffin, 2006; Lorenz, 2009). The realistic representation of relationships used in some agent-based models may allow for a variety of scenarios to be addressed. Being able to represent individual variation (Huston et al., 1988), capture complex relationships, and show visualization to audiences are strengths of the method. Methods are diverse, but a common pathway is joining one or more process-based ecosystem model, such as a hydrology and a vegetation growth model, with a rule-based (agent-based) human decision-making model.

An example of coupled systems modeling with process-based and agent-based components is the linking of the SAVANNA model and the agent-based household model DECUMA (Boone et al., 2011). SAVANNA is a comprehensive tool that is spatially explicit and simulates dynamics in soils, vegetation, and herbivores. The DECUMA model is a fairly complete representation of decision making for households in pastoral systems. At each monthly time step, SAVANNA passes information to DECUMA that allows herders to distribute their livestock reasonably, and that information is returned to SAVANNA. SAVANNA then provides to DECUMA the amount of energy animals acquired given their grazing patterns, which allows DECUMA to simulate livestock dynamics (Boone et al., 2011). Boone and Lesorogol (2016) and Lesorogol and Boone (2016) used these linked models to address eight scenarios reflecting changes ongoing in the Samburu region of Kenya. In Siambu, a region of Samburu, for example, access to grazinglands is rapidly shrinking as these high-elevation areas are cultivated by those from outside the area. They simulated declining grazing access caused by this fragmentation, limiting mobility by changing how far herders may have traveled from 10 km each day down to 0.2 km. The number of livestock that could be supported declined rapidly, as expected. But with the coupled tools, they also quantified expanding shrubs, decreasing milk energy available to families, and increased livestock sales (Lesorogol and Boone, 2016).

4.5.3 Use of Advanced Analytic Techniques for Model Analysis

During the last ten years we have made major advances in the use of advanced statistical techniques to parameterize models, determine error analysis of model results, and perform sensitivity analysis of our models. Model building at NREL traditionally emphasized predictions of state variables and fluxes based on estimates of parameters, estimates that were usually obtained from experiments and field studies analyzed by maximum likelihood methods. This tradition is broadly known as forward modeling. Parameter estimates were subjectively "tuned" to bring observations of state variables and fluxes into agreement with model predictions. Sensitivity analysis was conducted to determine the magnitude of responses of model output to changes in parameter values. There was no formal statistical foundation for model tuning and sensitivity analysis.

In contrast to forward modeling, the inverse modeling approach uses data on state variables to estimate model parameters. Traditional statistical analyses are examples of inverse modeling; for example, simple linear regression estimates intercept and slope of a line and associated uncertainties using data on a response and a predictor variable. Inverse models have a strong statistical foundation in statistical theory based on maximum likelihood and Bayes' theorem.

The advent of cheap, fast computing has allowed the application of inverse methods to problems of high dimension, like the simulation models historically developed at the NREL. Examples of these applications using maximum likelihood include using Akaike's information criterion modified for small sample sizes to select between 1, 2, and 3 pool models of litter decomposition, as affected by initial litter chemistry, decomposition rates, and a climate decomposition index (Adair et al., 2008). Decomposition data from the Long-Term Intersite Decomposition Experiment Team were used to parameterize and select the best model for global, long-term decomposition dynamics, yielding the model structured to include three carbon pools representing labile, cellulose, and recalcitrant litter defined by initial lignin and N content (Adair et al., 2008). Straube et al. (2018) used a variation of the Markov Chain Monte Carlo to optimize model parameters for the DayCent model using a long time series of AmeriFlux observed daily NEE and AET data from the Niwot Ridge site.

Bayesian methods are also being used for inverse modeling. These approaches allow detailed information on parameters obtained from process studies to be assimilated with formal model fitting so that inference on parameters emerges as a compromise between the previous results, represented in prior distributions, and the current data, represented in the data distributions, also known as likelihoods. Multiple sources of data can be used to fit parameters and unobserved quantities.

Examples of Bayesian applications include N. T. Hobbs' and colleagues work on modeling Brucellosis in the Yellowstone bison population (Hobbs et al., 2015). Nine sex, age, and disease states were modeled using 40 years of data on total population size and demography as well as data on the serological status of individuals. Prior data on recruitment by age and disease state and adult survival were included in the model. The work was the first to estimate the net reproductive ratio of brucellosis and the transmission rate of the disease. Results from the model have been directly applied to decisions on bison management in the Greater Yellowstone ecosystem.

Complex process-based ecosystem models like DayCent present several challenges to the use of Bayesian methods. DayCent includes hundreds of model parameters, many with conceptual definitions that lack clear connections to measurable values. While advanced computing brings feasibility to the application of Bayesian methods to such highly dimensional models, the availability of data to constrain the high numbers of model parameters becomes a bottleneck. This has motivated recent developments in multi-model comparisons and advanced open-source data-model integration systems – for example the Predictive ECosystem ANalyzer (PEcAn) Project, where a version of DayCent will be housed – which aims to aggregate diverse datasets and simplify the connection between data and multiple models to leverage more information (from both data collection and modeling) to more robustly constrain model parameters (Deitze et al., 2013; LeBauer et al., 2013). However, soil organic matter processes present unique challenges to these efforts, including (1) the disconnect between conceptual definitions of modeled soil pools and measurable soil organic matter fractions, (2) the extreme range of temporal scales in soil organic matter dynamics, as well as high lateral and vertical spatial variability, and (3) the difficulty measuring changes in the slowest-cycling organic matter, which tends to dominate soil organic matter on a mass basis. Collectively, these constrain the ability to leverage Bayesian methods to inform process-based ecosystem model parameters. Past efforts using DayCent limited the application of Bayesian methods to a subset of model parameters or model functions, for example to initialize the distribution of C across DayCent three soil C pools (Yeluripati et al., 2009).

An alternative approach is to use Bayesian methods on submodels within larger ecosystem models, where model structure and available datasets can make the application of Bayesian methods more tractable. An example of this approach includes Campbell et al.'s (2016) work using Bayesian methods to develop the LItter DEcomposition and Leaching (LIDEL) model. The LIDEL model uses lignin and N controls on microbial processes to simulate litter decomposition, leaching, and the generation of dissolved organic carbon that can subsequently enter the soil profile. The LIDEL model was proposed as new litter submodel that could be used in process-based ecosystem models like DayCent, by having a generalized and computationally simplistic structure, but incorporated new understanding of microbial controls on litter decomposition dynamics. This model was more directly connected to measureable values and was parameterized using a Bayesian approach to leverage experimental data collected by Soong et al. (2015), as well as data published by Adair et al. (2008) and Parton et al. (2007). This analysis illustrated the extent to which available data could inform LIDEL model parameters and structure, for example demonstrating the need for developing the experimental evaluation of litter-soluble fractions and the generation of dissolved organic matter early during decomposition to better inform a model parameter that was both highly sensitive and poorly constrained by the available data.

4.5.4 Model Independent Parameter Estimation and Uncertainly Software Package

PEST (the Model Independent Parameter Estimation and Uncertainly software package) (Doherty, 2015) has recently been used by several authors to perform sensitivity analysis, model parameterization, and error analysis for the DayCent model (Rafique et al., 2013, 2014; Necpálová et al., 2015; Asao et al., 2018). The parameters are optimized using an inverse modeling procedure where model parameters are estimated using nonlinear regression based on least squares minimization. Asao et al. (2018) successfully used PEST to parameterize the DayCent model for an annual grassland system in California using a long time series of AmeriFlux NEE and AET data. Similarly, Necpálová et al. (2015) showed that model performance was substantially improved for N_2O emission after calibration with PEST for a corn/soy system in Iowa and identified sensitive parameters. Rafique et al. (2014) first calibrated DayCent using PEST, then applied the model to investigate the impacts of a climate change scenario on CO_2, CH_4, and N_2O fluxes.

4.6 Time Series of Model Development and Applications

Figure 4.6 shows a summary of the time series of model development and applications at NREL during the last 50 years. The ELM grassland model was first model developed during the 1970s followed by the development of the Ruminant, Pathway, Century, SAVANNA, Food Web, and PHOENIX models during the 1980s. The major activity during the 1990s included extensive model comparison (VEMAP, N_2O, and plant production) research and climate change work along with the development of the daily version of Century (DayCent) which predicted full greenhouse gas fluxes for all biomes. Agent-based grassland and savanna model work started in the first decade of the 2000s, while the DayCent model was used to do extensive regional US and global modeling of the impact of agricultural management practices and biofuels on greenhouse gas fluxes (CO_2, N_2O, and CH_4) from agricultural systems from 2010 to the present time. The most recent model development includes the use of the Grass-Cast model to simulate seasonal forecasts of aboveground grass production (ANPP) for ranchers in the Great Plains. The DayCent model is used to simulate cumulative April to July actual evapotranspiration (AET) for all of the Great Plains counties using observed daily weather data and seasonal forecasts of precipitation

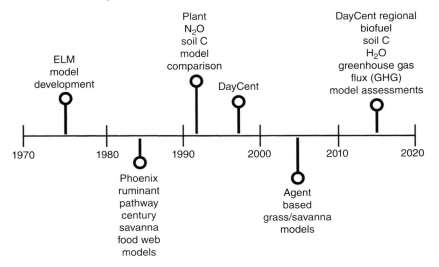

Figure 4.6 Time series of model development from 1970 to 2018 for NREL model development.

as input to the DayCent model. The Grass-Cast model uses the DayCent predictions of county-level AET as inputs to county-specific regressions of ANPP to AET and makes predictions of ANPP for all of the Great Plains counties starting in early May. Grass-Cast predictions of ANPP are updated every two weeks using current observations of precipitation. The accuracy of the Grass-Cast forecasts increases rapidly in May with the inclusion of more observed precipitation data. The development of the Grass-Cast model achieves one of the major goals of the ELM grassland model from 1970s by providing a tool for making spring seasonal predictions of grassland production for all of the grasslands in the Great Plains.

4.7 Current and Future Research Efforts

Given that models represent simplified versions of reality, decisions will always need to be made regarding where to concentrate resources allotted for model improvements. One area that is currently of concern is the depth of SOM that should be simulated. Most models represent SOM dynamics only in the top 20–30 cm soil layer because deeper SOM was thought to be stable and thus not vulnerable to change in response to land management choices. But some recent studies suggest that deeper

SOM is dynamic and decomposition of deep organic C makes a significant contribution to soil surface CO_2 emissions (e.g., Campbell and Paustian, 2015; Alcántara et al., 2016; Pries et al., 2017). In response, DayCent model developers are currently exploring how to incorporate deep SOM dynamics into the model. In addition to simply extending the current SOM cycling submodel to deeper layers, effective modeling of deep SOM dynamics requires better representation of processes such as movement of dissolved organinc carbon (Campbell et al., 2016).

Another issue currently being debated is the degree to which microbial populations and biological, physical, and chemical processes should be explicitly represented in models. To a large extent this is a conceptual question. Ecosystem models such as DayCent represent microbial populations and some physical processes (e.g., soil gas diffusion) more or less implicitly, while DNDC (Li, 1996) is somewhat more complex in that it explicitly represents soil redox potential while the Ecosys model (Grant, 2001) is still more complex and explicitly represents functional microbial populations as well as physical processes such as phase transitions, solute transport, gas diffusion, and other biogeochemical processes. Some recent studies suggests that changes in the microbial community due to climate change (e.g., Melillo et al., 2017) can impact processes that control respiration and SOC levels. Fujita et al. (2014) showed that including site-specific microbial biomass data into a Century-type modeling approach improved representation of N-mineralization and soil respiration, but sufficiently reliable microbial data is not typically available to conduct regional and larger scale simulations. This suggests that more complexity in models is necessary. However, limited comparisons involving relatively small numbers of models (2–4) and experimental sites with trace gas flux observations (1–3) do not provide strong evidence that more explicit representation of biological, chemical, and physical processes leads to better results than simpler approaches (Abdalla et al., 2010; Wu and Zhang, 2014; Grant et al., 2016). Comprehensive comparisons using a larger number of models and available multi-site observational data sets such as the Australian N_2O network[1] and the USDA ARS GRACEnet project[2] would help to determine what degree of model complexity is optimal.

---

[1] www.n2o.net.au/about-us/.

[2] http://usdaars.maps.arcgis.com/apps/MapSeries/index.html?appid= 9415d09247f64ae5bde462a3a9292e6c.

Model "predictive ability," interactive biophysical models, socio-cultural models, and linking biogeochemical models to economic models are some of the latest advancements in the use of ecosystem models. The use of Bayesian methods for model selection and model parameterization has the great potential for improving our ecosystem models with the current rapid advances in computer technology. The Agricultural Model Inter-comparison and Improvement Project (AgMIP)[3] tested the abilities of different models to represent wheat and yields and found that ensemble simulations using either the mean or median values of model outputs tended to give better estimates than the individual models. Methods used by AgMIP and those initially developed for ensemble climate models could also be used to guide model comparisons and developments of ensemble models to better predict current concerns regarding land management impacts on GHG fluxes, air quality, and water pollution. Databases with complete model driver and testing information using standardized formatting such as the GRACEnet/REAP system (Del Grosso et al., 2013) could help to facilitate needed model comparison and ensemble studies.

4.8 Summary

The types of questions that originally generated interest in ecosystem modeling (how much C and N are cycled within the earth system; how are human activities modifying these flows?) remain, but estimates of key C and nutrient fluxes have greatly improved form the 1970s to the current time. Both measuring and modeling methods have contributed to these improvements. Models represent the essence of systems ecology in that they embody accumulated knowledge and generate hypotheses to test understanding of processes. Initially, ecosystem models were primarily used to improve our understanding about how ecosystems operate; however, current ecosystem models are widely used to make accurate predictions about how climate change and management practices impact ecosystem dynamics and the potential impacts of these changes on economic activity and inform national policy making. Model failure can occur for various reasons: process-level understanding could be faulty; understanding could be correct but not properly implemented in models; both understanding and implementation could be correct, but

---

[3] https://research.csiro.au/foodglobalsecurity/our-research-2/global-change/agricultural-model-intercomparison-improvement-project-agmip/.

model inputs for all required variables may not be available at appropriate temporal and spatial scales. In reality, all of these factors probably contribute to some degree when model outputs diverge from observations. In sum, ecosystem models remain our best mechanism to integrate diverse types of knowledge regarding how the Earth system functions and to make quantitative predictions that can be confronted with observations of reality. Forrester (1968) suggested models should not be judged against some assumed perfection, instead they should be judged compared to other ways of describing a system of interest. Woodmansee (1978) expanded on this concept by suggesting that simulation models with well-documented and transparent assumptions should be compared to mental models, word models, photographs, or drawings as tools for describing systems. The recent development of the Grass-Cast models shows how our improved ecosystem model can be used to help ranchers anticipate the amount of grass production available for consumption by their cattle in the spring and provide information about how management practices and potential future changes in the climate will impact ecosystem dynamics and greenhouse gas fluxes.

References

Abdalla, M., Jones M., Yeluripati, J., et al. (2010). Testing DayCent and DNDC model simulations of N_2O fluxes and assessing the impacts of climate change on the gas flux and biomass production from a humid pasture. *Atmospheric Environment*, 44(25), 2961–70.

Adair, E. C., Parton, W. J., Del Grosso, S. J., et al. (2008). Simple three-pool model accurately describes patterns of long-term litter decomposition in diverse climates. *Global Change Biology*, 14(11), 2636–60.

Adler, P. R., Spatari, S., D´Ottone, F., et al. (2017). Legacy effects of individual crops affect N_2O emissions accounting within crop rotations. *Global Change Biology – Bioenergy*, 10(2),123–36.

Alcántara, V., Don, A., Well, R., and Nieder, R. (2016). Deep ploughing increases agricultural soil organic matter stocks. *Global Change Biology*, 22(8), 2939–56.

Asao, S., Parton, W. J., Chen, M., and Gao, W. (2018). Photodegradation accelerates ecosystem N cycling in a simulated California grassland. *Ecosphere*, 9(8), e02370.

Bachelet, D., Hunt, H. W., and Detling, J. K. (1989). A simulation model of intraseasonal carbon and nitrogen dynamics of blue grama swards as influenced by above-and belowground grazing. *Ecological Modelling*, 44(3–4), 231–52.

Billari, F. C., Fent, T., Prskawetz, A., and Scheffran, J. (2006). Agent-based computation modeling: An introduction. In *Agent-based Computational Modeling, Contributions to Economics*, ed. F. C. Billari, T. Fent, A. Prskawetz, and J. Scheffran. Heidelberg, Germany: Physica-Verlag, 1–16.

Bista, P., Machado, S., Del Grosso, S. J., Ghimire, R., and Reyes-Fox, M. (2016). Simulating influence of long-term crop residue and nutrient management on soil organic carbon and wheat yield using the DAYCENT model. *Agronomy Journal*, 108(6), 2554–65.

Boone, R. B., Coughenour, M. B., Galvin, K. A., and Ellis, J. E. (2002). Addressing management questions for Ngorongoro Conservation Area using the Savanna Modeling System. *African Journal of Ecology*, 40, 138–50.

Boone, R. B., and Galvin, K. A. (2014). Simulation as an approach to social-ecological integration, with an emphasis on agent-based modeling. In *Understanding Society and Natural Resources: Forging New Strands of Integration Across the Social Sciences*, ed. M. Manfredo, J. J. Vaske, A. Rechkemmer, and E. A. Duke. Dordrecht, Heidelberg, New York, London: Springer, 179–202.

Boone, R. B., Galvin, K. A., BurnSilver, S. B., et al. (2011). Using coupled simulation models to link pastoral decision making and ecosystem services. *Ecology and Society*, 16(2), Article 6.

Boone, R. B., Galvin, K. A., Coughenour, M. B., et al. (2004). Ecosystem modeling adds value to a South African climate forecast. *Climatic Change*, 64, 317–40.

Boone, R. B., Lackett, J. M., Galvin, K. A., Ojima, D. S., and Tucker, C. J. (2007). Links and broken chains: Evidence of human-caused changes in land cover in remotely sensed images. *Environmental Science & Policy*, 10(2), 135–49.

Boone, R. B., and Lesorogol, C. K. (2016). Modelling coupled human–natural systems of pastoralism in East Africa. In *Building Resilience of Human–Natural Systems of Pastoralism in the Developing World: Interdisciplinary Perspectives*, ed. S. Dong, K.-A. S. Kassam, J. F. Tourrand, and R. B. Boone. Switzerland: Springer, 251–80.

Bormann, F. H., and Likens, G. E. (1967). Nutrient cycling. *Science*, 155(3761), 424–9.

Burke, I. C., Yonker, C. M., Parton, W. J., et al. (1989). Texture, climate, and cultivation effects on soil organic matter context in U.S. grassland soils. *Soil Science Society of America Journal*, 53(3), 800–5.

Campbell, E. E., Parton, W. J., Soong, J. L., et al. (2016). Using litter chemistry controls on microbial processes to partition litter carbon fluxes with the litter decomposition and leaching (LIDEL) model. *Soil Biology and Biochemistry*, 100, 160–74.

Campbell, E. E., and Paustian, K. (2015). Current developments in soil organic matter modeling and the expansion of model applications: A review. *Environmental Research Letters*, 10(12), Article 123004.

Capinera, J. L., Detling, J. K., and Parton, W. J. (1983). Assessment of range caterpillar (*Lepidoptera:Saturniidae*) effects with a grassland simulation model. *Journal of Economic Entomology*, 76(5), 1088–94.

Chen, D. X., Hunt, H. W., and Morgan, J. A. (1996). Responses of a C3 and C4 perennial grass to CO2 enrichment and climate change: Comparison between model predictions and experimental data. *Ecological Modeling*, 87, 11–27.

Coleman, D. C., Cole, C. V., and Elliott, E. T. (1983). Decomposition, organic matter turnover, and nutrient dynamics in agroecosystems. In *Nutrient Cycling in Agricultural Ecosystems*, ed. R. R. Lowrance, R. L. Todd, L. E. Asmussen, and

R. A. Leonard. Special Publication No. 23. Athens, GA: University of Georgia, College of Agriculture Experiment Stations.

Coughenour, M. B. (1981). Sulfur dioxide deposition and its effect on a grassland sulfur-cycle. *Ecological Modeling*, 13, 1–16.

(1992). Spatial modeling and landscape characterization of an African pastoral ecosystem: A prototype model and its potential use for monitoring drought. In *Ecological Indicators*, vol. 1, eds. D. H. McKenzie, D. E. Hyatt, and V. J. McDonald. London and New York: Elsevier Applied Science, 787–810.

(1993). *SAVANNA – Landscape and Regional Ecosystem Model: Model Description*. Fort Collins, CO: Natural Resource Ecology Laboratory, Colorado State University.

(2000). Ecosystem modeling of the Pryor Mountain Wild Horse Range, executive summary. In *United States Geological Survey – USDI: Managers' Summary – Ecological Studies of the Pryor Mountain Wild Horse Range, 1992–1997*, compiled by F. J. Singer and K. A. Schoenecker. Fort Collins, CO: US Geological Survey, Midcontinent Ecological Science Center, 125–31.

Coughenour, M. B., and Chen, D. X. (1997). An assessment of grassland ecosystem responses to atmospheric change using linked ecophysiological and soil process models. *Ecological Applications*, 7, 802–27.

Coughenour, M. B., Ellis, J. E., Swift, D. M., et al. (1985). Energy extraction and use in a nomadic pastoral ecosystem. *Science*, 230, 619–24.

Coughenour, M. B., and Singer, F. J. (1996). Elk population processes in Yellowstone National Park under the policy of natural regulation. *Ecological Applications*, 6(2), 573–93.

Cramer, W., Kicklighter, D. W., Bondeau, A., et al. (1999). The intercomparison, and participants of the Potsdam NPP Model. Comparing global models of terrestrial net primary productivity (NPP): Overview and key results. *Global Change Biology*, 5(S1), 1–15.

Davis, S. C., Parton, W. J., Del Grosso, S. J., et al. (2012). Impact of second-generation biofuel agriculture on greenhouse gas emissions in the corn-growing regions of the US. *Frontiers in Ecology and the Environment*, 10(2), 69–74.

De Ruiter, P. C., Neutel, A. M., and Moore, J. C. (1995). Energetics, patterns of interaction strengths, and stability in real ecosystems. *Science*, 269(5228), 1257–60.

Del Grosso, S. J., Gollany, H. T., and Reyes-Fox, M. (2016). Simulating soil organic carbon stock changes in agro-ecosystems using CQESTR, DayCent, and IPCC Tier 1 Methods. In *Synthesis and Modeling of Greenhouse Gas Emissions and Carbon Storage in Agricultural and Forest Systems to Guide Mitigation and Adaptation*, ed. S. J. Del Grosso, L. Ahuja, and W. J. Parton. Madison, WI: American Society of Agronomy, Crop Science Society of America, Soil Science Society of America, 89–110.

Del Grosso, S. J., Ogle, S. M., Parton, W. J., and Breidt, F. J. (2010). Estimating uncertainty in N_2O emissions from US cropland soils. *Global Biogeochemical Cycles*, 24, Article GB1009.

Del Grosso, S. J., Parton, W. J., Adler, P. R., et al. (2012). DayCent model simulations for estimating soil carbon dynamics and greenhouse gas fluxes from agricultural production systems. In *Managing Agricultural Greenhouse Gases: Coordinated Agricultural Research through GRACEnet to Address Our Changing Climate*, ed. M. Liebig, A. J. Franzluebbers, and R. F. Follett. London: Academic Press, 241–50.

Del Grosso, S. J., Parton, W. J., Mosier, A. R., et al. (2000a). General CH_4 oxidation model and comparisons of CH_4 oxidation in natural and managed systems. *Global Biogeochemical Cycles*, 14(4), 999–1019.

et al. (2000b). General model for N_2O and N_2 gas emissions from soils due to denitrification. *Global Biogeochemical Cycles*, 14(4), 1045–60.

Del Grosso, S. J., White, J. W., Wilson, G., et al. (2013). Introducing the GRACEnet/REAP data contribution, discovery and retrieval system. *Journal of Environmental Quality*, 42(4), 1274–80.

Dietze, M. C., Lebauer, D. S., and Kooper, R. (2013). On improving the communication between models and data. *Plant, Cell & Environment*, 36(9), 1575–85.

Doherty, J. (2015). *Calibration and Uncertainty Analysis for Complex Environmental Models. PEST: Complete Theory and What It Means for Modelling the Real World*. Brisbane: Watermark Numerical Computing.

Ellis, J. E., and Swift, D. M. (1988). Stability of African pastoral ecosystems: Alternate paradigms and implications for development. *Journal of Range Management*, 41, 450–9.

Ellis, J. E., Wiens, J. A., Rodell, C. F., and Anway, J. C. (1976). A conceptual model of diet selection as an ecosystem process. *Journal of Theoretical Biology*, 60(1), 93–108.

EPA. (2017). *Inventory of U.S. greenhouse gas emissions and sinks: 1990–2015.* Washington, DC: USEPA. www.epa.gov/ghgemissions/inventory-us-green house-gas-emissions-and-sinks.

Fitton, N., Datta, A., Hastings, A., et al. (2014). The challenge of modelling nitrogen management at the field scale: Simulation and sensitivity analysis of N_2O fluxes across nine experimental sites using Daily DayCent. *Environmental Research Letters*, 9(9), Article 095003.

Forrester, J. W. (1968). *Principles of Systems*. Cambridge, MA: Wright-Allen Press.

Frolking, S. E., Mosier, A. R., Ojima, D. S., et al. (1998). Comparison of N_2O emissions from soils at three temperate agricultural sites: Simulations of year-round measurements by four models. *Nutrient Cycling in Agroecosystems*, 52 (2), 77–105.

Fujita, Y., Witte, J.-P. M., and Bodegom, P. M. (2014). Incorporating microbial ecology concepts into global soil mineralization models to improve predictions of carbon and nitrogen fluxes. *Global Biogeochemical Cycles*, 28(3), 223–38.

Fullman, T. J., Bunting, E. L., Full, G. A., and Southworth, J. (2017). Predicting shifts in large herbivore distributions under climate change and management using a spatially-explicit ecosystem model. *Ecological Modeling*, 352, 1–18.

Gilmanov, T. G., Parton, W. J., and Ojima, D. S. (1997). Testing the CENTURY ecosystem level model on data sets from eight grassland sites in the former USSR representing wide climatic/soil gradient. *Ecological Modelling*, 96(1–3), 191–210.

Grant, B. B., Smith, W. N., Campbell, C. A., et al. (2016). Comparison of DayCent and DNDC models: Case studies using data from long-term experiments on the Canadian prairies. In *Synthesis and Modeling of Greenhouse Gas Emissions and Carbon Storage in Agricultural and Forest Systems to Guide Mitigation and Adaptation*, ed. S. J. Del Grosso, L. Ahuja, and W. J. Parton. Madison, WI: American Society of Agronomy, Crop Science Society of America, Soil Science Society of America, 21–58.

Grant, R. F. (2001). A review of the Canadian ecosystem model ecosys. In *Modeling Carbon and Nitrogen Dynamics for Soil Management*, ed. M. J. Shaffer. Boca Raton, FL: CRC Press, 173–264.

Griffin, W. A. (2006). Agent-based modeling for the theoretical biologist. *Biological Theory*, 1(4), 404–9.

Hall, D. O., Ojima, D. S., Parton, W. J., and Scurlock, J. M. O. (1995). Response of temperate and tropical grasslands to CO_2 and climate change. *Journal of Biogeography*, 22, 537–47.

Hilbers, J. P., Van Langevelde, F., Prins, H. H. T., et al. (2015). Modeling elephant-mediated cascading effects of water point closure. *Ecological Applications*, 25, 402–15.

Hobbs, N. T., Baker, D. L., Ellis, J. E., and Swift, D. M. (1981). Composition and quality of elk winter diets in Colorado. *Journal of Wildlife Management*, 45, 156–71.

Hobbs, N. T., Geremia, C., Treanor, J., et al. (2015). State-space modeling to support management of brucellosis in the Yellowstone bison population. *Ecological Monographs*, 85(4), 525–56.

Hudiburg, T. W., Wang, W., Khanna, M., et al. (2016). Impacts of a 32-billion-gallon bioenergy landscape on land and fossil fuel use in the US. *Nature Energy*, 1, Article 15005.

Hunt, H. W., Coleman, D. C., Ingham, E. R., et al. (1987). The detrital food web in a shortgrass prairie. *Biology and Fertility of Soils*, 3(1), 57–68.

Hunt, H. W., and Parton, W. J. (1986). The role of mathematical models in research on microfloral and faunal interactions in natural and agroecosystems. In *Microfloral and Faunal Interactions in Natural and Agroecosystems*, ed. M. J. Mitchell and J. P. Nakas. Dordrecht: M. Nyhoff/Dr. W. Junk Publishers, 443–94.

Hunt, H. W., Trlica, M. J., Redente, E. F., et al. (1991). Simulation model for the effects of climate change on temperate grassland ecosystems. *Ecological Modelling*, 53, 205–46.

Huston, M., Deangleis, D., and Post, W. (1988). New computer-models unify ecological theory-computer-simulations show that many ecological patterns can be explained by interactions among individual organisms. *Bioscience*, 38(10), 682–91.

Innis, G. S., ed. (1978). *Grassland Simulation Model*. Ecological Studies, 26. New York: Springer.

Kelly, R. H., Parton, W. J., Crocker, G. J., et al. (1997). Simulating trends in soil organic carbon in long-term experiments using the Century model. *Geoderma*, 81, 75–90.

Kim, Y., Talucder, M. S. A., Kang, M., et al. (2016). Interannual variations in methane emission from an irrigated rice paddy caused by rainfalls during the aeration period. *Agriculture, Ecosystems & Environment*, 223, 67–75.

Kirchner, T. B. and Whicker, F. W. (1983/1984). Validation of PATHWAY, a simulation model of the transport of radionuclides through agroecosystems. *Ecological Modeling*, 22, 21–44.

Kittel, T. G. F., Ojima, D. S., Schimel, D. S., et al. (1996). Model GIS integration and data set development to assess terrestrial ecosystem vulnerability to climate change. In *GIS and Environmental Modeling: Progress and Research Issues*. Canada: John Wiley and Sons, 293–7.

LeBauer, D. S., Wang, D., Richter, K. T., Davidson, C. C., and Dietze, M. C. (2013). Facilitating feedbacks between field measurements and ecosystem models. *Ecological Monographs*, 83(2), 133–54.

Lesorogol, C. K., and Boone, R. B. (2016). Which way forward? Using simulation models and ethnography to understand changing livelihoods among Kenyan pastoralists in a "new commons." *International Journal of the Commons*, 10, 747–70.

Li, C. (1996). The DNDC model. In *Evaluation of Soil Organic Matter Models Using Existing, Long-Term Datasets, NATO ASI Series I*, vol. 38, ed. D. S. Powlson, P. Smith, and J. U. Smith. Heidelberg: Springer, 263–7.

Liedloff, A. C., Coughenour, M. B., Ludwig, J. A., and Dyer, R. (2001). Modelling the trade-off between fire and grazing in a tropical savanna landscape, northern Australia. *Environmental International*, 27(2–3), 173–80.

Lorenz, T. (2009). Epistemological aspects of computer simulation in the social sciences. *Lecture Notes in Computer Science*, 5466, 141–52.

Malone, S. L., Keough, C., Staudhammer, C. L., et al. (2015). Ecosystem resistance in the face of climate change: A case study from the freshwater marshes of the Florida Everglades. *Ecosphere*, 6(4), Article 57.

May, R. M. (1973). Qualitative stability in model ecosystems. *Ecology*, 54(3), 638–41.

McGill, W. B., Hunt, H. W., Woodmansee, R. G., and Reuss, J. O. (1981). *Phoenix, a Model of the Dynamics of Carbon and Nitrogen in Grassland Soils*. Ecological Bulletin, 33. Stockholm: Swedish Natural Science Research Council, 49–115 .

Melillo, J. M., Frey, S. D., DeAngelis, K. M., et al. (2017). Long-term pattern and magnitude of soil carbon feedback to the climate system in a warming world. *Science*, 358(6359), 101–5.

Metherell, A. K., Cambardella, C. A., Parton, W. J., et al. (1995). Simulation of soil organic matter dynamics in dryland wheat-fallow cropping systems. In *Soil Management and Greenhouse Effect*, ed. R. Lal, J. Kimball, E. Levine, and B. A. Stewart. Boca Raton, FL: CRC Press, 259–70.

Migliorati, M. D. A., Parton, W. J., Del Grosso, S. J., et al. (2015). Legumes or nitrification inhibitors to reduce N_2O emissions in subtropical cereal cropping systems? A simulation study. *Agriculture, Ecosystems and Environment*, 213, 228–40.

Moore, J. C., Berlow, E. L., Coleman, D. C., et al. (2004). Detritus, trophic dynamics and biodiversity. *Ecology Letters*, 7(7), 584–600.

Moore, J. C., and de Ruiter, P. C. (2012). Models of simple and complex systems. In *Energetic Food Webs: An Analysis of Real and Model Ecosystems*. New York: Oxford University Press, 27–53.

Moore, J. C., de Ruiter, P. C., and Hunt, H. W. (1993). Influence of productivity on the stability of real and model-ecosystems. *Science*, 261(5123), 906–8.

Moore, J. C., McCann, K., Setala, H., and de Ruiter, P. C. (2003). Top-down is bottom-up: Does predation in the rhizosphere regulate aboveground dynamics? *Ecology*, 84(4), 846–57.

Mosier, A., Schimel, D. S., Valentine, D., Bronson, K., and Parton, W. J. (1991). Methane and nitrous oxide fluxes in native, fertilized and cultivated grasslands. *Nature*, 350, 330–2.

Moore, J. C., Walter, D. E., and Hunt, H. W. (1988). Arthropod regulations of microbiota and meso biota in belowground detrital food webs. *Annual Review of Entomology*, 33, 419–39.

Necpálová, M., Anex, R. P., Fienen, M. N., et al. (2015). Understanding the DayCent model: Calibration, sensitivity, and identifiability through inverse modeling. *Environmental Modelling & Software*, 66, 110–30.

Ojima, D. S., Schimel, D. S., Parton, W. J., and Owensby, C. (1994). Long- and short-term effects of fire on N cycling in tallgrass prairie. *Biogeochemistry*, 24, 67–84.

Pan, Y., Melillo, J. M., McGuire, A. D., et al. (1998). Modeled responses of terrestrial ecosystems to elevated atmospheric CO_2: A comparison of simulations by the biogeochemistry models of the vegetation/ecosystem modeling and analysis project (VEMAP). *Oecologia*, 114, 389–404.

Parton, W. J., Coughenour, M. B., Scurlock, J. M. O., Ojima, D. S., Gilmanov, T. G., Scholes, R. J., Schimel, D. S., Kirchner, T. B., Menaut, J. C., Seasteadt, T., Garcia-Moya, E., Kamnalrut, A., Kinyamario, J. I., and Hall, D. O. (1996). Global grassland ecosystem modeling: Development and test of ecosystem models for grassland systems. In *Global Change: Effects on Coniferous Forests and Grasslands*, ed. A. I. Breymeyer, D. M. Hall, J. M. Melillo, and G. I. Agren, SCOPE. Hoboken, NJ: John Wiley and Sons Ltd., 229–66.

Parton, W. J., Gutmann, M. P., Merchant, E. R., et al. (2015). Measuring and mitigating agricultural greenhouse gas production in the US Great Plains, 1870–2000. *Proceedings of the National Academy of Sciences of the United States of America*, 112(34): E4681–E4688.

Parton, W. J., Hartman, M., Ojima, D., and Schimel, D. (1998). DAYCENT and its land surface submodel: Description and testing. *Global and Planetary Change*, 19, 35–48.

Parton, W. J., Holland, E. A., Del Grosso, S. J., et al. (2001). Generalized model for NO_x and N_2O emissions from soils. *Journal of Geophysical Research-Atmospheres*, 106, 17403–20.

Parton, W. J., Neff, J. and Vitousek, P. M. (2005). Modelling phosphorus, carbon and nitrogen dynamics in terrestrial ecosystems. In *Organic Phosphorus in the Environment*, ed. B. L. Turner, E. Frossard, and D. S. Baldwin. CAB International, 325–44.

Parton, W. J., and Rasmussen, P. E. (1994). Long-term effects of crop management in a wheat/fallow system: II. Modelling change with the CENTURY model. *Soil Science Society of America Journal*, 58, 530–6.

Parton, W. J., and Risser, P. G. (1979). Simulating impact of management practices upon the tallgrass prairie. In *Perspectives in Grassland Ecology*, ed. N. R. French. New York: Springer Verlag, 135–56.

(1980). Impact of management practices on the tallgrass prairie. *Oecologia*, 46(2), 223–34.

Parton, W. J., Schimel, D. S., Cole, C. V., and Ojima, D. (1987). Analysis of factors controlling soil organic levels of grasslands in the Great Plains. *Soil Science Society of America Journal*, 51, 1173–9.

Parton, W. J., Schimel, D. S., and Ojima, D. S. (1994). Environmental change in grasslands: Assessment using models. *Climatic Change*, 28, 111–41.

Parton, W. J., Scurlock, J. M. O., Ojima, D. S., et al. (1995). Impact of climate change on grassland production and soil carbon worldwide. *Global Change Biology*, 1, 13–22.

Parton, W., Silver, W. L., Burke, I. C., et al. (2007). Global-scale similarities in nitrogen release patterns during long-term decomposition. *Science*, 315(5810), 361–64.

Parton, W. J., Singh, J. S., and Coleman, D. C. (1978). A model of production and turnover of roots in shortgrass prairie. *Journal of Applied Ecology*, 47, 515–42.

Parton, W. J., Stewart, J. W. B., and Cole, C. V. (1988). Dynamics of C, N, P, and S in grassland soils: A model. *Biogeochemistry*, 5, 109–31.

Peinetti, H. R., Menezes, R. S. C., and Coughenour, M. B. (2001). Changes induced by elk browsing in the aboveground biomass production and distribution of willow (Salix monticola Bebb): Their relationships with plant water, carbon, and nitrogen dynamics. *Oecologia*, 127(3), 334–42.

Plumb, G. E., White, P. J., Coughenour, M. B., and Wallen, R. L. (2009). Carrying capacity and migration of Yellowstone bison: Implications for conservation. *Biological Conservation*, 142, 2377–87.

Pries, C. E. H., Castanha, C., Porras, R. C., and Torn, M. S. (2017). The whole-soil carbon flux in response to warming. *Science*, 355(6332), 1420–2.

Probert, M. E., Keating, B. A., Thompson, J. P., and Parton, W. J. (1995). Modelling water, nitrogen, and crop yield for a long-term fallow management experiment. *Australian Journal of Experimental Agriculture*, 35, 941–50.

Rafique, R., Fienen, M. N., Parkin, T. B., and Anex, R. P. (2013). Nitrous oxide emissions from cropland: A procedure for calibrating the DayCent biogeochemical model using inverse modelling. *Water, Air, & Soil Pollution*, 224(9), Article 1677.

Rafique, R., Kumar, S., Luo, Y., et al. (2014). Estimation of greenhouse gases (N_2O, CH_4 and CO_2) from no-till cropland under increased temperature and altered precipitation regime: A DAYCENT model approach. *Global and Planetary Change*, 118, 106–14.

Rooney, N., McCann, K., Gellner, G., and Moore, J. C. (2006). Structural asymmetry and the stability of diverse food webs. *Nature*, 442(7100), 265–9.

Sala, O. E., Parton, W. J., Joyce, L. A., and Lauenroth, W. K. (1988). Primary production of the Central Grassland Region of the United States. *Ecology*, 69(1), 40–5.

Savage, K. E., Parton, W. J., Davidson, E. A., Trumbore, S. E., and Frey, S. D. (2013). Long-term changes in forest carbon under temperature and nitrogen amendments in a temperate northern hardwood forest. *Global Change Biology*, 19(8), 2389–400.

Scheer, C., Del Grosso, S. J., Parton, W. J., Rowlings, D. W., and Grace, P. R. (2014). Modeling nitrous oxide emissions from irrigated agriculture: Testing DayCent with high-frequency measurements. *Ecological Applications*, 24(3), 528–38.

Schimel, D. S., Braswell, B. H., McKeown, R., et al. (1996). Climate and nitrogen controls on the geography and timescales of terrestrial biogeochemical cycling. *Global Biogeochemical Cycles*, 10, 677–92.

Schimel, D. S., Braswell, B. H., and Parton, W. J. (1997a). Equilibrium of the terrestrial water, nitrogen, and carbon cycles. *Proceedings of the National Academy of Sciences of the United States of America*, 94(16), 8280–3.

Schimel, D. S., Coleman, D. C., and Horton, K. A. (1985). Soil organic-matter dynamics in paired rangeland and cropland topsequences in North-Dakota. *Geoderma*, 36(3–4), 201–14.

Schimel, D. S., Emanuel, W., Rizzo, B., et al. (1997b). Continental scale variability in ecosystem processes: Models, data, and the role of disturbance. *Ecological Monographs*, 67(2), 251–71.

Schimel, D. S., Kittel, T. G. F., and Parton, W. J. (1991). Terrestrial biogeochemistry cycles: Global interactions with the atmosphere and hydrology. *Tellus*, 43AB, 188–203.

Schimel, D. S., Melillo, J. M., Tian, H., et al. (2000). Contribution of increasing CO_2 and climate to carbon storage by ecosystems in the United States. *Science*, 287(5460), 2004–6.

Smith, P., Smith, J. U., Powlson, D. S., et al. (1997). A comparison of the performance of nine soil organic matter models using datasets from seven long-term experiments. *Geoderma*, 81, 153–225.

Soong, J. L., Parton, W. J., Calderon, F., Campbell, E. E., and Cotrufo, M. F. (2015). A new conceptual model on the fate and controls of fresh and pyrolized plant litter decomposition. *Biogeochemistry*, 124, 27–44.

Straube, J. R., Chen, M., Parton, W. J., et al. (2018). Development of the DayCent-Photo model and integration of variable photosynthetic capacity. *Frontiers of Earth Science*, 12(4), 765–78.

Sun, H., Zhou, S., Fu, Z., et al. (2016). A two-year field measurement of methane and nitrous oxide fluxes from rice paddies under contrasting climate conditions. *Scientific Reports*, 6.

Swift, D. M. (1983). A simulation-model of energy and nitrogen-balance for free-ranging ruminants. *Journal of Wildlife Management*, 47(3), 620–45.

VEMAP, et al., Melillo, J. M., Borchers, J., et al. (1995). Vegetation/ecosystem modeling and analysis project: Comparing biogeography and biogeochemistry models in a continental-scale study of terrestrial ecosystem responses to climate change and CO_2 doubling. *Global Biogeochemical Cycles*, 9, 407–37.

Wagner-Riddle, C., Congreves, K. A., Abalos, D., et al. (2017). Globally important nitrous oxide emissions from croplands induced by freeze-thaw cycles. *Nature Geoscience*, 10(4), 279–83.

Wagner-Riddle, C., Hu, Q. C., Van Bochove, E., and Jayasundara, S. (2008). Linking nitrous oxide flux during spring thaw to nitrate denitrification in the soil profile. *Soil Science Society of America Journal*, 72(4), 908–16.

Weisberg, P. J., and Coughenour, M. B. (2003). Model-based assessment of aspen responses to elk herbivory in Rocky Mountain National Park, USA. *Environmental Management*, 32(1), 152–69.

Wiens, J. A., and Innis, G. S. (1974). Estimation of energy flow in bird communities: A population energetics model. *Ecology*, 55(4), 730–46.

Woodmansee, R. G. (1978). Critique and analyses of the grassland ecosystem model ELM. In *Grassland Simulation Model*, ed. G. S. Innis. New York: Springer Verlag.

Wu, X., and Zhang, A. (2014). Comparison of three models for simulating N_2O emissions from paddy fields under water-saving irrigation. *Atmospheric Environment*, 98, 500–9.

Xiao, X., Ojima, D. S., Parton, W. J., Zuozhong, C., and Du, C. (1995). Sensitivity of Inner Mongolia grasslands to global climate change. *Journal of Biogeography*, 22, 643–8.

Yeluripati, J. B., van Oijen, M., Wattenbach, M., et al. (2009). Bayesian calibration as a tool for initialising the carbon pools of dynamic soil models. *Soil Biology and Biochemistry*, 41(12), 2579–2583.

5 · *Advances in Technology Supporting the Systems Ecology Paradigm*

DAVID S. SCHIMEL

5.1 Introduction

The concept of big science pioneered at Colorado State University (CSU) (see Chapter 3) was always hospitable to infusion of highly technical approaches. The systems ecology paradigm (SEP) (see Chapter 1) was based on eventually capturing data into models (see Chapter 4) that provided integration, prediction, and analysis of feedbacks not directly susceptible to experimental test, and this mindset led to a different attitude toward technology infusion than in other groups active at the time.

SEP could not have developed had it not been for advances in experimental, observational, and computing technology. In the late 1960s, mainframe computers (CDC6400) occupying entire rooms and buildings, carried out calculations at speeds slow in comparison to today's smartphones, laptops, and desktops. Chemical analyses were done primarily using glassware and titration chemistry. The ability to "see" inside soil particles has evolved from the desktop optical microscope to computer imaging. Now, with modern spectroscopy and imaging both precision and accuracy have advanced exponentially. Remote sensing evolved from photogrammetry from airplanes. Now we have high-resolution imaging, spectral imaging, and lidar from satellites, manned aircraft, and drones. Geographic information systems (GIS) have developed from research tools to powerful but commodity technologies manipulating and displaying massive amounts data on handheld devices, laptops, and desktop computers. Information management has moved from storage on massive paper files to digital and searchable storage measured in terabytes, petabytes, and larger. Search engines such as Google make much of that information available from almost anywhere on Earth. Now, all of these technologies are interconnected through vast digital networks. Systems ecologists have both adopted and developed new technology and these advances have gone hand in hand with conceptual change.

Over the decades, CSU investigators and collaborators associated with the Natural Resource Ecology Laboratory (NREL), advanced ecosystem science and SEP through highly technical investigations taking advantage of advances in computing and computer networks, GIS, gas exchange systems, flux measurements, stable and radioactive isotopes, new techniques from analytical chemistry, and genomic techniques, have made major contributions to large-scale field campaigns and global remote sensing missions.

Technology development and infusion at CSU and NREL resulted from both indigenous technology investigations and early adoption of technical developments made elsewhere (see Chapters 6–8). The innovations began during the US International Biological Program (USIBP) Grassland Biome studies of the structure and functioning of ecosystems (see Chapter 3). While the discipline of ecology has not been known for aggressive adoption of technology, and its sponsors have mostly not invested in technology until recently, and certainly this has affected CSU investigators seeking advanced approaches, at the same time the history of NREL shows a fascination with technology as a way to unravel otherwise intractable problems. In this short chapter I won't try to cover all of the interactions of ecosystem science and technology centered at CSU, but rather illustrate the advances through the theme of increasing scale, the aspect I know best. References throughout this book will guide readers to specific examples.

5.2 A Personal Note

When I arrived at CSU in the summer of 1979, I had been working as a technician at an oceanographic and ecosystem research center, and had been exposed to highly technical geochemical measurements as well as the then-state of the art in computing, Digital Equipment Corporation mini-computers and one of the first Cray supercomputers, as well as early automated chemical analysis systems. After seeing oceanography's enthusiastic embrace of technology, I was thrilled to discover a like-minded group at CSU. My advisor was developing a field spectrometer for measuring ammonia flux, still a great challenge today, the lab had a complete computing infrastructure and the team had a great respect for meticulous analysis.

The heart and soul of the NREL analytical laboratories was found in a tiny office on the same corridor as the laboratories, for chemistry, isotopes, plant physiology, and soil preparation and analysis, in David Bigelow's office. Dave, a technician initially trained during the Grassland Biome studies, managed the laboratories and mentored the students, most ill-prepared for exacting analyses, in the art of precise and accurate measurement. Dave was responsible for the ammonia measurement, the instrument, and the complex chambers that had to replicate local boundary layer conditions over the shortgrass steppe so as not to modify the flux.

Although the instrumentation we used then to make measurements were almost unimaginably crude by today's standards, and the procedures manual to a degree today's graduate students can't comprehend, the data produced there has stood the test of time and the exhortation from Dave Bigelow as we washed glassware – "Three hot, three cold, three deionized" – still plays in the back of my head when I use, today, vastly more advanced instruments. The principles of calibration, cleanliness, and avoidance of contamination apply as much to a hundred-million-dollar sensor in space as to a test tube of soil extract in the laboratory.

Dave went on to ensure measurement integrity and precision in many scientific and monitoring programs, among his many other accomplishments, before his untimely passing, and as I have myself worked with instruments of greater and greater complexity, his lessons remain bedrock and I do feel him peering over my shoulder, friendly but skeptical, as I process experimental data.

5.3 Technology and the Spatial Dimension of Ecosystems

Systems ecology at CSU began with a strong process focus, examining plant–soil, plant–herbivore, soil–vegetation–atmosphere and microbial coupled processes. Process-oriented researchers initially not focused on the spatial dimension, but instead building on an abstracted notion of coupling between system components, quickly recognized that ecosystem processes had spatial dimensions (see Chapters 1, 6, and 7).

Several threads emerged. Scientists found that sometimes averaging over highly heterogeneous processes is needed to gain understanding, leading to a need for many, many observations or inherently integrating technology. This motivated efficiency and/or automation, and also measurements that are themselves spatial averages, such as eddy covariance and remote-sensing approaches.

A second thread involved the role of heterogeneity, where different facets of the landscape functioned differently and added function at the scale of the landscape itself. This particularly emerged in plant–animal studies, where mobile animals used different parts of the landscape differently and even more dramatically in the study of human interactions with ecosystems in spatially heterogeneous environments, such as in South Turkana and Mongolia (see Chapter 9).

A third thread of research emerged as the role of ecosystems in the Earth system became more and more evident, with researchers discovered more and more ways in which water, energy, trace gas exchange, and other processes at the land surface influence climate and weather (see Chapter 8).

Each of these three threads, pursued by systems ecologists to their logical end, motivated the adoption and advancement of a wide range of technologies, and other technologies, such as isotopic and genomic analysis, originally developed for other science questions, were often woven back in.

5.4 Technology for Scaling, Extrapolation, and Landscapes

In the 1980s a number of seminal grassland studies revealed the importance of landscapes in controlling ecosystem dynamics (see Chapters 1 and 6). Such work emerged across ecology around that time, but was woven seamlessly into systems ecology at NREL. How do landscapes, with heterogeneity, transport of materials, and hydrology function differently than would be inferred from plot (ecological site) or nonspatial studies? NREL scientists studied landscape function, mainly in grasslands and agroecosystems, at many levels. Many of these studies involved the linkage of patches (ecological sites) across landscapes by grazing animals, such as in work on biogenic patches created by grazers (Hobbs, et al., 1982; Coppock and Detling 1986) or landscapes created by geomorphic processes (Yonker et al., 1988). Other studies looked at human use of landscapes, for example, by nomadic pastoralists in Africa and Mongolia (Ellis and Swift, 1988; Reid et al., 2008; Ojima and Chuluun, 2008), how humans use various facets of a landscape, and in turn how they cause landscape change.

From the very outset, scaling or extending, extrapolating process-level understanding required fusion of traditional ecological measures, such as energy balance and food web techniques, to much larger spatial areas, in ways that challenged both information gathering and data management. Researchers were quick to adopt new technologies for both remote sensing and GIS. NREL installed one of the first academic GIS systems in the mid-1980s, perhaps the first in an ecosystem science laboratory, and early applications included supporting grassland and pastoral systems research. Long before geospatial data were readily available, before the internet, ecosystem scientists used airborne photography and early satellite observations (LANDSAT TM) to characterize landscapes as a template to extend meticulous field observations to entire landscapes and regions.

These technologies for geospatial analysis, cutting-edge breakthroughs in the 1980s, are pervasive today and have transitioned from research to routine application in ecosystem management. The impact of the view from above – space and aircraft imagery – on land management cannot be overstated, and as resources for field monitoring have declined, the importance of remote sensing has only increased, as has the ability to integrate multiple data sources in GIS. While remote sensing does not replace process research, it extends it and adds data in hard-to-access regions, areas inaccessible or challenging because of terrain and topography, distance, ownership, or simply limited personnel.

Geospatial technology gives access to immediate data on, for example, proximity of human use to critical habitat, fragmentation over landscapes, disturbance, and a comprehensive view of urban–rural transition zones. These approaches, widely deployed, owe a significant debt to early ecosystem science research, at NREL and elsewhere, as well as the advancements in both space-based sensors and geospatial analysis. While today the use of imagery and GIS is so common as to be ubiquitous, and almost invisible, the contrast with attempts to characterize landscapes with two-dimensional transects, field sampling, and other approximations is dramatic. A next revolution is likely with new remote sensing technologies, such as lidar for ecosystem structure (Lefsky et al., 2002) and its fusion with other innovative technologies allows fieldwork to be extended to landscapes and larger (Saatchi et al., 2015).

5.5 Ecosystems in the Earth System

Ecologists began to see ecosystems playing a role in the Earth system as concern about global change increased in the 1980s. At NREL, interest in trace gases, especially nitrogenous ones, which had begun with studies of gases as vectors for nutrient loss and/or redistribution (Woodmansee,

1978) shifted to concern about greenhouse gases (Mosier et al., 1988, 1993; see Chapters 4, 6, and 8). Other aspects of atmosphere–biosphere interactions also gained attention, including those mediated through the exchange of water and energy (Lu et al., 2001). Studies of ecosystem–atmosphere interaction in the Earth system were a prime motivator for technology adoption and development.

These technologies tended to fall into three areas. First were flux measurements since most atmosphere–ecosystem interactions occur via exchanges of matter and energy at the land surface. Second were techniques for spatial extrapolation, since the interactions occurred through processes that are heterogeneous and not necessarily well-captured by local measurements (Rosswall et al., 1988; Schimel et al., 1988). Third, since ecosystem–atmosphere exchange affects the Earth system by processes occurring over large regions and long periods of time, traditional approaches, process studies, flux measurements, and manipulative experiments had to be strongly complemented by simulation modeling. In fact, much of the standard role of experiments in inferring cause and effect for ecosystem impacts on the climate system had to be replaced by simulation models, informed by process studies, observations, and experiments.

NREL scientists were innovators in making early flux measurements, initially using chambers (Detling et al., 1978; Schimel et al., 1986) supplemented by isotope mass balances and tracers to diagnose specific mechanisms (Mosier et al., 1988) as well as other experimental techniques that, unlike early trace gas research conducted by atmospheric chemists, clearly embedded the gas fluxes in an ecosystem process context. Quickly, though, chamber techniques were complemented, or replaced entirely, by aerodynamic techniques, especially eddy covariance (Hanan et al., 2005), methods which scaled over local micro-heterogeneity and could be directly compared to models, or even used to inform them directly (Braswell et al., 2005).

Techniques for spatial extrapolation built on advances in remote sensing, using initially newly available vegetation indices (the Normalized Difference Vegetation Index), applied to global time series from the advanced very-high-resolution radiometer (AVHRR) instrument, a technique developed by Compton Tucker at the NASA Goddard Space Flight Center, himself a CSU graduate. These studies often built on light use efficiency (LUE) models, estimating absorbed photosynthetically active radiation from the vegetation index and then applying a light use efficiency to scale estimates of productivity over large regions (Hanan et al., 1995). LUE models gained in credibility and importance when one of NASA's first large field experiments explored LUE models and their link to remote sensing (Blad and Schimel, 1992), and were connected to some of the very first long-term (seasonal or longer) eddy covariance measurements. The fusion of eddy covariance and vegetation indices is now as fundamental to ecosystem science as field plots and biomass harvests once were and underpin the global operational estimate of productivity (Running et al., 2004) developed by CSU graduate Steve Running.

Many of these technologies, remote sensing, flux measurements, and integration by modeling came together in the North American Carbon Program's Mid-Continent Intensive Campaign (MCI), a field campaign aimed at comparing atmospheric and ecosystem inventory estimates of carbon budgets in an intensively inventoried region. The MCI was a large, multi-investigator study and one that played to CSU's strengths in modeling, atmosphere–ecosystem interactions, and collaborative ecosystem science (Ogle et al., 2015). The MCI not only informed carbon cycle methodology, but also advanced understanding of agroecosystem carbon budgets (Li et al., 2014).

5.6 Summary: The Role of Computing

Almost all of the science and advances mentioned above (and many more) involved capturing concepts, processes, and mechanisms understood or hypothesized from data into simulation models. NREL scientists pioneered both deeper levels of mechanism in ecosystem models, spatial extrapolation using models, and model–data fusion techniques. Doing so, moving from in-depth process models to gridded, geospatial models of landscape to global processes, required riding Moore's law and utilizing cutting-edge computing, from early adoption of PCs, later workstations and clusters, and later still high-performance and cloud computing. NREL systems ecologists, from its earliest days, used forefront computing approaches, whether those were remote card entry or distributed virtual computing. Models formed the group's "common currency" for integrating and making use of ever more advanced technology. NREL's fluency in modeling gave scientists there an enormous advantage in staying at the cutting edge of systems ecology. As measurement technology advanced and data sets grew larger, fluency in computing became more and more important to actually making use of new data, linking the advances documented here to Chapter 4.

References

Blad, B. L., and Schimel, D. S. (1992). An overview of surface radiance and biology studies in FIFE. *Journal of Geophysical Research: Atmospheres*, 97(D17), 18829–35.

Braswell, B. H., Sacks, W. J., Linder, E., and Schimel D. S. (2005). Estimating diurnal to annual ecosystem parameters by synthesis of a carbon flux model with eddy covariance net ecosystem exchange observations. *Global Change Biology*, 11(2), 335–55.

Coppock, D. L., and Detling, J. K. (1986). Alteration of bison and black-tailed prairie dog grazing interaction by prescribed burning. *The Journal of Wildlife Management*, 50(3), 452–5.

Detling, J. K., Parton, W. J., and Hunt, H. W. (1978). An empirical model for estimating CO_2 exchange of Bouteloua gracilis (H.B.K.) Lag. in the shortgrass prairie. *Oecologia*, 33(2), 137–47.

Ellis, J. E., and Swift, D. M. (1988). Stability of African pastoral ecosystems: Alternate paradigms and implications for development. *Rangeland Ecology & Management/Journal of Range Management Archives*, 41(6), 450–9.

Hanan, N. P., Berry, J. A., Verma, S. B., et al. (2005). Testing a model of CO_2, water and energy exchange in Great Plains tallgrass prairie and wheat ecosystems. *Agricultural and Forest Meteorology*, 131(3–4), 162–79.

Hanan, N. P., Prince, S. D., and Bégué A. (1995). Estimation of absorbed photosynthetically active radiation and vegetation net production efficiency using satellite data. *Agricultural and Forest Meteorology*, 76(3–4), 259–76.

Hobbs, N. T., Baker, D. L., Ellis, J. E., Swift, D. M., and Green, R. A. (1982). Energy-and nitrogen-based estimates of elk winter-range carrying capacity. *The Journal of Wildlife Management*, 46(1),12–21.

Lefsky, M. A., Cohen, W. B., Parker, G. G., and Harding, D. J. (2002). Lidar remote sensing for ecosystem studies: Lidar, an emerging remote sensing technology that directly measures the three-dimensional distribution of plant canopies, can accurately estimate vegetation structural attributes and should be of particular interest to forest, landscape, and global ecologists. *BioScience*, 52(1), 19–30.

Li, Z., Liu, S., Tan, Z., et al. (2014). Comparing cropland net primary production estimates from inventory, a satellite-based model, and a process-based model in the Midwest of the United States. *Ecological Modelling*, 277, 1–2.

Lu, L., Pielke, Sr., R. A., Liston, G. E., Parton, W. J., Ojima, D., and Hartman, M. (2001). Implementation of a two-way interactive atmospheric and ecological model and its application to the central United States. *Journal of Climate*, 14(5), 900–19.

Mosier, A. R., Parton, W. J., and Schimel, D. S. (1988). Nitrous oxide production by nitrification and denitrification in a shortgrass steppe. *Biogeochemistry*, 6, 45–58.

Mosier, A., Valentine, D., Schimel, D., Parton, W., and Ojima, D. (1993). Methane consumption in the Colorado short grass steppe. *Mitteilungen der Deutschen Bodenkundlichen Gesellschaft*, 69, 219–26.

Ogle, S. M., Davis, K., Lauvaux, T., et al. (2015). An approach for verifying biogenic greenhouse gas emissions inventories with atmospheric CO_2 concentration data. *Environmental Research Letters*, 10(3), 034012.

Ojima, D., and Chuluun, T. (2008). Policy changes in Mongolia: Implications for land use and landscapes. In *Fragmentation in Semi-arid and Arid Landscapes*, ed. K. A. Galvin, R. S. Reid, R. H. Behnke, Jr., and N. T. Hobbs. Dordrecht: Springer, 179–93.

Reid, R. S., Galvin, K. A., and Kruska, R. S. (2008). Global significance of extensive grazing lands and pastoral societies: An introduction. In *Fragmentation in Semi-arid and Arid Landscapes*, ed. K. A. Galvin, R. S. Reid, R. H. Behnke, Jr., and N. T. Hobbs. Dordrecht: Springer, 1–24.

Rosswall, T., Woodmansee, R. G., and Risser, P. G., eds. (1988). *Scales and Global Change: Spatial and Temporal Variability in Biospheric and Geospheric Processes*. Scientific Committee on Problems of the Environment (SCOPE) of the International Council of Scientific Unions (ICSU). New York: John Wiley.

Running, S. W., Nemani, R. R., Heinsch, F. A., Zhao, M., Reeves, M., and Hashimoto, H. (2004). A continuous satellite-derived measure of global terrestrial primary production. *Bioscience*, 54(6), 547–60.

Saatchi, S., Mascaro, J., Xu, L., et al. (2015). Seeing the forest beyond the trees. *Global Ecology and Biogeography*, 24(5), 606–10.

Schimel, D. S., Parton, W. J., Adamsen, F. J., Woodmansee, R. G., Senft, R. L., and Stillwell, M. A. (1986). The role of cattle in the volatile loss of nitrogen from a shortgrass steppe. *Biogeochemistry*, 2(1), 39–52.

Schimel, D. S., Simkins, S., Rosswall, T., Mosier, A. R., and Parton, W. J. (1988). Scale and the measurement of nitrogen-gas fluxes from Terrestrial Ecosystems. In *Scales and Global Change*, ed. T. Rosswall, R. G. Woodmansee, and P. G. Risser. SCOPE 35. New York: John Wiley and Sons, 179–93.

Woodmansee, R. G. (1978). Additions and losses of nitrogen in grassland ecosystems. *Bioscience*, 28(7), 448–53.

Yonker, C. M., Schimel, D. S., Paroussis, E., and Heil, R. D. (1988). Patterns of organic carbon accumulation in a semiarid shortgrass steppe, Colorado. *Soil Science Society of America Journal*, 52(2), 478–83.

6 · Emergence of Cross-Scale Structural and Functional Processes in Ecosystem Science

RANDALL B. BOONE, ROBERT G. WOODMANSEE, JAMES K. DETLING, DANIEL BINKLEY, THOMAS J. STOHLGREN, MONIQUE E. ROCCA, WILLIAM H. ROMME, PAUL H. EVANGELISTA, SUNIL KUMAR, AND MICHAEL G. RYAN

6.1 Introduction

The history of the Natural Resource Ecology Laboratory (NREL) mirrors the growing appreciation of ecosystem science as it relates to the importance of scale and its interconnectivity of elements within systems. Carbon and energy, nutrients, water, soils, weather, and climate interact at multiple scales to support the populations and communities that provide the ecosystem services that humans rely on. Here we provide an overview of the research conducted by NREL scientists into the interactive and interrelated nature of ecosystems. However, we emphasize that many of the discoveries and breakthroughs were accomplished in collaboration with other scientists around the world (see Chapter 1). Interdisciplinary teams of researchers have integrated field and laboratory studies and statistical and simulation modeling to discover the underpinnings of our ecosystems. This knowledge can improve sustainable resource management.

Here we present some terminology commonly used by ecosystem scientists, describe key points or components, and define essential processes of ecosystems. The concepts are the everyday language of scientists, educators, and managers but not lay readers. The concepts are essential for understanding ecosystem productivity, resilience, and sustainability. Where appropriate, we have emphasized concepts for lay readers that have withstood both peer-reviewed scientific inquiry and practical experience.

This chapter is divided into sections which define and discuss the important spatial scales: organism, ecological site, landscape, and regional and global levels. The organism scale emphasizes primary production and plant-level processes that ultimately influence the functioning of higher-level systems. At the ecological site level (i.e., plot, patch, or stand), we describe basic ecosystem processes. Ecological site-level descriptions address primary and secondary production, some of which include decomposition, nutrient cycling, water dynamics, and diversity. Some of the topics addressed at landscape scales include cumulative effects of ecological site processes, disturbance, and species–habitat selection. The linkages among landscape elements are emphasized at regional scales.

Much of the discussion that follows is well-established science discovered over the past five decades, especially at organismal and ecological scales. We make no attempt to cite the overwhelming number of scientific publications that have contributed to our current understanding. Rather, we will summarize our knowledge and reference only key textbooks, synthesis and review documents, and seminal publications mostly related to NREL research that will lead readers to our current state of ecosystem knowledge.

6.2 Scales and Ecological Hierarchies

Throughout this chapter, we will use a common perspective of how ecosystems are organized in space, time, and societally (Figure 6.1; see Chapters 1 and 2). During most of the twentieth century, ecosystem studies were conducted at scales of $1 \, m^2$ or below (Kareiva and Andersen, 1988). Results from the study of such "plots" were summarized and taken to represent regional conditions. Such work is still common today, but is enhanced by many studies at landscape, regional, and even global scales. At lower spatial dimensions (Figure 6.1), definition of scales is relatively easy and generally accepted by scientists. As spatial scales increase in size, definition becomes more complicated. We begin with a discussion of biophysical functioning within ecosystems, and specifically link (1) carbon, water, and nutrient dynamics; (2) primary and secondary production; (3) decomposition; and (4) energy flow to soil and climate properties across spatial scales. Temporal scales are also referenced throughout the book. Humans are introduced as interactive components of ecosystems in the Chapters 2, 7, 9, 10, and 13 that cover landscapes and larger geographic areas. This topic is part of the culture of NREL researchers, and is more specifically discussed in Chapter 9. Of critical

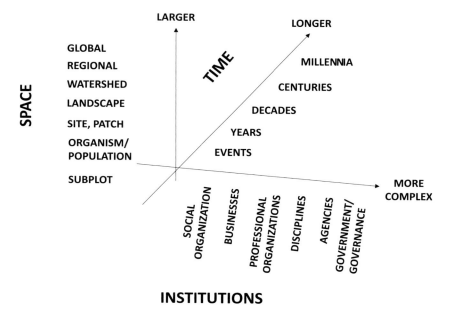

Figure 6.1 Some hierarchical dimensions needing specific attention when evaluating and managing ecological/social ecosystems. Specific discussions of these dimension are found in Section 1.9.

importance is a clear definition of the problems or questions of scientific focus. This will determine the appropriate levels of space, time, and institutional scales for investigation. Problems and questions often require integration of knowledge from multiple scales, with each being independently defined (O'Neil, 1988).

Ecosystems have been variously defined at multiple scales, for example from human eyebrows and the mites that inhabit them to the Earth itself. However, in recent years the linkages between more commonly considered ecosystem scales have been a focus. Researchers seek to understand how small-scale observations and experimental results produce or modify large-scale processes (Nash et al., 2014). Methodologies, such as tracking the fate of energy through ecosystems and applying a systems thinking approach, have proven critical in understanding systems across scales. Broader, and even global, analyses have driven research in recent decades (Ojima et al., 1994; Brown, 1995). Cross-scale effects and feedbacks have been a focus in the study of ecosystem science and sustainability (Briske and Heitschmidt, 1991; Holling, 1992; Ellis and

Galvin, 1994; MacDonald, 2000; Carpenter et al., 2009; Currie, 2011). Conceptualization and computer modeling of coupled systems to address complex responses have promoted the need to think across scales (see Chapter 4). Comprehensive modeling approaches may incorporate into a single application the physiology of plants and animals at fine spatial scales, and behavior, animal demography, community dynamics, and principles of ecosystem ecology at progressively larger scales. Ways in which information and understanding are distorted as we move across scales is a pressing research topic. For example, analyses at regional scales are usually coarser in spatial resolution than those at landscape or eco-logical site scales. Ways in which spatial data are scaled up or down in those analyses may affect research outcomes (Wiens, 1989).

Elements of the ecosystem cross scales more literally. Landscapes are linked by migrating animals, wind-blown dust and debris, blowing snow, and the movement of species that may become invasive. Dust that blows to the west from the Sahara in northern Africa may deposit on glaciers in South America, reducing the albedo of the ice, and increasing the melting rate. Runoff and groundwater link river basins, nutrients in fertilizer are transported long distances hydrologically, and nitrogen is transported in the atmosphere and deposited far from its source (Baron et al., 2000).

Recent studies claim that we are experiencing the sixth mass extinc-tion event on our planet, this one caused by human actions (Ceballos et al., 2015). Understanding ecosystem services, species distributions, abundances, movements, and control of biodiversity of plants, animals, and soil organisms often requires analyses at regional scales. Understanding how these and other factors interrelate across scales will improve our forecasting of, and response to, events that may cascade across ecosystem scales and become catastrophic (Peters et al., 2007). We may be certain that slowing the loss of biodiversity, managing global change, and monitoring water use and other ecosystem services in a sustainable way will require an increased understanding of our ecosys-tems at multiple scales (Baron et al., 2002).

6.2.1 Ecosystem Interactions

One way of viewing the holistic nature of ecosystem dynamics is to adopt a cross-scale perspective (Figure 6.2). On the left-hand side of the figure, interactions of structural attributes, such as biotic communities, species diversity, and population dynamics, are portrayed. The essential functional properties of ecosystems, for example the interactions and

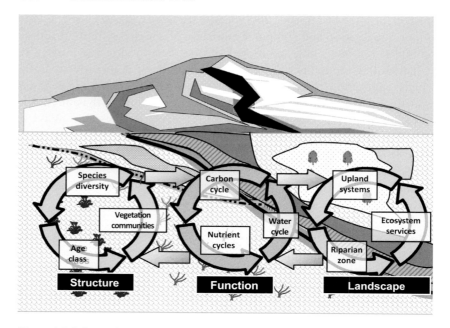

Figure 6.2 Schematic representing interactions of some biophysical attributes (structure and function) of ecological sites within landscapes. The emphasis is on dynamics in space and time and the interactions of the attributes. A black and white version of this figure will appear in some formats. For the color version, please refer to the plate section.

interdependencies of the carbon cycle and energy flow pathways, and the water and nutrient cycles, are shown in the center of the figure. On the right-hand side of Figure 6.2 is a representation of the interactions of upland ecological site scale ecosystems with riparian ecological sites focusing on the concept of ecosystem services (MEA, 2005). These services include the full suite of benefits humans receive from landscapes, grouped into (1) provisioning services that include material products from ecosystems, (2) regulating services such as erosion control, (3) supporting services such as carbon, water, and nutrient cycling, and (4) cultural services that capture religious and aesthetic appreciation of ecosystems.

6.2.2 Functional Scales of the C, N, P, and Water Cycles

Biological systems require many chemical elements, providing the macro and micronutrients that support life. They include carbon (C), hydrogen

(H), oxygen (O), nitrogen (N), phosphorus (P), calcium, magnesium, sulfur, potassium, iron, and several others. Understanding the cycling of C, N, and P and the flow of energy in ecosystems requires an understanding of processes that occur within and between the individual plants and organisms within ecosystems (Archer and Smeins, 1991; Heitschmidt and Stuth, 1991; Bedunah and Sosebee, 1995; Lauenroth and Burke, 2008; Chapin et al., 2011).

Some of the components and processes of the C and N cycles of a rangeland ecosystem, are shown in Figures 6.3 and 6.4. Remember, a system is a *grouping of parts that operate together for a common purpose or function.* To be defined as a system, the components must be described in common units such as grams of something per meter squared, numbers of individuals per area, or weight per volume of fluid (Forrester, 1968; Meadows, 2008). All components are composed of the same matter (here, carbon-based molecules containing carbon and nitrogen). All processes move matter – carbon-based molecules.

Since the chemical backbone of every living thing on this planet is carbon, it is fundamentally important to understand how this element

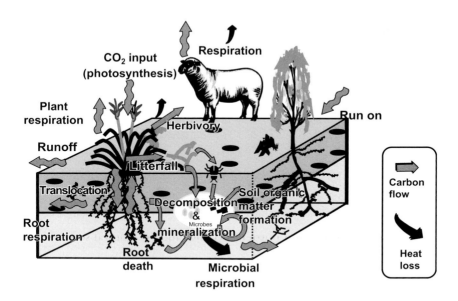

Figure 6.3 Cartoon of a rangeland ecological site showing the primary components and processes or transfer pathways in the carbon cycle. A black and white version of this figure will appear in some formats. For the color version, please refer to the plate section.

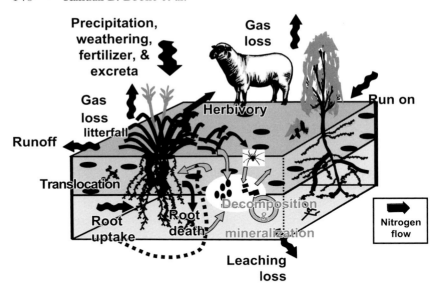

Figure 6.4 The nitrogen cycle. These processes or flows are basically the same as those for carbon (see Figure 6.3). Differences are explained in the text. Don't forget carbon compounds are the backbone for life. Nitrogen and most other nutrients are part of carbon molecules as they move through ecosystems.

works in ecosystems. Carbon is the basic building block of sugars, starches, fats, proteins, amino acids, DNA, plant and animal tissues, microorganisms, us, and all of our friends (and enemies). In addition to giving life its structural form, carbon-based chemicals carry energy in chemical bonds that allows living things to survive, grow, and reproduce. Understanding how ecosystems work – that is, how the parts of the system interact and, indeed, describing and explaining the parts themselves – requires knowledge of a few basic concepts related to the carbon cycle and how energy is passed through the system.

However, before the complexity depicted in Figures 6.2–6.4 can be introduced, we step down to the scale of a single plant because green plants are the source of almost all of the carbon and captured energy needed to sustain life in terrestrial ecosystems.

6.3 Organism Scale

The basic, pragmatic unit in the biophysical realm of a grazingland, forest, or agricultural ecosystem is a *plant* in a *subplot* (Figure 6.5). The

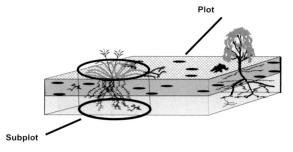

Figure 6.5 A plot representing an ecological site with a "subplot" contained therein. In the real world this plot and subplot would have intermingled root systems, aboveground and soil animals, bacteria and fungi, rocks, soil water, minerals, ions, etc. The processes such as those depicted in Figures 6.3 and 6.4 would be interacting.

subplot concept is one plant in its soil and climate environment. Plants may be grouped into different categories that yield different types of understanding, such as life-form, functional, and taxonomic groups (Milchunas et al., 2008). Plants share life-forms, such as grasses, shrubs, and trees. They may be classified into functional groups, dependent on the role the plant plays in the ecosystem (e.g., forage plants, medicinal plants). And of course, plants may be classified taxonomically into species, genus, families, etc. Regardless of whether we choose life-forms, functional groups, or taxonomic groups, the central building blocks of life on Earth are processes that occur within a single autotrophic plant or microorganism.

All life within a terrestrial ecosystem is dependent on the chemical energy and organic carbon-based compounds that are produced by green plants and a few bacteria and algae via the process of photosynthesis (Figure 6.6). Following photosynthesis and the synthesis of organic compounds, those compounds are translocated and some recirculated within the plant to meet the metabolic needs of stems, roots, leaves, and flowering parts.

Plants shed dead and dying parts that become debris (dead roots and litter) and "food" for microorganisms near the plant. Some plant parts may be eaten by herbivores and transported away from the subplot. Early studies in the US IBP Grasslands Biome Program (Coleman et al., 2004) era described these processes (see Chapter 3). A plethora of mathematical models have been produced that simulate these dynamics (Van Dyne and Anway, 1976), including the Century and DayCent models (Parton et al., 1983, 1998; see Chapter 4) – a major achievement of scientific research.

Photosynthesis
(CO$_2$)

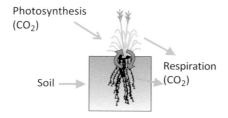

Respiration
(CO$_2$)

Soil

Figure 6.6 Basic concept of a plant (organism) in a soil and climate environment. In this idealized image the plant tops, roots, and flowering parts reside in a soil body. The plant tops fix carbon from the atmosphere into carbon-based compounds. Those compounds are translocated to various parts of the plant meet the metabolic needs of stems, roots, leaves, and flowering parts and some are recycled within the plant. At every chemical transformation along the way some CO$_2$ is lost through respiration. As plant parts die or are eaten carbon is lost to the environment.

6.3.1 Capturing the Essential Elements for Life in Plants

Carbon compounds are the backbone of life. Most nutrients are incorporated in carbon-based molecules as they move through ecosystems (Coyne et al., 1995). All living things need food to grow, replace parts, and reproduce to survive. The sources of that food are ultimately the chemical products of photosynthesis for almost all organisms (some interesting exceptions are organisms that make their living breaking down hydrogen sulfide chemical bonds around deep ocean thermal vents). Photosynthesis is one of the most studied processes in plant physiology and is referenced in myriad textbooks and online. Carbon dioxide (CO$_2$) is processed by plant leaves, some stems, and a few types of algae and bacteria in the presence of sunlight, water, and essential enzymes to form simple sugars. Chemical transformations and reactions take place following photosynthesis yielding sugars, starches, proteins, DNA, RNA, lignin, and cellulose. Chemical energy is stored in chemical bonds of the organic compounds. *The only source of C for autotrophic plants is atmospheric CO$_2$.* The organisms that do the processing are called primary producers.

One of the earliest research projects in the Grassland Biome IBP was to measure photosynthesis so that primary production and energy flow through a grassland ecosystem could be quantified. This proved to be very difficult (Brown and Trilica, 1977; Detling et al., 1978; Williams and Kemp, 1978). Early attempts to model ecosystems focused on modeling energy flow (Van Dyne, 1969; Van Dyne and Anway, 1976). However, it soon became clear that carbon may be more precisely modeled than energy (Innis, 1978).

Factors that control photosynthesis are temperature, nutrients, and plant water content. These factors are in turn dependent on various conditions, such as: (1) soil water availability if the primary producer is a terrestrial plant, (2) season, (3) life stage and plant health, (4) quantity of radiant energy, and (5) other environmental factors that may influence organism growth. In semi-arid and arid regions, water availability is the most important controller of photosynthesis.

6.3.2 Gross Primary Production

Gross primary production (GPP) is the total amount of carbon-based compounds produced by photosynthesis in a single organism or in a given area (ecological site scale) in a given period of time (Gough, 2012). However, all chemical transformations in plants come at a cost. To function, all living cells must have an energy source stored in carbon bonds, oxygen (with some exceptions), and water. For a plant to live, the process of photosynthesis and all subsequent chemical transformations needed to build new structural parts, maintain its living cells, defend itself, and reproduce the required energy that comes from the breaking of chemical bonds stored in some of the carbon compounds it previously manufactured. The result of this work is respiration (R), which releases CO_2, H_2O, and heat. Unlike nutrients that cycle, the flow of energy through ecosystems is unidirectional; that is, every metabolic process requires chemical energy, but heat (degraded energy) and CO_2 are lost with each transformation (Ryan, 1991; Coyne et al., 1995).

Carbon-based compounds that remain after carbon has been lost via plant respiration are transformed into structural parts, reproductive parts, and sugars and starches needed for subsequent energy and structural and metabolic transformations. Other biochemical reactions in the primary producers form organic compounds that contain nitrogen, phosphorus, and micronutrients to produce amino acids, proteins, DNA, vitamins, and essential chemicals that support life. Details of specific plant physiological processes have generally been beyond the scope of "ecosystem-level" studies except where specific information has been needed for modeling studies.

6.3.3 Net Primary Production

The quantity of chemical compounds that remains after respiration is called net primary production (NPP). The results of these chemical reactions are what we see, feel, weigh, and measure as wood, leaves, roots, seeds, or autotrophic microorganisms. This organic matter is often called biomass. The amount present at any instant is called standing crop.

Thousands of empirical studies and scientific papers have been dedicated to identifying and measuring these structures and compounds in plants found in grazinglands, forests, and agricultural ecosystems. Far fewer studies have attempted to determine the dynamics of structures and compounds through time and how they interact with other critical functions, such as secondary production in animals and microorganisms, land and atmospheric carbon and nitrogen exchanges, greenhouse gas mitigation, and ecosystem services. Such dynamic studies require a systems ecology approach that emphasizes mathematical modeling because the problems are too complex to address thoroughly using empirical approaches only (see Chapter 4).

Among the most significant contributions of NREL scientists and their collaborators over the past five decades to the body of knowledge of ecosystem science has been the quantification of GPP, NPP, and R and many of the ecosystem processes and functions derived from that research (Woodmansee, 1978; Lauenroth, 1979; Milchunas and Lauenroth, 1992; Lauenroth et al., 1999, 2008; Del Grosso et al., 2008; Li et al., 2014; Conant et al., 2016 and hundreds of others). Those contributions were dependent on the application of the systems ecology approach that demanded the integration of modeling, field, and laboratory research (see Chapter 1).

Formal simulation modeling efforts have been essential for integrating information from targeted field and laboratory studies, the literature, and expert experience (Coughenour et al., 1979; McGill et al., 1981; Parton et al., 2007). Without using these models, the enormous complexity of real ecosystems would be overwhelming. An example of the complexity is determining the annual production of roots in a grazingland ecosystem, information needed to determine the role of roots in C, N, P, or S cycles (e.g., Woodmansee et al., 1978; Lauenroth and Burke, 2008). A standing crop of roots (the amount of biomass present at any instant) is needed, and then the turnover rate of the roots (the number of times the standing crop is replaced in a given growing season) must be determined. To estimate either the standing crop or turnover rate, we need to distinguish between species of roots, between living, senescing, and dead roots, and then determine the vertical distribution of roots by species. Linking to the biogeochemical cycles requires determining labile compounds that are easily broken down (sugars, starches, small amino acids, etc.) versus structural parts of roots that take longer to decompose. Further complicating the analysis is the reality that some of the labile C, N, P, and S can be recycled within plants until it is fixed into structural parts or lost to the atmosphere as in the case of carbon (Clark, 1977). Modeling is the only practical method of dealing with this complexity.

6.3.4 Sources of Nutrients for Plants

We are generally taught that N–fixation in the roots of legumes and some microorganisms add nitrogen to ecosystems. Some atmospheric nitrogen (N_2) is converted into biologically active forms by lightning or fire. These processes convert atmospheric nitrogen into biologically useful forms such as ammonium ions, ammonia, and ultimately nitrate.

Unfortunately, life isn't that simple. Biological and lightning N–fixation do occur, of course, and in mesic ecosystems these may be important processes. But in healthy, functioning arid and semi–arid ecosystems, other factors, such as deposition of ions in rain and snow (wet deposition) and in dust and aerosols (dry deposition), are equally or more important (Woodmansee, 1978; Coyne et al., 1995; Baron et al., 2014; see Chapter 8). Weathering of minerals from rock is the original source of numerous nutrients for self-maintaining natural and agricultural ecosystems. Nutrients such as phosphorus, iron, calcium, and potassium are made available through these weathering processes. However, weathering is a very slow process and is thus inefficient for supporting annual biomass production (Clark, 1977; Woodmansee, 1978).

Nutrient additions from the atmosphere are the major sources of nitrogen and sulfur for self-maintaining ecosystems (Woodmansee et al., 1978; Burke et al., 1998; Baron et al., 2014; see Chapter 8). These sources are natural and are also waste products from fossil fuel burning for transportation, industry, and power generation. In many locations, especially in urban areas, the amounts added from the human–influenced sources exceed those from biological nitrogen fixation and natural background atmospheric levels (Ojima et al., 1994).

Intensively managed ecosystems, such as croplands, urban parks, golf courses, and lawns, may have massive amounts of nutrients added as fertilizer rather than from atmospheric and biologic sources. However, the vast majority of self-maintaining ecosystems are not fertilized. Some areas are fertilized from excreta of animals that feed elsewhere and deposit their wastes on a given site, which can be of local importance (Senft et al., 1987).

6.3.5 Plant Nutrient Uptake

Plants take up the nutrients required to support life in the form of ions in soil solution as NH_4^+, NO_3^-, $H_2PO_4^-$, HPO_4^{-2} and SO_4^{-2} (Clark, 1977; Coyne et al., 1995). The term *uptake* refers to the movement of nutrient ions into plant roots. Mineral ions, such as ammonium, nitrate, and phosphate, are present in soil water and move to the roots as the plant takes up water. Important controls of uptake are plant and soil water content, temperature, season, life stage of the plant, and availability of nutrient ions. Once inside the plant, the ions are chemically combined with carbon compounds to form organic matter.

6.3.6 Root Production and Death

Models are essential for unraveling complex interactions within plants because leaves are not just green objects that grow on grasses, forbs, shrubs, and trees, leading to the photosynthetic process (Figure 6.3). They are chemical structures that contain complex organic compounds, such as lignin and cellulose, that give cells structure; and simple molecules, such as sugars, starches, and amino acids which provide cell contents with energy and nutrients. The proportions and availability of these different compounds have a profound influence on overall ecosystem functioning, especially for above and belowground secondary productivity (i.e., productivity of the organisms that consume primary production). Likewise, roots are not just structures that attach leaves and stems to the soil to then be cut off and measured (Figure 6.3). In the real world, some roots are living and some are dead, yet are still attached to a root mass. Different parts of roots have different chemical compositions. Some roots are old and some are young, some may have different functions and relationships to soil layers, and some are extremely difficult to measure and quantify.

An essential concept (*ecological rule*) is that *carbon, nitrogen, and other nutrients tend to maintain a balance* (Redfield, 1934). For example, carbon and nitrogen ratios have a critical relationship in a multitude of ecosystem interactions. The so-called Liebig's law of the minimum may apply, where water or a nutrient such as nitrogen or phosphorus may be limiting the growth of plants. Adding a nutrient that is super-abundant may have little effect on production. However, if a specific nutrient or carbon that is limiting is added or lost from the system, then the other parts will adjust. If nitrogen is added, growth may be stimulated if adequate water is available. If nitrogen is lost, growth may be retarded. Models are needed to keep track of the assumptions required to understand and communicate these interactions. The factors that control both carbon and nutrient cycling include: (1) temperature; (2) plant water content, which in turn is dependent on available water in the soil if the primary producer is a terrestrial plant; (3) C/N/P/S ratios; (4) season of the year; and (5) life stage and "health" of the organisms (Bell et al., 2014).

6.3.7 Translocation of Carbon and Nutrients within Plants

The term *translocation* refers to the partitioning and movement of carbon and nutrients throughout the plant (Figure 6.6). This process is essential for moving carbon, energy, and nutrients to locations in the plant where growth, storage, and metabolism occur, that is, roots, leaves, reproductive tissues, and support and storage structures (Clark, 1977; Woodmansee et al., 1978; Coyne et al., 1995). As nutrient-bearing compounds move throughout the plant, further chemical transformations take place as dictated by the genetic rules of allocation within the plant. Important controls of translocation are plant water content, temperature, season, life stage of the plant, reproductive status, and injury, such as herbivory, harvest, or disease.

6.3.8 Internal Recycling

Perennial plants generally require far more essential nutrients for growth, metabolism, and reproduction than they take up from the soil during any growing season. Nutrients not physically or chemically part of newly produced structures are remobilized and translocated elsewhere for use – they are recycled (Clark, 1977; Woodmansee et al., 1978). Perennial plants have also evolved the capability of "sensing" when their parts are injured, old, and beginning to die, or when the plant is preparing to go dormant due to the onset of drought, seasonal changes in temperature, or other environmental factors. During this "dormancy preparation" process, most available nutrients, and some sugars and other carbohydrates, are mobilized and translocated to storage sites in roots, root crowns, stems, or other storage structures. These storage compounds become the nutrients and energy sources to begin the next growth cycle when environmental conditions are favorable (e.g., Ryan and Asao, 2014).

Once carbon is fixed into chemical bonds by photosynthesis, it is stored in carbon compounds of the cell walls in leaves, stems, roots, or in the contents of cells. These compounds become the source of energy and the carbon structures, including nutrients in all living organisms in the ecological site (Figure 6.3). They are used to build structural parts and meet the metabolic needs of plants, animals, and microorganisms. Due to the close relationship between the carbon and nutrient cycles and water, ecological site scale understanding is essential.

6.3.9 Connecting the Organism to Ecological Site Scale Ecosystems

A cautionary note: while the arboreal parts of a single plant are relatively easy to define, the plant root system and its encompassing soil environment are not. In nature, root systems of different plants intermingle and overlap as do soil fauna and microorganisms. Therefore, we can conceptualize a plant in its soil environment and position a physical sampling device to enclose a single plant aboveground; however, in nature we cannot be certain we are sampling one specific plant in its environment. Furthermore, imagine a dead root that is still attached to its living plant. The plant root is dead, but it is likely infused with bacteria, fungi, nematodes, etc. Is the dead root really dead? How can an ecologist determine its status?

Critical belowground ecological processes occur at the cm^3, mm^3, and nm^3 scales in the soil of a subplot (e.g., Figures 6.3 and 6.5). These processes have been the subjects of a great deal of research at the NREL as well as in the broader community (Coleman and Wall, 2014; Paul, 2015). Those studies focused on microbial/soil fauna interactions, belowground food webs, root production and death, decomposition, soil organic matter formation and dynamics, mineralization, soil and litter C, N, P, and S dynamics, soil aggregate formation and function, interactions of C, N, and P cycles, and relationships within soils (Bolin and Cook, 1983). Additionally, C, N, and P budgets and processes, nutrient exchanges and transport, and plant and microbe competition have connected these belowground and aboveground linkages.

Death and the shedding of aboveground plant parts is typically termed litterfall, a catch-all term that encompasses the entire shedding process of dead plant parts, sometimes even the roots which don't fall anywhere. Both litter and dead roots vary enormously in origin (leaves, stems, old roots, young roots, etc.), chemical composition, age, layers, and relationship to soil layers. Both are difficult to measure. These dead plant parts are the source of carbon, energy, and nutrients for biotic functions and processes external to plants and autotrophic microorganisms.

Before the death of perennial plant parts, many essential nutrients are remobilized from their associated carbon molecules and translocated to living parts where they are stored for later use. The remainder of dead or foraged plant parts becomes "food" and energy that drives secondary production and nutrient cycling in soil biota, aboveground herbivores, and ultimately in carnivores. The importance of this process cannot be overstated. Dead plant parts are the primary source of carbon, energy, and nutrients for microorganisms and small animals that recycle nutrients, form soil organic matter, and detoxify chemicals. Death and sloughing are controlled by: (1) the life and growth stages and health of plants; (2) weather conditions such as drought, flooding, and freezing; (3) damage by animals or disease; and (4) herbivory.

6.4 Ecological Site Scale (i.e., Patch, Stand)

The concept of an ecological site is an idealized homogeneous plant community and interrelated soil polypedon (an identifiable soil with distinct characteristics found in a location) (Anderson et al., 1983; Woodmansee, 1990). The plant community and its soil body are defined in space by plant community boundaries, soil type, and natural disturbances such as fire, floods, pests, and diseases, and human land-use activities such as fences, crop type, grazing and forest management, and construction. The concept of an ecological site suggests random sampling using plots that will yield similar probabilities of encountering members of the same plant community or soil characteristics. Sampling in other sites will result in other probabilities of similar or different species and soil characteristics. The plant community is made up of groupings of individual plants whose root systems are intermingled in the soil milieu within the site.

Many of the major contributions to ecosystem science by NREL scientists and collaborators have focused on the ecological site scale of organization. These contributions include: definition of spatial and temporal boundaries (Rosswall et al., 1988; Woodmansee, 1990); site scale C, N, P, S, and H_2O processes and budgets (e.g., Woodmansee, 1978; Coughenour et al., 1979; Cole and Heil, 1981; Parton et al., 1983; Ojima et al., 1994, 1999, 2000; Schimel et al., 2000; Kampf and Burges, 2007; Del Grosso et al., 2009; Fassnacht et al., 2016); carbon evolution and sequestration (Ogle et al., 2005; Conant et al. 2016); functional group diversity needed to accomplish all necessary biophysical processes, and ecosystem services (e.g., Ojima et al., 1991; Boone et al., 2007).

Plant succession and state-and-transition models used by the USDA Natural Resource Conservation Service (NRCS) Web Soil Survey and the Ecological Site Information System have also had their origins based in ecosystem science (WSS, 2018). This discussion has focused on the ever present and central process of photosynthesis. A prime ecological rule is: given a suitable site – that is, something that resembles soil containing a few nutrients – and given some water, some organism capable of committing photosynthesis will occupy that site. Basically, "Nature abhors a vacuum." That organism (desirable or undesirable) will thrive until pushed out by some other organism (plant competition) or some external force (e.g., humans).

6.4.1 Components of Ecological Site Scale Ecosystems

Scientists and enlightened managers often break the world down into two categories: the world of the living or *biotic* components and the realm of the nonliving or *abiotic* components. Figure 6.3 depicts examples of the parts or components of carbon-based, or biotic, and abiotic components of ecological site scale ecosystems. The arrows used in the figure show the transfer pathways. Figure 6.4 illustrates nitrogen processes that are similar to these carbon pathways.

The term biotic refers to anything that is now or once was alive. The biotic elements in a system are things like plants, animals, microorganisms, *and* their remains in soils and sediments (systems components). Abiotic means everything else, including weather, minerals, water, and radiation (often thought of as driving variables).

Remember, there's more than meets the eye in deciding what's alive and what isn't! Most of us don't think of things like soil and surface water as being alive, but both absolutely team with living, functioning organic life. "Dead" roots are likewise infused with living microorganisms and soil fauna.

The organisms depicted in Figures 6.7 and 6.8 can be viewed as actors. The actors are: producers, or autotrophs (*auto* = "self" and *tropho* = "nourishment") and consumers, or heterotrophs (*hetero* = "different"). Consumers are primary (herbivores, plant eaters) and secondary (carnivores, animal eaters). Omnivores eat both plants and animals whereas

Figure 6.7 Examples of carbon-based or biotic components of ecosystems. The term biotic refers to anything that is now or once was alive. Biotic elements in a system are things like plants, animals, microorganisms, *and* their remains in soils and sediments (systems components). Abiotic means everything else. Abiotic factors often include weather, minerals, water, and radiation (often thought of a driving variables).

detritivores eat nonliving plant and animal remains. Decomposers or saprovores break down organic matter.

6.4.2 Ecological Site Scale Processes

Our goal here is to briefly describe the processes and cite references that synthesize findings from the research conducted by NREL scientists and their collaborators. The publications that synthesize concepts derived from more than 50 years of ecosystem research (McGill et al., 1981; Bedunah and Sosebee, 1995; Lauenroth and Burke, 2008; Chapin et al., 2011; Paul, 2015; Robertson and Groffman, 2015) are of primary significance (see Chapter 4). For a listing of publications synthesizing current research, see NREL (2018, "Research").

The flow of energy through ecosystems is unidirectional (Figure 6.8). This means that once an energy source is used and converted to heat, that same energy loses its usefulness to the system. However, some carbon is recycled, but ultimately is lost as CO_2 via respiration (Odum and Odum,

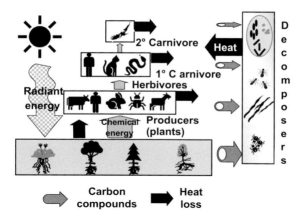

Figure 6.8 Energy flow in ecosystems. All life within terrestrial ecosystems is dependent on radiant energy that is transformed into chemical energy and organic carbon-based compounds that are produced by green plants and a few bacteria and algae (producers) via the process of photosynthesis. Once carbon and energy are "fixed" in simple sugars an astonishing number of chemical transformations and transfers (gray arrows) take place using the energy contained in those chemicals. Energy, as heat (black arrows), is lost from producers as they respire meeting their metabolic needs. CO_2 is also released during respiration. Some of the chemical compounds are eaten by herbivores but most are transferred to decomposers when plant parts die. Herbivores are eaten by carnivores meeting their metabolic needs and likewise meeting their energy and carbon needs. To survive, all living things need food to grow, replace parts, reproduce, and just plain survive.

1963). Most nitrogen and essentially all phosphorus and sulfur are recycled within ecological sites.

Another fundamental concept in ecosystem science is ecosystem productivity. We usually dissect this "system"-level idea into smaller parts, such as timber or forage productivity, livestock production, blue grama grass productivity, or bacteria production. Understanding the cycling of carbon and nutrients and the flow of energy in ecological site scale ecosystems requires knowledge about processes that occur within and between the individual plants and microorganisms within those ecological site scale ecosystems.

Ecological site scale processes depicted in this chapter involve carbon (Figure 6.3), nitrogen (Figure 6.4), and water cycles (Figure 6.9). Note that the similarities between the C and N cycles occur because N is primarily bound to C molecules. The primary differences between the cycles occur because carbon as CO_2 is assimilated via photosynthesis and

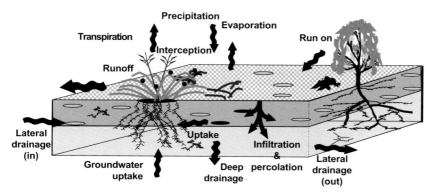

Figure 6.9 The ecological site scale water cycle. The critically important processes or flow paths are indicated with black arrows. The precipitation, evaporation, transpiration, interception, uptake, and infiltration and percolation pathways are internal to the ecological site ecosystem. The run-on, runoff, lateral drainage in and out, groundwater uptake, and deep drainage flow paths are connectors to other ecological sites within a landscape. A black and white version of this figure will appear in some formats. For the color version, please refer to the plate section.

lost primarily through respiration as CO_2 by all biota in the ecological site ecosystem. Nitrogen can be added from the atmosphere as NH_4^+, NO_3^-, and through N-fixation by microorganisms and can be lost as the gases NH_3, N_2O, and N_2, and leached from the system as NO_3^-. Otherwise, the flow pathways are very similar.

6.4.2.1 Ecological Site Scale Net Primary Production: Gross Photosynthesis Minus Respiration

Photosynthesis was discussed in Section 6.3. At the ecological site scale the cumulative amount of carbon assimilated by all plants (gross photosynthesis) within the site less carbon lost through plant respiration is ecological site net primary production (NPP) (Lauenroth et al., 2008; Chapter 12). Respiration and its production of CO_2 is the result of the metabolism of carbon compounds by living organisms – it's the cost of staying alive. However, microbial respiration is the dominant process for returning carbon into the atmosphere as CO_2 (Paul, 2015).

Photosynthesis generally exceeds respiration during a "growing season," but only for a short period of time ("sustainable growth" is an oxymoron in this context). Growth (accumulation of biomass) is offset by respiration except where plant biomass (especially trees), soil organic matter, and ocean and freshwater sediments are allowed to accumulate (carbon sequestration). Except for coal and oil for extended timescales, a fundamental ecological rule is that balance is maintained.

6.4.2.2 Decomposition

Decomposition is the process by which plants, microorganisms, and animal organic residues are biotically and abiotically transformed into simpler matter (e.g., simple organic molecules, CO_2, NH_4^+), and form soil organic matter (Paustian et al., 1998; Lauenroth and Burke, 2008; Chapin et al., 2011; Paul, 2015; see Chapter 4). Decomposition is a general term for a collection of processes that includes the fragmentation and churning action of biomass by aboveground and soil animals and the metabolism of dead organic matter by microorganisms and animals (Wall et al., 2008; Wallenstein and Hall, 2012; Cotrufo et al., 2015). The primary source of organic matter is plant debris or "fallen litter," but a substantial fraction of decomposition is the metabolizing of dead microorganisms. Decomposition will continue until all usable energy and organic matter is utilized, and CO_2 is released into the atmosphere or fresh organic matter is introduced. Important factors controlling decomposition are temperature, soil water, oxygen availability, abundance and viability of microorganism populations, and nutrient status of the soil environment.

Nutrients such as nitrogen and phosphorus, however, are not lost in respiration and remain behind in the soil or bound in living or dead organic matter (Paul, 2015). The "left-over" nutrients in the soil are then available for plant or microbial uptake – the most important source of nutrients in ecosystems dominated by perennial plants (and indeed most perennial crop ecosystems). In this discussion, we will focus more on nitrogen and less on phosphorus (Cole and Heil, 1981) and sulfur (Coughenour et al., 1979) because, for practical purposes, N is the most important limiting nutrient in arid and semi-arid terrestrial ecosystems. Each element has its own unique properties and its own cycling pattern. The primary differences between the nitrogen and phosphorus cycles are: (1) N has several gaseous forms, that is, NH_3 (can be added or lost), N_2O, NO_2, and N_2 (can be lost), and N_2 (can be transformed by microbial fixation and lightning); (2) N can be mobile in soil solution as NO_3^- and can be lost via leaching; (3) phosphorous has no gaseous phase of any significance, thus it is added to the system from the weathering of soil parent material or atmospheric wet and dry deposition; and (4) phosphorus does not have an ionic form that is mobile in soil solution, and is not easily leached from the soil. Sulfur as SO_4^{-2} is slightly mobile in soil solution and can be lost as H_2S and HS^- under rare, anaerobic conditions.

6.4.2.3 Secondary Production

Secondary production is the total amount of primary production (energy and/or biomass) consumed by herbivores, omnivores, and decomposers (animals and microorganisms) minus respiration and waste (Figure 6.7). Some factors that control secondary production include the amount of plant or microorganism NPP; the amount, type, and physiological state of consumers and decomposers; and temperature.

When photosynthesis is completed by primary producers, *the bulk of the real work of ecosystems is accomplished by decomposers, especially the microbes.* Decomposition of dead organic matter by microorganisms in soils and sediments and in the digestive systems of animals (e.g., ruminants, monogastrics, insects, birds, and reptiles.) is the dominant function of ecological site scale ecosystems.

Nutrients move through ecosystems along the same pathways as carbon compounds. However, there is a substantial difference in the fates of the nutrient elements. Carbon is returned to the atmosphere as CO_2 and energy is lost as heat. Nutrients are recycled in all self-maintaining and perennial "cropped" ecosystems and some annual tillage systems. In fact, because annual nutrient additions are so small compared to the growth, reproduction, and maintenance needs of organisms, nutrients must be recycled to meet those needs.

Plants and animals recycle nutrients within their own bodies (Houpt, 1959; Moir, 1970; Clark, 1977; Woodmansee et al., 1981; Kandylis, 1984; Goselink et al., 2014; see organism scale processes, Section 6.3). However, when plants or their parts or microbes die, or when animals die or excrete wastes, the nutrients they contain are consumed and metabolized by other microbes and converted into their own new cells, thereby keeping the nutrients in the system. In addition, the ecosystem of the ecological site recycles and conserves nutrients within the system. In other words, just as plants and animals tend to reutilize the nutrients they acquire, so do ecological site scale ecosystems.

6.4.2.4 Mineralization

The nutrients remaining in dead parts of animals, microorganisms, and perennial plants, and all nutrients in annual plants, are available for metabolism by decomposers (Figure 6.4; Woodmansee et al., 1981; Lauenroth and Burke, 2008; Chapin et al., 2011; Robertson and

Groffman, 2014; and see Chapter 4). The fragmentation and metabolism or decomposition of dead organic matter by animals and microorganisms leads to the release of biologically active, inorganic nutrients. This process is called mineralization. In self-maintaining ecological site scale ecosystems, availability of nutrient ions is largely dependent on mineralization by microbes.

Organic matter disappears during decomposition and mineralization because microbes release CO_2 through their respiration. Mineral nutrients are left behind as either living microbial cells or as waste products. The end product of these wastes are the original mineral ions (e.g., NH_4^+ (ammonium), Ca^{++}, K^+, PO_4^{-3}) – *the exact chemicals used in some types of fertilizer*. These ions are then available in soil solution to be taken up by plant roots or soil microorganisms.

6.4.2.5 Ammonification, Nitrification, and Gaseous Nitrogen Loss

The mineral form released in the mineralization of N is ammonium (NH_4^+) (Figure 6.4), which is readily taken up by most plants (Schimel et al., 1986; Coyne et al., 1995; Mosier et al., 2008; Chapin et al., 2011; Robertson and Groffman, 2014; see Chapter 4). Most N taken up by wildland plants is in the form of NH_4^+, not NO_3^- as indicated in many naïve publications. Free NH_4^+ in N deficient soils will almost certainly be taken up immediately if soil water and temperatures are suitable for growth (Clark, 1981; Woodmansee et al., 1981). If NH_4^+ is not taken up immediately by a plant, bacterium, fungus, or other microorganism, and is present in soil solution for an extended time period (hours to days), specialized bacteria (nitrifiers) will use it for their own needs and release NO_3^- as a by-product.

The fate of mineralized N is critical for many reasons. If nitrified, the nitrate ions are highly mobile in the soil solution and can be leached out if sufficient water is present to move through the profile. In addition, if nitrate resides for an extended length of time, and if the soils become saturated with water, the NO_3^- can be attacked by *denitrifying bacteria* and converted into atmospheric N_2. Along the chemical conversion pathway, greenhouse gases, such as N_2O and other NO_xs, can be released (see Chapter 4).

Animal wastes, especially urine, some plant processes, and fertilizer additions lead to the loss of ammonia (NH_3) into the atmosphere (Woodmansee et al., 1978; Schimel et al., 1986). This process can be locally significant.

6.4.2.6 Microbial Uptake

Microbial waste products are mineral nutrient ions in soil water and are available for plant uptake. However, the microorganisms that produced them need these same nutrients and typically have initial access (Paul, 2015). As an *ecological* rule, if carbon compounds are available, microbes will use (take up) all or most of the nutrients available. Consider how garden plants become nutrient deficient when wood chips are used as a compost. Due to the massive carbon availability, the microbes capture all available nutrients (immobilization) to support their own living habits. Few, if any, nutrients are left over for the plants.

6.4.2.7 Soil Organic Matter Formation

Soil organic matter is far and away the largest component of carbon and nitrogen in grazing ecosystems and many forest ecosystems (Paul et al., 1997; Clark and Rosswall 1981; Burke et al., 2008; see Chapter 4). As microorganisms metabolize plant debris and dead microorganisms, they evolve carbon dioxide and heat, and form microaggregates (Six et al., 2000, 2002). However, not all carbon and energy is utilized completely as some is inefficiently converted, some is processed and converted to waste products, and some is difficult to metabolize due to its chemical complexity. This residual carbon and associated nutrients become new soil organic matter – a vital component of all ecosystems (Cotrufo et al., 2013, 2015). Organic matter that is not completely respired may remain in the ecosystem for an extended length of time. The remaining organic matter becomes critical for nutrient storage on chemical exchange sites and for water-holding capacity.

The primary controllers of soil organic matter formation are temperature, soil water, chemical composition of the source organic matter, and nutrients. The nature of their interactions is complicated, but a new urgency to better understand controls on soil organic carbon has arisen due to climate change and nitrogen loading from the atmosphere and use of fertilizers (see Chapter 8). Soils have the potential to sequester (or store over long periods) vast quantities of the carbon released into the atmosphere due to the burning of fossil fuels (Parton et al., 1987). Management decisions on agricultural lands can either increase the loss of soil organic carbon or increase storage of soil carbon (Ogle et al., 2003; Six et al., 2004; Ogle et al., 2005; Smith et al., 2008). For example, conventional tilling of soils decreases carbon, whereas so-called no-till practices can help increase soil organic carbon. Likewise, proper management of grasslands can potentially store organic carbon (Parton et al., 1987; Conant et al., 2001, 2016).

6.4.2.8 Herbivory and Carnivory

Herbivory is the consumption of plants by animals, called herbivores, some of which include warm-blooded birds and mammals, cold-blooded insects, nematodes, and reptiles. Herbivory is the process by which herbivores meet their metabolic and nutrient requirements. The process of animals eating plants to satisfy their metabolic needs seem simple. It's not! Why do animals select one plant to eat but not another? Is the animal a large or small mammal or a small soil arthropod or nematode? How does plant chemical composition influence the animal? What influence does the animal foraging have on the growth, development, and metabolism of the plant? These are questions that have complex answers and are essential for understanding the functioning of ecological sites and landscape ecosystems. The type and quantity of plants; the type, number, and size of herbivores; and other environmental factors, such as management systems, control the process.

The ecological site scale concept is essential for integrating the relationship of primary production from plant communities and herbivore grazing and food selection/diets (Woodmansee et al., 1981; Senft et al., 1987; Ellis and Swift, 1988; Coughenour, 1991; Detling et al., 1998; Klein et al., 2007; Lauenroth and Burke, 2008). The ways in which grazers affect primary production within plant communities and plants compensate for disruption by herbivores are questions appropriate for the organism and ecological site scales of spatial resolution.

Carnivory is the process of animals eating other animals, or in rare cases plants eating animals. Relative to the carbon cycle or energy flow processes, carnivory is trivial in terrestrial ecosystems.

6.4.2.9 Erosion and Harvest

Carbon and nutrients can be removed from an ecosystem by water runoff or carried away by wind (Milchunas et al., 2008; Thurow, 1991). Another loss pathway is through harvest by humans or animals that remove biomass from an ecological site. When ecosystems are disturbed, this loss mechanism can be extremely important. An additional loss pathway is through harvest by humans or other animals (beavers, for example) that remove biomass from the site.

6.4.2.10 Run On, Fertilization, and Excreta Deposition

In the same manner as for removal, carbon and nutrients can be deposited into an ecosystem by water, wind, or urine, feces, or the dead bodies of animals. Human additions of organic fertilizer can also add carbon and nutrients – *in fact, without such additions modern agriculture would not be possible.*

6.4.2.11 Hydrology and Water Flows

In ecosystem science we concern ourselves with water and its movement at several spatial and temporal scales (Figure 6.9; see Chapter 4; Thurow, 1991). Precipitation in an area may be intercepted by vegetation and not reach the soil surface or may flow down the leaves and stems of plants to reach the soil. Water that reaches the soil surface may infiltrate, moving into the soil and downhill or toward groundwater. It may form runoff and move toward ponds or streams and flow out of the patch or landscape. Alternatively, water may evaporate from the soil or water surface. Water that moves through plant tissues and then turns into water vapor is said to be transpired and, combined with evaporation, we speak of evapotranspiration.

Early modeling efforts at the NREL conceptualized the flow of water through soil as moving through layers. The model used the rates of infiltration and runoff, precipitation required for runoff, and the "tipping bucket model," where the soil column is represented by a series of layers; water not used by plants descends through those layers until it reaches an unsaturated layer or moves to deep drainage (see Chapter 4). Plant roots may be in most or all these layers, with a variation in root biomass distribution. Plant types may then compete for water based on the biomass of these roots. For example, grasses and shrubs have quite different rooting depths which allows for the simultaneous presence of the two types because water that escapes the rooting zone of the grasses is available to the shrubs.

6.4.3 Plant Diversity

Ecologists interested in assessing ecological sites and landscapes typically measure biomass, cover, and the density or frequency of various key species. Measurements of plant diversity from plots, supposedly representing ecological sites, to regions have been conducted by researchers at the NREL (Stohlgren, 2007). One feature of the work was to point out the way landscapes were often depicted or imagined in sampling methods' papers and books. In homogeneous units (ecological sites), many sampling designs might easily capture plant diversity (Figure 6.10). However, environmental gradients, disturbances, rock outcrops, heterogeneous areas, riparian zones, ecotones, plant and animal

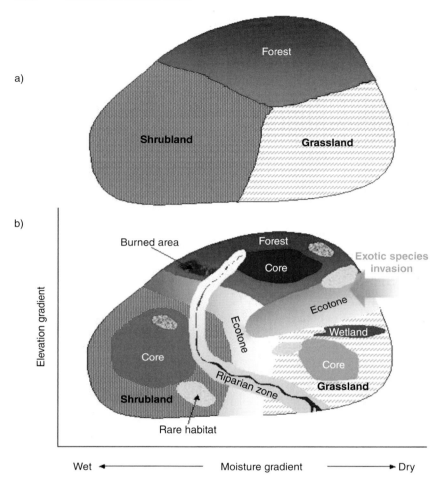

Figure 6.10 (a) The way landscapes are commonly portrayed or imagined for sampling; (b) the complex way landscapes appear in real life. A black and white version of this figure will appear in some formats. For the color version, please refer to the plate section.

invasions, disease, herbivory, among numerous other factors, influence the patterns of plant diversity at ecological site, landscape, and regional scales (Figure 6.11). Thus, sampling designs that capture only the most common and widely distributed species may be inadequate for detecting and mapping rare or patchily distributed species. A case in point, many of the ecological site-level sampling techniques commonly used by forest and rangeland plant ecologists for decades were incapable of detecting these plant species. For

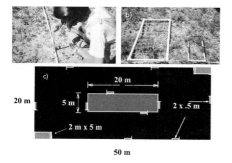

Figure 6.11 Three common sampling designs used to plant diversity. (a) The Parker loop. The Parker loop area is about the size of a quarter, placed along 100-foot line-transects, and every one foot you look down into the loop and describe what plant species you've encountered, or if you've hit bare ground. It's a tiny area of sampling. When you get back to the office you would have looked at a < 1 meter square area. (b) Various plant diversity "quadrats." Daubenmire used a quadrat, 20 cm by 50 cm, which is still pretty small when you consider the patchy distribution of plant species on the landscape. Others have recommended the use of transects as long as you use a larger quadrat. (c) The modified Whittaker multiscale sampling plot. A black and white version of this figure will appear in some formats. For the color version, please refer to the plate section.

example, when line-transect (Figure 6.11a) and small-quadrat sampling techniques (Figure 6.11b) were compared to larger, multiscale sampling techniques (Figure 6.11c), the researchers found that the small-area techniques commonly missed half of the native species and half of the nonnative plant species in each larger plot (Stohlgren et al., 1998). However, it all begins with more complete sampling of plant diversity at the ecological site scale. Early detection of harmful plant invaders requires that sampling designs detect species of concern with minimal survey and monitoring techniques (Stohlgren et al., 1999). When a multiscale framework was used in the USDA Forest Service Forest Health Monitoring program, dozens of harmful invasive species were detected (Stohlgren et al., 2003). The most important question about the efficacy of the sampling design wasn't "What did we capture in the field?" rather it was "What did we miss?" Many of the older sampling techniques missed a lot!

6.5 Landscape–Scale Interactions

Understanding landscape-scale dynamics requires integrating the influences of ecological sites within the landscape, evaluating the exchanges among sites, and determining the impact on "outputs," such as ecosystems services, land and water health, and the productive capacity of farms, ranches, and forests.

Research at the NREL has embraced two landscape concepts. For practical research purposes, geographic barriers, institutional or political boundaries, or human development and management boundaries define landscapes spatially. The definition of a landscape must also include a time frame of concern because landscapes can change through time (see Section 1.9.1.3).

One concept of a landscape is a geographic area composed of ecological sites that are connected by material that flows from one ecological site to another or through information controls among the sites within the landscape (i.e., one site provides potential cover for a herbivore who will choose to graze or drink water nearby (Woodmansee, 1981, 1990; Bailey et al., 1996). Ecological sites in landscapes can be linked by water (interflow, run-on/runoff, erosion/sedimentation), wind (erosion/sedimentation), animals, including humans (food selection, removal, disposal, and redistribution; urination; and defecation), animal influence on plant community distribution and diversity, and animal influence on CH_4, NH_3, and N_2O production. Common aggregations of ecological sites within this concept of landscapes are catenas (a sequence of soil profiles down a slope), watering locations, and fence corners (Schimel et al., 1985). Humans can dramatically influence these interactions.

Another concept of a landscape emphasizes the pattern of ecological sites within the defined landscape and the influence of that pattern on habitat use by animals and humans (Coughenour et al., 1985; Risser, 1990; Reid et al., 2008; Reid, 2012; Stabach et al., 2016). The patches composed of plant communities, indigenous and mobile animals, including humans, and microorganisms all function to provide necessary ecosystem services for those included. Important concepts within this view of landscapes are plant and animal biodiversity, migration patterns and corridors, and use of landscapes by people. People, as well as large and mobile animals, use whole landscapes, not just the patches therein.

Most human activities directly dealing with land use occur at the landscape scale in the ecological hierarchy. Small watersheds, farming, ranching, forest management, urban development, and outdoor recreation activities, such as hunting, skiing, and hiking, occur at landscape scales. Management decisions are typically applied to landscapes.

Earlier research in ecosystem science and the systems ecology approach focused on the ecological site and smaller hierarchical scales. As the science and the approach evolved, more emphasis was given to landscape, regional, and larger scales. The following sections are examples of the trend to focus on landscapes.

6.5.1 Habitat Studies

Habitat studies have followed arcs familiar to ecologists with a long-term view, moving from small-scale studies of the last century to macroecology (e.g., Brown, 1995; Boone and Krohn, 2000c; Mingyang et al., 2008). Variability in ecosystems has gained greater importance in research relative to a focus on equilibria and nonlinearity, and discontinuities are of interest (Wiens, 1984; Ellis and Swift, 1988; Nash et al., 2014). An emphasis is now placed on cross-scale relationships and the matrix within which habitats fall (Rodewald, 2003). Humans are also now more often perceived as elements of coupled systems rather than bothersome sources of variability to be controlled in experiments (Coughenour et al., 1985; Reid and Ellis, 1995; Boone et al., 2002; Galvin et al., 2004; Boone and Galvin, 2014). For example, in the past we considered urban areas as interruptions to the natural systems of interest, but now ecology of, by, and for cities is of great interest (McHale et al., 2013, 2015; Pickett et al., 2016).

Mapping habitat selection by species is an important step in planning, allowing conservation efforts to be prioritized. Biophysical filters formed the basis of popular species-habitat modeling approaches (Boone and Krohn, 2000a). For decades, an ongoing project within the US Geological Survey (USGS), called the Gap Analysis Program, has worked to map and protect the habitats of common species. Matrices that list habitat types on one dimension and species along another record habitats used by each species in a state or region. A map of land-cover types and other ancillary data are compiled to delineate habitat types. The ranges of species are defined based on occurrence data or expert review. Subsequently, the occurrences of species are predicted in a geographic information system. The predicted occurrences are then stacked, and the species density is compared to a conservation network to ensure adequate protection of common species (Boone and Krohn, 2000b).

The mapping of species–habitat occurrences has advanced greatly since the development of the Gap Analysis Program. Remote sensing and spatial data provide the foundation of regional mapping of species–habitat associations, with a dramatic improvement observed in the use of these sources. For example, the Landsat program now has a more than 40-year collection of moderate resolution Earth images available, the Moderate Resolution Imaging Spectroradiometer Program (MODIS) provides a series of products at coarse resolution since the turn of this century, and very high-resolution images are now readily available commercially.

These data have been used to map changes in species occurrences associated with oil and gas development in the western US (Homer et al., 2013). Species occurrence data sets have expanded as well, such as from the remarkable USGS Breeding Bird Survey, a stratified randomly distributed set of thousands of 50-stop routes along secondary roads that have been surveyed for 50 years (Sauer et al., 2017). Modeling may use resource selection functions to quantify species use of habitats in a rigorous way at landscape scales (e.g., Stabach et al., 2016). Those methods may be combined hierarchically to refine selection at ecological site scales, such as modeling the Gunnison sage-grouse (*Centrocercus urophasianus*) nesting habitat (Aldridge et al., 2012), and modeling habitat selection through different seasons (Fedy et al., 2014, for the same species).

Biophysical limitations to the distributions of species were formalized as niche dimensions in a way that people found compelling when Hutchinson (1957) spokes of axes in n-dimensional hypervolumes. Temperatures or their extremes, water or energy availability, food availability, land-cover type – and the occurrence of all other species – may comprise axes that together delineate a volume within which a species may exist. This point of view has led to niche envelop modeling and mapping techniques that are popular in NREL and elsewhere. Tools such as MaxEnt (Phillips et al., 2004; Phillips and Dudik, 2008) use the distribution of occurrence data for a species to identify its niche envelope, the hypervolume in which it may occur given the spatial data used in modeling (Figure 6.12). From that, the method allows distributions to be extrapolated across space, mapping the agreement between pixels in images used in modeling and their agreement with the hypervolume defined. NREL scientists have used this method to map invasive species, forecast their spread through time (see below), and predict changes in species distributions under climate change (e.g., Evangelista et al., 2008; Kumar et al., 2009, 2014; Graham et al., 2011). This is done by creating models with current-day climate as candidates for entry in the definition of the niche envelop. If climate proves useful in defining species distributions, forecasted future climate surfaces may replace the current surfaces and the relationships remapped using the same niche envelope.

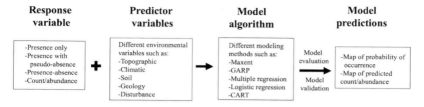

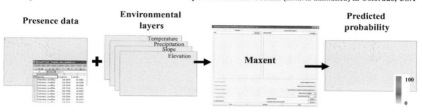

Figure 6.12 Schematic of the tool MaxEnt used to predict species invasions (or any species migrations) in space and time. A black and white version of this figure will appear in some formats. For the color version, please refer to the plate section.

Biotic filters include competition that dictates whether or not a species will occupy an area – the species must be capable of competing well with members of its own and with other species. These relationships are not included in the modeling approaches we have described. Boone, Kumar, and Stabach have adapted speciation methods used on plants to simulate interspecific competition in birds using an agent-based model that includes an evolutionary computational perspective (Boone, 2017). Bird species across the US have niche dimensions defined that may change slightly with each generation due to selective pressure to occupy new landscapes.

6.5.2 Wildlife and Livestock Abundances

Extensive surveys of wildlife and livestock abundances in Maasai Mara National Reserve were conducted from 1989 to 2003 (Ogutu et al., 2009). Advanced statistical methods were used to analyze those animal counts that showed persistent declines in animal populations associated with land-use change in surrounding landscapes. Similar methods were used to ask if wildlife were attracted to or repelled by households of Maasai in the region (Bhola et al., 2012).

The effects of fragmentation have been a focus of research at the NREL (Galvin et al., 2008; Hobbs et al., 2008). Some of these have been local-scale analyses tracking the movements of individual livestock herds through space (BurnSilver et al., 2003) or of collared wildebeest across fragmented landscapes (Stabach et al., 2016). Other analyses have been synthetic, studying the ways in which livestock and wildlife require broad access to semi-arid and arid lands to meet their needs, and the nature of external inputs into fragmented areas that enabled them to persist (Figure 6.13; Coughenour, 1991; Galvin et al., 2008). Sometimes access implies simply being able to locate sufficient water, forage, and cover, which Boone (2007) and Boone et al. (2005) have addressed for livestock. Other cases include migration, where seasonal, food, or mating triggers prompt longer-distance movements of animals. Reid et al. (2008)

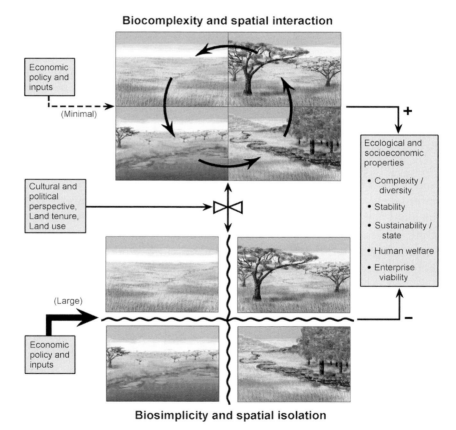

Figure 6.13 Conceptualization of the effects of fragmentation in semi-arid and arid areas (Hobbs et al., 2008). A black and white version of this figure will appear in some formats. For the color version, please refer to the plate section.

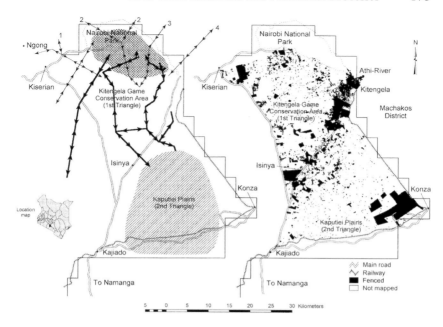

Figure 6.14 Fragmentation of the Kitengela region of Kajiado County, Kenya. The broad arrows (a) show past pathways of migratory animals between the Athi-Kapatuiei Plains and Nairobi National Park. The fragments mapped in 2004 (b) and subsequent fragmentation has stopped that migration. Adapted from Reid et al. (2008).

mapped the fragmentation of the Kitengela area of Kajiado County, Kenya (Figure 6.14) relative to animal migration. Like many African parks, Nairobi National Park was defined decades ago to be a relatively small park, with the assumption that surrounding areas would be available to wildlife. However, that is often no longer the case, as people have constructed fences, buildings, and other infrastructure. The migratory pathways used by animals in the area in the past are no longer active (Stabach et al., 2016).

6.5.3 Estimating Animal Abundance and Condition

Often ecologists seek to make inferences regarding changes in abundance or conditions of animals using information that on its face is either too sparse or too noisy to draw conclusions. N. T. Hobbs has advanced methods and training in Bayesian modeling techniques that use probability theory and repeated sampling to infer outcomes that include error estimates for complex problems (Hobbs and Hooten, 2015). For example, long-term surveys of animal populations may be used to infer rates of change in a rigorous way, such as for reindeer (Hobbs et al., 2012). Hobbs led a research project to understand the change in frequency of chronic wasting disease within Larimer County mule deer (*Odocoileus hemionus*). Proteins called prions that affect animals may have misfolded and become resistant to any breakdown. A misfolded protein prompts other proteins to misfold. These malformed proteins then build within an animal, causing death. The Hobbs research project tracked dozens of animals using radio and GPS collars, which were then captured each year to assess their disease state. Statistical analyses used that repeated sampling data to confirm that the disease would not spread through the entire herd.

Several projects have used tracking devices to deduce the movements of animals. Cutting-edge work has developed a means to track horses using GPS tags attached to the horses' tails (S. King and K. Schoenecker, unpub. data). R. Boone led a project called Gnu Landscapes that assessed the effects of fragmentation and more frequent droughts on wildebeest and also tracked the hourly movements of 36 wildebeest in Kenya. As part of that work, the stress levels of wildebeest inhabiting areas differing in their human disturbance was quantified using fecal analysis (Stabach et al., 2016).

Many populations of a species are isolated, but only to a degree. They are separated by areas unoccupied by the species, either through biophysical limitations, historical accident, or through human activities that fragment once-habitable areas. If individuals move between populations occasionally, but not so frequently as to be considered one population, they are termed a metapopulation (Levins, 1969). Occasional movements can be important, with dispersing individuals providing a possibility to restore populations that have become locally extinct. There are also important genetic repercussions for occasional mixing of individuals. Boone et al. (2006) provides an example, where an individual-based model was used to look at the likelihood that wood frogs (*Rana sylvatica*) would move between populations in vernal pools in Minnesota being isolated through forest harvest.

6.5.4 Species–Habitat Relationships

A species requires food, water, cover, and space to occupy an area – these attributes and others comprise habitat for the species (i.e., habitat is species-specific, although habitat type is a term sometimes used in an overarching way). Differences in those attributes may favor the occurrence of one species over another. For example, water is not a uniform resource – a high mountain stream in the Rockies may be home to an American dipper (*Cinclus mexicanus*) hunting for aquatic insects in the fast-moving water, whereas an open reservoir may be patrolled for fish by a bald eagle (*Haliaeetus leucocephalus*). The occurrence of yucca (*Yucca* sp.) requires the presence of their obligate pollinators, yucca moths (within the family Prodoxidae). The moths in turn occur only if the species with which they coevolved are present. Space and cover too may limit species occurrence, such as the presence of special habitat features such as standing dead trees supporting the presence of cavity-nesting birds.

Collectively, these requirements may be viewed as the biophysical constraints on species entry into local assemblages. This is a hierarchical process, in which a regional species pool is filtered by biogeographic constraints, such as mountain ranges or large water bodies, preventing a species from reaching a region. Various physiological filters also limit species occurrence (Rahel, 2002), for example the occurrence of birds is limited by energy availability and temperature (Root, 1988) given that some species may not tolerate areas that are too hot or too cold. Additionally, some species have broad tolerances for biophysical requirements and are habitat generalists, such as red foxes (*Vulpes vulpes*) and American crows (*Corvus brachyrhynchos*) that inhabit rural and urban areas of the US and feed on a wide variety of foods. Some species have narrow tolerances and are habitat specialists, such as red crossbills (*Loxia curvirostra*), which, as their name implies, are so specialized in their diets that their bills have crossed tips for prying apart conifer cones to access seeds. Lastly, we should not think of habitat selection as static through space, time, or close taxonomic relatedness. For example, pikas (*Ochotona princeps*) in the Rocky Mountains are habitat specialists, inhabiting cliffs and rocky outcrops above 3,350 m (11,000 ft) – a distribution that leaves them vulnerable to shifting conditions due to climate change. However, a related species, the plateau pikas (*Ochotona curzoniae*) of Tibet, are very common and share many ecosystem roles with the prairie dog (*Cynomys* spp.) of North America.

Loss of habitat is the most pressing threat to maintaining biodiversity. Identifying habitats important to species is also critical work currently underway by many NREL researchers along with their students and other colleagues. Citing just a few examples, the implications of climate change for white-tailed ptarmigan (*Lagopus leucura*) in the high-elevation Rocky Mountains has been a focus of research by NREL staff (Wann et al., 2016). Ways in which greater sage-grouse (*Centrocercus urophasianus*) use habitat impacted by oil and gas extraction has been studied (e.g., Aldridge and Boyce, 2007; Aldridge et al., 2012). Important work on the habitat use of mountain nyala (*Tragelophus buxtoni*), a rare antelope species of the Ethiopian highlands, has been accomplished (Evangelista et al., 2007, 2008).

6.5.5 Disturbance, Succession, and State-and-Transition

Ecosystem disturbance and succession were central issues in ecology during the first two-thirds of the twentieth century. These topics have retained their prominence up to the present, although our actual ways of thinking about disturbance and succession have changed profoundly since the 1960s to the point where some ecologists now suggest that the very terms themselves need to be discarded as hindrances to clear thinking (Binkley et al., 2015). In this section, we briefly examine dominant thinking about these topics in the 1960s, then look at several key empirical and theoretical developments in ecology that have undermined the paradigm of the time, and conclude with what we think may be our current understanding of ecosystem dynamics.

Mainstream ecological theory in the 1960s characterized communities as generally stable and highly coevolved assemblages of organisms, which are occasionally disturbed or damaged by various natural and anthropogenic agents. Following disturbance, the universal ecological process of succession proceeds until the community recovers into a mature climatic state (Christensen, 2014). The basic framework of succession had been formulated by Frederick Clements half a century earlier (Clements, 1916). It was then elaborated upon and expanded by Odum (1969) whose "strategy of ecosystem development" outlined a long list of generalized successional trends in community diversity, life histories, energetics, and stability. These ideas were enthusiastically imparted to students in the sciences and natural resource management fields. An example of succession was commonly the centerpiece of the ecology section included in a general biology textbook. Land managers also embraced the paradigm that typically regarded wildfire and insect-caused tree mortality as undesirable disturbances to be avoided. Conservationists scoured the landscape for good examples of climax communities to be preserved.

There were, of course, early critics of the succession paradigm: (1) H. A. Gleason (1926, 1939) rejected Clements' "organismic" concept of the coevolved plant associations early on, arguing instead for an "individualistic" model where species distributions fluctuate largely independently of each other along environmental gradients; (2) A. S. Watt (1947) pointed out that one could find all of the supposed stages of succession as patches within what were classified as mature or climax forests; (3) the Wisconsin School of Plant Ecology argued that vegetation composition varied along an abiotic gradient as a continuum of change rather than a sequence of discrete types (Curtis, 1959; Whittaker, 1975); (4) Connell and Slatyer (1977) added a mechanistic perspective and proposed three models of endogenous drivers of vegetation change, only one of which was Clementsian "facilitation" (which was probably less common than the competition and tolerance models); and (5) Egler (1975, 1981) offered a large donation to charity on behalf of anyone who could demonstrate examples of successional turnover of plant communities, so-called relay floristics (Egler, 1954). He apparently never had to pay. But these critics were unable to sway the prevailing acceptance of successional theory, perhaps because the theory seemed so intuitively appealing, so universal, and because the critics never offered a suitably compelling alternative paradigm to replace succession.

One of the great values of Odum's (1969) synthesis was that nearly all of his "trends in ecosystem development" were stated as empirically testable hypotheses. Furthermore, in the 1970s ecologists began to energetically test them (Drury and Nisbet, 1973). The results were not pretty for anyone married to the dominant paradigm; in almost every case the empirical evidence did not support the hypothesized trend. Species diversity was often found to be greatest in early or middle stages of forest succession, not in the oldest stages (Loucks, 1970; Connell, 1978). In North American conifer forests, species regarded as indicative of both the early and the mature stages of succession were found to be present in stands of all ages. The former were simply more abundant or conspicuous soon after a fire and the latter were more so after several decades had passed (Egler, 1954; Johnson and Fryer, 1989; Romme et al., 2016). It was further found that old forests were not the most stable stages of development, but were actually more susceptible to fire and insect-caused mortality than younger forests (Safranyik, 1974; Clark, 1989; Romme, 1982).

It had been recognized early on that true "climax" communities were relatively uncommon, but this was thought to be explained simply by the widespread disturbing influence of modern humans (Clements, 1935). However, tree ring studies in western North American conifer forests revealed that fires had recurred for centuries prior to the arrival of Europeans, and were responsible for some of the characteristic features of those forests (Baisan and Swetnam, 1990; Swetnam, 1993). Land managers began to recognize that complete elimination of natural disturbances would not protect, but would actually compromise the very ecosystems they were trying to sustain. Managers of large national parks in the Sierra Nevada began to restore low-severity fire in their forests (Kilgore, 1973). The "historical range of variation" (Keane et al., 2009) came to provide a benchmark of natural ecological conditions for management and restoration of ecosystems in national forests, grasslands, and other public lands.

Even in the modern world, natural disturbance of ecosystems – by fire, wind, herbivores, and diseases – was found to be a universal phenomenon. Even mature moist tropical forests, long regarded as some of the best examples of a climax state, were in fact opened up on a regular basis by large trees falling and creating canopy gaps, where early successional species flourished and contributed substantially to the famous diversity of those forests (Brokaw and Busing, 2000). Much of the storied African savanna exists in places where climate is favorable for closed woodland. It is only chronic disturbance by fire and herbivory that maintains the open habitat and distinctive wildlife of this ecosystem (Sankaran et al., 2005). In pristine grasslands, prairie dogs regularly removed the climax grasses and created patches of bare ground, the specific locations of which shifted over time (Augustine et al., 2008). Adding another nail to the succession paradigm's coffin, new rigorous studies of postglacial vegetation changes revealed that trees did not move northward from glacial refugia as discrete and stable communities, as predicted by the Clementsian theory. Rather, species migrated individualistically, such that newly created specie assemblages were unlike those of the glacial period (Davis and Shaw, 2001).

In addition to these kinds of empirical studies, ecologists began approaching the subject of community/ecosystem dynamics from new theoretical perspectives. Spatial and temporal scale took center stage as a critical defining characteristic of any analysis (Levin, 1992), and some heated arguments about vegetation dynamics turned out to be primarily differences in the scale at which ecologists were thinking. For example, is species composition of the forests of the southern Appalachian Mountains stable? If we look at a 0.25 ha plot over a century, the composition is not stable: shade-tolerant trees may gradually replace shade-intolerant trees, or a windstorm may topple the canopy and promote a pulse of shade-intolerant species. Even so, species composition at the scale of a 1,000 ha watershed may remain stable over several hundred years, despite the continuing cyclic changes that occur at finer spatial scales. Bormann and Likens (1979) formalized this idea in their concept of a "shifting mosaic steady state." Turner et al. (1993) offered a predictive model of the spatial and temporal scales at which an ecosystem would exhibit equilibrium and long-term stability, but with either high or low variability within shorter time frames, or instability and transition to a fundamentally different state.

Other key theoretical developments were the explicit recognition of multiple stable states (Holling, 1973) and stochastic influences on vegetation dynamics. For example, state–and–transition models permit vegetation to change in multiple directions in response to multiple environmental influences (Westoby et al., 1989). Empirically derived probabilities could be assigned to each kind of transition between states, and ecosystem dynamics of a system could be projected forward through time. The models could be formulated at a fine scale, for example a single stand or ecological site (Horn, 1975), or at a broad landscape scale, as an aggregation of multiple stands, each going through the same probabilistic dynamics over time (Baker, 1989; Westoby et al., 1989; Briske et al., 2005). State-and-transition models have been increasingly applied to land management decision making on both rangelands (Bestelmeyer et al., 2011; WSS, 2018) and forests (e.g., the LANDFIRE program, Rollins, 2009), representing an acknowledgment that management based on the outdated successional paradigm often led to resource damage via overgrazing and fire suppression.

The new theoretical models added welcomed complexity and nuance to what had come before, but many retained overtones of inherent stability and predictability in processes of ecosystem change over time – one just had to view the system at a broad enough spatial or temporal scale and at least some form of stability would emerge. While it was widely acknowledged that transition probabilities would change if fundamental characteristics of the environment changed, such as when global climate changed at the end of the Pleistocene, it was not yet recognized that such changes were imminent again. In the first decade of the twenty-first century, it became unmistakably apparent that substantial climate change was already under way, and that by the end of this century the magnitude of change could even approach that of the glacial transition 12,000 years ago. Any notion of equilibrium, or even predictability based on the past, was suddenly questionable: as the title of an influential article exclaimed, "stationarity is dead" (Milly et al., 2008).

And what about those words "disturbance" and "succession"? Some ecologists have become uncomfortable with them, even finding them deeply troubling. The word disturbance can imply a disruption of something that was previously stable, healthy, and desirable – all very Clementsian in overtone. Pickett et al. (2009) recommended referring to vegetation dynamics instead of succession to avoid all of the intellectual baggage of Clements' and Odum's concepts. Similarly, the editors of *Forest Ecology and Management* (Binkley and Fisher, 2012) questioned why we keep talking about disturbance and succession when all we really mean is change. Change may be fast or it may be slow and it may result from many different types of stimuli and may go in many different directions. Throwing all of that into a single notion of "succession" merely blurs important distinctions, the very distinctions that ecologists should be focusing on (Binkley et al., 2015). Yet many ecologists argue that we all know what we mean by disturbance and succession, that we have moved far beyond the simplistic concepts of Clements and Odum, and that these are merely handy terms to distinguish change in ecosystems from other kinds of changes in the world.

So, what is the state of our science in 2021? Most ecologists today would agree with Christensen (2014) that a grand unifying theory or strategy of succession is illusive. We have moved away from the holistic paradigms of earlier generations to a more reductionist research paradigm, documenting exactly how organisms, environments, and ecosystems respond to different stimuli, requiring empirical evidence to support our interpretations, and adding environmental change and stochasticity to our predictive models. Basic biogeography and paleoecology, subfields that generally were not in the forefront of late twentieth-century research, have been reenergized as key approaches for understanding and predicting how species and ecosystems will respond to novel environments of the not-so-distant future. We have amazing new satellite-based capacities for acquiring high-resolution data over broad spatial scales, and powerful computing tools to handle the complexity of new data and theory. It is an exciting time to be an ecologist – and also an important time to be an ecologist, if we are to help prevent or minimize the ecological degradation that could be awaiting future generations.

6.5.6 Landscape–Level Plant Diversity

Ecological site–level descriptions of plant diversity are useful. However, it has become increasingly important to measure species richness and diversity, patterns of plant diversity, species–environment relationships, and species distributions on the scale of landscapes to regions in order to monitor the effects of climate change, changes in land-use and disturbance regimes, and the invasion of harmful plants, animals, and diseases. Multiscale sampling designs linked to remote sensing data and spatial-temporal models were needed to protect rare and native species and important habitats for conservation, or to model harmful species invasions to guide control efforts (Figure 6.12; Stohlgren, 2007). Of course, such an ambitious undertaking requires accurate field data. Multiscale methods for measuring plant diversity, such as the modified Whitaker sampling technique, which includes four scales and measurements (1, 10, 100, and 1000 m^2 plots) commonly linked to remotely sensed information, were designed or redesigned. This allowed ecologists to extrapolate fine-grained sampling methods to landscapes and regions (Stohlgren, 2007).

Regarding invasive species, scientists had argued that areas of low diversity would be quickly and easily invaded because areas of high diversity should exhibit competitive exclusion. However, the opposite holds true. Across many landscapes, including grasslands, shrublands, riparian zones, and Rocky Mountain ecosystems, species-rich areas were more prone to invasion. This "rich get richer" pattern of invasion was true across the United States for plants, fishes, and birds (Stohlgren et al., 2006), and has been confirmed elsewhere. Thus, natural resource managers in national parks, wildlands, and waterways began to target monitoring programs in species-rich areas and frequently disturbed habitats.

6.5.7 Forest Biology and Structure

The structure and change of forests has been a focus of research at the NREL. An important volume describing soils in forested systems contains information about forest ecosystem structure and functioning (Binkley and Fisher, 2012). In other studies, Lefsky et al. (1999) found that canopy structure can be inferred by energy emitted by an aerial- or spaced-based device, and reflected by trees, shrubs, and soil in a system called Lidar. The time required for a signal to return to the sensor is shorter from the tree canopy than from the soil, thus canopy height and structure can be inferred. From those results and a mix of species based on field visits or remotely sensed information, one can estimate canopy volume, carbon stored, etc.

6.5.8 Invasive Species

Invasive species are now widely recognized as a leading cause of native species decline, extirpation, and extinction. NREL scientists have been international leaders in the field of biological invasions for the past 20 years (Stohlgren et al., 1999, 2006, 2014; Evangelista et al., 2009). Gaps in knowledge on invasive species were evaluated and focused on three major needs: (1) improving multi-scale sampling techniques to better scale results from landscapes to regions and beyond (Stohlgren, 2007); (2) developing new spatial and temporal modeling techniques to better assess the current and future distributions on harmful species given changes in land use, climate, and human-assisted migrations (Kumar et al., 2014; Wakie et al., 2016); and (3) working cooperatively with international colleagues, government agencies, universities, tribes, and the public to develop a "community for action" (Stohlgren and Schnase (2006). This focus has contributed to better sampling designs, stronger links to remote-sensing information, and new modeling techniques for mapping and predicting invasive species distributions at landscape, regional, and national scales.

6.5.9 Landscape–Scale Water Research

Movement of water across landscapes yields drainage pathways that combine to form watersheds. The ways in which water moves across landscapes has been of interest to NREL researchers dating back to the first years of the US IBP and research conducted on microwatersheds. Work in that regard expanded greatly following the joining of watershed scientists with the NREL in the last decade (e.g., MacDonald et al., 1991; Kampf et al., 2005; Covino and McGlynn, 2007; Kampf and Burges, 2007; Fassnacht et al., 2017). For example, MacDonald and Huffman (2004) described patterns of decline in water repellency after a fire in northern Colorado. A fire volatilizes organic material in and on the soil, which adheres to the soil surface causing it to repel water. The authors described repellency as being related to fire severity and declining within a year of a fire. Snow and its properties have been a focus of S. Fassnacht, including means of interpolating snow depths across space based on a series of field-based point measurements (Fassnacht et al., 2003) and measurements of the roughness of snow surfaces (Fassnacht et al., 2009). Physical hydrological processes and methods of modeling water movement through landscapes have been compared and advanced (Kampf and Burges, 2007). S. Kampf has recently leveraged the help of citizens in monitoring water flow in intermittent streams in a project called Stream Tracker (Kampf et al., 2018).

6.6 Regional and Global Drivers of Change

Many questions remain about how landscapes are linked into regions (see Chapter 2), but macroecology (Brown, 1995) and global sustainability science (Liu et al., 2015) have leveraged broad-scale sampling, readily available remotely sensed data over the last 40 years, and simulation to study regional and global drivers of change. General circulation models simulate past and future climate and their interaction with oceans and land cover, with results famously published in the Intergovernmental Panel on Climate Change reports and elsewhere, to which NREL scientists have contributed. A constellation of Long-term Ecological Research sites included the Shortgrass Plains LTER. Currently, 28 sites comprise the network, with results that have helped researchers understand ecological changes over the long term and across regions. The National Ecological Observatory Network (NEON) is a large effort by the US government to collect ecological data in systematic ways at 81 representative terrestrial and aquatic sites across the continent and to make those data freely available to everyone. These data, which include more than 180 response variables, are to be collected for at least the next 30 years, providing an extraordinary record of the state of our ecosystems and their changes.

Regional and global analyses are now common at NREL. For example, the unit includes a program supported by the US Department of Agriculture called the UV-B Monitoring and Research Program. The director, W. Gao, oversees a network of climatological measurement sites that establishes the spatial and temporal characteristics of UV-B irradiance. The network follows a grid-based design which divides the country into 26 regions of approximately equal area. This form of ultraviolet radiation can damage crops, and thus the program is furnishing basic information necessary to support evaluations of the potential damaging effects of UV-B to agricultural crops and forests (e.g., Gao et al., 2004; Reddy et al., 2004). Ogle et al. (2005) used meta-analyses of more than 100 analyses to quantify changes in soil organic carbon storage in temperate and tropical regions. Recently, Ogle has conducted annual inventories of soil organic carbon change in countries across the US that summarize results from thousands of individual simulations (see Chapter 4), using methods his team helped to develop (e.g., Ogle et al. 2003). Global analyses of rangeland responses to climate change have highlighted concerns for African rangelands, potential for carbon storage, greenhouse gas fluxes, and challenges to livestock production (Del Grosso et al., 2008, 2009; Henderson et al., 2015; Boone et al., 2018). In a more than 30-year research program, J. Baron has quantified the effects of nitrogen deposition on landscapes from local to regional and national scales (Baron et al., 2000; Fenn et al., 2003).

Other active regional and larger-scale projects at NREL include large-scale nitrogen transport and loading (see Chapter 8), modeling the Great Plains ecosystems (see Chapter 4), and the establishment of a USDA Regional Climate Center (see Chapter 7).

Box 6.1 *Early plant–animal interaction studies*

The Wind Cave Project grew out of a previous NSF-supported Plant–Animal Interaction project. One major hypothesis of the project was that at intermediate (optimal) grazing intensities, above-ground net primary production (ANPP) would be maximized (i.e., the so-called grazing optimization hypothesis; McNaughton, 1979, Hilbert et al., 1981). A former MS student on the project, D. Layne Coppock, set out to conduct a field study at Wind Cave National Park (WCNP) to evaluate the first hypothesis by measuring NPP along a presumed bison (*Bison bison*) grazing intensity gradient at various distances from the water sources they used. As often happens, this approach looked much better when drawn up on paper at NREL than it did when Layne arrived at his field site; thus, his original project proved unfeasible.

Over the next several weeks, Layne observed bison grazing throughout WCNP (more than 11,000 ha of predominantly northern mixed-grass prairie). In doing so, he noticed that bison appeared to be found on prairie dog (*Cynomys ludovicianus*) colonies to a greater extent than would be expected if they were using the grassland habitat randomly. He then set up a sampling routine for the remainder of that summer and the following growing season to determine whether his initial impressions held up. A vegetation-sampling scheme was also used to compare a variety of vegetation attributes from prairie dog colonies with those on colonies of several known ages (from < two years old up to > 26 years old). Similar to McNaughton's (1976) African savanna study of grazing facilitation between wildebeest and Thomson's gazelle, Coppock's study demonstrated rather convincingly that: (1) bison selected prairie dog colonies (particularly those still totally or partially dominated by graminoids) as foraging sites during the summer growing season (Coppock et al., 1983b), and (2) forage quality, both in terms of leaf (N) and in vitro digestibility, was greater on prairie dog colonies than on noncolonized sites, even though grass biomass was lower on the prairie dog colonies (Coppock et al., 1983a). This suggests a potential causal explanation for bison preference of colonies. This research also demonstrated that plant species diversity and richness were greatest in prairie dog colonies that had been colonized for intermediate periods (3–8 years), thus conforming to Connell's (1978) "intermediate disturbance hypothesis." Finally, bison increased their use of a noncolonized site and reduced their use of a colonized site following a spring prescribed burn in the noncolonized site (Coppock and Detling, 1986).

Aboveground/Belowground Linkages

Coppock's research served as the basis for the follow-up NSF-funded Wind Cave project which investigated prairie dog colonies as patches or "hotspots" of intensified biological activity within the noncolonized grassland matrix, and emphasized the importance of studying aboveground/belowground linkages in this grassland ecosystem. The research included integrated greenhouse/growth chamber experiments, field observations, manipulative field experiments, and simulation modeling.

Intensive grazing by prairie dogs and other herbivores aboveground reduced plant root biomass belowground. The extent of the reduction increased with time of occupation by prairie dogs (Whicker and Detling, 1988; Detling, 1998). Heavy grazing aboveground apparently facilitated feeding and population growth by some classes of both root-parasitic nematodes and nematodes that consumed soil microorganisms (Ingham and Detling, 1984). In a later field experiment, we estimated that root-feeding nematodes reduced ANPP by 16 times more than the biomass they consumed (Ingham and Detling,

1990). Belowground rates of net nitrogen mineralization were higher in soils from prairie dog colonies than in soils from adjacent noncolonized grassland (Holland and Detling, 1990). Possibly, in part, due to higher N-mineralization rates on prairie dog colonies, net aboveground plant N-yield was greater on prairie dog colonies than on noncolonized grassland, even though ANPP was similar (Whicker and Detling, 1988). However, increases in aboveground N-yield also were observed in field (Green and Detling, 2000) and laboratory (Jaramillo and Detling, 1988; Polley and Detling, 1989) leaf-clipping experiments, suggesting that defoliation-induced changes in plant physiology may be involved in increased N-uptake as well.

Another line of research examined the potential for natural selection of "grazing ecotypes" of grasses on heavily grazed prairie dog colonies, and the potential consequences of such ecotypic differentiation (i.e., within species biodiversity) for grassland ecosystem function. Individuals of four species of grasses collected from prairie dog colonies were shorter and more prostrate than those from either nearby, lightly grazed noncolonized sites or from a long-term (50 years) grazing exclosure. The morphological differences were maintained for several growing seasons after being transplanted to a common environment (Painter et al., 1993). Using the Century simulation model, Holland et al. (1992) explored how different physiological responses of "on-colony" and "off-colony" populations to defoliation intensity regulates nutrient flow in the grassland ecosystem. The simulation results suggested that differences in the physiological responses of the two populations might have substantial ecosystem consequences for control of nitrogen losses from the system.

Prairie Dog Grazing Effects on Microclimate

One distinct characteristic of landscape patches heavily grazed by prairie dogs is a shorter and more open plant canopy and lower amount of surface litter than the surrounding, more lightly grazed, noncolonized grassland. These structural changes in the plant canopy resulted in higher daytime air temperatures and wind speed in the canopy on prairie dog colonies (Day and Detling, 1994). However, even with a warmer microclimate and higher evaporative demand on colonies, there was greater available soil moisture, probably due to the reduced transpiring leaf area and absorptive root biomass. As a result, leaf conductances to water vapor and leaf water potentials were higher on the colonies (Archer and Detling, 1986; Day and Detling, 1994).

Urine Patch Dynamics

Grazing ungulates return significant quantities of available N to soil via urination (Detling, 1988), and in doing so create large numbers of small, N-rich patches across grassland landscapes. Our studies at WCNP (Day and Detling, 1990a, 1990b) and the High Plains Grasslands Research Station, WY (Jaramillo and Detling, 1992a, 1992b) indicate that these urine patches differ from the surrounding grassland matrix in several ways, including: (1) a higher leaf (N), (2) higher leaf biomass, and (3) relative abundance of C_3 vs. C_4 grasses. Over time, following a urination event, these patches are grazed more frequently and intensively than plants in the surrounding matrix. For example, in one WCNP experimental area in which patches were created by applying artificial bovine urine, patches covering just 2 percent of the study area provided 7 percent of the biomass and 14 percent of the N consumed by aboveground herbivores through-out the summer (Day and Detling, 1990a).

References

Aldridge, C. L., and Boyce, M. S. (2007). Linking occurrence and fitness to persistence: Habitat-based approach for endangered Greater Sage-grouse. *Ecological Applications*, 17, 508–26.

Aldridge, C. L., Saher, D. J., Childers, T. M., Stahlnecker, K. E., and Bowen, Z. H. (2012). Crucial nesting habitat for Gunnison Sage-grouse: A spatially explicit hierarchical approach. *Journal of Wildlife Management*, 76, 391–406.

Anderson, D. W., Heil, R. D., Cole, C. V., and Deutsch, P. C. (1983). *Identification and Characterization of Ecosystems at Different Integrative Levels*. Special Publication. Athens, GA: University of Georgia, Agriculture Experiment Stations.

Archer, S., and Detling, J. K. (1986). Evaluation of potential herbivore mediation of plant water status in a North American mixed-grass prairie. *Oikos*, 47, 287–91.

Archer, S., and Smeins, F. E. (1991). Ecosystem-level processes. In *Grazing Management: An Ecological Perspective*, ed. R. K. Heitschmidt and J. W. Stuth. Portland, OR: Timber Press, 109–39.

Augustine, D. J., Matchett, M. R., Toombs, T. B., Cully, J. F., Johnson, T. L., and Sidle, G. (2008). Spatiotemporal dynamics of black-tailed prairie dog colonies affected by plague. *Landscape Ecology*, 23, 255–67.

Bailey, D. W., Gross, J. E., Laca, E. A., et al. (1996). Mechanisms that result in large herbivore grazing distribution patterns. *Journal of Range Management*, 49, 386–400.

Baisan, C. H., and Swetnam, T. W. (1990). Fire history on a desert mountain range – Rincon Mountain Wilderness, Arizona, USA. *Canadian Journal of Forest Research-Revue Canadienne De Recherche Forestiere*, 20, 1559–69.

Baker, W. L. (1989). A review of models of landscape change. *Landscape Ecology*, 2, 112–34.

Baron, J. S., Barber, M. C., Adams, M., et al. (2014). The effects of atmospheric nitrogen deposition on terrestrial and freshwater biodiversity. In *Nitrogen Deposition, Critical Loads, and Biodiversity*, ed. M. K. Sutton, L. Mason, H. Sheppard, et al. Dordrecht: Springer, 465–80.

Baron, J. S., Poff, N. L., Angermeieret, P. L., et al. (2002). Meeting ecological and societal needs for freshwater. *Ecological Applications*, 12, 1247–60.

Baron, J. S., Rueth, H. M., Wolfe, A. M., et al. (2000). Ecosystem responses to nitrogen deposition in the Colorado Front Range. *Ecosystems*, 3, 352–68.

Bedunah, D. J., and Sosebee, R. E. eds. (1995). *Wildland Plants: Physiological Ecology and Developmental Morphology*. Denver, CO: Society for Range Management.

Bell, C. W., Tissue, D. T., Loik, M. E., et al. (2014). Soil microbial and nutrient responses to 7 years of seasonally altered precipitation in a Chihuahuan Desert grassland. *Global Change Biology*, 20, 1657–73.

Bestelmeyer, B. T., Goolsby, D. P., Archer, S. R. (2011). Spatial perspectives in state-and-transition models: A missing link to land management? *Journal of Applied Ecology*, 48, 746–57.

Bhola, N., Ogutu, J. O., Piepho, H. -P., et al. (2012). Comparative changes in density and demography of large herbivores in the Masai Mara Reserve and its surrounding human-dominated pastoral ranches in Kenya. *Biodiversity and Conservation*, 21, 1509–30.

Binkley, D., Adams, M., Fredericksen, T., Laclau, J. P., Makinen, H. H., and Prescott C. (2015). Editors note: Clarity of ideas and terminology in forest ecology and management. *Forest Ecology and Management*, 349, 1–3.

Binkley, D., and Fisher, R. (2012). *Ecology and Management of Forest Soils*. New York: John Wiley and Sons.

Bolin, B., and Cook, R. B. ed. (1983). *The Major Biogeochemical Cycles and Their Interactions* (SCOPE Report 21). Chichester, published on behalf of the Scientific Committee on Problems of the Environment (SCOPE) of the International Council of Scientific Unions (ICSU). New York: John Wiley.

Boone, R. B. (2007). Effects of fragmentation on cattle in African savannas under variable precipitation. *Landscape Ecology*, 22, 1355–69.

(2017). Evolutionary computation in zoology and ecology. *Current Zoology*, 63, 675–86.

Boone, R. B., BurnSilver, S. B., Thornton, P. K., Worden, J. S., and Galvin, K. A. (2005). Quantifying declines in livestock due to subdivision. *Rangeland Ecology & Management*, 58, 523–32.

Boone, R. B., Conant, R. T., Sircely, J., Thornton, P. K., and Herrero, M. (2018). Climate change impacts on selected global rangeland ecosystem services. *Global Change Biology*, 24, 1382–93.

Boone, R. B., Coughenour, M. B., Galvin, K. A., and Ellis, J. E. (2002). Addressing management questions for Ngorongoro Conservation Area using the Savanna Modeling System. *African Journal of Ecology*, 40, 138–50.

Boone, R. B., Galvin, K. A. (2014). Simulation as an approach to social–ecological integration, with an emphasis on agent-based modeling. In *Understanding Society and Natural Resources: Forging New Strands of Integration across the Social Sciences*, ed. M. Manfredo, et al. New York: Springer, 179–202.

Boone, R. B., Johnson, C. M., and Johnson, L. B. (2006). Simulating wood frog movement in central Minnesota, USA using a diffusion model. *Ecological Modelling*, 198, 255–62.

Boone, R. B., and Krohn, W. B. (2002a). An introduction to modeling tools and accuracy assessment. In *Predicting Species Occurrences: Issues of Accuracy and Scale*, ed. J. M. Scott, J. H. Haglung, M. L. Morrison, et al. Washington, DC: Island Press, 265–70.

(2000b). Predicting broad-scale occurrences of vertebrates in patchy landscapes. *Landscape Ecology*, 15, 63–74.

(2000c). Relationship between avian range limits and plant transition zones in Maine. *Journal of Biogeography*, 27, 471–82.

Boone, R. B., Lackett, J. M., Galvin, K. A., Ojima, D. S., Tucker III, C. J. (2007). Links and broken chains: Evidence of human-caused changes in land cover in remotely sensed images. *Environmental Science & Policy*, 10, 135–49.

Bormann, F. H., and Likens, G. E. (1979). *Pattern and Process in a Forest Ecosystem: Disturbance, Development, and the Steady State Based on the Hubbard Brook Ecosystem Study*. New York: Springer.

Briske, D. D., Fuhlendorf, S. D., and Smeins, F. E. (2005). State-and-transition models, thresholds, and rangeland health: A synthesis of ecological concepts and perspectives. *Rangeland Ecology & Management*, 58, 1–10.

Briske. D. D., and Heitschmidt, R. K. (1991). An ecological perspective. In *Grazing Management: An Ecological Perspective*, ed. R. K. Heitschmidt and J. W. Stuth. Portland, OR: Timber Press.

Brokaw, N., and Busing, R. T. (2000). Niche versus chance and tree diversity in forest gaps. *Trends in Ecology and Evolution*, 15, 183–8.

Brown, J. H. (1995). *Macroecology*. Chicago: University of Chicago Press.

Brown, L. F., and Trlica, M. J. (1977). Interacting effects of soil water, temperature and irradiance on CO_2 exchange rates of two dominant grasses of the shortgrass prairie. *Journal of Applied Ecology*, 14, 197–204.

Burke, I. C., Lauenroth, W. K., and Wessman, C. A. 1998. Progress in understanding biogeochemistry at regional to global scales. In *Successes, Limitations, and Challenges in Ecosystem Science*, ed. P. Groffman and M. Pace. New York: Springer Verlag.

Burke, I. C., Mosier, A. R., Hook, P. B., et al. (2008). Organic matter and nutrient dynamics of shortgrass steppe. In *Ecology of the Shortgrass Steppe: A Long-Term Perspective*, ed. W. K. Lauenroth and I. C. Burke. Oxford: Oxford University Press.

BurnSilver, S., Boone, R. B., and Galvin, K. A. (2003). Linking pastoralists to a heterogeneous landscape: The case of four Maasai group ranches in Kajiado District, Kenya. In *Linking Household and Remotely Sensed Data: Methodological and Practical Problems*, ed. J. Fox, V. Mishra, R. Rindfuss, and S. Walsh. Boston: Kluwer Academic Publishing, 173–99.

Carpenter, S. R., Mooney, H. A., Agard, J., et al. (2009). Science for managing ecosystem services: Beyond the Millennium Ecosystem Assessment. *Proceedings of the National Academy of Science USA*, 106, 1305–12.

Ceballos, G., Ehrlich, P. R., Barnosky, A. D. A., et al. (2015). Accelerated modern human-induced species losses: Entering the sixth mass extinction. *Science Advances*, 1(5), e1400253.

Chapin, F. S., Chapin, M. C., Matson, P. A., and Vitousek P. (2011). *Principles of Terrestrial Ecosystem Ecology*. New York: Springer.

Christensen, N. L. (2014). An historical perspective on forest succession and its relevance to ecosystem restoration and conservation practice in North America. *Forest Ecology and Management*, 330, 312–22.

Clark, F. E. (1977). Internal cycling of ^{15}nitrogen in shortgrass prairie. *Ecology*, 58, 1322–33.

(1981). The nitrogen cycle: Viewed with poetic licence. In *Terrestrial Nitrogen Cycles: Processes, Ecosystem Strategies, and Management Impacts*, ed. F. E. Clark and T. Rosswall. Ecological Bulletin, 33. Stockholm: Swedish Natural Science Research Council (NRF).

Clark, F. E. and Rosswall, T., ed. (1981). *Terrestrial Nitrogen Cycles, Processes, Ecosystem, Strategies and Management Impacts*. Ecological Bulletin, 33. Stockholm: Swedish Natural Science Research Council (NRF).

Clark, J. S. (1989). Ecological disturbance as a renewal process: Theory and application to fire history. *Oikos*, 56, 17–30.

Clements, F. E. (1916). *Plant Succession: An Analysis of the Development of Vegetation*. Publication No. 242. Washington, DC: Carnegie Institute of Washington.

(1935). Experimental ecology in the public service. *Ecology*, 16, 342–63.

Cole, C. V., and Heil, R. D. (1981). Phosphorus effects on terrestrial nitrogen cycling. In *Terrestrial Nitrogen Cycles: Processes, Ecosystem, Strategies and Management Impacts*, ed. F. E. Clark and T. Rosswall. Ecological Bulletin, 33. Stockholm: Swedish Natural Science Research Council, 363–74.

Coleman, D. C., Swift, D. M., and Mitchell, J. E. (2004). From the frontier to the biosphere: A brief history of the USIBP Grasslands Biome program and its impacts on scientific research in North America. *Rangelands*, 26, 8–15.

Coleman, D. C., and Wall, D. H. (2014). Soil fauna: Occurrence, biodiversity, and roles in ecosystem function. In *Soil Microbiology, Ecology and Biochemistry*, ed. E. A. Paul. London: Academic Press.

Conant, R. T., Cerri, C. E. P., Osborne, B. B., and Paustian, K. (2016). Grassland management impacts on soil carbon stocks: A new synthesis. *Ecological Applications*, 27, 662–8.

Conant, R. T., Paustian, K., and Elliot, E. T. (2001). Grassland management and conversion into grassland: Effects on soil carbon. *Ecological Applications*, 11, 343–55.

Connell, J. H. (1978). Diversity in tropical rain forests and coral reefs. *Science*, 199, 1302–10.

Connell, J. H, and Slatyer, R. O. (1977). Mechanisms of succession in natural communities and their role in community stability and organization. *American Naturalist*, 111, 1119–44.

Coppock, D. L., and Detling, J. K. (1986). Alteration of bison/prairie dog grazing interaction by prescribed burning. *Journal of Wildlife Management*, 50, 452–5.

Coppock, D. L., Detling, J. K., Ellis, J. E., and Dyer, M. I. (1983a). Plant–herbivore interactions in a North American mixed-grass prairie: I. Effects of black-tailed prairie dogs on seasonal aboveground plant biomass and nutrient dynamics and plant species diversity. *Oecologia*, 5, 1–9.

(1983b). Plant–herbivore interactions in a North American mixed-grass prairie: II. Responses of bison to modification of vegetation by prairie dogs. *Oecologia*, 56, 10–15.

Cotrufo, M. F., Soong, J. L., Horton, A. J., et al. (2015). Soil organic matter formation from biochemical and physical pathways of litter mass loss. *Nature Geosciences*, 8(10), 1–4.

Cotrufo, M. F., Wallenstein, M., Boot, M. C., Denef, K., and Paul, E. A. (2013). The Microbial Efficiency-Matrix Stabilization (MEMS) framework integrates plant litter decomposition with soil organic matter stabilization: Do labile plant inputs form stable soil organic matter? *Global Change Biology*, 19, 988–95.

Coughenour, M. B. (1991). Spatial components of plant–herbivore interactions in pastoral, ranching, and native ungulate ecosystems. *Journal of Rangeland Management*, 44, 530–42.

Coughenour, M. B., Dodd, J. L., Coleman, D. C., and Lauenroth, W. K. (1979). Partitioning of carbon and SO_2 sulfur in a native grassland. *Oecologia*, 42, 229–40.

Coughenour, M. B., Ellis, J. E., Swift, D. M., et al. (1985). Energy extraction and use in a nomadic pastoral ecosystem. *Science*, 230, 619–25.

Covino, T. P., and McGlynn, B. L. (2007). Stream gains and losses across a mountain-to-valley transition: Impacts on watershed hydrology and stream water chemistry. *Water Resources Research*, 43: W10431.

Coyne, P. I., Trlica, M. J., and Owensby, C. E. (1995). Carbon and nitrogen dynamics in range plants. In *Wildland Plants: Physiological Ecology and Developmental Morphology*, ed. D. J. Bedunah and R. E. Sosebee. Denver, CO: Society for Range Management: 59–167.

Currie, W. S. (2011). Units of nature or processes across scales? The ecosystem concept at age 75. *New Phytologist*, 190, 21–34.

Curtis, J. T. (1959). *The Vegetation of Wisconsin*. Madison: University of Wisconsin Press.

Davis, M. B., and Shaw, R. G. (2001). Range shifts and adaptive responses to climate change. *Science*, 292, 673–9.

Day, T. A., and Detling, J. K. (1994). Water relations of *Agropyron smithii* and *Bouteloua gracilis* and community evapotranspiration following long-term grazing by prairie dogs. *American Midland Naturalist*, 132, 381–92.

(1990a). Grassland patch dynamics and herbivore grazing preference following urine deposition. *Ecology*, 71, 180–8.

(1990b). Changes in grass leaf water relations following urine deposition. *American Midland Naturalist*, 123, 171–8.

Del Grosso, S., Ojima, D. S., Parton, W. J., et al. (2009). Global scale DAYCENT model analysis of greenhouse gas emissions and mitigation strategies for cropped soils. *Global and Planetary Change*, 67, 44–5.

Del Grosso, S., Parton, W., Stohlgren, T., et al. (2008). Global potential net primary production predicted from vegetation class, precipitation, and temperature. *Ecology*, 89, 2117–26.

Detling, J. K. (1988). Grasslands and savannas: Regulation of energy flow and nutrient cycling by herbivores. In *Concepts of Ecosystem Ecology*, ed. L. R. Pomeroy and J. J. Alberts. Ecological Studies, 67. New York: Springer Verlag, 131–48.

(1998). Mammalian herbivores: Ecosystem-level effects in two grassland national parks. *Wildlife Society Bulletin*, 26, 438–48.

Detling, J. K., Parton, W. J., and Hunt, H. W. (1978). An empirical model for estimating CO_2 exchange of *Bouteloua gracilis* (H.B.K.) Lag. in the shortgrass prairie. *Oecologia*, 33, 137–47.

Drury, W. H., and Nisbet, I. C. T. (1973). Succession. *Journal of the Arnold Arboretum*, 54, 331–68.

Egler, F. E. (1954). Vegetation science concepts: 1. Initial floristic composition, a factor in old-field vegetation development. *Vegetatio*, 4, 412–17.

(1975). *Plight of the Right of Way Domain*. Mt. Kisco, NY: Futura Press.

(1981). Untitled letter to the editor. *Bulletin of the Ecological Society of America*, 62, 230–2.

Ellis, J. E., and Galvin, K. A. (1994). Climate patterns and land-use practices in the dry zones of Africa. *BioScience*, 44, 340–9.

Ellis, J. E., and Swift, D. M. (1988). Stability of African pastoral ecosystems: Alternate paradigms and implications for development. *Journal of Range Management*, 41, 450–9.

Evangelista, P. H., Kumar, S., Stohlgren, T. J., et al. (2008). Modelling invasion for a habitat generalist and a specialist plant species. *Diversity and Distributions*, 14, 808–17.

Evangelista, P. H., Norman, J., Berhanu, L., Kumar, S., and Alley, N. (2008). Predicting habitat suitability for the endemic mountain nyala (*Tragelaphus buxtoni*) in Ethiopia. *Wildlife Research*, 35, 409–16.

Evangelista, P., Stohlgren, T. J., Morisette, J. T., and Kumar, S. (2009). Mapping invasive tamarisk (Tamarix): A comparison of single-scene and time-series analyses of remotely sensed data. *Remote Sensing, Ecological Status and Change by Remote Sensing special issue*, 1, 519–33.

Evangelista, P., Swartzinski, P., and Waltermire, R. (2007). A profile of the mountain nyala (*Tragelophus buxtoni*). *African Indaba*, 5(2), special report.

Fassnacht, S. R., Dressler, K. A., and Bales, R. C. (2003). Snow water equivalent interpolation for the Colorado River Basin from snow telemetry (SNOTEL) data. *Water Resources Research*, 39(8), 1208.

Fassnacht, S. R., Sexstone, G. A., Kashipazha, A. H., et al. (2016). Deriving snow-cover depletion curves for different spatial scales from remote sensing and snow telemetry data. *Hydrological Processes*, 30, 1708–17.

Fassnacht, S. R., Web, R. W., and Sanford, W. E. (2017). Headwater regions – physical, ecological, and social approaches to understand these areas: Introduction to special issue. *Frontiers of Earth Science*, 11(3), 443–6.

Fassnacht, S. R., Williams, M. W., and Corrao, M. V. (2009). Changes in the surface roughness of snow from millimetre to metre scales. *Ecological Complexity*, 6, 221–9.

Fedy, B. C., Doherty, K. E., Aldridge, C. L., et al. (2014). Habitat prioritization across large landscapes, multiple seasons, and novel areas: An example using Greater Sage-Grouse in Wyoming. *Wildlife Monographs*, 190, 1–39.

Fenn, M. E., Baron, J. S., Allen, E. B., et al. (2003). Ecological effects of nitrogen deposition in the western United States. *BioScience*, 53, 404–20.

Forrester, J. W. (1968). *Principles of Systems*. Cambridge, MA: Wright-Allen Press.

Galvin, K. A., Reid, R. S., Behnke, Jr., R. H., and Hobbs, N. T. (eds) (2008). *Fragmentation in Semi-arid and Arid Landscapes*. Dordrecht: Springer.

Galvin, K. A., Thornton, P. K., Boone, R. B., and J. Sunderland. (2004). Climate variability and impacts on East African livestock herders. *African Journal of Range and Forage Sciences*, 21,183–9.

Gao, W., Zheng, Y. F., Slusser, J. R., et al. (2004). Effects of supplementary ultraviolet-B irradiance on maize yield and qualities: A field experiment. *Photochemistry and Photobiology*, 80, 127–31.Gleason, H. A. (1926). The individualistic concept of the plant association. *Bulletin of the Torrey Botanical Club*, 53, 7–26.

Gleason, H. A. (1939). The individualistic concept of the plant association. *American Midland Naturalist*, 21, 92–110.

Goselink, R., Klop, G., Dijkstra, J., and Bannink, A. (2014). Phosphorus metabolism in dairy cattle: A literature study on recent developments and missing links. *Livestock Research, Livestock Research Report 910*. Wageningen: Wageningen University and Research Centre.

Gough, C. (2012). Terrestrial primary production: Fuel for life. *Nature Education Knowledge*, 3, 28.

Graham, J., Jarnevich, C., Young, N., Newman, G., and Stohlgren, T. (2011). How will climate change affect the potential distribution of Eurasion tree sparrows *Passer montanus* in North America? *Current Zoology*, 57, 648–54.

Green, R. A., and Detling, J. K. (2000). Defoliation-induced enhancement of total aboveground nitrogen yield of grasses. *Oikos*, 91, 280–4.

Heitschmidt, R. K., and Stuth, J. W. (1991). *Grazing Management: An Ecological Perspective*. Portland, OR: Timber Press.

Henderson, B. B., Gerber, P. J., Hilinski, T. E., et al. (2015). Greenhouse gas mitigation potential of the world's grazing lands: Modeling soil carbon and nitrogen fluxes of mitigation practices. *Agriculture, Ecosystems & Environment*, 207, 91–100.

Hilbert, D. W., Swift, D. M., Detling, J. K., and Dyer, M. I. (1981). Relative growth rates and the grazing optimization hypothesis. *Oecologia*, 51, 14–18.

Hobbs, N. T., Andrén, H., Persson, J., Aronsson, M., and Chapron, G. (2012). Native predators reduce harvest of reindeer by Sámi pastoralists. *Ecological Applications*, 22, 1640–54.

Hobbs, N. T., Galvin, K. A., Stokes, C. J., et al. (2008). Fragmentation of range-lands: Implications for humans, animals, and landscapes. *Global Environmental Change* 18, 776–85.

Hobbs, N. T., and M. B. Hooten. (2015). *Bayesian Models: A Statistical Primer for Ecologists*. Princeton, NJ: Princeton University Press.

Holland, E. A., and Detling, J. K. (1990). Plant response to herbivory and below-ground nitrogen cycling. *Ecology*, 71, 1040–9.

Holland, E. A., Parton, W. J., Detling, J. K., and Coppock, D. L. (1992). Physiological responses of plant populations to herbivory and their consequences for ecosystem nutrient flow. *American Naturalist*, 140, 685–706.

Holling, C. S. (1973). Resilience and stability of ecological systems. *Annual Review of Ecology and Systematics*, 4, 1–23.

(1992). Cross-scale morphology, geometry, and dynamics of ecosystems. *Ecological Monographs*, 62, 447–502.

Homer, C., Meyer, D. K., Aldridge, C. L., and Schell, S. J. (2013). Detecting annual and seasonal changes in a sagebrush ecosystem with remote sensing-derived continuous fields. *Journal of Applied Remote Sensing*, 7(1), 10.1117/1.JRS 7.073508.

Horn, H. S. (1975). Forest succession. *Scientific American*, 232, 90–8.

Houpt, T. R. (1959). Utilization of blood urea in ruminants. *American Journal of Physiology*, 197, 115–20.

Hutchinson, G. E. (1957). Concluding remarks. *Cold Spring Harbor Symposium on Quantitative Biology*, 22, 415–27.

Ingham, R. E., and Detling, J. K. (1984). Plant–herbivore interactions in a North American mixed-grass prairie: III. Soil nematode population and root biomass dynamics on a black-tailed prairie dog colony and an adjacent uncolonized area. *Oecologia*, 63, 307–13.

(1990). Effects of root-feeding nematodes on aboveground net primary production in a North American grassland. *Plant and Soil*, 121, 279–81.

Innis, G. S., ed. (1978). *Grassland Simulation Model*. Ecological Studies, 26. New York: Springer.

Jaramillo, V. J., and Detling, J. K. (1988). Grazing history, defoliation, and competition: Effects on shortgrass production and nitrogen accumulation. *Ecology*, 69, 1599–608.

(1992a). Small-scale heterogeneity in a semiarid North American grassland I: Tillering, N uptake and retranslocation in simulated urine patches. *Journal of Applied Ecology*, 29, 1–8.

(1992b). Small scale heterogeneity in a semiarid North American grassland II: Cattle grazing of simulated urine patches. *Journal of Applied Ecology*, 29, 9–13.

Johnson, E. A., and Fryer, G. I. (1989). Population dynamics in lodgepole pine–Engelmann spruce forests. *Ecology*, 70, 1335–45.

Kampf, S. K., and Burges, S. J. (2007). A framework for classifying and comparing distributed hillslope and catchment hydrologic models. *Water Resources Research*, 43, W05423.

Kampf, S. K., Strobl, B., Hammond, J., et al. (2018). Testing the waters: mobile apps for crowdsourced streamflow data. EOS 99, https://doi.org/10.1029/2018EO096355.

Kampf, S. K., Tyler, S. W., Ortiz, C. A., Muñoz, J. F., and Adkins, P. L. (2005). Evaporation and land surface energy budget at the Salar de Atacama, Northern Chile. *Journal of Hydrology*, 310, 236–52.

Kandylis, K. (1984). The role of sulphur in ruminant nutrition: A review. *Livestock Production Science*, 11, 611–24.

Kareiva, P., and Andersen, M. (1988). Spatial aspects of species interactions: The wedding of models and experiments. In *Community Ecology*, ed. A. Hasting. New York: Springer, 38–54.

Keane, R. E., Hessburg, P. F., Landres, P. B., and Swanson, F. J. (2009). The use of historical range and variability in landscape management. *Forest Ecology and Management*, 258, 1025–37.

Kilgore, B. M. (1973). The ecological role of fire in Sierran conifer forests: Its application to National Park management. *Quaternary Research*, 3, 496–513.

Klein, J. A., Harte, J., and Zhao, X.-Q. (2007). Experimental warming, not grazing, decreases rangeland quality on the Tibetan Plateau. *Ecological Applications*, 17, 541–57.

Kumar, S., Graham, J., West, A. M., and Evangelista, P. H. (2014). Using district-level occurrences in MaxEnt for predicting the invasion potential of an exotic insect pest in India. *Computers and Electronics in Agriculture*, 103, 55–62.

Kumar, S., Neven, L. G., and Wee, Y. L. (2014). Evaluating correlative and mechanistic niche models for assessing the risk of pest establishment. *Ecosphere*, 5(7), 86.

Kumar, S., Spaulding, S. A., Stohlgren, T. J., et al. (2009). Potential habitat distribution for the freshwater diatom *Didymosphenia geminata* in the continental US. *Frontiers in Ecology and the Environment*, 7, 415–20.

Lauenroth, W. K. (1979). Grassland primary production: North American grasslands in perspective. In *Perspectives on Grassland Ecology*, ed. N. R. French. Ecological Studies, 32. New York: Springer Verlag, 3–24.

Lauenroth, W. K., and Burke, I. C., eds. (2008). *Ecology of the Shortgrass Steppe: A Long-Term Perspective*. Oxford: Oxford University Press.

Lauenroth, W. K., Burke, I. C., and Gutmann, M. (1999). The structure and function of ecosystems in the central North American grassland region. *Great Plains Research*, 9, 223–59.

Laurnroth, W. K., Milchunas, D. G., Sala, O. E., Burke, I. C., and Morgan, J. A. (2008). Net primary production in the Shortgrass Steppe. In *Ecology of the Shortgrass Steppe: A Long-Term Perspective*. W. K Lauenroth and I. C. Burke. Oxford: Oxford University Press, 270–305.

Lefsky, M. A., Cohen, W. B., Acker, S. A., et al. (1999). Lidar remote sensing of the canopy structure and biophysical properties of Douglas-fir western hemlock forests. *Remote Sensing of Environment*, 70, 339–61.

Levin, S. A. (1992). The problem of pattern and scale in ecology: The Robert H. MacArthur Award lecture. *Ecology*, 73, 1943–67.

Levins, R. (1969). Some demographic and genetic consequences of environmental heterogeneity for biological control. *Bulletin of the Entomological Society of America*, 15, 237–40.Li, Z., Liu, S., Tan Z., et al. (2014). Comparing cropland net primary production estimates from inventory, a satellite-based model, and a process-based model in the Midwest of the United States. *Ecological Modelling*, 277, 1–12.

Liu, J., Mooney, H., Hull, V., et al. (2015). Systems integration for global sustainability. *Science*, 347, 1258832.

Loucks, O. L. (1970). Evolution of diversity, efficiency, and community stability. *American Zoologist*, 10, 17–25.

MacDonald, L. H. (2000). Evaluating and managing cumulative effects: Process and constraints. *Environmental Management*, 26, 299–315.

MacDonald, L. H., and Huffman, E. L. (2004). Post-fire soil water repellency: Persistence and soil moisture thresholds. *Soil Science Society of America Journal* 68: 1729–34.

MacDonald, L. H., Smart, A. W., and Wissmar, R. C. (1991). Monitoring guidelines to evaluate effects of forestry activities on streams in the Pacific Northwest and Alaska. EPA/910/9–91–001. Seattle, WA: US Environmental Protection Agency.

McGill, W. B., Hunt, H. W., Woodmansee, R. G., and Reuss, J. O. (1981). Phoenix: A model of the dynamics of carbon and nitrogen in grassland soils. In *Terrestrial Nitrogen Cycles: Processes, Ecosystem, Strategies and Management Impacts*, ed. F. E. Clark and T. Rosswall. Ecological Bulletin, 33. Stockholm: Swedish Natural Science Research Council, 49–115.

McHale, D. N., Bunn, M. R., Pickett, S. T. A., and Twine, W. (2013). Urban ecology in a developing world: Why advanced socioecological theory needs Africa. *Frontiers in Ecology and the Environment*, 11, 556–64.

McHale, M. R., Pickett, S. T. A., Barbosa, O., Bunn, D. N., and Cadenasso, M. L. (2015). The new global urban realm: Complex connected, diffuse, and diverse social-ecological systems. *Sustainability*, 7, 5211–40.

McNaughton, S. J. (1976). Serengeti migratory wildebeest: Facilitation of energy flow by grazing. *Science*, 191, 92–4.

   (1979). Grazing as an optimization process: Grass–ungulate relationships in the Serengeti. *American Naturalist*, 113, 691–703.

MEA (Millennium Ecosystem Assessment). (2005). *Ecosytems and human well-being synthesis*. Washington, DC: Island Press.

Meadows, D. H. (2008). *Thinking in Systems: A Primer*. White River Junction, VT: Chelsea Green Publishing.

Milchunas, D. G., and Lauenroth, W. K. (1992). Carbon dynamics and estimates of primary production by harvest, C-14 dilution, and C-14 turnover. *Ecology*, 73, 593–607.

Milchunas, D. G., Lauenroth, W. K., Burke, I. C., and Detling, J. K. (2008). Effects of grazing on vegetation. In *Ecology of the Shortgrass Steppe: A Long-Term Perspective*, ed. W. K. Lauenroth and I. C. Burke. Oxford: Oxford University Press.

Milly, P. C. D., Betancourt, J., Falkenmark, M., et al. (2008). Climate change – Stationarity is dead: Whither water management? *Science*, 319, 573–4.

Mingyang, L., Yunwei, J., Kumar, S., and Stohlgen, T. J. (2008). Modeling potential habitats for alien species Dreissena polymorpha in continental USA. *Acta Ecological Sinica*, 28, 4253–8.

Moir, R. J. (1970). Implications of the N:S ratio and differential recycling. In *Symposium: Sulphur in Nutrition*, ed. O. H. Muth and J. E. Oldfield. Westport, CT: AVI Publishing Co.

Mosier, A. R., Parton, W. J., Martin, R. E., et al. (2008). Soil–atmosphere exchange of trace gasses in the Colorado shortgrass steppe. *Ecology of the Shortgrass Steppe: A Long-Term Perspective* ed. W. K. Lauenroth and I. C. Burke. Oxford: Oxford University Press.

Nash, K. L., Allen, C. R., Angeler, D. G., et al. (2014). Discontinuities, cross-scale patterns, and the organization of ecosystems. *Ecology*, 95, 654–67.

NREL. (2018). Natural Resource Ecology Laboratory. www.nrel.colostate.edu (accessed June 6, 2018).

Odum, E. P. (1969). The strategy of ecosystem development. *Science*, 164, 262–70.

Odum, E. P., and Odum, H. T. (1963). *Fundamentals of Ecology*, 2nd edn. E. P. Odum in collaboration with H. T. Odum. Philadelphia and London: W. B. Saunders.

Ogle, S. M., Breidt, F. J., Eve, M. D., and Paustain, K. (2003). Uncertainty in estimating land use and management impacts on soil organic matter storage for US agricultural lands between 1982 and 1997. *Global Change Biology*, 9, 1521–42.

Ogle, S. M., Breidt, F. J., and Paustain, K. (2005). Agricultural management impacts on soil organic carbon storage under moist and dry climatic conditions of temperate and tropical regions. *Biogeochemistry*, 72, 87–121.

Ogutu, J. O., Piepho, H.-P., Dublin, H. T., Bhola, N. and Reid, R. S. (2009). Dynamics of Mara-Serengeti ungulates in relation to land use changes. *Journal of Zoology*, 278, 1–14.

Ojima, D. S., Galvin, K. A., and Turner, B. L. (1994). The global impact of land-use change. *BioScience*, 44, 300–4.

Ojima, D., Garcia, L., Elgaali, E., et al. (1999). Potential climate change impacts on water resources in the Great Plains. *Journal of the American Water Resources Association*, 35(6), 1443–54.

Ojima, D. S., Kittel, T. G. F., Rosswall, T., and Walker, B. H. (1991). Critical issues for understanding global change effects on terrestrial ecosystems. *Ecological Applications*, 1, 316–25.

Ojima, D., Mosier, A., DelGrosso, S. J., and Parton, W. J. (2000). TRAGNET analysis and synthesis of trace gas fluxes. *Global and Biogeochemical Cycles*, 14, 995–7.

Ojima, D. S., Schimel, D. S., Parton, W. J., and Owensby, C. W. (1994). Long- and short-term effects of fire on nitrogen cycling in tallgrass prairie. *Biogeochemistry*, 24, 67–84.

O'Neill, R. V. (1988). Hierarchy theory and global change. In *Scales and Global Change: Spatial and Temporal Variability in Biospheric and Geospheric Processes*, ed. T. Rosswall, R. G. Woodmansee, and P. G. Risser. SCOPE Series 38. Hoboken, NJ: John Wiley and Sons, 29–45.

Painter, E. L., Detling, J. K., and Steingraeber, D. A. (1993). Plant morphology and grazing history: Relationships between native grasses and herbivores. *Vegetatio*, 106, 37–62.

Parton, W. J., Anderson, D. W., Cole, C. V., and Stewart, J. W. B. (1983). Simulation of soil organic matter formation and mineralization in semiarid agroecosystems. In *Nutrient Cycling in Agricultural Ecosystems*, ed. R. R. Lowrance, R. L. Todd, L. E. Asmussen, and R. A. Leonard. Special Publication No. 23. Athens, GA: University of Georgia, College of Agriculture Experiment Station.

Parton, W. J., Hartman, M., Ojima, D., and Schimel, D. (1998). DAYCENT and its land surface submodel: Description and testing. *Global and Planetary Change*, 19, 35–48.

Parton, W. J., Schimel, D. S., Cole, C. V., and Ojima, D. S. (1987). Analysis of factors controlling soil organic matter levels in Great Plains grasslands. *Soil Science Society of America Journal*, 51, 1173–9.

Parton, W., Silver, W. L., Burke, I. C., et al. (2007). Global-scale similarities in nitrogen release patterns during long-term decomposition. *Science*, 315, 362–4.

Paul, E. A., ed. (2015). *Soil Microbiology, Ecology and Biochemistry Academic Press*, 4th edn. Burlington, MA: Academic Press .

Paul, E. A., Paustian, K., Elliott, E. T., and Cole, C. V., eds. (1997). *Soil Organic Matter in Temperate Ecosystems*. Boca Raton, FL: CRC Press.

Paustian, K., Cole, C. V., Sauerbeck, D., and Sampson, N. (1998). CO_2 mitigation by agriculture: An overview. *Climatic Change*, 40, 135–62.

Peters, D. P. C., Sala, O. E., Allen, C. D, Covich, A., and Brunson, M. (2007). Cascading events in linked ecological and socioeconomic systems. *Frontiers in Evolution and the Environment*, 5, 221–4.

Phillips, S. J., and Dudik, M. (2008). Modeling of species distributions with Maxent: New extensions and a comprehensive evaluation. *Ecography*, 31, 161–75.

Phillips, S. J., Dudik, M., and Schapire, R. E. (2004). A maximum entropy approach to species distribution modeling. *Proceedings of the 21st International Conference on Machine Learning*. New York: ACM Press, 655–62.

Pickett, S. T. A., Cadenasso, M. L., Childers, D. L., McDonnell, M. J., and Zhou, W. (2016). Evolution and future of urban ecological science: Ecology in, of, and for the city. *Ecosystem Health and Sustainability*, 2(7), e01229.

Pickett, S. T. A., Cadenasso, M. L., and Meiners, S. J. (2009). Ever since Clements: From succession to vegetation dynamics and understanding to intervention. *Applied Vegetation Science*, 12, 9–21.

Polley, H. W., and Detling, J. K. (1989). Defoliation, nitrogen, and competition: Effects on plant growth and nitrogen nutrition. *Ecology*, 70, 721–7.

Rahel, F. J. (2002). Homogenization of freshwater faunas. *Annual Review of Ecology, Evolution, and Systematics*, 33, 291–315.

Reddy, K. R., Kakani, V. G., Zhao, D., Koti, S., and Gao, W. (2004). Interactive effects of ultraviolet-B radiation and temperature on cotton physiology, growth, development and hyperspectral reflectance. *Photochemistry and Photobiology*, 79, 416–27.

Redfield, A .C. (1934). On the proportions of organic derivatives in sea water and their relation to the composition of plankton. *James Johnstone Memorial Volume*. Liverpool: Liverpool University Press, 176–92.

Reid, R. S. (2012). *Savanas of Our Birth*. London: University of California Press.

Reid, R. S., Gichohi, H., Said, M. Y., et al. (2008). Fragmentation of a peri-urban savanna, Athi-Kaputiei Plains, Kenya. In *Fragmentation in Semi-Arid and Arid Landscapes*, ed. K. A. Galvin, R. S. Reid, R. H. Behnke Jr., and N. T. Hobbs. Dordrecht: Springer, 195–224.

Reid, R. S., and Ellis, J. E. (1995). Impacts of pastoralists on woodlands in South Turkana, Kenya: Livestock-mediated tree regeneration. *Ecological Applications*, 5, 978–92.

Risser, P. G. (1990). Landscape pattern and its effects on energy and nutrient distribution. In *Changing Landscapes: An Ecological Perspective*, I. S. Zonneveld and R. R. T. Forman. New York: Springer, 45–56.

Robertson, G. P., and Groffman, P. M. (2015). Nitrogen transformations. In *Soil Microbiology, Ecology and Biochemistry*, ed. E. A. Paul. Burlington, MA: Academic Press, 421–46.

Rodewald, A. D. (2003). The importance of land uses within the landscape matrix. *Wildlife Society Bulletin*, 31, 586–92.

Rollins, M. G. (2009). LANDFIRE: A nationally consistent vegetation, wildland fire, and fuel assessment. *International Journal of Wildland Fire*, 18, 235–49.

Romme, W. H. (1982). Fire and landscape diversity in subalpine forests of Yellowstone National Park. *Ecological Monographs*, 52, 199–221.

Romme, W. H., Whitby, T. G., Tinker, D. B., and Turner, M. G. (2016). Deterministic and stochastic processes lead to divergence in plant communities 25 years after the 1988 Yellowstone fires. *Ecological Monographs*, 86, 327–51.

Root, T. (1988). Environmental factors associated with avian distributional limits. *Journal of Biogeography*, 15, 489–505.

Rosswall, T., Woodmansee, R. G., and Risser, P. G. (1988). *Scales and Global Change: Spatial and Temporal Variability in Biospheric and Geospheric Processes*. Scope Series (Book 38). Hoboken, NJ: John Wiley and Sons.

Ryan, M. G. (1991). Effects of climate change on plant respiration. *Ecological Applications*, 1, 157–67.

Ryan, M. G., and Asao, S. (2014). Phloem transport in trees. *Tree Physiology*, 34, 1–4.

Safranyik, L., Shrimpton, D. M., and Whitney, H. S. (1974). *Management of lodgepole pine to reduce losses from the mountain pine beetle*. Forestry Technical Report 1. Victoria, BC: Natural Resources Canada, Canadian Forest Service, Pacific Forestry Centre.

Sankaran, M., et al. (2005). Determinants of woody cover in African savannas. *Nature*, 438, 846–9.

Sauer, J. R., Niven, D. K., Hines, J. E., et al. (2017). *The North American Breeding Bird Survey, Results and Analysis 1966–2015. Version 2.07.2017*. Laurel, MD: USGS Patuxent Wildlife Research Center.

Schimel, D. S., Melillo, M., Tian, H., et al. (2000). Contribution of increasing CO_2 and climate to carbon storage by ecosystems in the United States. *Science*, 287, 2004–6.

Schimel, D. S., Parton, W. J., Adamsen, F. J., et al. (1986). Role of cattle in the volatile loss of nitrogen from a shortgrass steppe. *Biogeochemistry*, 2, 39–52.

Schimel, D. S., Stillwell, M. A., and Woodmansee, R. G. (1985). Biogeochemistry C, N, and P in a soil catena of the shortgrass steppe. *Ecology*, 66, 276–82.

Senft, R. L., Coughenour, M. B., Bailey, D. W., et al. (1987). Large herbivore foraging and ecological hierarchies. *BioScience*, 37, 789–99.

Six, J., Conant, R. T., Paul, E. A., and Paustian, K. (2002). Stabilization mechanisms of soil organic matter: Implications for C-saturation of soils. *Plant and Soil*, 241, 155–76.

Six, J., Elliott, E. T., and Paustian, K. (2000). Soil microaggregate turnover and microaggregate formation: A mechanism for C sequestration under no-tillage agriculture. *Soil Biology and Biochemistry*, 32, 2099–103.

Six, J., Ogle, S. M., Conant, R. T., Mosier, A. R., and Paustian, K. (2004). The potential to mitigate global warming with no-tillage management is only realized when practiced in the long term. *Global Change Biology*, 10, 155–60.

Smith, P., Martino, D., Cai, Z., et al. (2008). Greenhouse gas mitigation in agriculture. *Philosophical Transactions of the Royal Society of London B: Biological Sciences*, 363, 789–813.

Stabach, J. A., Wittemyer, G., Boone, R. B., Reid, R. S., and Worden, J. S. (2016). Variation in habitat selection by white-bearded wildebeest across different degrees of human disturbance. *Ecosphere*, 7(8), e01428.

Stohlgren, T. J. (2007). *Measuring Plant Diversity: Lessons from the Field*. New York: Oxford University Press.

Stohlgren, T. J., Barnett, D., Flather, C., et al. (2006). Species richness and patterns of invasion in plants, birds, and fishes in the United States. *Biological Invasions*, 8, 427–57.

Stohlgren, T. J., Barnett, D., and Kartesz, J. (2003). The rich get richer: Patterns of plant invasions in the United States. *Frontiers in Ecology and the Environment*, 1 (1), 11–14.

Stohlgren, T. J., Binkley, D., Chong, G. W., et al. (1999). Exotic plant species invade hot spots of native plant diversity. *Ecological Monographs*, 69, 25–46.

Stohlgren, T. J., Bull, K. A., and Otsuki, Y. (1998). Comparison of rangeland sampling techniques in the Central Grasslands. *Journal of Range Management*, 51, 164–72.

Stohlgren, T. J., and Schnase, J. L. (2006). Risk analysis for biological hazards: What we need to know about invasive species. *Risk Analysis*, 26, 163–73.

Stohlgren, T. J., Szalanski, A. L., Gaskin, J., et al. (2014). From hybrid swarms to swarms of hybrids. *Environment and Ecology Research*, 2(8), 311–18.

Swetnam, T. W. (1993). Fire history and climate-change in giant sequoia groves. *Science*, 262, 885–9.

Thurow, T. L. (1991). Hydrology and erosion. In *Grazing Management: An Ecological Perspective*, ed. R. K. Heitschmidt and J. W. Stuth. Portland, OR: Timber Press.

Turner, M. G., Romme, W. H., Gardner, R. H., O'Neill, R. V., and Kratz, T. K. (1993). A revised concept of landscape equilibrium: Disturbance and stability on scaled landscapes. *Landscape Ecology*, 8, 213–27.

Van Dyne, G. M., ed. (1969). *The Ecosystem Concept in Natural Resource Management*. New York: Academic Press.

Van Dyne, G. M., and Anway, J. C. (1976). Research program for and process of building and testing grassland ecosystem models. *Journal of Range Management*, 29, 114–22.

Wakie, T. T., Laituri, M., and Evangelista, P. H. (2016). Assessing the distribution and impacts of Prosopis juliflora through participatory approaches. *Applied Geography*, 66, 132–43.

Wall, D. H., Bradford, M. A., St. John, M. G., et al. (2008). Global decomposition experiment shows soil animal impacts on decomposition are climate-dependent. *Global Change Biology*, 14, 2661–77.

Wallenstein, M. D., and Hall, E. K. (2012). A trait-based framework for predicting when and where microbial adaptation to climate change will affect ecosystem functioning. *Biogeochemistry*, 109, 35–47.

Wann, G. T., Aldridge, G. L., and Braun, C. E. (2016). Effects of seasonal weather on breeding phenology and reproductive success of alpine ptarmigan in Colorado. *PLoS ONE*, 11(7), e0158913.

Watt, A. S. (1947). Pattern and process in the plant community. *The Journal of Ecology*, 35: 1–22.

Westoby, M., Walker, B., and Noymeir, I. (1989). Opportunistic management for rangelands not at equilibrium. *Journal of Range Management*, 42, 266–74.

Whicker, A. D., and Detling, J. K. (1988). Ecological consequences of prairie dog disturbances. *BioScience*, 38, 778–85.

Whittaker, R. H. (1975). *Communities and Ecosystems*, 2nd edn. New York: Macmillan.

Wiens, J. A. (1984). On understanding a non-equilibrium world: Myth and reality in community patterns and processes. In *Ecological Communities: Conceptual Issues and the Evidence*, ed. D. R. Strong, D. Simberloff, L. G. Abele, and A. B. Thistle. Princeton, NJ: Princeton University Press.

(1989). Spatial scaling in ecology. *Functional Ecology*, 3, 385–97.

Williams III, G. J., and Kemp, P. R. (1978). Simultaneous measurement of leaf and root gas exchange of shortgrass prairie species. *International Journal of Plant Sciences*, 139, 150–7.

Woodmansee, R. G. (1978). Additions and losses of nitrogen in grassland ecosystems. *BioScience*, 28, 448–53.

(1990). Biogeochemistry cycles and ecological hierarchies. In *Changing Landscapes: An Ecological Perspective*, ed. I. S. Zonneveld and R. R. T. Forman. New York: Springer, 57–71.

Woodmansee, R. G, Dodd, J. L., Bowman, R. A., Clark, F. E., and Dickinson, C. E. (1978). Nitrogen budget of a shortgrass prairie ecosystem. *Oecologia*, 34, 363–76.

Woodmansee, R. G., Vallis, I., and Mott, J. J. (1981). Grassland nitrogen. In *Terrestrial Nitrogen Cycles: Processes, Ecosystem Strategies, and Management Impacts*, ed. F. E. Clark and T. Rosswall. Ecological Bulletin, 33. Stockholm: Swedish Natural Science Research Council, 443–62.

WSS. (2018). Web Soil Survey. USDA Natural Resource Conservasion Service. https://websoilsurvey.sc.egov.usda.gov/App/HomePage.htm (accessed June 5, 2018).

7 · Evolution of the Systems Ecology Paradigm in Managing Ecosystems

ROBERT G. WOODMANSEE,
MICHAEL B. COUGHENOUR,
KEITH PAUSTIAN, WILLIAM J. PARTON,
THOMAS J. STOHLGREN,
WILLIAM H. ROMME,
PAUL H. EVANGELISTA,
CAMERON ALDRIDGE, DENNIS S. OJIMA,
WILLIAM LAUENROTH, INGRID BURKE,
KATHLEEN GALVIN, AND ROBIN REID

7.1 Introduction

The management of grazingland, forest, and cropland ecosystems has dramatically changed during the past 50 years. Governmental land-use policies and associated management practices have changed based on the knowledge gained from research, such as that described in Chapter 6 using the systems ecology paradigm. Modern land and water management is evolving toward ecosystem-based thinking that is reliant upon many aspects of the systems ecology paradigm. Systems thinking (Forrester, 1961, 1968; von Bertalanffy, 1968; Van Dyne, 1969; Meadows et al., 1972), simulation models (see Chapter 4), and advanced spatial analyses (see Chapter 5), combined with the warehouse of knowledge in ecosystem science (see Chapters 6 and 8) have resulted in new management paradigms (National Research Council, 1994, 2010; Williams, 2005). Ecosystem research has expanded knowledge of above and belowground primary and secondary production, decomposition and nutrient cycling pathways, plant and animal interactions, the hydrologic cycle, and the inclusion of human populations as stakeholders and interactive components of ecosystems that receive ecosystem services (see Chapter 1). Humans are no longer viewed simply as drivers of system structure and functioning in grazinglands, croplands, and forestlands

(Paul, 2015; Franklin, 2017; Franklin et al., 2017; Baron, 2002; see Chapters 1 and 9). These concepts have changed the calculus involved in management and decision making. Ecosystem-based management that uses the systems ecology approach will be the management paradigm of the future.

7.2 Native Land Management before the Late 1960s

Ecosystems dominated by native or naturalized vegetation include grasslands, shrublands, and forestlands. Of these, about 63 percent of the Earth's land surface can be classified as grazinglands (Suttie et al., 2005). The World Bank estimates that forestlands occupy about 30 percent (World Bank, 2018). A portion of both of these land types is cultivated.

Different views of lands dominated by native vegetation before the 1970s are represented in Figure 7.1. Each discipline had separate perspectives (silo views) of what we now call ecosystems and landscapes. Land managers and scientists focused on production goals and objectives expressed in terms of measurements of objects that could be seen,

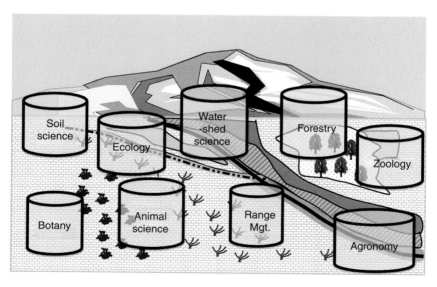

Figure 7.1 Different professional perspectives of managing ecosystem. Before the 1970s the silos were very rigid. Due largely to the influence of the systems ecology paradigm the rigidity has been lessening. Now, ecosystem-based management is becoming the standard practice with all perspectives being considered.

touched, weighed, and counted. For example, range managers and scientists focused on forage production measured as kilograms or pounds per hectare or acre, and livestock measurements, such as pounds gained and animal units per months of grazing. Management interventions and manipulations, such as vegetation control treatments, pest and predator removal, and other interventions, were introduced to enhance production goals. Chemical treatments and machinery were applied for increased livestock production and were utilized in efforts to increase profitability. Less attention was given to the consequences of overgrazing.

Agronomists and farmers focused on crop production, for example bushels per ha, fertilizer rates, pesticide costs, and machinery costs. Many considered soils to be a "free" and unlimited resource. Foresters focused on yield as board feet per ha and regeneration, and yield tables. Forests were cut, fires suppressed, and roads built to maximize timber yield. Ecologists measured "things" as what could be observed aboveground, for example plants or animals, biomass, or millimeters of precipitation. They focused on things that could be seen, touched, felt, weighed, and counted. Ecologists speculated about plant succession and animal population dynamics. Mining activities, including oil and gas exploration and development, were conducted without regard to their effects on surrounding lands. The consequences of these production-driven activities led to significant degradation of our forests, rangelands, croplands, and wetlands. Federal agencies supported management activities that exploited specific natural resources with little or no regard for broader environmental systems.

The emphasis on measurable aboveground components and productivity and narrow disciplinary perspectives (e.g., livestock, grass, trees, crops) resulted in few interactions across disciplines. Academic departments in universities and colleges and within land management agencies were loath to interact with one another and professional societies were focused on their particular disciplinary perspectives. Exacerbating the problem was the widespread publication model adopted by scientific societies and academic departments and agencies that emphasized single- or dual-authored research papers about narrow disciplinary topics. Scientific success was measured by individual achievement. The result was a limited knowledge of the environment as a whole, its broader impacts, and the activities that could lead to a better understanding of the total, multidimensional environment.

Results of the silo views of the land and the focus on aboveground production showed an ignorance of ecosystem processes, the landscape,

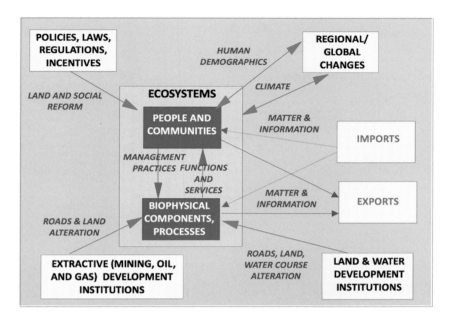

Figure 1.1 Ecosystems – the relationship of people and communities (societies) to the biophysical components and interactions (land, water, and air) in an ecosystem context.

Figure 1.10 An ecological site within a landscape. Photo by R. G. Woodmansee.

Figure 1.12 Example of a landscape ecosystem that illustrates many ecological sites. A sagebrush community is in the foreground, an aspen forest is adjacent, with a subalpine forest positioned behind, and alpine tundra on the horizon. Each may be a distinct ecological site, yet many different ecological sites are intermixed.

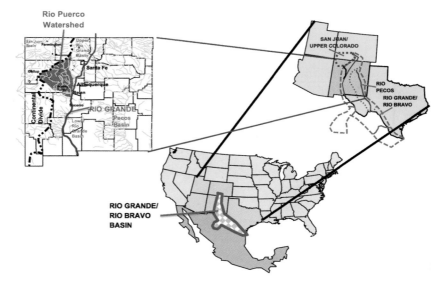

Figure 1.15 Representation of watershed (small region), regions, and subcontinental-scale ecosystems. The Rio Puerco watershed is in New Mexico, USA. Headwaters of the Rio Grande/Rio Bravo Basin are in the USA and Mexico.

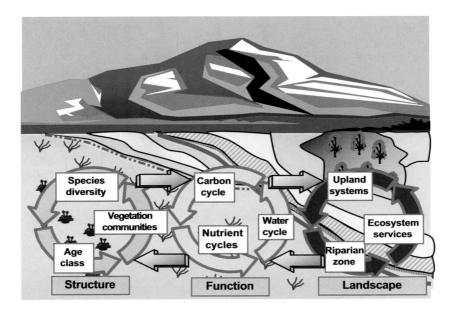

Figure 6.2 Schematic representing interactions of some biophysical attributes (structure and function) of ecological sites within landscapes. The emphasis is on dynamics in space and time and the interactions of the attributes.

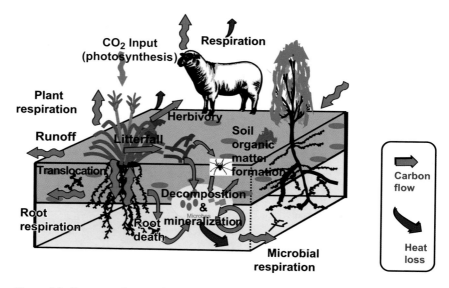

Figure 6.3 Cartoon of a rangeland ecological site showing the primary components and processes or transfer pathways in the carbon cycle.

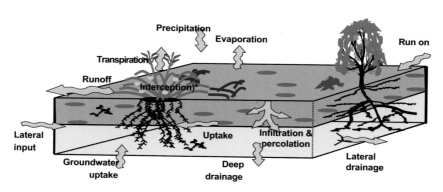

Figure 6.9 The ecological site scale water cycle. The critically important processes or flow paths are indicated with black arrows. The precipitation, evaporation, transpiration, interception, uptake, and infiltration and percolation pathways are internal to the ecological site ecosystem. The run-on, runoff, lateral drainage in and out, groundwater uptake, and deep drainage flow paths are connectors to other ecological sites within a landscape.

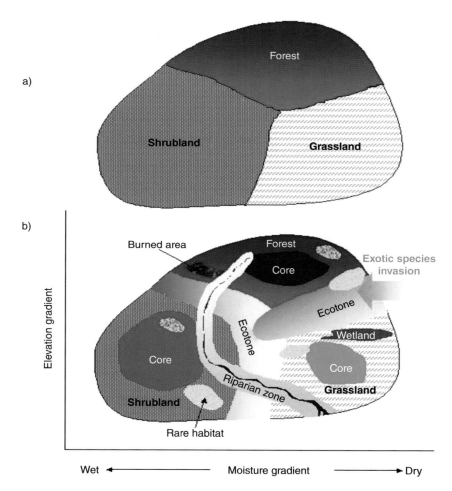

Figure 6.10 (a) The way landscapes are commonly portrayed or imagined for sampling; (b) the complex way landscapes appear in real life.

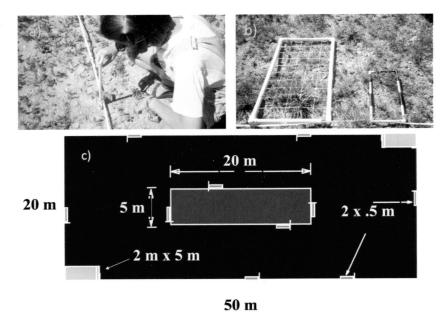

Figure 6.11 Three common sampling designs used to plant diversity. (a) The Parker loop. The Parker loop area is about the size of a quarter, placed along 100-foot line-transects, and every one foot you look down into the loop and describe what plant species you've encountered, or if you've hit bare ground. It's a tiny area of sampling. When you get back to the office you would have looked at a < 1 meter square area. (b) Various plant diversity "quadrats." Daubenmire used a quadrat, 20 cm by 50 cm, which is still pretty small when you consider the patchy distribution of plant species on the landscape. Others have recommended the use of transects as long as you use a larger quadrat. (c) The modified Whittaker multiscale sampling plot.

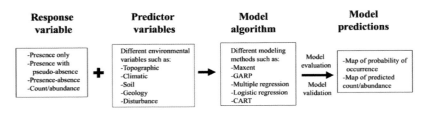

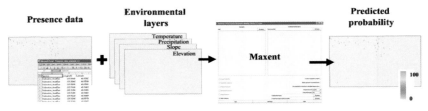

Figure 6.12 Schematic of the tool MaxEnt used to predict species invasions (or any species migrations) in space and time.

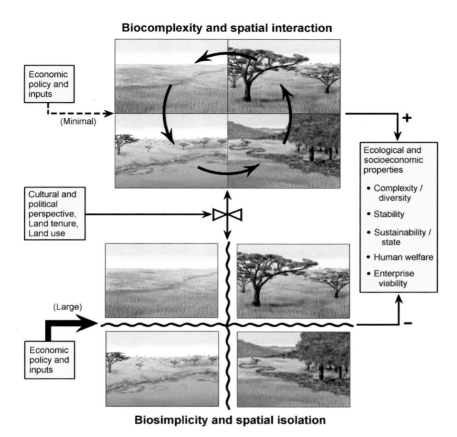

Figure 6.13 Conceptualization of the effects of fragmentation in semi–arid and arid areas (Hobbs et al., 2008).

Figure 8.2 (a) Early photosynthesis/CO_2 chamber exposed to sun – could not control radiation load. (b) Early photosynthesis/CO_2 chamber – even when cooling infrastructure insulated, radiation load was difficult to control.

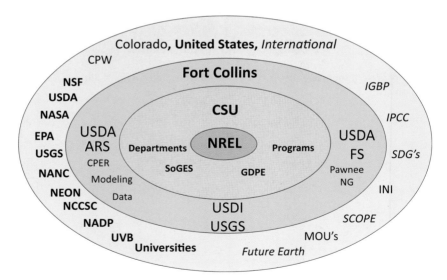

Figure 12.1 Diagram showing some of the relationships of the NREL with organizations within CSU; Fort Collins, Colorado; the State of Colorado; the United States; and internationally.

Figure 13.5 Illustration of digital technology in farming. Photo courtesy of USDA Natural Resource Conservation Service.

Figure 13.6 Maasai herder using cell phone for entertainment, herd management tips, and marketing information. Photo origin unknown – used on many African websites.

and regional scales, in addition to a lack of appreciation of belowground ecosystem functioning. This ignorance often led to disastrous consequences of land degradation, which in turn prompted public outcry on the current management of private and public lands and waters.

During the early 1900s, perspectives were emerging about plant ecology that would lead to the dismantling of silo views of ecosystem management, and eventually led to the development of the systems ecology paradigm. Appendix 7.1 presents a vignette of the development of plant ecology in North America that would profoundly influence the systems ecology paradigm and modern ecosystem management.

7.3 The Evolution of Modern Land–Use Management

The US passage of the Multiple Use and Sustained Yield Act of 1960 mandates that national forests be "administered for outdoor recreation, range, timber, watershed, and wildlife and fish purposes," and marks the beginning of a transformation in land management practices (see Box 7.1). The National Environmental Policy Act (NEPA) was passed and signed into law by President Nixon in 1969. It became the model for environmental policies around the world and created the formal process for environmental impact assessments on federal lands. A year later, the Environmental Protection Agency (EPA), whose mission is to "protect human health and the environment," was created to consolidate many of the requirements of NEPA. The Federal Land Use and Management Act of 1976 directed the Bureau of Land Management (BLM) to manage lands for multiple uses and to preserve their natural resources.

Box 7.1 *Examples of major US policies influencing ecosystem-based management of public and private lands*

- Multiple Use and Sustained Yield Act – 1960, United States Forest Service (USFS)
- National Environmental Policy Act (NEPA) – 1969
- Environmental Protection Agency (EPA) – 1970
- Clean Air Act – 1970, EPA
- Clean Water Act – 1972, EPA
- Federal Land Use Policy and Management Act – 1976, BLM
- Farm Bills

Concurrently, with adoption of new federal policies, numerous publications that greatly influenced public thought. Some of these publications include: Rachael Carson's *Silent Spring* appeared (Carson, 1962); Garrett Harden's "Tragedy of the commons" (Harden, 1968); Paul Erlich's *The Population Bomb* (Ehrlich, 1968); James Lovelock and Lynn Margulis' "Gaia hypothesis" (Lovelock and Margulis, 1974); and Dennis Meadows et al.'s *The Limits to Growth* (Meadows et al., 1972). "Earth Day" was subsequently established in 1970. Internationally, the Scientific Committee on Problems of the Environment (SCOPE) was established in 1969, UNESCO's Man and the Environment Program in 1971, followed by the launch of the United Nations Environmental Program (UNEP) 1972. Subsequent to the establishment of these environmental programs, and as evidenced by research conducted locally, there has been an increased awareness of the Earth's environment as it relates to its land, water, and atmosphere.

These events were the initial steps leading toward recognition of the need for new management concepts for the health and sustainability of our environment and natural resources. By the 1980s, policies were adopted that mandated public lands be managed for multiple purposes with a focus on environmental and natural resource protection and sustainability. But how?

Where was the knowledge to meet these goals? A new way of thinking was needed about the complex reality of land management, as were the data and knowledge bases to support these new perspectives. The novel approach to answering these questions was through the systems ecology paradigm – systems thinking and methodologies of holistically analyzing complex environmental and natural resource problems and challenges of forests, grasslands, shrublands, croplands, streams, and rivers. Ecosystem science was born through the study of these systems, the interactions of each component, and the external factors that influence them. Ecosystem science matured during the 1980s and 1990s and has produced a vast warehouse of sound scientific knowledge relevant to the land management goals mandated by federal laws (Box 7.1).

7.4 Emergence of "Ecosystem Management": 1968–1980

One of the first products of the immerging International Biological Program's Grassland Biome was a book organized and edited by George Van Dyne entitled *The Ecosystem Concept in Natural Resource*

Management (Van Dyne, 1969). It introduced the notion of the "systems ecology approach" to issues of natural resource management. Van Dyne used the term "ecosystem approach" in the introduction to that volume. Major topics in the book included range management, forestry, fish and game management, and watershed management. The book also included a chapter that introduced the ecosystem concept in academic training. This volume foreshadowed the integration of simulation modeling and field and laboratory research into applications to ecosystem management.

A holistic view of grazingland ecosystems emerged from the linkage between the IBP Grassland Biome, the Natural Resource Ecology Laboratory (NREL), the Range Science Department, and the Agronomy Department at Colorado State University, and with the USDA Agricultural Research Service in Fort Collins, Colorado. Whole ecological systems and their function, not just structure and production, were to become the focus of grazingland management in the United States and numerous other countries across the globe (Williams, 2005). The phrase "whole-system functioning" meant understanding above and belowground processes (above and belowground primary and secondary production, decomposition processes, nutrient cycling pathways, plant and animal interactions, ecological site scale and landscape hydrology, erosion, and sedimentation). Many of these processes are now considered "ecosystem services." Spatial and temporal scaling (ecological hierarchies) were identified as essential for both grazingland and agricultural ecosystem management (Anderson et al., 1983; Woodmansee, 1990). Simulation models were essential for the development of the concepts that integrated these interactions (see Chapter 4). The early focus and success of NREL was the discovery of how ecosystems function using field laboratory research, data analysis and integration, and simulation modeling.

During the late 1960s and 1970s, Colorado State University became known as a world leader in ecosystem science and range management (Rykiel, 1999). The Range Science Department and the Grassland Biome established training for federal land managers in the concepts of ecosystem structure and functioning using graduate and undergraduate curricula and "Ecosystem Management Short Courses" (see Chapter 11). These courses emphasized modules in primary production, decomposition, nutrient cycling, soils, secondary production, enterprise economics, statistics, and systems ecology and ecosystem modeling. Many prominent leaders in ecosystem science and management were trained in those and subsequent programs (see Chapters 3 and 11). The stage was set for the infusion of basic ecosystem science into applied science and management (see Appendix 7.1).

7.5 Ecosystem Science and Management: The Turning Point, Early 1980s

The systems ecology paradigm was established by the early 1980s with the completion of the International Grassland Biome studies and the publication of the Grassland Ecosystem Model (Innis, 1978). New research using ecosystem science for better understanding of C, N P, and S cycling, structure and functioning of belowground biomass and food webs, plant and animal interactions, landscape dynamics, humans as components of ecosystems, agroecosystems, and long-term ecological research were underway (see Chapters 3 and 6). The systems ecology approach and simulation modeling were integral to all of these programs. An emerging warehouse of knowledge about ecosystem functioning was infiltrating policy and management perspectives of both public and private lands (Williams, 2005). This approach pointed the way toward deeper research and understanding as well as guidance for management.

7.5.1 Emergence of Ecosystem Management: 1980s to Present

The demand for new approaches for federal land management, and the emerging knowledge generated by ecosystem science, converged in the mid to late 1980s with the evolving concept of ecosystem management. Ecosystem management, as discussed on page 145 of *The USDA Forest Service: The First Century* (Williams, 2005), is often characterized as a holistic approach for managing natural resources and the ecological processes that serve our social, economic, and cultural values. The goal is to manage ecosystems as a whole so that ecological services and biological and soil resources are maintained and/or achieved. This "new" management paradigm was founded on the "realization by many researchers and public land managers that an ecosystem science approach to managing public lands is the only logical way to proceed in the future" (Williams, 2005: 145).

Ecosystem management, the driving force behind current policies adopted by US federal agencies, such as the USDA Forest Service, US Department of the Interior (USDI BLM), and to some extent the EPA and The Nature Conservancy (TNC, 2018), combines science, enterprise profitability, philosophy, conservation, economics, ecology, environmentalism, politics, and public involvement. Below are some examples of the foundational principles in ecosystem management:

- Ecosystem management is an experience and science-based process open to all stakeholders.
- Healthy, functioning ecosystems are the key to achieving optimal goods (products), services (i.e., clean water, clean air, recreational opportunities), and ecological processes (i.e., nutrient cycling, carbon sequestration, soil health, control of the hydrologic cycle) from our lands and waters.
- People are parts of ecosystems as regulators, beneficiaries of goods and services, and stakeholders in decision making.
- Adaptation to changing conditions, such as changing climates, economic considerations, and political turmoil are best addressed by collaboration among stakeholders.
- Ecosystems often transcend administrative and political boundaries; therefore, interagency cooperation at the federal, state, and local levels, as well as the private sector, is essential.
- Cultural norms, such as human attitudes, beliefs, and values are important in determining the future of ecosystems.

Scientific and experience-based models of ecosystem management, that is, the new forestry (Franklin, 1989), ecosystem health (Christensen et al., 1996), rangeland health (National Research Council, 1994), adaptive management (Holling, 1978), and Forest Restoration (2018), are evolving and maturing. Regardless of the name, these concepts underpin current policies that drive land use and management in the US and influence the development of policies in Australia, Canada, and many other countries. However, these increasingly successful models are continuously threatened by governmental policies and special interest groups that support resource extraction, profitability, and deregulation, in addition to the inadequate funding of agencies and programs responsible for land management and the environment. Finding a balance between immediate and short-term human goals and long-term sustainability of global ecosystems is a tenuous and ever-evolving challenge.

The current management policies that address ecosystem challenges, for example native, dryland grazinglands and forests, represent a tremendous interplay of ecosystem research results, simulation modeling, creative ideas, traditional knowledge, and experience. Collaboration among scientists, managers, policy makers, and stakeholder groups, locally,

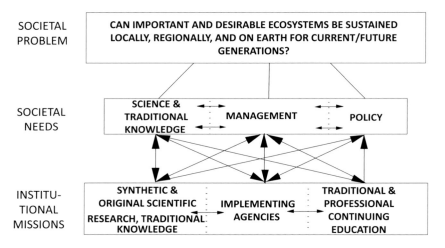

SOCIETAL PROBLEM

SOCIETAL NEEDS

INSTITU-TIONAL MISSIONS

Figure 7.2 Ideal relationship of science and traditional knowledge, based on facts and evidence, management, and policy sectors in addressing societal problems, issues, and goals. In a perfect world, the arrows representing knowledge sharing between the science, management, and policy sectors would be transparent and interactive. To accomplish the ideal state, many research, outreach, and education institutions must contribute reliable knowledge to policy makers and management agencies.

regionally, and maybe internationally (Figure 7.2), is essential. For example, teams of researchers and collaboration among teams within SCOPE, UNEP, and the International Geosphere-Biosphere Program (IGBP), have greatly influenced concepts and increased the understanding of ecosystem functioning, for example "ecosystem services," the importance of nutrient cycling, belowground ecosystems, and biodiversity. Policy making and implementation of management options based on collaborative decision making are products of community efforts (BLM, 2016; USFS, 2016). However, all management is local, even if policies are broad sweeping.

Identifying the precise linkage of research results to specific federal policies is difficult due to the diffusion of agencies and individuals in management processes. What is possible is showing how the integration of ecosystem science knowledge and the systems ecology paradigm have influenced public and private policy in the US and elsewhere in the world (National Research Council, 1994; Christensen et al., 1996; NFF, 2016; BLM, 2018; TNC, 2018; USFS, 2018). For example, the USDA Forest Service and USDI BLM and the National Park Service (NPS) land management goals and strategies are based on ecosystem science and application of the systems ecology approach. Likewise, TNC's management philosophy embraces both.

Modern ecosystem management embraces multiple-use concepts and emphasizes healthy, functioning ecosystems. According to a growing body of experience and scientific evidence, properly managed, healthy ecosystems are more productive and profitable for traditional users than old, single-product-focused management models (Teague, 2009a, 2009b). Accomplishing successful ecosystem management requires hard work on the part of land managers and participating stakeholders, in addition to policies and adequate funding support.

7.5.2 Examples of Ongoing Research Involving Ecosystem Management

The early focus and success of NREL, in conjunction with other national and international ecosystem research programs, was simply to gain a better understanding of how ecosystems function. Specific research projects focused on grassland ecosystems, agroecosystems, pastoral social systems, belowground or soil ecosystems, wildlife management, invasive species, species conservation, biodiversity, and forest and high-elevation and high-latitude ecosystems. With the basic knowledge established by the early 1990s, the modern concepts of ecosystem management began developing as described in "The report of the Ecological Society of America Committee on the scientific basis for ecosystem management" (Christensen et al., 1996).

7.5.2.1 Long-Term Research

Long-term research on ecosystem dynamics and processes has been, and continues to be, a priority with NREL scientists. Most notable are the Shortgrass Steppe Long-Term Ecological Research Program (SSLTER) (Lauenroth and Burke, 2008) and the long-term research on the Loch Vale Watershed (LVWS) project in Rocky Mountain National Park (Baron et al., 2009).

The SSLTER Program, located at the Central Plains Experimental Range (CPER) of the USDA Agricultural Research Service, was initiated in the early 1980s and continued until 2014 (Lauenroth and Burke, 2008). The SSLTER was the continuation and expansion of research started by the USDA Forest Service in the late 1930s and transferred to the USDA Agricultural Research Service in the 1950s. The CPER was created to conduct research to improve grazing management practices on fragile grasslands. With the establishment of the US IBP Grassland Biome in the late 1960s, the CPER became the principle research site (Pawnee Site) for studies of the structure and functioning of grassland ecosystems. Many of the studies conducted at the CPER and described in this book represent the marriage of basic and applied research that have led directly to the management and policy transformations described in this chapter. Many of these research programs are now conducted at the National Ecological Observatory Network (NEON, 2018) and the USDA Agricultural Research Service (USDA ARS, 2018).

The LVWS project tracks and interprets trends in biogeochemical, hydrologic, and biological processes to provide knowledge to the NPS of the consequential threats external to park boundaries (Baron, 1992; LVWSP, 2018). Established in 1983, the program has provided an increased understanding of high-elevation alpine and subalpine ecosystems. The objectives are: (1) provide a greater understanding and differentiate natural processes from unnatural, human-caused drivers of change; (2) understand and quantify the effects of atmospheric deposition and climate variability/change on high-elevation ecosystems; (3) share knowledge with managers. The LVWS project adopted an ecosystem approach from the beginning, attempting to quantify biogeochemical processes, particularly those related to nitrogen and carbon cycling. A variety of research approaches were and are employed, including: (1) long-term monitoring (e.g., Baron et al., 2009, Mast et al., 2014); (2) field and laboratory experiments (Reuth et al., 2003; Lafrancois et al., 2004; Nydick et al., 2004; Elser et al., 2009); (3) ecosystem modeling (Baron et al., 1994, 2000); (4) spatial comparison (Baron et al., 2000; Meixner et al., 2000; Hartman et al., 2014; O'Reilly et al., 2015); and (5) reconstructions of past conditions using proxy indicators of past changes preserved in lake sediments (Wolfe et al., 2003; Enders et al., 2008). A number of biogeochemical and biological effects from atmospheric deposition of nitrogen have been discovered, reported, and used to set regional air quality policies (CDPHE, 2018). Monitoring now continues to determine the efficacy of these policies. Recent observations of increased alpine lake primary production have prompted further research into the interactions of atmospheric deposition and climate warming (Baron et al., 2009).

7.5.2.2 Research Supporting Ecosystem Management
Identifying best management practices to maintain ecosystem resilience in the face of climate change. The North Central Climate Adaptation Science Center (NCCASC) is one of eight regional climate centers created by the US Department of Interior to help meet the changing needs of land and

resource managers across the US. The center brings together the latest data, tools, and knowledge on the impacts of climate change. It works directly with resource managers to promote climate-informed conservation and provides researchers with an opportunity to work with an engaged and proactive applied management community (NCCASC, 2018). This project aims to identify different ways that natural resource managers can adapt to these changes and deal with the uncertainties associated with climate change (NREL, 2018a; NCCASC, 2018). Their work on this project and others has provided a large body of scientific research to assist in climate-smart planning across the North Central Region of the US.

Invasive species management. NREL scientists have pioneered invasive species science and management in terrestrial, aquatic, and marine environments (Stohlgren et al., 1999; Evangelista et al., 2008; see Chapter 6; NREL, 2018a). Their research includes studies at both local and global scales on native and nonnative species interactions, effects on ecological processes, and impacts on livelihoods and economies. In addition, their efforts have engaged stakeholders through citizen science programs, development of new tools and technologies, and online resources to support the early detection and rapid response to manage new invasions (Newman et al., 2012).

Examining the wildland/urban interface and responding to wildfire and bark beetle epidemics across North America. Over the past few decades, wildfires and bark beetle outbreaks have dramatically altered forest structure throughout most of western North America.

The impacts of these large, severe disturbances on ecosystem processes and biological resources have been studied in great depth at NREL (Romme et al., 2016; NREL, 2018a). Researchers documented spatial patterns and temporal trends in the regrowth of forest vegetation for over 25 years following the 1988 Yellowstone fires. This research revealed that Rocky Mountain forests were remarkably resilient to that fire and to historic fires that resulted in a rapid recovery of prefire species composition and ecosystem processes, such as nutrient cycling. However, more recently fires are burning with shorter intervals between fires, followed by warmer temperatures. New studies are being conducted to evaluate future ecosystem resiliency in the face of changing climate and increasing fire frequency.

In 2006, the location, extent, and trends of expansion of the wildland–urban interface (WUI) (areas where urban development presses against private and public wildlands) were examined by Dave Theobald and Bill

Romme (Theobald and Romme, 2007). They reported that in 2000 the WUI covered over 719,000 km^2, and contained 39 percent of all housing units in the continental US. They also predicted that the area in the WUI would continue to expand as urban areas expanded. The WUI occurs disproportionately in the eastern US, yet nationally typical involvement is observed on privately owned wildlands. One of the biggest forest management issues within the WUI is forest fires due to both the firefighting and management interventions required to reduce their likelihood and severity.

Because of the dominance of private land ownership in the WUI, a reevaluation of polices was suggested to potentially shift more of the forest management and firefighting costs, now largely absorbed by the public, to private landowners.

Indirect human impacts on ecosystems: human activities may create an unsuspected impact on neighboring ecosystems. Nitrogen is a by-product of energy production, transportation, and food production, and can harm ecosystems when present in large amounts. Responding to this threat, the NPS, in collaboration with the EPA and the State of Colorado, developed a plan to reduce emissions of this pollutant to reverse the damage and restore park resources (NREL, 2018a).

Bioenergy Alliance Network of the Rockies (BANR, 2018). This project explores the use of beetle-kill and other forest biomass as a bioenergy feedstock and provides rigorous scientific underpinnings to support a sustainable renewable energy industry. During the past decade infestations of pine and spruce bark beetles led to widespread tree death in coniferous forests across the Rocky Mountains, with ~42 million hectares of US forests impacted since 1996. This trend is likely to intensify with future global climate change. The resulting beetle-killed wood represents a vast bioenergy resource that requires no cultivation, circumvents food vs. fuel concerns, and may have a highly favorable carbon balance compared to other forestry feedstocks. However, beetle-killed biomass is typically located far from urban industrial centers in relatively inaccessible areas with challenging topography. Transportation costs have been a key barrier to more widespread productive utilization of this vast resource.

Promoting citizen science through data collection: engaging citizens through community-based wildlife monitoring. Community engagement and promoting science is a priority at NREL. Investigators work alongside various community stakeholders and often employ volunteers to assist in scientific data collection (NREL, 2018b). One of the major goals of the project is to provide data that support wildlife management decisions.

Land fragmentation and resource extraction in the American West: human development and its impact on population and species biodiversity. Sage-grouse is an iconic bird species in the American West that has become the focal point for land management controversy. Sage-grouse populations have declined over the past century due to habitat degradation from land fragmentation, oil and gas development, and environmental change. Sage-grouse habitats overlap with areas of human activity, prompting efforts to engage wildlife managers, conservationists, politicians, recreationists, and land developers for their protection and conservation (NREL, 2018b).

7.5.2.3 Current Research Supporting Wildlife Management

Savanna ecosystems in East Africa: vegetative productivity in ecosystems and their effect on pastoral communities. Pastoral communities, often leading nomadic lifestyles and herding livestock, rely on healthy ecosystems to support their livelihoods. However, due to increased human development grazing areas are often fragmented, creating additional stressors to a landscape already threatened by fire and drought. Thus, these communities are forced to seek ways to adapt to the changing landscape (Boone, 2007; NREL, 2018a).

Estimating population size in wildlife communities: studying the grazing ecology of ungulate species to assess habitat viability. NREL scientists have conducted research on population dynamics and grazing ecology of ungulates (hooved animals) and domestic livestock in North America and Africa for many years (NREL, 2018b). In the southwestern US, researchers have focused their studies on creating a better understanding of wild burro population demography and their social and reproductive behavior. Complimentary research on the African wild ass in Ethiopia and Somaliland is being developed. This work will impact the conservation of endangered equids, especially wild asses, globally.

Land appropriation, endangered species and the human–wildlife conflict in sub-Saharan Africa: researchers use an interdisciplinary approach to address the complex questions surrounding wildlife management (NREL, 2018b). Studies using species distribution models of the demographics and habitat of an endangered antelope species (mountain nyala) endemic to Ethiopia are ongoing. The research has been able to produce maps of the mountain nyala population extent, which the Ethiopian Wildlife Conservation Authority has used to develop best management practices.

For the last two decades, researchers have been tracking wildebeest in the savanna ecosystems in East Africa. They were able to track migratory patterns over time and produce spatial maps of the migratory corridors. From these results, it has become clear how environmental factors, such as precipitation and fire, in addition to human development, affect wildebeest migration. Their models uncovered traditional migratory pathways that had been broken due to fencing and land fragmentation, thus obstructing the former migration routes.

Research in South Africa has involved the human–wildlife conflict surrounding Kruger National Park. These studies are exploring the intersection of race, ethnicity, and conservation management. A major goal is to identify how local human populations will be included in the development of this conservation area.

Forecasting population dynamics of large herbivores in national parks: NREL researchers work with NPS wildlife managers to sustainably manage wildlife populations. Models using Bayesian statistical methods to predict ungulate population dynamics were developed for national park wildlife managers (NREL, 2018b). These models assimilated data from a census to predict population size and composition change over time. The models forecast future behavior of ungulate populations that managers are actively using to make decisions with the goal of sustaining viable, healthy wildlife populations in national parks.

Population and community ecology and the management of large herbivores has been an additional research focus at the NREL (Bradford and Hobbs, 2008; Hobbs et al., 2008). This work emphasizes two major themes: population modeling and understanding influences of herbivores on ecosystems. Contributions to basic theories that link animal populations to their environment and the application of scientific knowledge to management and policy have emerged making important conceptual contributions toward understanding how population dynamics are influenced by spatial heterogeneity of landscapes and habitat fragmentation.

Large herbivore studies in East Africa have also been intensely studied by NREL scientists (Milne et al., 2015). Studies include movement and foraging behavior of wildebeest in Kenya and Tanzania, tracking their response to fragmented landscapes and extreme climates (Galvin et al., 2008; Reid, 2012). The ways wildlife and livestock use landscapes, and how changing landscapes may affect them, are of interest. Computer modeling is used to address these questions by modifying conditions in simulations to reflect landscape or policy changes, and then reporting on those outcomes.

7.5.2.4 The Need for the Systems Ecology Paradigm in Large Herbivore Management

Most of the current research noted in Section 7.5.2.3 is linked to the co-development of simulation modeling and field research described in this section. We have chosen to highlight this large herbivore management story to illustrate the extensive time, effort, and interconnection of research projects needed to develop major ecosystem research programs. Similar stories can be told about other programs discussed in this chapter.

Management of native large herbivores in national parks and other nature reserves requires an understanding of their roles in ecosystems. Herbivores alter vegetation structure, abundance and species composition. They affect nutrient cycling and hydrology by altering vegetation. They return nutrients directly back to the soil, which enhances nutrient availability to plants. In some cases, native herbivores have been viewed as "ecosystem engineers" or "keystone species" that markedly alter ecosystem structure and functioning. Removing herbivores or managing their abundance to overly low or high levels can bring about a vegetation type that is atypical of the site. Native herbivores maintain vegetation in states that can be considered "natural" inasmuch as they existed prior to the arrival of Europeans. Many plant species coevolved with herbivores and are adapted to withstand herbivory.

Conversely, herbivores are affected by ecosystem processes. Forage availability is affected by all the factors which determine vegetation productivity and composition, including water and nutrient availabilities. These in turn are influenced by soil physical properties and processes involved in nutrient cycling, particularly decomposition. Herbivores are additionally affected by other species, through competition for food, or through their effects on vegetation and habitat structure. Predation must also be considered. Thus, herbivores, vegetation, soils, and predators are all parts of a dynamic system with multiple feedback loops. Focusing solely on herbivore population dynamics is insufficient as herbivore population size impacts vegetation and vegetation responses feed back on herbivore population dynamics via food availability. Indirect causality is important in such systems. For example, predators may influence vegetation and soils indirectly by reducing herbivore numbers and distributions.

Perhaps the most pervasive management issue with large herbivores in national parks is the determination of natural, appropriate, or sustainable numbers. A simplistic way to frame the question is to ask what the "carrying capacity" is for large herbivores. However, unlike the management of domestic livestock operations, in which a manager can assess total forage availability and exert complete control over herbivore numbers, the situation in national parks is more complex. First of all, national parks are managed for "naturalness." This objective constrains how much human interference there can be with natural processes of herbivore population regulation. Second, herbivores interact with other species. They may compete with other herbivores for forage and they are influenced by the presence, or lack of presence, of predators. Third, what constitutes desirable or acceptable herbivore impacts on vegetation are different from what is desirable or acceptable for a livestock system.

While a primary goal of national parks is the preservation of natural processes, humans have affected these ecosystems in many ways. Even very large parks having vast areas without human development and very low levels of human presence can be affected. For example, historical human impacts prior to park establishment can have lasting effects. These might include residual effects of heavy hunting pressures, including market hunting, extermination of predators such as wolves and grizzly bears, timber harvesting, and overgrazing by domestic livestock. Human impacts outside of park boundaries can affect processes within the boundaries. Wildlife are mobile and most large parks are unfenced. For example, hunting outside of parks affects herbivore populations that migrate between areas inside and outside of park boundaries.

Thus, the determination of "carrying capacity" for herbivores in national parks requires an assessment of ecosystem functioning prior to modern human settlement and ecosystem functioning under minimal management intervention. At the same time, it is necessary to consider the normal effects of herbivores on ecosystems and the processes that determine ecosystem dynamics and herbivore population sizes with minimal human intervention. It requires an assessment of the effects of past and present human influence on herbivores and ecosystem processes inside and outside of park boundaries. Finally, it requires an assessment of management interventions which might be necessary to mitigate human impacts such as predator eradication and restrictions on herbivore movements.

Due to this complexity, large herbivore management in national parks has often been controversial. Most notably, controversy has arisen regarding possible herbivore overabundance and resultant negative impacts on vegetation. Elk numbers in Yellowstone and Rocky Mountain National Parks and bison numbers in Yellowstone increased after the National Park Service implemented a policy of natural regulation in 1968. The objective of this policy was to preserve natural processes and minimize human intervention in herbivore population dynamics. An underlying hypothesis was that large herbivore populations can be naturally regulated through food limitation, even without predators. In turn, higher levels of elk and bison herbivory significantly altered the vegetation, especially woody vegetation. Some observers contended that these changes are unnatural and destructive, often pointing to the lack of predators and restrictions on herbivore movement as factors preventing natural regulation.

The Involvement of the NREL in Large Herbivore Ecosystem Science
Controversy and uncertainty resulted in the US Congress directing the NPS in 1986 to initiate a research program to address the issue of potential overgrazing and elk overabundance on Yellowstone's northern elk winter range (Despain et al., 1986; Yellowstone National Park 1997). The NPS subsequently sought scientific expertise to carry out the research. Scientists at the NREL were identified as being leading experts in grazing ecosystems. NREL scientist James K. Detling and colleagues had recently carried out research on prairie dog grazing in Wind Cave National Park (Detling, 1998; see also Chapter 6). Francis Singer, a large-herbivore ecologist at Yellowstone, contacted Detling in 1986 for recommendations regarding a study of grassland responses to herbivory on the northern range. Detling referred Singer to Michael B. Coughenour, who had carried out ecosystem modeling and plant ecology research on the Serengeti grazing ecosystem in Tanzania with Samuel McNaughton, an ecosystem scientist at Syracuse University (McNaughton, 1976, 1979; Coughenour, et al., 1984). At the time, Coughenour was at the NREL, involved in research on a pastoral ecosystem in northern Kenya (see Chapter 9). He carried out field research in Yellowstone in 1987 and 1988 (Coughenour, 1991). This study led to population and ecosystem modeling of vegetation–elk interactions (Coughenour, 1994; Coughenour and Singer, 1996a), and elk and vegetation responses to the Yellowstone fires of 1988 (Coughenour and Singer, 1996b).

Singer also enlisted McNaughton and his student Douglas Frank to study the northern range (Frank and McNaughton, 1992). McNaughton's previous research in the Serengeti documented the stable coexistence of grassland vegetation and very large, naturally regulated ungulate populations (McNaughton, 1979). Moreover, there was considerable evidence that the most abundant Serengeti herbivores, wildebeest, were naturally regulated by food limitation rather than predation. His research supported the idea that African grasses and herbivores had coevolved and that the grasses were well adapted to withstand herbivory. This research was an excellent model for an assessment of the Yellowstone grazing ecosystem which was essentially undergoing an experiment in natural regulation (Coughenour and Singer, 1996a).

Singer led numerous studies on Yellowstone elk and vegetation ecology during 1987–93 (Yellowstone National Park, 1997; Singer et al., 1998a). This led to subsequent research projects funded by the NPS and the US Geological Survey (USGS) during 1993–2005 on elk and bison ecology in Rocky Mountain (RMNP), Grand Teton (GTNP), and Wind Cave National Parks (WCNP), and wild horses on the Pryor Mountain Wild Horse Range (PMWHR) in Bighorn Canyon National Recreation Area, all of which involved NREL researchers including Detling, Coughenour, Kate Schoenecker, and N. T. Hobbs. After the Yellowstone research, Singer was posted to the USGS in Fort Collins and worked at the NREL where he carried out his PhD research and led a large project on elk, vegetation, and ecosystem processes in RMNP (Singer et al., 2002a; Zeigenfuss et al., 2002b). These projects supported ecosystem modeling studies of the PMWHR, RMNP, WCNP, and GTNP ecosystems as described in Box 7.2. Sadly, Francis Singer passed away prematurely in 2005.

Box 7.2 *The modeling process: an ecosystem model for large herbivore management*

Modeling could be used not only to simulate herbivore population dynamics, but also the natural processes involved in population regulation and the interactions of herbivores with other components of the ecosystem. The basic idea is to develop a process-based ecosystem-level model that simulates vegetation, soil processes, herbivores, and predators, and then use the model to simulate ecosystem dynamics in a "natural" presettlement state as well as scenarios involving alternative levels of herbivore population management and human impacts. For national parks, the objective would be to use the ecosystem model to identify and maintain natural processes that give rise to ecosystem dynamics and the ways that the ecosystem affects and is affected by large herbivores.

An ecosystem model that assesses large herbivores in ecosystems would need to have a number of characteristics, some of which might differ from a model designed for other purposes.

Overall structure. The temporal resolution must be one week or less in order to capture seasonal dynamics. The model must be spatially explicit to simulate heterogeneous vegetation and foraging conditions. This requires the capability to read geographic information systems (GIS) data into the model at the outset. The model must also be driven by spatially variable temperature and precipitation data. Obviously, the model must simulate vegetation and herbivores, but a paramount requirement is that herbivore population dynamics are affected by forage availability.

Vegetation submodels. The vegetation model must represent temporal and spatial variations in forage quantity and quality. Forage production is determined by soil moisture and nutrient contents as well as temperature. Forage biomass varies seasonally and interannually depending on conditions. Forage quality also varies seasonally as plants green up, reach peak biomass, and then dry out and senesce. Multiple types or species of plants must be simulated because of differences in growth form, phenology, and palatability. Fundamental processes involved in plant growth include photosynthesis, nitrogen uptake, allocation of C and N to various tissues, transpiration, and senescence. Plants should realistically respond to herbivory via its impacts on photosynthetic tissue. Carbon and nitrogen stored within the plant is important for regrowth in the spring and recovery from herbivory. Compensatory growth may occur due to a number of mechanisms.

Soil submodels. Because of the important role of soil moisture in driving plant growth, soil water balance must be simulated. This necessitates simulating precipitation inputs and losses due to transpiration, evaporation, and runoff. Soil nitrogen availability must be simulated, which requires simulation of decomposition and soil organic matter dynamics.

Snow model. Snowpack dynamics must be represented for several reasons. First, it is how winter precipitation is stored until snowmelt. Second, snow has extremely important impacts on forage availability. Third, it covers herbaceous plants which determines the time of green-up. Fourth, it is spatially variable, particularly with elevation in mountainous environments. Together, these factors determine where herbivores move and forage across the landscape, how much forage is available, where, and when, and thus how many herbivores can be supported.

Herbivore foraging and energy balance. The rate of forage consumption determines the degree to which a herbivore can meet its energetic requirements, and thus whether it is gaining weight, losing weight, starving, or in good condition. The model must therefore simulate factors which affect intake rate including forage biomass, dietary composition, and snow cover. In turn, the model must simulate herbivore energy balance and body condition, which is determined both by forage intake and energetic requirements.

Herbivore movement. Large herbivores move voluntarily in response to the distributions of forage, snow, topography, water, and other habitat variables. Herbivore movements may also be impacted by humans via fencing, hunting, and land use. Herbivore location relative to available forage has consequences for forage intake, energy balance, population dynamics, and the impacts of herbivory on vegetation. The model must consequently simulate dynamic herbivore spatial distributions as affected by these factors.

Herbivore population dynamics. A key feature of the model must be a linkage between forage abundance and herbivore population dynamics. This can be mechanistically achieved by making population variables such as birth and death rates responsive to body condition, which in turn is affected by forage intake and thus forage availability. Population dynamics are consequently affected by spatial and temporal variations in forage quantity and quality, and snow cover. Human management intervention by culling or permitted hunting can readily be modeled.

Predator submodel. In some cases, predators are or were present and have significant impacts on herbivore populations with consequences for vegetation. Predator numbers and distributions could be specified or simulated dynamically in response to prey availability and prey consumption.

Model Applications

Over a number of years, an ecosystem modeling approach was developed to assess the role of large herbivores in landscape ecosystems (Coughenour, 1992; Weisberg et al., 2002, 2006). A model having many of the necessary characteristics was developed during 1984–92 to study a pastoral ecosystem in northern Kenya (Coughenour, 1992). The feasibility of using this model for assessing large herbivore carrying capacity was first demonstrated during the Yellowstone northern elk winter range research efforts (Coughenour, 1994). The issue of elk overabundance due to the natural regulation policy was very controversial and there was a need to understand why elk numbers had increased to unprecedented levels. The model was parameterized and driven by a wealth of data from various research efforts on the northern range (e.g., Coughenour, 1991; Coughenour and Singer, 1996a). GIS data were also beginning to be available (e.g., soil, vegetation, and fire maps). The feasibility of the ecosystem modeling approach was also demonstrated as part of an assessment of the effects of the 1988 fires on elk carrying capacity (Coughenour and Singer, 1996b). The fires resulted in a conversion of forests to herbaceous vegetation thus potentially increasing forage biomass. The model was used to estimate elk body condition and population dynamics under pre- and post–fire scenarios.

The second application was an assessment of carrying capacity in the Pryor Mountain Wild Horse Range (Coughenour, 1999, 2000, 2002a, 2012). Wild horse management was, and remains, controversial, with horse advocates calling for a more or less unmanaged "wildness," and range managers conservatively calling for reductions to prevent range degradation. The model was parameterized and verified using an exceptional data set of vegetation biomass dynamics inside and outside of grazing exclosures (Fahnestock and Detling, 1999a, 1999b; Gerhardt and Detling, 2000) as well as detailed data on horse numbers and distributions (Singer et al., 1998b; Gerhardt and Detling 2000). Scenarios were run with different horse population sizes. The model was also run to a dynamic equilibrium with no management removals of horses. Resultant horse numbers could be considered to be the true food-limited carrying capacity. Impacts on herbaceous vegetation were simulated and with no management reductions grazing reduced biomass but vegetation still persisted. This assessment was a marked departure from traditional methods used by the Bureau of Land Management to set "appropriate management levels" for horse numbers (National Research Council, 2013).

The third application aimed to assess elk carrying capacity and impacts on vegetation in Rocky Mountain National Park (Coughenour, 2002b). A large research project led by Francis Singer included studies of herbaceous, willow, and aspen productivities and responses to elk herbivory along with studies of elk population dynamics and distributions (Singer et al., 1998b, 2002a, 2002b; Zeigenfuss et al., 2002a, 2002b; USDI, 2007). As with elk in Yellowstone National Park and horses in

PMWHR, this was a controversial situation with differences in views about the need to preserve natural processes and those arguing that pure natural regulation was not feasible due to conflicting land uses and a lack of predators. Several modeling experiments were conducted with SAVANNA. Experiments for 1949–98 included a simulation with unmanaged elk populations. The populations grew to their food-limited carrying capacities and stabilized. There was about 10 percent less grass and 30 percent less forb biomass on drylands than in the control run by the end of the period. Willow cover also decreased. Beaver and water table depths were simulated as well, in order to examine the hypothesis that reduced beaver numbers, possibly due to reduced willow and aspen, would lower water tables which would negatively affect willows. A factorially designed experiment was conducted in which elk and beaver densities were varied in all possible combinations to assess their relative effects on plants. Alternative elk management and elk exclosure scenarios were simulated by running the model for 50 years starting in 1994. There were three elk reduction scenarios. Aspen and willow within the park boundary were either unfenced or fenced to exclude elk and deer. Increasing water table heights had little positive benefit when elk were not reduced, and willow were unprotected by fencing. Simulations were performed to examine sensitivities to the wolf submodel parameters. It was possible to find plausible parameter values which resulted in diminished or no effects of predation on elk population size. The model showed that the situation in RMNP is more complex than the simple plant–herbivore equilibrium predicted by natural regulation theory. While the elk-grassland subsystem may reach an equilibrium, that equilibrium would probably not have developed in the presence of wolves and other predators. Instead, a different dynamic equilibrium would be expected with elk numbers being regulated by vegetation as well as wolves. Other more focused modeling studies were carried out to investigate willow growth and responses to elk and beaver herbivory (Peinetti et al., 2009), competition between elk and beaver for willow (Baker et al., 2012), and elk herbivory impacts on aspen (Weisberg and Coughenour, 2003).

As a result of the many field and modeling studies on the Singer project and many other research projects and assessments, the NPS developed an elk and vegetation management plan and environmental impact statement to address the problem (USDI, 2007). A major element of the plan was a call for the construction of several very expansive elk exclosures in willow and aspen communities within the park. These fenced exclosures were constructed in 2008. Since then there has been significant recovery of aspen and willow within them. At full recovery, the exclosures will be removed. The plan also called for elk numbers to be reduced through limited culling operations to levels that might have existed prior to settlement and wolf extirpation. The culls were carried out, but elk have also increasingly migrated to lower elevations outside the park. Due to both of these factors, population sizes are now lower than previously.

A fourth major application of SAVANNA in a national park was an assessment of bison carrying capacity in Yellowstone (Coughenour, 2005a, 2005b, 2005c, 2006; Plumb et al., 2009). Like elk, bison numbers increased since the implementation of natural regulation; however, unlike elk there were periodic large removals when they migrated outside the park, justified primarily by the fact that they carry brucellosis, which purportedly could be spread to surrounding livestock operations (Yellowstone National Park, 1997). With increasing numbers of bison, more were migrating outside of the park boundary and being culled at the boundary. This was yet another controversial situation, with bison advocates arguing for minimal management and allowance for free-ranging behavior beyond park boundaries on one side, and livestock concerns arguing for strict control on bison numbers and distributions on the other. Increased outmigration led some to claim that this was due to the fact that bison numbers had exceeded the carrying capacity of the park. The SAVANNA model was consequently used to examine this assertion. The model was already pre-adapted for use in Yellowstone due to previous work on the northern elk range. A considerable amount of newer data had also been collected, particularly on bison population dynamics and distributions. Bison ranges expanded markedly and previously separate subpopulations increasing intermixed. The model needed to represent these changes. The model needed to simulate both elk and bison because they compete for same forage: elk numbers affect bison numbers and vice versa. Another key requirement was to simulate snow cover dynamics and distributions, because snow affects bison and elk seasonal distributions and forage availability.

The modeling exercise provided insight into the causes and consequences of bison population growth and dispersal beyond park boundaries. The model indicated that bison had not reached a theoretical food-limited carrying capacity. However, the traditional concept of carrying capacity is overly simplistic for bison. The observed patterns of range expansion and dispersal in response to increased density relative to food supply and winter weather suggests that bison have a tendency to move in search of food well before they begin to starve and die due to food limitation. It is infeasible and contrary to policy to fence the bison inside the park. Thus, the model showed that while the park could support more bison if they were confined to the park, this will not occur due to bison dispersal tendencies and open boundaries. Thus, management removals to achieve some population objective will continue to be necessary. It was concluded that a population of 2500–4500 bison should satisfy collective interests concerning the park's forage base, bison movement ecology, retention of genetic diversity, brucellosis risk management, and prevailing social conditions (Plumb et al., 2009).

SAVANNA was also applied in other national parks with large herbivores, including Elk Island National Park in Alberta, Wind Cave National Park, and Grand Teton National Park. However, these applications did not reach full maturity due to funding limitations. In East Africa, the model has been used in the Ngorongoro Conservation Area (Boone et al., 2002), Kajiado, Kenya (Boone, 2007), Serengeti National Park (Metzger et al., 2005; Coughenour unpubl.), and Kruger National Park in South Africa (Hilbers et al., 2015; Fullman et al., 2017). It has also been used to assess elk management in northern Colorado (Weisberg et al., 2002), fire and grazing on cattle operations in Australia (Liedloff et al., 2001; Ludwig et al., 2001), and livestock grazing in Inner Mongolia (Christensen et al., 2006) and on the Tibetan Plateau (Boone et al. unpublished). The model has also been coupled with models of pastoral household economies with interactive feedbacks between humans and other components of the ecosystem (Galvin et al., 2006; Thornton et al., 2006; Boone et al., 2011).

Ecosystem modeling can be used in an adaptive management approach (Williams, 2011; Williams and Brown, 2012) to manage ungulates in national parks and elsewhere. In this approach, the model is used as an embodiment of our current understanding of ecosystem functioning. Management is used as a tool to test our hypotheses via models of those hypotheses. We then learn from agreements or disagreements between the model and observed responses to management, and we improve our models accordingly. This approach was recommended to improve the management of brucellosis in elk and bison in the Yellowstone ecosystem (NAS, 2017), and more generally to facilitate the use ecosystem science in natural resource management (Williams, 2013).

7.6 Agricultural Ecosystems: Cropland Management before 1968

Cropland management in the US Great Plains prior to the 1970s generally consisted of plowing native grasslands, followed by annual plowing to control weeds and prepare seedbeds, and often leaving portions of fields fallow for a year to store water in the soil profile (National Research Council, 2010). The consequences of these management practices were dramatic losses of soil organic carbon through respiration as CO_2 and nitrogen via volatilization of NH_3, N_2O, and N_2 and leaching of NO_3^-. Carbon, nitrogen, phosphorus, and other nutrients were also lost through water and wind erosion. These practices led to losses of soil fertility that were replaced with increasing applications of fertilizer.

7.6.1 Emergence of Agroecosystem Management: 1968–1980

A transformation in tillage agriculture began along with the development of the ecosystem concept and the systems ecology paradigm in grazing-land science and management. Several soil scientists from various institutions (Colorado State University, USDA Agricultural Research Service, University of Saskatchewan, University of Alberta) associated with the IBP Grassland Biome developed an understanding of the dynamics of soil functioning and health (belowground ecosystems). These scientists, along with US and international systems ecology collaborators, laid the scientific basis for modern crop agriculture: agroecosystems (Lowrance et al., 1984).

As awareness of "belowground ecosystems" emerged, basic research at the NREL, funded by the National Science Foundation and the USDA ARS, deciphered the roles of soil fauna, bacteria, and fungi, the dynamics of carbon, nitrogen, and phosphorus, and the role of soil structure and soil aggregates in soils of the western Great Plains (Coleman et al., 1983; see Chapter 6). Simulation modeling was established as an essential part of research programs (Cole and Heil, 1981; McGill et al., 1981; Parton et al., 1983; see Chapter 4). Research to this point in time had focused on the ecological site or smaller scales of ecological resolution (see Chapter 6), which posed limitations requiring further exploration (Anderson et al., 1983; Schimel et al., 1985; Woodmansee, 1990). Limitations within landscapes and adjacent ecological sites or patches, based on vegetation communities and soil polypedons, can have dramatically different structural and functional properties (see Chapters 1 and 6). And yet, these differences are the norm, and conclusions based on a generalized ecological site can be very misleading (Woodmansee, 1990). Emerging from these studies were concepts of ecological hierarchies – ecological site, catena, landscape, and larger "regional" ecosystems. The landscape-scale ecosystem was first introduced in NSF-funded programs: the Nitrogen Cycling project (Woodmansee, unpublished data, 1978, funded NSF proposal; Schimel et al., 1985), Shortgrass Steppe LTER project (Woodmansee, unpublished data, 1982, funded NSF proposal), and in the Great Plains project (Cole, unpublished data, 1983, funded NSF proposal).

The Great Plains project was a collaborative effort of scientists from the NREL, USDA ARS, and numerous other departments from Colorado State University and other universities. The project goals included the study and evaluation of various tillage and no-tillage practices on the H_2O, C, N, and P dynamics of agricultural ecosystems or agroecosystems. Field experiments, laboratory studies, and modeling were used for the study at several locations in the Great Plains. The project helped lay the scientific and theoretical foundation for modern agroecosystem management practices, not only in the US but also in many locations around the world (see Chapters 3 and 4).

Examples of contributions from the Great Plains Project are:

- Quantification of the processes and their controls involving C, N, P, and H_2O under various tillage practices (Paustian et al., 1997; see Chapter 4).
- Quantification of pools of organic matter and nutrients in agroecosystems (Cole et al., 1993).
- Expansion of ecological-scale system behavior to landscapes and regions (Burke et al., 1990).

7.6.2 Emergence of Agroecosystem Management: 1980s to 1990s

Research findings emerged from many locations around the world supporting the notion that these new agricultural practices could greatly improve "soil health," lower the costs of fertilizer, reduce erosion and pollution, and reduce fossil fuel consumption (National Research Council, 2010). Toward the end of the twentieth century, the role of agriculture as a contributor to global change (e.g., through greenhouse gas emissions, carbon sequestration, and nitrogen loading into the atmosphere, groundwater, rivers, streams, and oceans) was being quantified. Much of the research was intertwined with mathematical models that were rapidly improving to the extent of near predictive ability (see Chapter 4). With the use of these models, the expansion of spatial scales from ecological sites to landscapes, regions, and the globe was made possible.

During the 1980s and 1990s, the acceptance by researchers of minimum or no-tillage agriculture became evident in many countries. Alternatively, the widespread acceptance by farmers and ranchers was slow to develop (see Chapter 13).

7.6.3 Expansion of Agroecosystem Management: 2000 to Present

Since the turn of the century, acceptance of the systems ecology approach to crop management and sustainability has become widespread. In 2010, the US National Research Council published a report, *Toward Sustainable Agriculture Systems in the 21st Century*, highlighting advances and challenges in agricultural systems since the 1990s (National Research Council, 2010). Key elements from that report are:

- Remarkable emergence of innovations and technological advances in sustainable agriculture have been made.
- The agricultural sector is expected to produce adequate food, fiber, and feed, and contribute to biofuels to meet the needs of a rising global population.
- The agricultural sector must continue to meet production demands while enduring diminished natural resources, climate disruptions, and negative consequences of some agricultural production practices.
- Societal expectations for improved environmental, community, labor, and animal welfare standards in agriculture are bringing increased political and economic pressures to bear the agricultural sector.

This report recognized the concept of "ecologically based farming systems," where tremendous progress has been made over the past two decades. The report also proposed four goals of sustainability:

- Satisfy human food, feed, and fiber needs, and contribute to biofuel needs.
- Enhance environmental quality and the resource base.
- Sustain the economic viability of agriculture.
- Enhance the quality of life for farmers, farm workers, and society as a whole.

These four goals are laudable, yet how are they to be achieved? We believe the systems ecology paradigm described in this book represents the right science at the right time to address the daunting current and future challenges mentioned above.

Interactions of agroecosystems with local-to-global changes, such as climate, the carbon, nitrogen, phosphorus, and hydrologic cycles, air and water pollution, and erosion and sedimentation, are all increasingly well understood. This can be largely attributed to the knowledge gained from basic and applied research, such as that described in Chapters 6 and 8, and the continued improvement and reliability of simulation and decision support models (see Chapter 4).

7.6.4 The Importance of the Systems Ecology Paradigm in Agriculture

The importance of the systems ecology approach and modeling to agroecosystem research and management cannot be overstated. Farming and ranching systems are too complex (too many variables) to comprehend without systematic and holistic analysis. This is especially true when evaluating landscape to regional to global scales of interactions.

7.6.5 Working Models Being Used for Agroecosystem Research and Management

One of the major research efforts from the Great Plains and Atmosphere Biosphere projects was the development of the Century model (see Chapter 4). The initial goal of the model was to simulate the impact of agricultural management practices in the Great Plains on crop yields and soil C and nutrient dynamics. The model was also designed to represent the impacts of rangeland management practices on ecosystem dynamics for Great Plains grasslands.

As discussed in Chapter 4, continued development of the Century model yielded the DayCent model that has been utilized to simulate soil C dynamics, crop yields, soil nutrient dynamics, and trace gas fluxes from all of the major crops and crop rotations (corn, wheat, barley, soybeans, sorghum, sugarcane, alfalfa). The simulations use observational data sets from sites across the globe (the US, Australia, China, Brazil, Argentina, Germany, the UK, Canada).

7.7 Status of Research, Management, and Policies Going Forward in the Twenty-First Century

An increased knowledge on belowground ecosystems, controls of plant production and decomposition, nutrient cycling in ecological site scale soils, landscape ecology, and the ability to build simulation models of ecosystem functioning has laid the biological and soil science foundation for reduced tillage or no-till management and precision agriculture. Precision agriculture is also dependent on satellite, aerial (now drone),

GIS, and GPS technology for implementation (see Chapters 4 and 5). The scientific and technological knowledge is now available with the potential to greatly improve modern agriculture and achieve these goals.

The COMET-Farm model (Paustian et al., 2012; NREL, 2018c) is a powerful example of the integration of science and technology through modeling. It is a decision support model that uses components of DayCent (see Chapter 4), and is a whole farm and ranch carbon and greenhouse gas accounting system. The tool guides users by describing their farm and ranch management practices, including alternative future management scenarios. Once complete, a report is generated that compares the carbon changes and greenhouse gas emissions between their current management practices and future scenarios (Paustian et al., 2010; see Chapter 4).

Another example is the recent focus on nonfood-based biofuels, such as switchgrass, miscanthus, poplar, and agricultural residues, and how they are incorporated into current farming practices. The feasibility of using these alternate crops is being evaluated using various models, such as DayCent (see Chapter 4).

A major goal of these efforts is to facilitate the adoption of improved land management practices to mitigate greenhouse gas emissions in an economically and environmentally sustainable fashion (see Chapter 8). Researchers will accomplish this by providing the knowledge and tools needed by land managers and policy makers to design and implement land use-based mitigation strategies, including greenhouse gas emission reductions, carbon sequestration, and bioenergy production (NAS, 2018). Implementing such strategies can provide a new source of income to farmers and ranchers, from both the emergence of emission reduction trading systems, currently under development, and as energy producers. Additional benefits of greenhouse gas mitigation practices include improved air, water, and soil quality.

7.8 Summary

This chapter gives a few examples of the strength of using the systems ecology paradigm to better comprehend grazingland, forestland, and agricultural ecosystems functions, which is essential to guide the development of "best management practices." The integration of basic and applied sciences to support policy and management decision making is likewise essential as we continue to seek long-term sustainability.

Appendix 7.1 Contribution of Plant Ecology to the Evolution of the Systems Ecology Paradigm

The metaphor of dwarfs standing on the shoulders of giants seems apropos here.[1] We also add that the dwarfs need to be propped up by colleagues and collaborators.

The evolution of the systems ecology paradigm and "ecosystem management" can be traced back to the development of plant ecology in North America (Figure 7.3). Late in the nineteenth century, Eugenius Warming, considered to by many to be the founder of plant ecology, published the first textbook on the subject, *Lehrbuch der ökologischen Pflanzengeographie* (Warming, 1896). This book, and other publications by Warming, had a strong influence on Henry Cowles and Frederic Clements, early founders of plant ecology in America (Humphrey, 1961). The dominant focus of plant ecology early in the twentieth century were the observations and descriptions of plants, plant

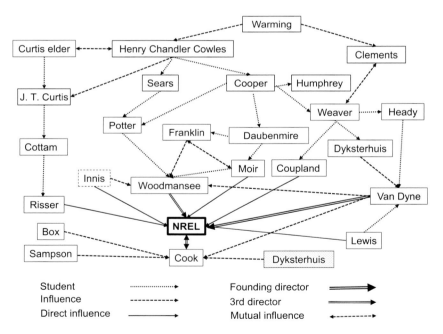

Figure 7.3 Diagram of the influence of western United States plant ecologists on the development of the NREL.

[1] https://en.wikipedia.org/wiki/Standing_on_the_shoulders_of_giants.

community structure, and structural dynamics or succession (Cowles, 1899; Cooper, 1913; Clements, 1916). The analyses were based on aboveground plant structures and plant communities in relation to their environment. Belowground components of plants and plant communities were largely unrecognized, with a few exceptions (e.g., Weaver and Clements, 1935).

Henry Cowles is best known for his descriptions of plant community succession on sand dunes in Indiana (Cowles, 1899). Clements is most noted for his concepts of ecological succession leading to "climax vegetation" (Clements, 1916) and his strong influence on the development of plant ecology in the Great Plains and the southwestern region of the US (Humphrey, 1961). He published many papers on vegetation in the West.

Cowles is also known for the students he mentored while at the University of Chicago, notably William Cooper and Paul Sears, both influential in the development of plant ecology in the western US. Also notable were the accomplishments of his graduate students, including western plant ecologists John Weaver, Rexford Daubenmire, Robert Humphrey, and Loren Potter.

Sears, most noted for *Deserts on the March* (Sears, 1935), was the major professor of Estella Leopold (PhD), daughter of Aldo Leopold and Loren Potter (MS). John Weaver published many papers and books describing the vegetation and ecology of the North American prairies (Weaver and Clements, 1938; Weaver, 1968). Rexford Daubenmire is most noted for his contribution to quantitative plant ecology, plant community classification, and the concept of potential vegetation at a given site. His book *Plant Communities: A Textbook of Plant Synecology* is a classic (Daubenmire, 1968). Robert Humphrey published many papers and a book, *Range Ecology* (Humphrey, 1962), covering an array of topics about the plant ecology of arid and semi-arid lands of the southwest US. Loren Potter was one of the few other classically trained plant ecologists in the southwest. His "Phytosociological study of San Augustin Plains, New Mexico" (Potter, 1957) was his most notable contribution.

As with their predecessors, early plant ecologists were classically trained academics who mentored younger scientists. However, by the mid-twentieth century, two parallel perspectives of plant ecology emerged; one basic, the other applied (range and forest management). John Weaver was the major professor for many notable young scientists who had a great impact on the field of plant ecology. E. J. Dyksterhuis was one of the most prominent and influential plant ecologists in the field of rangeland management (Dyksterhuis, 1951). Robert Coupland became a leading plant ecologist in Canada and was one of the founders of the Canadian Grassland Biome of the IBP. Harold Heady was one of the founders of the Society for Range Management, co-author of *Rangeland Ecology and Management* (Heady and Child, 1999), and the major advisor of George Van Dyne, founder of the NREL and first Director of the US Grassland Biome, US IBP.

Rexford Daubenmire, another Cooper student, was a major professor for Jerry Franklin, known as the "father of the new forestry" (Franklin, 2017) and William Moir, who had a short but influential tenure with the Grassland Biome and the Range Science Department at Colorado State University. He later became a prominent plant ecologist with the US Forest Service (Moir et al., 1997; Moir and Block, 2001). Moir was Robert G. Woodmansee's major professor (PhD). Loren Potter was Woodmansee's MS degree advisor. Woodmansee became a postdoc on the grassland ecosystem modeling team (ELM), a Professor of Range Science, and the third Director of the NREL.

Arthur Sampson and C. Wayne Cook were notable scholars, although not from the linage of plant ecologists described above, yet they had a significant influence on the development of ecosystem science. Sampson has been called the first range ecologist and the father of range management. His book, *Range and Pasture Management*, was the first applied plant ecology textbook dealing with arid and semi-arid lands (Sampson, 1923). The early emphasis in range management was to maximize livestock production or forage production – the focus was on aboveground components (structure).

During the 1950s and 1960s, the ecological focus of plant ecology shifted from descriptive ecology and ecological succession to energy flow in ecosystems (Odum and Odum, 1963) and above and belowground ecological processes (Chapter 6). The shift in range management transitioned from maximum production and forage to optimization, taking into account other rangeland resources – now called ecosystem services (Chapter 6). Central to this shift was an emphasis on the ecophysiology of plants, for example primary production and plant nutrition, and the recognition of the importance of roots and of carbon as the backbone of primary production rather than energy flow – a vastly important concept in modeling (DayCent, Chapter 4; Savanna, Chapter 9) and nutrient cycling.

C. Wayne Cook, a prominent range scientist and plant ecologist at Utah State University, came to Colorado State University in 1968 to establish a Rangeland Ecosystem Science (RES) program in the Range

Science Department. Cook's concept was to build graduate and undergraduate programs based on transdisciplinary studies of primary and secondary producers, decomposers, soils, hydrology, and economics. The program was based on both applied and basic science and was complimentary and interactive with the developing NREL. Several RES faculty contributed to the IBP Grassland Program from which many NREL staff and students received their degrees. Some of these graduates went on to obtain academic appointments in the department.

A blending of basic and applied plant ecology and systems ecology occurred during the 1970s a result of the research, training, and outreach at the NREL, the Range Science Department, and their national and international collaborators. This led to a focus on concepts such as processes that control primary production (Chapter 6), use of livestock as a tool for managing vegetation (Chapter 6), and optimization of ecosystem services and rangeland health (National Research Council, 1994).

The emerging understanding of fundamental ecosystem processes (primary production, nutrient cycling, hydrologic cycle) brought about by the systems ecology approach, supported by simulation modeling, led to the transformation of policies and practices of grazingland management in the US, Canada, and Australia, among others.

References

Anderson, D., Heil, R. C., Cole, C. V., and Deutsch, P. (1983). Identification and characterization of ecosystems at different integrative levels. In *Nutrient Cycling in Agricultural Ecosystems*, ed. R. R. Lowrance, R. L. Todd, L. E. Asmussen, and R. A. Leonard. Special Publication No. 23. Athens, GA: University of Georgia, College of Agriculture Experiment Stations.

Baker, B. W., Peinetti, H. R., Coughenour, M. B., and Johnson, T. L. (2012). Competition favors elk over beaver in a riparian willow ecosystem. *Ecosphere*, 3 (11), 95.

BANR (2018). Bioenergy Alliance Network of the Rockies. Natural Resource Ecology Laboratory. http://banr.nrel.colostate.edu/ (accessed June, 25, 2018).

Baron, J. S., ed. (1992). *Biogeochemistry of a Subalpine Ecosystem: Loch Vale Watershed.* New York: Springer Verlag.

  ed. (2002). *Rocky Mountain Futures: An Ecological Perspective.* Washington, DC: Island Press.

Baron, J. S., Hartman, M. D., Band, L. E., et al. (2000). Sensitivity of a high-elevation rocky mountain watershed to altered climate and CO2. *Water Resources Research*, 36(1), 89–99.

Baron, J. S., Ojima, D. S., Holland, E. A., et al. (1994). Analysis of nitrogen saturation potential in Rocky Mountain tundra and forest: Implications for aquatic systems. *Biogeochemistry*, 27(1), 61–82.

Baron, J. S., Rueth, H. M., Wolfe, A. M., et al. (2000). Ecosystem responses to nitrogen deposition in the Colorado Front Range, ed. J. Baron. *Ecosystems*, 3 (4), 352–68 (2002).

Baron, J. S., Schmidt, T. W., and Hartman, M. D. (2009). Climate-Induced Changes in High Elevation Stream Nitrate Dynamics. *Global Change Biology*, 15: 1777–1789.

BLM. (2016). Little Snake Resource Management Plan. USDI Bureau of Land Management. https://eplanning.blm.gov/epl-front-office/eplanning/planAndProjectSite.do?methodName=dispatchToPatternPage&currentPageId=93686 (accessed June, 25, 2018).

Boone, R. B. (2007). Effects of fragmentation on cattle in African savannas under variable precipitation. *Landscape Ecology*, 22, 1355–69.

Boone, R. B., Coughenour, M. B., Galvin, K. A., and Ellis, J. E. (2002). Addressing management questions for Ngorongoro Conservation Area, Tanzania, Using the Savanna Modeling System. *African Journal of Ecology*, 40, 138–58.

Boone, R. B., Galvin, K. A., BurnSilver, S. B., Thornton, P. K., Ojima, D. S., and Jawson, J. R. (2011). Using coupled simulation models to link pastoral decision making and ecosystem services. *Ecology and Society* 16(2), 6. www.ecologyandsociety.org/vol16/iss2/art6/.

Bradford, J. B., and Hobbs, N. T. (2008). Regulating overabundant ungulate populations: An example for elk in Rocky Mountain National Park, Colorado. *Journal of Environmental Management*, 86, 520–8.

Bureau of Land Management (BLM) (2018). Moving toward an ecosystem services and management framework among federal agencies. USDI Bureau of Land Management. https://nespguidebook.com/ecosystem-services-and-federal-agencies/introduction/.

Burke, I. C., Schimel, D. S., Yonker, C. M., et al. (1990). Regional modeling of grassland biogeochemistry using GIS. *Landscape Ecology*, 4(1), 45–54.

Carson, R. (1962). *Silent Spring*. Boston: Houghton Mifflin Company.

CDPHE. (2018). Rocky Mountain National Park Initiative. Colorado Department of Public Health and Environment. www.colorado.gov/pacific/cdphe/rocky-mountain-national-park-initiative (accessed June, 25, 2018).

Christensen, L., Burnsilver, S., and Coughenour, M. (2006). Integrated assessment of the dynamics, stability, and resilience of the Inner Mongolian grazing ecosystems. *Nomadic Peoples*, 9, 131–45.

Christensen, N. L., Bartuska, A. M., Brown, J. H., et al. (1996). The report of the Ecological Society of America committee on the scientific basis for ecosystem management. *Ecological Applications*, 6(3), 665–91.

Clements, F. E. (1916). *Plant Succession: An Analysis of the Development of Vegetation*. Publication No. 242. Washington, DC: Carnegie Institute of Washington.

Cole, C. V., and Heil, R. D. (1981). Phosphorus effects on terrestrial nitrogen cycling. In *Terrestrial Nitrogen Cycles: Processes, Ecosystem, Strategies and Management Impacts*, ed. F. E. Clark and T. Rosswall. Ecological Bulletin, 33. Stockholm: Swedish Natural Science Research Council, 363–74.

Cole, C. V., Paustian, K., Elliott, E. T., et al. (1993). Analysis of agroecosystem carbon pools. *Water, Air and Soil Pollution*, 70, 357–71.

Coleman, D. C., Cole, C. V., and Elliott, E. T. (1983). Decomposition, organic matter turnover, and nutrient dynamics in agroecosystems. In *Nutrient Cycling in Agricultural Ecosystems*, ed. R. R. Lowrance, R. L. Todd, L. E. Asmussen, and R. A. Leonard. Special Publication No. 23. Athens, GA: University of Georgia, College of Agriculture Experiment Stations.

Cooper, W. S. (1913). The climax forest of Isle Royale, Lake Superior, and its development. *Botanical Gazette*, 55, 1–44.

Coughenour, M. B. (1991). Grazing responses of upland steppe in Yellowstone's Northern winter range. *Journal of Applied Ecology*, 28, 71–82.

   (1992). Spatial modeling and landscape characterization of an African pastoral ecosystem: A prototype model and its potential use for monitoring drought. In *Ecological Indicators*, vol. 1, ed. D. H. McKenzie, D. E. Hyatt, and V. J. McDonald. London and New York: Elsevier Applied Science, 787–810.

   (1994). Elk carrying capacity on Yellowstone's northern elk winter range: Preliminary modeling to integrate climate, landscape, and elk nutritional requirements. In *Plants and Their Environments: Proceedings of the First Biennial Scientific Conference on the Greater Yellowstone Ecosystem, Mammoth Hot Springs, 1991*, Technical Report NPS/NRYELL.NRTR-93/XX, ed. D. Despain. Denver: USDI/NPS, 97–112.

   (1999). *Ecosystem Modeling of the Pryor Mountain Wild Horse Range*. Final Report to US Geological Survey. Fort Collins, CO: National Park Service, and Bureau of Land Management, Biological Resources Division.

   (2000). Ecosystem modeling of the PMWHR: Executive summary. In *Managers' Summary: Ecological Studies of the Pryor Mountain Wild Horse Range, 1992–1997*, ed. F. J. Singer and. K. A. Schoenecker. Fort Collins, CO: US Geological Survey, Midcontinent Ecological Science Center, 125–31.

   (2002a). Ecosystem modeling in support of the conservation of wild equids: The example of the Pryor Mountain Wild Horse Range. In *Equids: Zebras, Asses and Horses: Status Survey and Conservation Action Plan*, ed. P. D. Moehlman. IUCN/SSC Equid Specialist Group. Gland, Switzerland and Cambridge: IUCN, 174.

   (2002b). Elk in the Rocky Mountain National Park Ecosystem: A model-based assessment. Final Report to USGS Biological Resources Division, Fort Collins, CO, and US National Park Service, Rocky Mountain National Park.

   (2005a). Plant biomass and primary production on bison and elk ranges in Yellowstone National Park: Data synthesis and ecosystem modeling. Part 1: Final report to US Geological Survey, Biological Resources Division, Bozeman, MT.

   (2005b). Interactions between grazing herbivores and herbaceous vegetation on a heterogeneous landscape: Yellowstone National Park. Part 2: Final report to US Geological Survey, Biological Resources Division, Bozeman, MT.

   (2005c). Bison and elk in Yellowstone National Park: Linking ecosystem, animal nutrition, and population processes. Part 3: Final report to US Geological Survey, Biological Resources Division, Bozeman, MT.

   (2006). Ecosystem research and modeling in protected areas with large mammals: Yellowstone as a case study. In *Wildlife in Shiretoko and Yellowstone National*

238 · **Robert G. Woodmansee et al.**

Parks: Lessons in Wildlife Conservation from Two World Heritage Sites, ed. D. R. McCullough, K. Kaji, and M. Yamanaka. Hokkaido, Japan: Shiretoko Nature Foundation, 165–75.

(2012). The use of ecosystem simulation modeling to assess feed availabilities for large herbivores in heterogeneous landscapes. In *Conducting National Feed Assessments*, ed. M. B. Coughenour and H. P. S. Makkar. Animal Production and Health Manual No. 15. Rome: FAO.

Coughenour, M. B., McNaughton, S. J., and Wallace, L. L. (1984). Simulation study of Serengeti perennial graminoid responses to defoliation. *Ecological Modeling*, 26, 177–201.

Coughenour, M. B., and Singer, F. J. (1996a). Elk population processes in Yellowstone National Park under the policy of natural regulation. *Ecological Applications*, 6, 573–93.

(1996b). Yellowstone elk population responses to fire: A comparison of landscape carrying capacity and spatial-dynamic ecosystem modeling approaches. In *The Ecological Implications of Fire in Greater Yellowstone*, ed. J. Greenlee. Fairfield, WA: International Association of Wildland Fire, 169–80

Cowles, H. C. (1899). *The Ecological Relations of the Vegetation on the Sand Dunes of Lake Michigan*. Chicago: University of Chicago Press.

Daubenmire, R. F. (1968). *Plants Communities: A Textbook of Plant Synecology*. New York, Evanston, London: Harper & Row.

Despain, D., Houston, D., Meagher, M., and Schullery, P. (1986). *Wildlife in Transition: Man and Nature on Yellowstone's Northern Range*. Boulder, CO: Roberts Rinehart.

Detling, J. K. (1998). Mammalian herbivores: Ecosystem level effects in two national parks. *Wildlife Society Bulletin*, 26, 438–48.

Dyksterhuis, E. J. (1951). Use of ecology on range land. *Journal of Range Management*, 4, 319–22.

Ehrlich, P. R. (1968). *The Population Bomb*. New York: Sierra Club/Ballantine.

Elser, J. J., Andersen, T., Baron, J. S., et al. (2009). Shifts in lake N: P stoichiometry and nutrient limitation driven by atmospheric nitrogen deposition. *Science*, 326 (5954), 835–7.

Enders, S. K., Pagani, M., Pantoja, S., et al. (2008). Compound-specific stable isotopes of organic compounds from lake sediments track recent environmental changes in an alpine ecosystem, Rocky Mountain National Park, Colorado. *Limnology and Oceanography*, 53(4), 1468–78.

Evangelista, P. H., Kumar, S., Stohlgren, T. J., et al. (2008). Modelling invasion for a habitat generalist and a specialist plant species. *Diversity and Distributions*, 14, 808–17.

Fahnestock, J. T., and Detling, J. K. (1999a). The influence of herbivory on plant cover and species composition in the Pryor Mountain Wild Horse Range, USA. *Plant Ecology*, 144, 145–57.

(1999b). Plant responses to defoliation and resource supplementation in the Pryor Mountains. *Journal of Range Management*, 52, 263–70.

Forest Restoration. (2018). Forest restoration. USDA Forest Service. www.fs.fed.us/restoration/index.shtml (accessed June 25, 2018).

Forrester, J. W. (1961). *Industrial Dynamics*. Cambridge, MA: MIT Press.

(1968). *Principles of Systems*. Cambridge, MA: Wright-Allen Press.

Frank, D., and McNaughton, S. J. (1992). The ecology of plants, large mammalian herbivores, and drought in Yellowstone National Park. *Ecology*, 73, 2043–58.

Franklin, J. F. (1989). Toward a new forestry. *American Forests*, 95, 11–12.

(2017). Understanding and managing forests as ecosystems: A reflection on 60 years of change, and a view to the Anthropocene. *The Pinchot Letter*, 19 (1), 24–9. www.pinchot.org/doc/612 (accessed June 25, 2018).

Franklin, J. F., Johnson, K. N., and Johnson, D. L. (2017). *Ecological Forest Management*. Chicago: Waveland Press.

Fullman, T. J., Bunting, E. L., Kiker, G. A., and Southworth, J. (2017). Predicting shifts in large herbivore distributions under climate change and management using a spatially-explicit ecosystem model. *Ecological Modeling*, 352, 1–18.

Galvin, K. A., Reid, R. S., Behnke, Jr., R. H., and Hobbs, N. T., eds. (2008). *Fragmentation in Semi-arid and Arid Landscapes: Consequences for Human and Natural Systems*. Dordrecht: Springer.

Galvin, K. A., Thornton, P. K., de Pinho, J. R., Sunderland, J., and Boone, R. B. (2006). Integrated modeling and its potential for resolving conflicts between conservation and people in the rangelands of East Africa. *Human Ecology*, 34, 155–83.

Gerhardt, T., and Detling, J. K. (2000). Summary of vegetation dynamics at the Pryor Mountain Wild Horse Range, 1992–1996. In *Managers' Summary-Ecological Studies of the Pryor Mountain Wild Horse Range, 1992–1997*, ed. F. J. Singer and K. A. Schoenecker. Fort Collins, CO: United States Geological Survey – USDI.

Harden, G. (1968). The tragedy of the commons. *Science*, 162(3859), 1243–8.

Hartman, M. D., Baron, J. S., Ewing, H. A., et al. (2014). Combined global change effects on ecosystem processes in nine US topographically complex areas. *Biogeochemistry*, 119(1–3), 85–108.

Heady, H., and Child, R. D. (1999). *Rangeland Ecology and Management*. New York: Avalon Publishing.

Hilbers, J. P., Van Langevelde, F., Prins, H. H. T., et al. (2015). Modeling elephant-mediated cascading effects of water point closure. *Ecological Applications*, 25, 402–15.

Hobbs, N. T., Galvin, K. A., Stokes, C. J., et al. (2008). Fragmentation of rangelands: Implications for humans, animals, and landscapes. *Global Environmental Change – Human and Policy Dimensions*, 18, 776–85.

Holling, C. S. (1978). *Adaptive Environmental Assessment and Management*. New York: John Wiley and Sons.

Humphrey, H. B. (1961). *Makers of North American Botany*. New York: Ronald.

Humphrey, R. R. (1962). *Range Ecology*. New York: Ronald Press Co.

Innis, G. S., ed. (1978). *Grassland Simulation Model*. Ecological Studies, 26. New York: Springer.

Lafrancois, B. M., Nydick, K. R., Johnson, B. M., et al. (2004). Cumulative effects of nutrients and pH on the plankton of two mountain lakes. *Canadian Journal of Fisheries and Aquatic Sciences*, 61(7), 1153–65.

Lauenroth, W. K., and Burke, I. C., eds. (2008). *Ecology of the Shortgrass Steppe: A Long-Term Perspective*. Oxford: Oxford University Press.

Liedloff, A. C., Coughenour, M. B., Ludwig, J. A., and Dyer, R. (2001). Modelling the trade-off between fire and grazing in a tropical savanna landscape, northern Australia. *Environment International*, 27, 173–80.

Lovelock, J., and Margulis, L. (1974). Atmospheric homeostasis by and for the biosphere: The Gaia hypothesis. *Tellus*, 26(1–2), 2–10.

Lowrance, R., Stinner, B. R., and House, G. J., eds. (1984). *Agricultural Ecosystems.* New York: John Wiley and Sons.

Ludwig, J. A., Coughenour, M. B., Liedloff, A. C., and Dyer, R. (2001). Modelling the resilience of Australian savanna systems to grazing impacts. *Environment International*, 27, 167–72.

LVWSP (2018). The Loch Vale Watershed Program. USDI USGS and Natural Resource Ecology Laboratory. www2.nrel.colostate.edu/projects/lvws/index .html (accessed June 25, 2018).

Mast, M. A., Clow, D. W., Baron, J. S., et al. (2014). Links between N deposition and nitrate export from a high-elevation watershed in the Colorado Front Range. *Environmental Science & Technology*, 48(24), 14258–65.

McGill, W. B., Hunt, H. W., Woodmansee, R. G., and Reuss, J. O. (1981). Phoenix: A model of the dynamics of carbon and nitrogen in grassland soils. In *Terrestrial Nitrogen Cycles: Processes, Ecosystem, Strategies and Management Impacts*, ed. F. E. Clark and T. Rosswall. Ecological Bulletin, 33. Stockholm: Swedish Natural Science Research Council, 49–115.

McNaughton, S. J. (1976). Serengeti migratory wildebeest: Facilitation of energy flow by grazing. *Science*, 191, 92–4.

(1979). Grassland–herbivore dynamics. In *Serengeti: Dynamics of an Ecosystem*, ed. A .R. E. Sinclair and M. Norton-Griffiths. Chicago: University of Chicago Press, 46–81.

Meadows, D. H., Meadows, D. L., Randers, J., and Benhrens III, W. W. (1972). *The Limits to Growth: A Report for the Club of Rome's Project on the Predicament of Mankind*. New York: New American Library.

Meixner, T., Bales, R. C., Williams, M. W., et al. (2000). Stream chemistry modeling of two watersheds in the Front Range, Colorado. *Water Resources Research*, 36(1), 77–87.

Metzger, K., Coughenour, M., Reich, R., and Boone, R. B. (2005). Effects of season of grazing on vegetation diversity, composition, and structure in a semi-arid ecosystem. *Journal of Arid Environments*, 61, 147–60.

Milne, E., Williams, S., Bationo, A., et al. (2015). *Grazing Lands, Livestock and Climate Resilient Mitigation in Sub-Saharan Africa*. www.vivo.colostate.edu/ lccrsp/reports/GrazingLandsLivestockClimateMitigation_Paper1_ Final6Aug2015editedv4a.pdf (accessed June 25, 2018).

Moir, W. H., and Block, W. M. (2001). Adaptive management on public lands in the United States: Commitment or rhetoric? *Environmental Management*, 28(2), 141–8.

Moir, W. H., Geils, B. W., Benoit, M. A., and Scurlock, D. (1997). Ecology of southwestern ponderosa pine forests: A literature. Gen. Tech. Rep. RM-292. Fort Collins, CO: US Department of Agriculture, Forest Service, Rocky Mountain Forest and Range Experiment Station. NAS (National Academies of Sciences, Engineering, and Medicine). (2017). *Revisiting Brucellosis in the*

Greater Yellowstone Area. Washington, DC: The National Academies Press. https://doi.org/10.17226/24750. www.nap.edu/catalog/24750/revisiting-brucellosis-in-the-greater-yellowstone-area (accessed August 12, 2020).

NAS (National Academies of Sciences, Engineering, and Medicine) (2018). *Negative Emissions Technologies and Reliable Sequestration: A Research Agenda*. National Academies of Sciences, Engineering, and Medicine. Washington, DC: The National Academies Press. https://doi.org/10.17226/25259 (accessed August 12, 2020).

National Research Council. (1994). *Rangeland Health: New Methods to Classify, Inventory, and Monitor Rangelands*. Washington, DC: The National Academies Press.

(2010). *Toward Sustainable Agricultural Systems in the 21st Century*. Washington, DC: The National Academies Press.

(2013). *Using Science to Improve the BLM Wild Horse and Burro Program: A Way Forward*. Washington, DC: The National Academy Press. www.nap.edu/catalog/13511/using-science-to-improve-the-blm-wild-horse-and-burro-program (accessed August 12, 2020).

NCCASC. (2018). North Central Climate Adaptation Science Center. Natural Resource Ecology Laboratory. http://nccsc.colostate.edu (accessed June 26, 2018).

NEON. (2018). Central Plains Experimental Range - CPER. www.neonscience.org/field-sites/field-sites-map/CPER (accessed June, 25, 2018).

Newman, G., Wiggins, A., Crall, A., et al. (2012). The future of citizen science: Emerging technologies and shifting paradigms. *Frontiers in Ecology and the Environment*, 10(6), 298–304.

NFF. (2016). Collaborative Restoration Workshop. The 2016 Collaborative Restoration Workshop, Denver Colorado, National Forest Foundation. www.nationalforests.org/collaboration-resources/collaborative-restoration-workshop (accessed August 17, 2018).

NREL. (2018a). Ecosystem management. Natural Resource Ecology Laboratory. www.nrel.colostate.edu/research/ecosystem-management/ (accessed June 25, 2018).

(2018b). Wildlife management. Natural Resource Ecology Labratory. www.nrel.colostate.edu/research/wildlife-management/ (accessed June 26, 2018).

(2018c). COMET-Farm. Natural Resource Ecology Laboratory and USDA. http://cometfarm.nrel.colostate.edu (accessed June 26, 2018).

Nydick, K. R., Lafrancois, B. M., Baron, J. S., et al. (2004). Nitrogen regulation of algal biomass, productivity, and composition in shallow mountain lakes, Snowy Range, Wyoming, USA. *Canadian Journal of Fisheries and Aquatic Sciences*, 61(7), 1256–68.

Odum, E. P., and Odum, H. T. (1963). *Fundamentals of Ecology*, 2nd edn. E. P. Odum in collaboration with H. T. Odum. Philadelphia and London: W. B. Saunders.

O'Reilly, C. M., Sharma, S., Gray, D. K., et al. (2015). Rapid and highly variable warming of lake surface waters around the globe. *Geophysical Research Letters*, 42 (24): 1–9.

Parton, W. J., Anderson, D. W., Cole, C. V., and Stewart, J. W. B. (1983). Simulation of soil organic matter formation and mineralization in semiarid agroecosystems. In *Nutrient Cycling in Agricultural Ecosystems*, ed. R. R. Lowrance, R. L. Todd, L. E. Asmussen, and R. A. Leonard. Special Publication No. 23. Athens, GA: University of Georgia, College of Agriculture Experiment Stations.

Paul, E. A. (2015). *Soil Microbiology, Ecology and Biochemistry*, 4th edn. San Diego, CA: Elsevier, Academic Press.

Paustian, K., Elliott, E. T., and Killian, K. (1997). Modeling soil carbon in relation to management and climate change in some agroecosystems in central North America. In *Soil Processes and the Carbon Cycle*, ed. R. Lal, J. M. Kimble, R. F. Follett, and B. A. Stewart. Boca Raton, FL: CRC Press, 459–71.

Paustian, K. H., Ogle, Stephen M., and Conant, Rich T. (2010). Quantification and decision support tools for US agricultural soil carbon sequestration. In *ICP Series on Climate Change Impacts, Adaptation, and Mitigation; Volume 1, Handbook of Climate Change and Agroecosystems Impacts, Adaptation, and Mitigation*, ed. D. Hillel and C. Rosenzweig. London: Imperial College Press, 307–41.

Paustian, K., Schuler, J., Killian, K., et al. (2012). COMET 2.0: Decision support system for agricultural greenhouse gas accounting. In *Managing Agricultural Greenhouse Gases: Coordinated Agricultural Research through GraceNet to Address Our Changing Climate*, ed. M. Liebig, A. Franzluebbers, and R. Follett. San Diego, CA: Academic Press, 251–70.

Peinetti, H. R., Baker, B. W., and Coughenour, M. B. (2009). Simulation modeling to understand how selective foraging by beaver can drive the structure and function of a willow community. *Ecological Modeling*, 220, 998–1012.

Plumb, G .E., White, P. J., Coughenour, M. B., and Wallen, R. L. (2009). Carrying capacity and migration of Yellowstone bison: Implications for conservation. *Biological Conservation* 142, 2377–87.

Potter, L. D. (1957). Phytosociological study of San Augustin Plains, New Mexico. *Ecology*, 27(2), 113–36.

Reid, R. S. (2012). *Savanas of Our Birth*. London: University of California Press.

Romme, W. H, Whitby, T. G., Tinker, D. B., and Turner, M. G. (2016). Deterministic and stochastic processes lead to divergence in plant communities 25 years after the 1988 Yellowstone fires. *Ecological Monographs*, 86, 327–51.

Rueth, H. M., Baron, J. S., and Allstott, E. J. (2003). Responses of Engelmann spruce forests to nitrogen fertilization in the Colorado Rocky Mountains. *Ecological Applications*, 13(3), 664–73.

Rykiel, E. (1999). Ecosystem science at the Natural Resource Ecology Laboratory. *BioScience*, 49(1), 69–70.

Sampson, A. W. (1923). *Range and Pasture Management*. New York: John Wiley.

Schimel, D. S., Stillwell, M. A., and Woodmansee, R. G. (1985). Biogeochemistry C, N, and P in a soil catena of the shortgrass steppe. *Ecology*, 66, 276–82.

Sears, P. B. (1935). *Deserts on the March*. Norman: University of Oklahoma Press.

Singer, F. J., Johnson, T., Ziegenfuss, L. C., Coughenour, M., Bowden, D., and Moses, M. (1998b). Population estimation, plant interactions, forage biomass, and consumption and carrying capacity estimation of elk in the Estes Valley. Final report to US National Park Service, Rocky Mountain National Park. Fort Collins, CO: Colorado State University and US Geological Survey.

Singer, F. J., Swift, D. M., Coughenour, M. B., and Varley, J. (1998a). Thunder on the Yellowstone revisited: An assessment of natural regulation management of native ungulates, 1968–93. *Wildlife Society Bulletin*, 26, 375–90.

Singer, F. J., Zeigenfuss, L. C., Lubow, B., and Rock, M. J. (2002a). Ecological evaluation of the potential overabundance of ungulates in U.S. national parks: A case study. In *Ecological Evaluation of the Abundance and Effects of Elk Herbivory in Rocky Mountain National Park, Colorado, 1994–1999*, ed. F. J. Singer and L. C. Zeigenfuss, 205–48. Open-File Report 02-208. Fort Collins, CO: US Geological Survey.

Singer, F. J., and Zeigenfuss, L. C., eds. (2002b). *Ecological Evaluation of the Abundance and Effects of Elk Herbivory in Rocky Mountain National Park, Colorado, 1994–1999*. Open-File Report 02-208. Fort Collins, CO: US Geological Survey.

Stohlgren, T. J., Binkley, D., Chong, G. W., et al. (1999). Exotic plant species invade hot spots of native plant diversity. *Ecological Monographs*, 69, 25–46.

Suttie, J. M., Reynolds, S. G., and Batello, C., eds. (2005). *Grasslands of the World*. Food and Agriculture Organization of the United Nations. Plant Production and Protection Series No. 34. www.fao.org/docrep/008/y8344e/y8344e00.htm (accessed June 25, 2018).

Teague, W. R., Kreuter, U. P., and Fox, W. E. (2009a). Economically efficient rangeland management to sustain ecosystem function and livelihoods. *Range and Animal Sciences and Resources Management*, vol. 2. www.eolss.net/Sample-Chapters/C10/E5-35-26.pdf (accessed July 18, 2018).

Teague, W. R., Kreuter, U. P., Grant, W. E., Diaz-Solis, H., and Kothmann, M. M. (2009b). Economic implications of maintaining rangeland ecosystem health in a semi-arid savanna. *Ecological Economics*, 68(5), 1417–29.

Theobald, D. M., and Romme, W. H. (2007). Expansion of the US wildland–urban interface. *Landscape and Urban Planning*, 83(4), 340–54.

Thornton, P. K., BurnSilver, S. B., Boone, R. B., and Galvin, K. A. (2006). Modelling the impacts of group ranch subdivision on agro-pastoral households in Kajiado, Kenya. *Agricultural Systems*, 87, 331–56.

TNC. (2018). The Nature Conservancy. www.nature.org/en-us/. (accessed October, 18, 2018).

US Department of Agriculture Agricultural Research Service (USDA ARS) (2018). Rangeland Resources and Systems Research: Fort Collins, CO. www.ars.usda.gov/plains-area/fort-collins-co/center-for-agricultural-resources-research/rangeland-resources-systems-research/docs/rrsr/central-plains-experimental-research-location/ (accessed June 25, 2018).

USDI (2007). Elk and vegetation management plan, Rocky Mountain National Park, Colorado. Washington, DC: US Department of the Interior, National Park Service. www.nps.gov/romo/learn/management/elk-and-vegetation-management-plan.htm (accessed August 12, 2020).

USFS. (2016). Northwest forest plan. USDA Forest Service. www.fs.fed.us/r6/reo/ (accessed June 25, 2018).

Van Dyne, G. (1969). *The Ecosystem Concept in Natural Resource Management*. New York: Academic Press.

Von Bertalanffy, L. (1968). *General Systems Theory: Foundations, Development, Applications*. New York: George Braziller.

Warming, E. (1896). *Lehrbuch der ökologischen Pflanzengeographie*. Berlin: Gebrüder Borntraeger.

Weaver, J. E. (1968). *Prairie Plants and Their Environment: A Fifty-Year Study in the Midwest*. Lincoln, NE: University of Nebraska Press.

Weaver, J. E., and Clements, F. E. (1938). *Plant Ecology*. New York: McGraw-Hill.

Weisberg, P., and Coughenour, M. (2003). Model-based assessment of aspen responses to elk herbivory in Rocky Mountain National Park, U.S.A. *Environmental Management*, 32, 152–69.

Weisberg, P., Coughenour, M., and Bugmann, H. (2006). Modelling of large herbivore–vegetation interactions in a landscape context. In *Large Herbivore Ecology and Ecosystem Dynamics*, ed. K. Danell, R. Bergstrom, P. Duncan, and J. Pastor. Cambridge: Cambridge University Press.

Weisberg, P., Hobbs, N. T., Ellis, J., and Coughenour, M. (2002). An ecosystem approach to population management of ungulates. *Journal of Environmental Management*, 65, 181–97.

Williams, B. K. (2011). Adaptive management of natural resources: Framework and issues. *Journal of Environmental Management*, 92, 1346–53.

Williams, B. K., and Brown, E. D. (2012). *Adaptive Management: The U.S. Department of the Interior Applications Guide*. Washington, DC: US Department of the Interior, Adaptive Management Working Group.

Williams, B. K., Wingard, G. L., Brewer, G., et al. (2013). U.S. Geological Survey ecosystems science strategy – Advancing discovery and application through collaboration: U.S. Geological Survey Circular 1383–C. Reston, VA: US Geological Survey.

Williams, G. W. (2005). *The USDA Forest Service: The First Century*. FS-650. Washington, DC: USDA Forest Service.

Wolfe, A. P., Van Gorp, A. C., and Baron, J. S. (2003). Recent ecological and biogeochemical changes in alpine lakes of Rocky Mountain National Park (Colorado, USA): A response to anthropogenic nitrogen deposition. *Geobiology*, 1(2), 153–68.

Woodmansee, R. (1990). Biogeochemical cycles and ecological hierarchies. In *Changing Landscapes: An Ecological Perspective*, ed. I. S. Zonneveld and R. T. T. Forman. New York: Springer, 57–71.

World Bank. (2018). Forest area (% of land area). World Bank. https://data .worldbank.org/indicator/AG.LND.FRST.ZS (accessed June 25, 2018).

Yellowstone National Park. (1997). *Yellowstone's Northern Range: Complexity and Change in a Wildland Ecosystem*. Mammoth Hot Springs, WY: USDI, National Park Service.

Zeigenfuss, L. C., Singer, F. J., and Bowden, D. (2002a). Vegetation responses to natural regulation of elk in Rocky Mountain National Park. Biological Science Report USGS/BRD/BSR-1999-0003. Denver: US Government Printing Office.

Zeigenfuss, L. C., Singer, F. J., Williams, S. A., and Johnson, T. L. (2002b). Influences of herbivory and water on willow in elk winter range. *Journal of Wildlife Management*, 66, 788–95.

8 · *Land/Atmosphere/ Water Interactions*

ROBERT G. WOODMANSEE,
MICHAEL B. COUGHENOUR, WEI GAO,
LAURIE RICHARDS, WILLIAM J. PARTON,
DAVID S. SCHIMEL, KEITH PAUSTIAN,
STEPHEN OGLE, DENNIS S. OJIMA,
RICHARD CONANT, AND
MATHEW WALLENSTEIN

No man is an island.

John Donne, 1572–1631

8.1 Introduction

This chapter describes ongoing research and outreach aimed at climate change, CO_2 dynamics and carbon sequestration, large-scale nitrogen dynamics, UV-B effects on ecosystems, and atmospheric deposition programs. The research described emphasizes activities conducted by the Natural Resource Ecology Laboratory (NREL) scientists and their collaborators. However, full recognition is acknowledged for the essential role played by the global network of cooperating scientists who conducted related activities. The phrase "No man is an island" noted at the beginning of the chapter is true now more than ever.

The emphasis herein is on regional to global challenges (see Chapter 2) and the various programs that have emerged to address them. These programs are based on fundamental understanding of the functioning of ecosystems and their management (Chapters 6 and 7) and the expanding knowledge on the interactions of croplands, grazinglands, and forests with surface waters and the atmosphere. Land-use changes and their interactions with changing climates, greenhouse gas dynamics, and altered nutrient fluxes are a central focus. Further research is vital for mitigation of and adaptation to changing climate and chemical and radiation environments.

The history of the development of the NREL and the expertise in land/atmosphere/water interactions shared by their collaborators is a

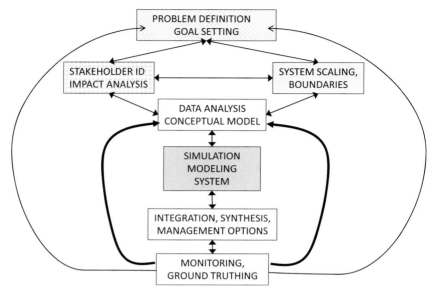

Figure 8.1 Steps in the system ecology approach used to collaboratively and systematically address important challenges facing society.

powerful demonstration of the application of the systems ecology approach (Figure 8.1; see Chapter 1). Over five decades the iterative nature of the approach ultimately led to an increased understanding of how ecosystems function and improved the confidence in predictive capability. The application of the approach over time demonstrated the power of long-term sustainability of a single research organization.

As with the other chapters in this book, we will cite only a few of the key publications that have been generated through these programs. The references in the works cited here will guide readers to more thorough literature reviews. Additionally, we will make liberal use of internet links to (1) current activities that describe ongoing research programs, (2) websites that describe governmental and institutional programs of relevance, and (3) resources for online data.

8.2 Early Work in the International Biological Program: 1967 through the Late 1970s

Measurements of net primary production in grasslands using CO_2 exchange chambers (Figure 8.2) were attempted in the earliest days

(a)  (b)

Figure 8.2 (a) Early photosynthesis/CO_2 chamber exposed to sun – could not control radiation load. For color version, please see plate section. A black and white version of this figure will appear in some formats. (b) Early photosynthesis/CO_2 chamber – even when cooling infrastructure insulated, radiation load was difficult to control. A black and white version of this figure will appear in some formats. For the color version, please refer to the plate section.

of the International Biological Program (IBP) (Brown and Trlica, 1977; Detling et al., 1978; Williams and Kemp, 1978). These site-scale measurements were intended to determine photosynthesis and plant respiration which proved to be extremely difficult due to insufficient technology for monitoring temperature, humidity, and radiation. Furthermore, the overwhelming importance of soil microbial respiration (Coleman et al., 1983; Paul, 2014) was not appreciated. However, these early studies and the simulation modeling of CO_2 exchange set the stage for more sophisticated field experiments and subsequent modeling.

Measurements of the abiotic driving variables for temperature, radiation, precipitation, evaporation, evapotranspiration, and runoff were the early emphases of the IBP efforts. These measurements were made at weather stations at many sites in the Grassland Biome network (Lauenroth and Burke, 2008; see Chapter 4) and were analyzed for a basic understanding of the H_2O dynamics of grasslands. Results from these analyses provided critical driving variable data for the Grassland Ecosystem Model – ELM (Innis, 1978).

These early studies, though crude compared to today's standards, were critical to increase the understanding of grassland ecosystems function (Lauenroth and Burke, 2008). They demonstrated how the blending of empirical field and laboratory science, in addition to the systems ecology approach and modeling, would lead to major breakthroughs in our awareness of the structure and function of ecosystems.

Equally important was the use of these results as critical driving variables of CO_2 dynamics (e.g., net primary production, soil respiration) to develop simulation models that would later promote the concept of land, atmosphere, and surface water interactions, that is, greenhouse gas dynamics, consequences of climate change in terrestrial ecosystems, nitrogen transport, and loading in ecosystems (see Chapter 4).

8.3 Expansion from the Late 1970s and 1980s to the Present

8.3.1 Interactions between Modeling, Field, and Laboratory Studies

Following the earlier learning experiences in ecosystem analysis and the systems ecology approach through the IBP, new lines of discovery related to gaseous exchanges of C, N, and S were opened up by the late 1970s based on the power of the following projects:

1. *Belowground Ecosystems* (1975), principal investigator (PI): DC Coleman, Co-PIs: C. V. Cole, D. Klein, and C. P. P. Reid, funded by NSF);
2. *Effects of SO$_2$ on Grasslands* (1976), PI: R. G. Woodmansee, Co-PI: J. L. Dodd, and later W. K. Lauenroth funded by US Environmental Protection Agency (EPA)
3. *Nitrogen Cycling in Grasslands* (1977), initially funded by NSF, PI: R. G.Woodmansee, Co-PIs: H. W. Hunt and J. L. Dodd; 1979 PI: R. G. Woodmansee, Co-PI: W. J. Parton and W. Laycock;
4. *Great Plains* (1981), PI: C. V. Cole, Co-PIs: G. Peterson, R. D. Heil, D. C. Coleman, and J. Doran, funded by NSF and the US Department of Agriculture (USDA) Agricultural Research Service (ARS).

The structures of the fundamental biogeochemical cycles, C, N, P, S, and H_2O had been articulated and modeled at ecological site scales of resolution (Woodmansee, 1975; Coughenour et al., 1979; Cole and Heil, 1981; McGill et al., 1981; Parton et al., 1983; Schimel et al., 1985). The importance of gaseous exchanges of C, N, and S were beginning to emerge, as was the vital role of soil microorganisms in C, N, and P transformations (Woodmansee, 1978; Woodmansee et al., 1978; Paul, 2014).

8.3.2 SO$_2$ and Grasslands

One of the first ecosystem-level research projects at the NREL after the IBP was a study funded by the EPA and led by NREL scientists Jerold Dodd and William Lauenroth (who were involved in the IBP research), to investigate the potential effects of sulfur dioxide (SO$_2$) pollution from coal-burning power plants on grasslands in southern Montana (Preston et al.,1981). This study ran from 1974 to 1979 and while it involved researchers from several institutions, most components were carried out by NREL scientists. The centerpiece of this project was an in-situ SO$_2$ exposure study in a southern Montana grassland in which large plots were continuously exposed to three different concentrations of SO$_2$ (Heitschmidt et al., 1978; Lauenroth et al., 1979). Studies were carried out on direct and indirect impacts of SO$_2$ on primary production, plant species composition, decomposition, nutrient cycling, forage quality, soil water dynamics, soil microbiota, and insects. Many of the study's methodologies and concepts were developed during the IBP Grassland Biome Program, and like the IBP studies this was a systems-level study that recognized the importance of interconnections among ecosystem processes. Ecosystem modeling was carried out using the follow-on version of the ELM model (Coughenour, 1978; Coughenour et al., 1980), which later came to be known as "strip-ELM" because it was used to study the impacts of coal strip-mining in Wyoming and Montana.

The study also investigated interactions between SO$_2$ and the terrestrial sulfur cycle (Coughenour, 1978; Coughenour et al., 1981). SO$_2$ sulfur can be incorporated into the sulfur cycle through gaseous dry deposition on leaves and soil. SO$_2$ is not only dry-deposited on surfaces, it is taken up through the stomatal openings of leaves and dissolved in plant moisture once it is inside the leaf (Coughenour et al., 1979; Lauenroth et al., 1979) and is translocated to roots (Coughenour, 1981). A model of these processes entails atmospheric processes, physics of gas transport, as well as biophysics and plant ecophysiology (Coughenour, 1981). From leaves, roots, litter, and soil it is cycled in parallel with nitrogen through plant uptake and tissue turnover to soil microbiota. Adding to an early version of the PHOENIX biogeochemical model (McGill et al., 1981), sulfur was modeled similarly to nitrogen.

Regulation of C/N/S ratios in plants and microbes was an important modeling concept as it provides feedback control over element flows to and from plants and microbes as well as affecting nutrient dynamics and thus ecosystem dynamics (Coughenour, 1981). Sulfur is an essential plant nutrient and it can limit plant growth under certain conditions, thus potentially affecting primary production and other processes. The study demonstrated that the terrestrial ecosystem interacts with the atmosphere through biogeochemical nutrient fluxes as well as through direct effects of gases on plant growth.

8.3.3 Second-Generation Studies of the N Cycle

Second-generation studies of the nitrogen cycle included additions and losses of N, especially gaseous NH_3 and N_2O from grazinglands (Schimel, 1986; see Chapter 4). At that time, N_2O was not well appreciated as a greenhouse gas. Additionally, the importance of within-landscape transfers and spatial variability in N dynamics was initiated (Hutchinson and Viets, 1969; Senft et al., 1987). The N dynamics model PHOENIX was completed during this period (McGill et al., 1981). This model linked C and N but did not include losses of NH_3 or N_2O. Later, versions of Century (DayCent), simulated N_2O production from ecosystems, with field studies and use of these models continuing today.

A principle goal of the Great Plains project was to examine the effect of various tillage practices on soil fertility, especially C, N, and P (see Chapter 7). The project was a superb example of the integration of field, laboratory, and modeling research and the application of the systems ecology approach. Although a primary focus of the project was soil fertility, it soon became recognized that a major issue facing agriculture was the loss of soil organic matter. As soil organic matter is decomposed, CO_2 is released. As soil organic matter is formed, C is chemically bound (sequestered). It would take a few more years before the importance of these dynamics in greenhouse gas gains and losses would be appreciated.

One of the most important products of the Great Plains Project was the development of the aforementioned simulation model, Century (see Chapter 4). The Century model, developed from the original grassland ecosystem model ELM, became the standard for models of C, N, and P dynamics, primary production (CO_2 uptake), and decomposition (microbial respiration and CO_2 production).

Shortly following the initiation of the Nitrogen Cycling and Great Plains projects, in 1982 the Shortgrass Steppe Long-Term Ecological Research Project (LTER) was funded by NSF, entitled *Ecology of the Shortgrass Steppe: A Long-Term Perspective* (R. G. Woodmansee, PI and W. K. Lauenroth and W. A. Laycock, Co-PIs).[1] In conjunction with USDA ARS researchers, new techniques were developed for field measurements of CO_2 and nitrogen gas exchange using chambers and eddy correlation techniques combined with modeling (Mosier et al., 2008).

Research in the late 1980s and 1990s utilized the systems ecology approach (Figure 8.1), setting the stage for the NREL and its collaborators to fully engage in national and international programs such as the Intergovernmental Panel on Climate Change. That engagement continues today.

8.3.4 Plant and Ecosystem Responses to Increasing CO_2 and Climate Change

As interest in global climate change began to heighten in the late 1980s and early 1990s, and interest in potential effects of rising atmospheric carbon dioxide (CO_2) concentrations on ecosystems also heightened. The US Department of Energy was particularly interested in this topic, given that fossil fuels are a primary source of CO_2 emissions. Both the climatic effects of rising concentrations of greenhouse gases and the direct physiological effects of elevated CO_2 were anticipated to have plant-through ecosystem-level consequences. Such ecological changes were in turn expected to have feedbacks to climate through their effects on biophysical properties of the land surface. Prediction of ecological responses to CO_2 and climate change was proposed to require simulation of the interaction of different ecological processes at multiple temporal scales. There was no modeling approach in 1988 that explicitly synthesized predictions at the scales of leaves, plants, communities (ecological sites), ecosystems (landscapes), and regions, although paradigms had been proposed (Kittel and Coughenour, 1988).

Scientists at the NREL were well-positioned to carry out assessments of potential impacts of rising CO_2 on ecosystems, given their whole-

---

[1] In early 1982, R. G. Woodmansee was recruited by the NSF to become program director for ecosystem studies. The NSF required him to relinquish his leadership of the Nitrogen Cycling project and the Shortgrass Steppe LTER Program. W. J. Parton assumed leadership of the former and W. K. Lauenroth the latter.

system approach that integrates plant ecophysiology, soil processes involved in carbon and nitrogen transformations, and soil moisture dynamics. For example, a model of plant growth (GRASS) that was originally developed in the early 1980s to mechanistically explain graminoid responses to herbivory and climate in the Serengeti ecosystem (Coughenour, 1984; Coughenour et al., 1984) could be useful to examine CO_2 impacts. This model was in disuse for nearly a decade, but with funding from the Department of Energy (DOE) in 1989–92 it was revitalized and revised to address grassland responses to CO_2 and climate (Coughenour et al., 1993). The original GRASS soil water and heat flow routine was replaced with a well-established model (Parton, 1978) which was used in a similar manner later and given the name "SoilWat" (Sala et al., 1992; Lauenroth and Bradford, 2006). In GRASS2, however, transpiration was explicitly simulated through stomatal functioning and transpiration and bare soil evaporation rates were calculated as part of leaf and soil surface energy balances. In order to represent CO_2 responses, a detailed C3 and C4 photosynthesis submodel was developed (Chen et al., 1993). Most herbs, trees, and cool-season grasses have the C3 photosynthetic pathway, but warm season and tropical grasses use the C4 pathway. The submodel for C3 photosynthesis was based on the model of Farquhar et al. (1980), while the C4 photosynthesis submodel was entirely original (Chen et al., 1993). Stomatal conductance was coupled with photosynthetic assimilation rate as in Ball et al. (1987), an approach used in many other subsequent land surface models. As in the original model, fixed carbon was partitioned to plant tissues and labile carbohydrate reserves were dynamically simulated. GRASS2 was also linked with a daily time step implementation of decomposition and nitrogen cycling processes in the Century soil organic matter model (CSOM) (Parton et al., 1987) to form what was subsequently referred to as the GRASS-CSOM model. The linked ecosystem model was applied to examine ecosystem-level responses to CO_2, temperature, precipitation, and global-warming scenarios in grasslands of Colorado, Kansas, and Kenya (Coughenour and Parton, 1995; Parton et al., 1996; Coughenour and Chen, 1997). The model predicted that increased temperatures would decrease primary production at current CO_2 levels, but decreases were reversed by doubling atmospheric CO_2 concentration (Coughenour and Chen, 1997). In addition to the "fertilizing" effect of CO_2 on C3 photosynthesis, an important component of CO_2 response was an increase in water use efficiency resulting from stomatal closure in both C3 and C4 species. At current atmospheric CO_2 levels, projected climate changes resulted in little change or decreased NPP and SOM; however, doubling CO_2 offset negative effects of climate change. A similar set of experiments was carried out with a subsequent version of the model (Chen et al., 1996). Although CO_2 and climate directly affect plant processes such as photosynthesis, the outcomes here were emergent, system-level responses involving numerous interactions and feedbacks among plant and soil processes, among carbon, nitrogen, and water flows, and involving energy and mass transfers between the atmosphere and the terrestrial ecosystem. For example, while CO_2 may stimulate photosynthesis, plant growth is constrained by nitrogen availability, and while CO_2 affects plant water use, plant water use affects soil moisture which may then affect decomposition rate. This type of modeling has developed considerably since then and has been widely used to assess the role of terrestrial ecosystems in the global carbon budget (see Chapters 4 and 7).

8.3.5 Modeling Atmosphere–Biosphere Interactions

The National Science Foundation in 1989 initiated a competition for National Science and Technology Centers. The NREL and the Department of Atmospheric Sciences (DAS) at Colorado State University (CSU) collaborated to propose the Center for Analysis of the Dynamics of Regional Ecosystems (CADRE). The total funding request was $27,500,000 for five years. The proposed principal investigators were R. G. Woodmansee (NREL), J. E. Ellis (NREL), T. H. Vander Haar (DAS), R. A. Pielke (DAS), and J. K. Detling (NREL). The primary theme of the proposal was to integrate ecosphere, atmosphere, and social interactions at the scale of the North American Great Plains using the systems ecology paradigm (SEP) as described in this book. CADRE ranked number three in the NSF competition. Two centers were funded. However, as Roger Pielke (personal communication) would later say, "CADRE was the most successful failed proposal I ever worked on." His comment was based on collaborations such as that described next and subsequent research efforts.

Our interests in ecosystem responses to atmospheric changes associated with greenhouse gases, particularly CO_2, coupled with our systems approach, naturally led to consideration of interactions between vegetation and land surface processes with atmospheric processes as being system-level processes involving bidirectional feedbacks between terrestrial ecosystems and atmospheric systems. Assuming such feedbacks exist, unidirectional assessments that do not consider them could lead to inaccurate conclusions. NREL scientists, in their traditional interdisciplinary fashion, collaborated with atmospheric scientists to consider these questions (Coughenour et al., 1993). Fortunately, a very strong team of atmospheric scientists at CSU were responsive. In particular, a team led by Roger Pielke in the Atmospheric Sciences Department had been carrying out research examining the effects of land surfaces and land surface changes on atmospheric processes (Pielke et al., 1991, 1993, 1999; Chase et al., 1999). This team developed a widely used model of atmospheric processes at mesoscales called RAMS (Regional Atmospheric Modeling System) that was well suited for studying the effects of land surfaces on the atmosphere due to its relatively high degree of spatial resolution (Pielke et al., 1992; Walko et al., 2000; Liston et al., 2001). Collaborative research between the Pielke team and NREL researchers began in the late 1980s (Kittel and Coughenour, 1988; Schimel et al., 1991; Pielke et al., 1993).

One of the first joint projects between NREL and Atmospheric Sciences was carried out with funding from the DOE during 1989–92 (Coughenour et al., 1993). In addition to developing the GRASS-CSOM ecosystem model (Coughenour and Chen, 1997), the researchers developed a biophysical land surface model (LSM) called the general energy and mass transport model (GEMTM) (Chen and Coughenour, 1994). GEMTM was what has since been recognized as a third-generation LSM. LSMs are key components of all climate models as they represent the surface energy balance and fluxes of water and energy between the atmosphere, soil, and vegetation. Water vapor flux from the land surface determines the partitioning of energy between latent and sensible heat fluxes. Pitman (2003) reviewed the evolution of LSMs, distinguishing between first-generation models which represented a single bulk surface resistance to water vapor flux, second-generation models which distinguished stomatal from physical controls on water vapor flux, and third-generation models which linked stomatal fluxes of water vapor to photosynthesis and carbon allocation in the plant, thereby enabling simulation of aboveground and belowground plant growth. Pitman referred to this as the "greening" of LSMs.

The development of a "greened" LSM set the stage for the work toward the ultimate goal of a coupled atmosphere–ecosystem model. A fully coupled model would enable assessments of the two-way interactions and feedbacks between the atmosphere, soil, and vegetation, and it would enable assessments of the effects of land-cover changes and vegetation responses to rising temperatures and CO_2 on weather and climate. This was the goal of a project carried out by NREL and CSU Atmospheric Science researchers during 1995–9. The project was funded by the Terrestrial Ecology and Global Change Program (TECO), an interagency collaboration by NSF, DOE, NASA, and USDA. The plant models contained in GEMTM (Chen and Coughenour, 1994) were integrated into a climate version of the Regional Atmospheric Modeling System (RAMS), with the coupled modeling system being called GEMRAMS. During the first two years of the project, D. X. Chen, M. Coughenour (NREL), and Bob Walko (DAS) completed the initial coupling. There was a considerable learning curve on the part of the ecologists to become familiar with the large, complex atmospheric model and its computer code. Chen then left the project and an atmospheric science graduate student, Joseph Eastman, picked up where Chen left off. This team used the coupled model to carry out several experiments on a regional scale to examine how elevated CO_2, ecological processes, and land-use change exhibit dominant effects on both meteorological and ecological states (Eastman et al., 2001a, 2001b). Such results had not been demonstrated with any other modeling system, and to our knowledge, at that time this was the only modeling system of its kind. Importantly, photosynthesis and stomatal functioning were simulated on a diurnal basis, a time step that is compatible with diurnal energy and water fluxes represented in RAMS. Furthermore, photosynthetic carbon was used to simulate plant growth and these plant processes were affected by soil moisture. Thus, the plant and RAMS models were fully interactive.

The first set of experiments examined the differences between current and potential natural vegetation, doubling of atmospheric CO_2 concentration, and changes in solar radiation due to a doubling of CO_2 in a region covering central US (Eastman et al., 2001a). Averaged across the region, natural vegetation produced lower temperatures and lower precipitation. Vegetation responses to a doubling of CO_2 produced lower maximum temperatures, higher minimum temperatures, and reduced precipitation. Changes in radiation due to a doubling of CO_2 were minimal. There was a high degree of variation in responses across the region, and there were interesting teleconnections with changes in vegetation in one area affecting climate in other areas. The second set of experiments examined the effects of grazing and CO_2 (Eastman et al., 2001b). The experiment was designed to examine climate responses to the presence of millions of bison that once roamed the Great Plains. In the absence of grazing, maximum temperatures were cooler and precipitation was reduced. The study showed that grazing does influence regional climate and needs to be accounted for in regions where grazing is significant. These two sets of experiments demonstrated the importance of plant responses to CO_2, land use, grazing, and subsequent feedbacks to the atmosphere due to changes in albedo and surface energy balances.

GEMRAMS was also used to examine the effects of land-use/land-cover changes on the atmosphere in southern South America (Beltrán-Przekurat et al., 2012). Shifts from grassland to agriculture caused cooler and wetter conditions. Conversion from wooded grasslands and forests to agriculture caused warmer temperatures. In Australia, GEMRAMS was used to investigate the potential significance of vegetation responses to elevated CO_2 and land-cover changes (Narisma et al., 2003; Narisma and Pitman, 2004). GEMRAMS simulates reduced stomatal conductance and increased vegetation growth under elevated CO_2, both of which can affect atmospheric processes. While a decrease in stomatal conductance may lead to decreased transpiration and elevated surface temperatures, an increase in leaf area may have the opposite effects. These authors referred to the combined response as the "biospheric feedback." Model experiments showed that biospheric feedbacks may reduce effects of land-cover change, therefore these feedbacks must be included to accurately project effects of land-cover changes. Similar conclusions were reached earlier by Betts et al. (1997).

8.4 Decision Support Systems

A vital key to the development of current land/atmosphere activities involving the NREL and their collaborators is the DayCent simulation model, the daughter of Century and granddaughter of ELM (see Chapter 4). DayCent model outputs include daily N-gas flux (N_2O, NO_x, N_2), CO_2 flux from heterotrophic soil respiration, soil organic C and N, NPP, H_2O and NO_3^+ leaching, and other ecosystem parameters.

Major projects led by local, regional, and global analysis researchers rely on DayCent to estimate greenhouse gas (Ogle et al., 2005; Paustian 2014), greenhouse gas mitigation methodologies (Conant et al., 2016), and agricultural decision support systems (COMET-Farm, 2018). COMET, an earlier version of COMET-Farm, is the USDA's official greenhouse gas quantification tool.

COMET-Farm (2018), developed by K. Paustian and colleagues at the NREL and the USDA Natural Resource Conservation Service

(NRCS), is a whole farm and ranch carbon and greenhouse gas accounting system. It uses management practices together with spatially explicit information on climate and soil conditions from USDA databases (automatically provided in the tool) to run a series of models that evaluate sources of greenhouse gas emissions and carbon sequestration. By integrating NRCS Soil Survey Geographic (SSURGO) database and site-specific climate data, locality-specific results are presented to COMET-Farm users. There are several modules nested within the model (i.e., croplands, livestock, agroforestry, energy). COMET-Farm relies on biogeochemical process models, Intergovernmental Panel on Climate Change (IPCC) methodologies, and a number of peer-reviewed research results. The tool guides users through a process to describe their farm and ranch management practices, including alternative future management scenarios. Once complete, a report is generated that compares the carbon changes and greenhouse gas emissions with the user's current management practices and future scenarios.

8.5 Global Changes

The following subsections highlight areas of research conducted by a few NREL scientists, in conjunction with their national and international collaborators and colleagues. John Donne, in 1624, said "No man is an island". This is absolutely true when discussing global change. Collaboration both locally and globally is essential.

8.5.1 Climate Change

Climate change touches everything on Earth: water, agriculture, grassland and forest health, fire and insect outbreaks, biodiversity, and human health. NREL scientists and collaborators are heavily involved in identifying potential impacts, seeking solutions to help mitigate climate change, and exploring strategies for adapting to a climate that will differ from the past.

The food, fuel, fiber, and energy demand of an expanding population have increased the release of gases into the atmosphere acting like the plastic covering over a greenhouse and radiating heat back onto the Earth's surface. This warming drives many other climate features, such as the timing and amount of precipitation and snowmelt, the length of forest growth and fire seasons, the frequency and severity of storms, and high temperature extremes. An increase in carbon dioxide (CO_2) can also directly affect plant growth. Climate change interacts with ecosystem management, sustainable development, and food and water security, and creates challenges for agriculture, forestry, and grazingland sustainability. All ecosystem services are influenced by climate change. Slowing its pace, preventing the worst expected impacts, and adapting to unpreventable changes are the most significant environmental management practices challenging society today. Researchers are tackling climate change methodically and pragmatically by monitoring national and global greenhouse gas emissions, studying the impacts of climate change on grassland, forest, arctic, and agricultural ecosystems, and investigating new ways to educate land and resource managers.

8.5.2 Greenhouse Gas Emissions and Sequestration

The future of greenhouse gas management lies in accurate and consistent measurement of the stocks and flows of carbon dioxide (CO_2), nitrous oxide (N_2O), and other greenhouse gases from agriculture, forests, and other land uses (Ogle, 2014; Paustian, 2014; see Chapter 4). These studies are vital to determining agricultural greenhouse gas emissions and their potential reduction through innovative management. Carbon sequestration, the capture and storage of atmospheric carbon dioxide by plants, oceans, and soil, is considered one of the least expensive options over the short term for reducing atmospheric greenhouse gas concentrations and their associated impact on the climate system.

8.5.3 Greenhouse Gas Mitigation

Greenhouse gas emissions and climate change pose two of the greatest long-term challenges to human society. While fossil fuel combustion is the single greatest source of greenhouse gas, land-use and agricultural activities contribute *almost one-third* of the human-induced warming of the planet. Hence, improved management practices are essential for reducing greenhouse gas (CO_2, N_2O, and CH_4) emissions from land use (Conant et al., 2016). Carbon sequestration – by which carbon dioxide (CO_2) is removed from the atmosphere through the buildup of carbon stocks in soils and biomass with improved land-use practices – is a low-cost, early action mitigation option, which also rebuilds soil fertility. Practices that improve the nitrogen use efficiency of crops can reduce nitrous oxide (N_2O) emissions and greatly enhance environmental quality. Currently, nearly a quarter of the nitrogen fertilizer used (11 million tonnes in the US) is lost from soils, resulting in nitrate pollution of groundwater, coastal "dead-zones," and degradation of pristine ecosystems. Reducing methane (CH_4) emissions from livestock production can increase animal productivity, yield renewable energy (CH_4 capture from manure storage), and improve air quality. Over the longer term, renewable energy from agricultural biomass offers great potential to reduce fossil fuel use. New crops and management systems for bioenergy production are needed to fully realize this potential in an environmentally sustainable way.

The major goal of this research is to facilitate the adoption of improved land management practices to mitigate greenhouse gas emissions in an economically and environmentally sustainable fashion.

8.5.4 Arctic Shrubs and Soil Microbes

In the Alaskan Arctic, the effects of rapid climate warming are appearing across the full spectrum of ecological trophic levels. Receding sea ice and changing wildlife behavior are among the most obvious impacts, but significant changes are also occurring beneath the soil surface. The effects of shrub expansion into the tundra and its influence on altering soil carbon stocks and microbial activity in the carbon–rich soils is an area of active research by NREL staff and collaborators (Wallenstein and Hall, 2012; Bailey et al., 2017). They have found that climate warming facilitates shrub expansion, increasing nitrogen availability and the efficiency of microbial metabolism. Together these factors can facilitate the formation of organic matter, highlighting the resilience and extraordinary carbon storage capacity of the tundra. By using field and laboratory experiments to quantify the interactions of biological, chemical, and physical controls, NREL researchers are gaining a better understanding of carbon cycles in Arctic soils and the complex impacts of climatic change.

8.5.5 The IPCC

NREL scientists have contributed substantially to a better understanding of the impacts of climate change on grassland and forest ecosystems through their research and contributions to the International Panel on Climate Change (IPCC) and the US National Climate Assessments (IPCC, 2018).[2] This team

---

[2] In 2007, current members Drs. Keith Paustian, Stephen Ogle, Kathleen Galvin, and Dennis S. Ojima were acknowledged for their contributions to the IPCC (2018) which received the 2007 Nobel Peace Prize.

of scientists provided estimates for soil CO_2 and N_2O emissions for the greenhouse gas inventory and the resulting climate change effects, and developed the accounting system for agricultural carbon sequestration used in the US voluntary emission reduction program. In addition, NREL studied how climate change will alter plant productivity, soil fertility, and biodiversity and species migration. The NREL documented the impacts of recent large severe fires and insect outbreaks on forest structure, tree regeneration, and carbon storage.

8.5.6 United Nations Framework Convention on Climate Change

Each year, NREL scientists conduct a national inventory of greenhouse gas emissions and carbon sequestration on agricultural lands that is reported to the United Nations Framework Convention on Climate Change (UNFCCC).[3] The annual assessment provides a detailed record of agricultural greenhouse gas emissions since 1990, including nitrous oxide emissions from fertilizers, methane emissions from rice cultivation, and carbon stock changes from both crop and grasslands.

8.5.7 North Central Climate Adaptation Science Center

The US Department of Interior (DOI) North Central Climate Adaptation Science Center (NC CASC)[4] is part of a federal network of eight regional DOI Climate Science Adaptation Centers created to provide scientific information, tools, and techniques that resource managers can use to anticipate, monitor, and adapt to climate change in their region. Dennis S. Ojima served as the NC CASC Director from 2011 to 2017 while housed at CSU. The NC CASC works with natural and cultural resource managers to gather scientific information and build the tools needed to help fish, wildlife, and ecosystems adapt to the impacts of climate change. Since the program's inception, that mandate has been extended to include land, energy, and cultural heritage resources. In addition to creating data sets and models, these centers work directly with resource managers to develop the skills and software needed to maintain resilient and sustainable ecosystems in a changing climate.

The NC CASC extends this vision to the specific regional needs of land and resource managers in the north-central region of the U.S. The

---

[3] ALU, www.nrel.colostate.edu/projects/alusoftware/home/; UNFCCC, https://unfccc .int.

[4] https://casc.usgs.gov/centers/northcentral.

collaborative center provides users with data, technology, and training to incorporate the best possible understanding of past, present, and future climate into the decision process.

The NC CASC seeks to meet the following four goals through cross-sector collaboration and iterative engagement with resource managers, decision makers, and the public.

- Compile existing climate data and projections for use in regional climate models that can inform short-term management objectives.
- Identify climate drivers and their impacts on key regional sectors: natural, cultural, and energy resource and ecosystem goods and services.
- Evaluate vulnerabilities through physical, ecological, and social perspectives, and consider adaptive capabilities with a focus on human livelihood, health, and safety.
- Develop user-driven decision-support tools to develop effective climate change response strategies and resilient management practices.

National and regional collaborators have agreed on a set of guiding principles to ensure that all efforts work toward the center's mission. As a result, the NC CASC strives to:

- Build on existing documents, assessments, indicators, and frameworks so as not to "reinvent the wheel."
- Inform resource managers on the implications of a nonstationary climate where temperature and precipitation events vary over time.
- Prioritize research that is useful for end-users.
- Maintain functionality of the center as a coordinated research team that focuses on regional initiatives.
- Respect the unique demands and constraints of all diverse stakeholders and research partners, each of whom is both limited and guided by different incentives and circumstances.

8.5.8 USDA Climate Hub

USDA's Climate Hubs (USDA CH)[5] is a unique collaboration of departmental agencies led by Agricultural Research Service and Forest Service senior directors located at ten regional locations. Other agencies that contribute to the programs include the Natural Resources

---

[5] www.climatehubs.oce.usda.gov.

Conservation Service, Farm Service Agency, Animal and Plant Health Inspection Service, and the Risk Management Agency. The USDA CH links USDA research and program agencies in their regional delivery of timely and authoritative tools and information to agricultural producers and professionals.

NREL partners with the USDA CH. The hubs develop and deliver information and technologies to agricultural and natural resource managers to enable climate-informed decision making, and to provide access to assistance to implement those decisions.

Vision – robust and healthy agricultural production and natural resources under increasing climate variability and climate change.

Mission – the mission of the Climate Hubs is to develop and deliver science-based, region-specific information and technologies, with USDA agencies and partners, to agricultural and natural resource managers that enable climate-informed decision making, and to provide access to assistance to implement those decisions. This is in alignment with the USDA mission to provide leadership on food, agriculture, natural resources, rural development, nutrition, and related issues based on sound public policy, the best available science, and efficient management.

The NREL provides the Northern Plains Climate Hub with information about how changing weather patterns and atmospheric CO_2 will impact rangeland grazing conditions so that livestock producers can adapt their practices as the climate changes.

8.6 Nitrogen: Another Major Type of Global Change

Nitrogen is essential for all life on Earth, being the stuff of DNA and proteins, but through much of Earth's evolutionary history it has been chronically limiting to the growth of plants and animals (Vitousek et al., 1997; Galloway et al., 2004). While 78 percent of the atmosphere is made up of nitrogen molecules, this elemental dinitrogen (N_2) is unreactive and unavailable for primary productivity. Prior to the advent of agriculture and the industrial revolution, reactive nitrogen was in short supply, coming from only two natural sources: lightning, which provided sufficient energy in the atmosphere to bust the N_2 bonds, and N-fixing organisms such as cyanobacteria and symbiotic N-fixing bacteria that coexist with legumes. Today, societal production of synthetic N fertilizers and combustion-produced reactive N from transportation and industry has far exceeded natural reactive N sources. While that has been a major stimulus to human population numbers, quality of life, and modern society, the unintentional loss of excess reactive nitrogen to the environment is a global-scale change equivalent to that caused by increased greenhouse gas emissions. During the last few decades, the global increase of reactive nitrogen by all human sources has far out-stripped production from all natural terrestrial systems. Since the 1960s, the rate of increase has accelerated sharply (see International Nitrogen Initiative [INI][6]).

Available reactive nitrogen has greatly increased both the human quality of life and population numbers. Approximately 40 percent of the world's population is fed by crops sustained by human-induced formation of reactive nitrogen. At the same time, reactive nitrogen can cascade all through the biosphere, damaging ecosystems and human health. Reactive nitrogen contributes to high concentrations of tropo-spheric, eutrophication of coastal ecosystems, acidification of the ocean, forests, soils, and freshwater streams and lakes, and losses of biodiversity. In the form of nitrous oxide, a greenhouse gas, nitrogen contributes to global warming and stratospheric ozone depletion.

The NREL has been involved with studies that seek to understand N cycling in an ecosystem context since the 1970s. That basic research has been foundational to biogeochemical knowledge and has led logic-ally to ongoing efforts to develop better ways of managing N for its beneficial uses while minimizing the damage caused by N pollution.

8.6.1 Pawnee, the Nitrogen Cycle Project

Nitrogen studies begun by R. G. Woodmansee and his students, in conjunction with the Shortgrass Steppe IBP program, provided some of the earliest studies of nitrogen cycling, whole ecosystem nitrogen budgets, and the responses of nitrogen to various ecosystem processes and disturbances. As mentioned earlier, these provided critical input and validation data for ecosystem models, such as ELM and Century, but the studies themselves stand on their own and continue to be referred to today. Nitrogen cycle and N budget studies described the critical roles of soil organic matter, hillslope geomorphology, and above and below-ground herbivory on soil fertility (Woodmansee et al., 1978; Schimel

---

[6] www.initrogen.org/.

et al., 1985, 1986; Holland and Detling, 1990). Further studies explored the role of fire and grazing on nitrogen cycling, concluding that these natural disturbances were necessary to the continued productivity of grasslands (e.g., Ojima et al., 1994; Milchunas and Lauenroth, 1995). Among other findings, these studies showed that animal waste and the residues of wildfires were important sources of N.

8.6.2 Loch Vale Watershed Study Project

Nitrogen cycling research was initiated in Rocky Mountain National Park (RMNP) with the establishment of the Loch Vale Watershed Long-term Ecological Research and Monitoring Program (LVWSP).[7] The instrumented watershed, ranging from 4,000 masl, down to 3,000 masl, was established in 1982 for the purpose of quantifying the sources and impacts of acidic atmospheric deposition (Baron, 1992). By interpreting data from the Loch Vale National Atmospheric Deposition Program (NADP)[8] site, paleoecological reconstructions of past atmospheric deposition, and from contemporary water quality studies, it became apparent that elevated atmospheric deposition of reactive nitrogen, not acid rain, was the cause of the ecological response (Baron et al., 1986, 2000). Nitrogen in deposition began to increase above background in the mid-twentieth century, caused by post–World War II population growth and development along Colorado's Front Range, and by a growing livestock industry that took advantage of a favorable climate, abundant water supplies from trans-mountain diversions, and corn and soy grown with cheap synthetic N fertilizers (Baron et al. 2004). Commensurate with the increase in N deposition was a shift in lake algal assemblages and an increase in lake productivity (Baron et al. 2000). Follow-on experiments in the alpine and subalpine forests also documented increased microbial N-mineralization rates, and enhanced grass and sedge biomass (Bowman and Steltzer, 1998; Rueth et al., 2003).

Many publications and an external review of the science (Burns, 2004; Baron et al., 2016) concluded that N deposition was affecting the biodiversity and water quality of alpine and subalpine ecosystems of RMNP, in violation of the Clean Air Act Amendments and the Wilderness Act. This prompted the National Park Service, the US EPA, and the State of Colorado to collaborate to develop the Nitrogen

[7] www2.nrel.colostate.edu/projects/lvws/index.html.
[8] http://nadp.sws.uiuc.edu/.

Deposition Reduction Plan (NDRP)[9] (Morris et al., 2014) that sets a trajectory of N emissions reductions from 2007 to 2032 to restore atmospheric deposition loads to at or below the critical load. This unprecedented collaboration calls for voluntary emissions reductions from energy companies, the transportation sector, and agriculture in an attempt to avoid regulatory actions. The final outcome remains to be seen, but stakeholder groups, including Colorado Dairy Farmers and Colorado Livestock Association, meet regularly with scientists and regulators to develop and implement best management practices that will reduce their contribution of pollution to RMNP.

The project is a cooperative effort between the US Geological Survey, National Park Service, and CSU. Major outcomes of the research to date include: (1) small increases in reactive N availability from atmospheric deposition have been found to be sufficient to transform algal assemblages and aquatic and freshwater primary productivity in regions where N had previously been scarce (Baron et al., 2000; Elser et al., 2009); (2) as with the Shortgrass Steppe, additional N altered soil microbial activity and food webs (Boot, et al., 2016); and (3) a socioecological approach toward management that includes local stakeholders, resource managers, and regulatory agencies, which can bring people together to work toward shared goals.

8.6.3 National and International Nitrogen Research

Excess reactive nitrogen poses a severe threat to biodiversity (Simkin et al., 2016), and also causes multiple additional threats to human health and the environment through pathways in the atmosphere, and surface and groundwaters (Vitousek et al., 1997; Galloway et al., 2004). Nitrous oxide released to the atmosphere from soils is a greenhouse gas that contributes to climate change (Pinder et al., 2012). Because so much of the nitrogen used to grow food for the world's population (80 percent) is lost to the environment due to inefficiencies in nitrogen management, it poses an existential threat to humans and the ecosystem on the scale of climate change (Grant et al., 2018).

The combined effects of excess reactive nitrogen from so many sources with so many consequences have made nitrogen excess a global threat (Sutton et al., 2011). Many nitrogen issues can be addressed at local,

---

[9] www.colorado.gov/pacific/cdphe/rocky-mountain-national-park-initiative.

regional, and national scales; however, providing real solutions, such as the one described above for RMNP, remains elusive. As a result, the International Nitrogen Initiative (INI) was established in 2003, with the aim of optimizing nitrogen use in food and energy production and minimizing the consequent harm to humans and the environment. The INI was co-sponsored by the Scientific Committee on Problems in the Environment (SCOPE) and the International Geosphere-Biosphere Program, and is now a sustained partner of Future Earth.[10] The INI is divided into five global regions. The North American Nitrogen Center is charged with assessing how human activity has altered nitrogen flows within North America, determining the environmental, human health, and economic consequences of this alteration, and helping to develop solutions to reduce the problem. Specific goals are to:

- Improve assessments of sources and causes of nitrogen pollution, with an emphasis on evaluating trends in fluxes and environmental exposure.
- Improve assessment of both the ecological and human health consequences of nitrogen pollution in North America.
- Foster the application of judgment of experts to existing knowledge concerning alteration of the nitrogen cycle in order to identify a scientifically credible potential solution.
- Communicate to the public the current scientific knowledge of problems and potential solutions to excess nitrogen in the environment in terms that are relevant to policy making and personal decisions.

Disruption of the global nitrogen cycle is a direct result of human activities, and because so much of it is connected with how people grow, process, transport, and consume their food, solutions by definition must be closely linked with people and society. Nitrogen cycling is a quintessential ecosystem-scale process, but nitrogen management is socioecological at its core. The scientists involved with the INI have been extraordinarily successful at raising awareness of nitrogen issues across Europe, with production of the European Nitrogen Assessment (ENA, 2018), and a number of other initiatives designed to make people and governments move toward improved nitrogen management. Recognizing that nitrogen is vital to our global food system, recent reports have begun to address the connections between diet, human

---

[10] www.futureearth.org/.

health issues such as obesity and heart disease, food waste, and climate change (e.g., Westhoek et al., 2014).

The International Nitrogen Management System (INMS)[11] began in 2017 with support from the Global Environmental Federation to support governments and others through international nitrogen policy processes. The four components of INMS are designed to provide tools for understanding and managing the nitrogen cycle, quantification of nitrogen flows, threats, benefits, and regional demonstrations of how countries can collaborate across boundaries for better understanding and management and raise awareness of nitrogen issues worldwide. INMS participants are inclusive of all parts of the world and all sectors of society. A North American Demonstration[12] project between Canada and the US addresses agricultural and other nitrogen source runoff into Bellingham Bay, and seeks to develop collaborative solutions among citizens, farmers, municipalities, and tribes that protect and enhance the quality of life and economy for all residents, while also improving the environment. By addressing better management across the nitrogen cycle, INMS hopes to contribute to improving economy-wide nitrogen use efficiency, while reducing surplus that would often be wasted as pollution.

8.6.4 National Atmospheric Deposition Program

In 1977, US State Agricultural Experiment Stations (SAES) organized a project, later titled the National Atmospheric Deposition Program (NADP)[13] to measure atmospheric deposition and study its effects on the environment. Jim Gibson, former director of the NREL, was the NADP program coordinator from 1978 to 1997.

Sites in the NADP precipitation chemistry network began operations in 1978 with the goal of providing data on the amounts, trends, and geographic distributions of acids, nutrients, and base cations in precipitation. The network grew rapidly in the early 1980s. Much of this expansion was funded by the National Acid Precipitation Assessment Program (NAPAP), established in 1981 to improve the understanding of the causes and effects of acidic precipitation. Reflecting the federal NAPAP role in the NADP, the network name was changed to NADP National Trends Network (NTN). Today, the NADP is the SAES National

---

[11] www.inms.international/.
[12] www.inms.international/north-america-demonstration/north-america-demonstration.
[13] http://nadp.sws.uiuc.edu/.

Research Support Project – 3. The NTN network currently has 250 sites.

A second network, the Atmospheric Integrated Research Monitoring Network (AIRMoN) joined the NADP in 1992, and currently has seven sites. Although measuring the same chemicals as NTN, AIRMoN sampling is daily rather than weekly. These higher-resolution samples enhance researchers' ability to evaluate how emissions affect precipitation chemistry using computer simulations of atmospheric transport and pollutant removal. This network also evaluates alternative sample collection and preservation methods.

A third network, the Ammonia Monitoring Network (AMoN), joined NADP in 2010. It began as a special study in 2007 and now comprises about 50 monitoring locations. AMoN is the only network that provides a consistent, long-term record of ammonia gas concentrations across the US.

8.6.5 USDA UV-B Monitoring and Research Program

Although ultraviolet (UV) radiation represents only small fraction of the solar radiation reaching the Earth's surface, the UV impacts on the environment, including agricultural crops like corn, soybean, cotton, as well as rangeland grasses and forests, are significant. Because Earth's ecosystems have evolved slowly under the influence of UV radiation, any modification of UV levels must be taken seriously by the scientific community. The Earth's surface has been shielded from harmful UV by the ozone layer in the stratosphere. Measurements in the mid-to-late twentieth century showed significant stratospheric ozone depletion over Antarctic regions (Farman et al., 1985), and similar, though less dramatic, ozone depletion over the Arctic (von der Gathen et al., 1995) driven by anthropogenic ozone-depleting, chlorofluorocarbon compounds. As a result, coincident increases in UV at the surface were observed in these polar regions (e.g., Bernhard et al., 2013). Concern regarding the expansion of these ozone holes, and therefore global increases in surface UV, prompted the creation of the Montreal Protocol in 1987, which initiated a global phase-out of ozone-depleting substances. Recent observations of ozone layer recovery highlight the success of the Montreal Protocol (e.g., Solomon et al., 2016). However, potential reductions in stratospheric ozone resulting from climate change and/or geoengineering (e.g., Shindell et al., 1998; Heckendorn et al., 2009) together with new emissions of certain ozone-depleting substances (e.g., Rigby et al., 2019) contribute to uncertainty of future surface UV radiation.

In response the concerns of increased surface UV radiation, the USDA investigated the need for a nationwide UV-monitoring activity in 1991. Positive responses from the scientific community prompted the USDA to initiate the UV-B Monitoring and Research Program (UVMRP)[14] (Bigelow et al., 1998). Located within NREL at CSU, the program is tasked with establishing a UV climatology and studying the effects of UV radiation on the health of agricultural interests including crop plants, rangelands, and forests. As of this writing, the UVMRP is the only nationwide network monitoring UV irradiance. The network currently consists of 37 climatological monitoring sites and four research sites, most of which are distributed across the US, with an additional site in both Canada and in New Zealand. The sites encompass 20 ecoregions.

The results of the UVMRP data collection and quality control efforts have produced over two decades of high-temporal-resolution surface UV and visible solar irradiances. These data have been used by program staff as well as researchers to address critical research topics in several disciplines including agricultural sciences, medicine, ecology, and atmospheric sciences. Examples include: (1) validation of satellite observations (Xu et al. 2010; Sun et al. 2015), (2) examination of trends of UV radiation across US (Zhang et al., 2019), (3) assessment of the relationship between skin cancer instances and surface UV (Chang et al., 2010), (4) retrieval of UV-related atmospheric parameters such as particulate matter optical properties (Corr et al., 2009) and column ozone (Gao et al., 2001), and (5) investigation of UV interception by tree canopies (Qi et al., 2003). Further, UV index and other derived products are frequently accessed by the agricultural communities and broader public. In total, the UVMRP has users from more than 300 different organizations, including national educational institutions, national governmental agencies, commercial enterprises, and international institutions.

In addition to maintaining climatology data collection, the UVMRP has expanded its objectives to include effects research and integrated assessment. Over a decade of controlled environmental chamber experiments conducted by the UVMRP and its collaborators have evaluated the impacts of factors such as UV, temperature, and water availability and their combined effects on agricultural crops. This includes investigations on the

---

[14] http://uvb.nrel.colostate.edu.

adverse effects of low temperature and drought on plants' physiological, morphological, and phenological parameters such as root structure and seed quality (Singh et al., 2018; Wijewardana et al., 2018). Studies have also identified the detrimental effects of UV exposure on crops (Reddy et al., 2003, 2013, 2016) and how temperature and CO_2 amplified and mitigated these UV effects, respectively (Reddy et al., 2004; Brand et al., 2016). The findings of these studies could allow for selection of cultivars with the best coping ability for future climate change environments.

The UVMRP and its collaborators are also developing a comprehensive predictive system for risk analysis, economic impacts evaluation, and strategic planning to achieve sustainable agricultural development in a changing environment. Recent economically focused analysis indicated a strong causal correlation between crop productivity parameters and environmental variables (Wu et al., 2015; Liang et al., 2017). Further, results suggest that projected climate change may reduce productivity to pre-1980 levels by 2050 under medium to high greenhouse emissions scenarios. Ongoing work involving the coupling of crop growth and climate models will also assess the feedbacks between the agricultural and climate systems under various climate conditions (Xu et al., 2005; Liang et al., 2012). Modeling efforts involving the impact of environmental stress factors on a broader range of plant types are also being conducted to investigate the impacts of these factors at the ecosystem scale. For instance, UV effects on decomposition and nitrogen cycling in semi-arid grasslands are being incorporated into biogeochemical models, with initial analysis showing improved agreement on various ecological variables (Chen et al., 2016; Asao et al., 2018).

References

Asao, S., Parton, W. J., Chen, M., and Gao, W. (2018). Photodegradation accelerates ecosystem N cycling in a simulated California grassland. *Ecosphere*, **9**(8), e02370–1–e02370–18.

Bailey, V. L., Bond-Lamberty, B., DeAngelis, K., et al. (2017). Soil carbon cycling proxies: Understanding their critical role in predicting climate change feedbacks. *Global Change Biology*, **24**(3), 1–11.

Ball, J. T., Woodrow, I. E., and Berry, J. A. (1987). A model predicting stomatal conductance its contribution to the control of photosynthesis under different environmental conditions. In *Progress in Photosynthesis Research*, vol. 4, ed. I. Biggins. Dordrecht: Martinees Nijhof, 222–4.

Baron, J. ed. (1992). *Biogeochemistry of a subalpine ecosystem: Loch Vale Watershed.* Ecological Study Series No. 90. New York: Springer Verlag.

Baron, J. S., Blett, T., Malm, W. C., Alexander, R., and Doremus, H. (2016). Protecting national parks from air pollution effects: Making sausage from science and policy. In *Science, Conservation, and National Parks*, ed. S. Beissinger, D. D. Ackerly, H. Doremus, and G. E. Machlis. Chicago: University of Chicago Press, 151–69.

Baron, J. S., Del Grosso, S., Ojima, D. S., Theobald, D. M., and Parton, W. J. (2004). Nitrogen emissions along the Colorado Front Range: Response to population growth, land and water use change, and agriculture. In *Ecosystems and Land Use Change*, ed. R. DeFries, G. Asner, and R. Houghton. Geophysical Monograph Series 153. Washington, DC: American Geophysical Union, Wiley, 117–27.

Baron, J., Norton, S. A., Beeson, D. R., and Hermann, R. (1986). Sediment diatom and metal stratigraphy from Rocky Mountain lakes with special reference to atmospheric deposition. *Canadian Journal of Fisheries and Aquatic Science*, **43**, 1350–62.

Baron, J. S., Rueth, H. M., Wolfe, A. M., et al. (2000). Ecosystem responses to Nitrogen deposition in the Colorado Front Range. *Ecosystems*, **3**, 352–68.

Beltrán-Przekurat, A., Pielke Sr., R. A., Eastman, J. L., Coughenour, M. B. (2012). Modeling the effects of land-use/land-cover changes on the near–surface atmosphere in southern South America. *International Journal of Climatology*, **32**, 1206–25.

Bernhard, G., Dahlback, A., Fioletov, V., et al. (2013). High levels of ultraviolet radiation observed by ground-based instruments below the 2011 Arctic ozone hole. *Atmospheric Chemistry and Physics*, **13**, 10573–90.

Betts, R. A., Cox, P. M., Lee, S. E., and Woodward, F. I. (1997). Contrasting physiological and structural vegetation feedbacks in climate change simulations. *Nature*, **387**, 796–9.

Bigelow, D. S., Slusser, J. R., Beaubien, A. F., and Gibson, J. H. (1998). The USDA Ultraviolet Radiation Monitoring Program. *Bulletin of the American Meteorological Society*, **79**(4), 601–15.

Boot, C. M., Hall, E. K., Denef, K., and Baron, J. S. (2016). Long-term reactive nitrogen loading alters soil carbon and microbial community properties in a subalpine forest ecosystem. *Soil Biology and Biochemistry*, **92**, 211–20.

Bowman, W. D., and Steltzer, H. (1998). Positive feedbacks to anthropogenic nitrogen deposition in Rocky Mountain alpine tundra. *Ambio*, **27**(7), 514–17.

Brand, D., Wijewardana, C., Gao, W., and Reddy, K. R. (2016). Interactive effects of carbon dioxide, low temperature, and ultraviolet-B radiation on cotton seedling root and shoot morphology and growth. *Frontiers of Earth Science*, **10**, 607–20.

Brown, L. F., and Trlica, M. J. (1977). Interacting effects of soil water, temperature, and irradiance on CO_2 exchange rates on two dominant grasses of the short-grass prairie. *Journal of Applied Ecology*, **14**, 197–204.

Burns, D. A. (2004). The effects of atmospheric nitrogen deposition in the Rocky Mountains of Colorado and southern Wyoming, USA: A critical review. *Environmental Pollution*, **127**(2), 257–69.

Chang, N., Feng, R., Gao, Z., and Gao, W. (2010). Skin cancer incidence is highly associated with ultraviolet-B radiation history. *International Journal of Hygiene and Environmental Health*, **213**(5), 359–68.

Chase, T. N., Pielke Sr., R. A., Kittel, T. G. F., Baron, J. S., and Stohlgren, T. J. (1999). Potential impacts on Colorado Rocky Mountain weather due to land use changes on the adjacent Great Plains. *Journal of Geophysical Research*, **104**, 16673–90.

Chen, D. X., and Coughenour, M. B. (1994). GEMTM: A general model for energy and mass transfer at land surfaces and its application at the FIFE sites. *Journal of Agricultural and Forest Meteorology*, **68**, 145–71.

Chen, D. X., Coughenour, M. B., Owensby, C., and Knapp, A. (1993). Mathematical simulation of C4 grass photosynthesis in ambient and elevated CO_2. *Ecological Modeling*, **73**, 63–80.

Chen, D. X., Hunt, H. W., and Morgan, J. A. (1996). Responses of a C3 and C4 perennial grass to CO_2 enrichment and climate change: Comparison between model predictions and experimental data. *Ecological Modeling*, **87**, 11–27.

Chen, M., Parton, W. J., Adair, E. C., Asao, S., Hartman, M. D., and Gao, W. (2016). Simulation of the effects of photodecay on long-term litter decay using DayCent. *Ecosphere*, **7**, e01631.

Cole, C. V., and Heil, R. D. (1981). Phosphorus effects on terrestrial nitrogen cycling. In *Terrestrial Nitrogen Cycles: Processes, Ecosystem, Strategies and Management Impacts*, ed. F. E. Clark and T. Rosswall. Ecological Bulletin, 33. Stockholm: Swedish Natural Science Research Council, 363–74.

Coleman, D. C., Reid, C. P. P., and Cole, C. V. (1983). Biological strategies of nutrient cycling in soil systems. *Advances in Ecological Research*, **13**, 1–55.

COMET-Farm (2018). What is Comet Farm? USDA, NRCS, Natural Resource Ecology Laboratory, Colorado State University. http://cometfarm.nrel .colostate.edu (accessed July 31, 2018).

Conant, R. T., Cerri, C. E. P., Osborne, B. B., and Paustian, K. (2016). Grassland management impacts on soil carbon stocks: A new synthesis. *Ecological Applications*, **27**, 662–8.

Corr, C. A., Krotkov, N., Madronich, S., et al. (2009). Retrieval of aerosol single scattering albedo at ultraviolet wavelengths at the T1 site during MILAGRO. *Atmospheric Chemistry and Physics*, **9**(15), 5813–5827.

Coughenour, M. B. (1978). Grassland sulfur cycle and ecosystem responses to low-level SO_2. PhD dissertation, Colorado State University.

(1981). Sulfur dioxide deposition and its effect on a grassland sulfur-cycle. *Ecological Modeling*, **13**, 1–16.

(1984). A mechanistic simulation analysis of water use, leaf angles, and grazing in East African graminoids. *Ecological Modeling*, **26**, 203–20.

Coughenour, M. B., and Chen, D. X. (1997). An assessment of grassland ecosystem responses to atmospheric change using linked ecophysiological and soil process models. *Ecological Applications*, **7**, 802–27.

Coughenour, M. B., Dodd, J. L., Coleman, D. C., and Lauenroth, W. K. (1979). Partitioning of carbon and SO_2 sulfur in a native grassland. *Oecologia*, **42**, 229–40.

Coughenour, M. B., Kittel, T. G. F., Pielke Sr., R. A., and Eastman, J. (1993). Grassland/atmosphere response to changing climate: coupling regional and local scales. Final report to US Department of Energy. DOE/ER 60932-3.

Coughenour, M. B., McNaughton, S. J., and Wallace, L. L. (1984). Modeling primary production of perennial graminoids: Uniting physiological processes and morphometric traits. *Ecological Modeling*, **23**, 101–34.

Coughenour, M. B., and Parton, W. J. (1995). Integrated mode models of ecosystem function: A grassland case study. In *Global Change and Terrestrial Ecosystems*, ed. B. H. Walker and W. L. Steffen. Cambridge: Cambridge University Press.

Coughenour, M. B., Parton, W. J., Lauenroth, W. K., Dodd, J. L., and Woodmansee, R. G. (1980). Simulation of a grassland sulfur-cycle. *Ecological Modeling*, **9**, 179–213.

Detling, J. K., Parton, W. J., and Hunt, H. W. (1978). An empirical model for estimating CO_2 exchange of *Bouteloua gracilis* (H.B.K.) Lag. in the shortgrass prairie. *Oecologia*, **33**, 137–47.

Eastman, J. L., Coughenour, M. B., and Pielke Sr., R. A. (2001a). The regional effects of CO_2 and landscape change using a coupled plant and meteorological model. *Global Change Biology*, **7**, 797–815.

Eastman, J. L., Coughenour, M. B., and Pielke Sr., R. A. (2001b). Does grazing affect regional climate? *Journal of Hydrometeorology*, **2**, 243–53.

Elser, J. J., Andersen, T., Baron, J. S., et al. (2009). Shifts in lake N:P stoichiometry and nutrient limitation driven by atmospheric nitrogen deposition. *Science*, **326** (5954), 835–7.

ENA (European Nitrogen Assessment) (2018). Nitrogen in Europe, Current Problems and Future Solutions. European Science Foundation. www.nine-esf.org/node/204/ENA.html (accessed July 31, 2018).

Farman, J. C., Gardiner, B. G., and Shanklin, J. D. (1985). Large losses of total ozone in Antarctica reveal seasonal ClO_X/NO_X interaction. *Nature*, **315**, 207–10.

Farquhar, G. D., Von Caemmerer, S., and Berry, J. A. (1980). A biochemical model of photosynthetic CO_2 assimilation in leaves in C_3 species. *Planta*, **149**, 78–90.

Galloway, J. N., Dentener, F. J., and Capone, D. G., et al. (2004). Nitrogen cycles: Past, present, and future. *Biogeochemistry*, **70**(2), 153–226.

Gao, W., Slusser, J., Gibson, J., et al. (2001). Direct-Sun column ozone retrieval by the ultraviolet multifilter rotating shadow-band radiometer and comparison with those from Brewer and Dobson spectrophotometers. *Applied Optics*, **40** (19), 3149–55.

Grant, S. B., Azizian, M., Cook, P., et al. (2018). Factoring stream turbulence into global assessments of nitrogen pollution. *Science*, **359**(6381), 1266–9.

Heckendorn, P., Weisenstein, D., Fueglistaler, S., et al. (2009). The impact of geoengineering aerosols on stratospheric temperature and ozone. *Environmental Research Letters*, **4**(4), 045108.

Heitschmidt, R. K., Lauenroth, W. K., and Dodd, J. L. (1978). Effects of controlled levels of sulphur dioxide on western wheatgrass in a south-eastern Montana grassland. *Journal Applied Ecology*, **15**, 859–68.

Holland, E. A., and Detling, J. K. (1990). Plant response to herbivory and below-ground nitrogen cycling. *Ecology*, **71**(3), 1040–9.

Hutchinson, G. L., and Viets Jr. F. G. (1969). Nitrogen enrichment of surface water by absorption of ammonia from cattle feedlots. *Science*, **166**, 514–15.

Innis, G. S., ed. (1978). *Grassland Simulation Model*. Ecological Studies, 26. New York: Springer.

IPCC (Intergovernmental Panel on Climate Change) (2018). Special Report on Global Warming of 1.5 °C (SR15). World Meteorological Organization and United Nations Environmental Program. www.ipcc.ch (accessed July 31, 2018).

Kittel, T. G. F., and Coughenour, M. B. (1988). Prediction of regional and local ecological change from global climate model results: A hierarchical modeling approach. In *Monitoring Climate for the Effects of Increasing Greenhouse Gas Concentrations*, ed. R. A. Pielke and T. G. F. Kittel. Fort Collins, CO. Cooperative Institute for Research in the Atmosphere, Colorado State University, 173–93.

Lauenroth, W. K., Bicak, C. J., and Dodd, J. L. (1979). Sulfur accumulation in western wheatgrass exposed to three controlled SO$_2$ concentrations. *Plant and Soil*, **53**, 131–6.

Lauenroth, W. K., and Bradford, J. B. (2006). Ecohydrology and the partitioning AET between transpiration and evaporation in a semiarid steppe. *Ecosystems*, **9**, 756–67.

Lauenroth, W. K., and Burke, I. C. (2008). *Ecology of the Shortgrass Steppe: A Long-Term Perspective*. New York: Oxford University Press.

Liang, X., Wu, Y., Chambers, R. G., et al. (2017). Determining climate effects on US total agricultural productivity. *Proceedings for the National Academy of Sciences of the United States of America (PNAS)*, **114**(12), E2285–E2292.

Liang, X., Xu, M., Gao, W., et al. (2012). Physical Modeling of U.S. Cotton Yields and Climate Stresses during 1979 to 2005. *Agronomy Journal*, **104**(3), 675–83.

Liston, G. E., and Pielke Sr., R. A. (2001), A climate version of the Regional Atmospheric Modeling System. *Theoretical Applied Climatology*, **68**, 155–73.

McGill, W. B., Hunt, H. W., Woodmansee, R. G., and Reuss, J. O. (1981). Phoenix: A model of the dynamics of carbon and nitrogen in grassland soils. In *Terrestrial Nitrogen Cycles: Processes, Ecosystem, Strategies and Management Impacts*, ed. F. E. Clark and T. Rosswall. Ecological Bulletin, 33. Stockholm: Swedish Natural Science Research Council, 49–115.

Milchunas, D. T., and Lauenroth, W. K. (1995). Inertia in plant community structure: State changes after cessation of nutrient-enrichment stress. *Ecological Applications*, **5**(2), 452–8.

Morris, K. A., Mast, M. A., Wetherbee, G., et al. (2014). *2012 Monitoring and Tracking Wet Nitrogen Deposition at Rocky Mountain National Park*. NPS Natural Resource Report NPS/NRSS/ARD/NRR–2014–757, 36.

Mosier, A. R., Parton, W. J., Martin, R. E., et al. (2008). Soil–atmosphere exchange of trace gases in the Colorado Shortgrass Steppe. In *Ecology of the Shortgrass Steppe: A Long-Term Perspective*, ed. W. K. Lauenroth and I. C. Burke. New York: Oxford University Press.

Narisma, G. T., Pitman, A. J., Eastman, J., Watterson, I. G., Pielke Sr., R., and Beltra'n-Przekurat, A. (2003). The role of biospheric feedbacks in the simulation of the impact of historical land cover change on the Australian January climate. *Geophysical Research Letters*, **30**(22), 2168.

Narisma, G. T., and Pitman, A. J. (2004). The effect of including biospheric responses to CO$_2$ on the impact of land-cover change over Australia. *Earth Interactions*, **8**(5), 1–28.

Ogle, S. M. (2014). Quantifying greenhouse gas sources and sinks from land use change. In *Quantifying Greenhouse Gas Fluxes in Agriculture and Forestry: Methods for Entity-Scale Inventory*, ed. M. Eve, D. Pape, M. Flugge, R. Steele, D. Man, M. Riley-Gilbert, and S. Biggar. Technical Bulletin 1939, July 2014. Washington, DC: US Department of Agriculture, 7.1–7.15.

Ogle, S. M., Breidt, F. J., and Paustain, K. (2005). Agricultural management impacts on soil organic carbon storage under moist and dry climatic conditions of temperate and tropical regions. *Biogeochemistry*, **72**, 87–121.

Ojima, D. S., Schimel, D. S., Parton, W. J., and Owensby, C. E. (1994). Long- and short-term effects of fire on nitrogen cycling in tallgrass prairie. *Biogeochemistry*, **24**(2), 67–84.

Parton, W. J. (1978). Abiotic section of ELM. In *Grassland Simulation Model*, ed. G. S. Innis. New York: Springer Verlag, 31–53.

Parton, W. J., Anderson, D. W., Cole, C. V., and Stewart, J. W. B. (1983). Simulation of soil organic matter formation and mineralization in semiarid agroecosystems. In *Nutrient Cycling in Agricultural Ecosystems*, ed. R. R. Lowrance, R. L. Todd, L. E. Asmussen, and R. A. Leonard. Special Publication No. 23. Athens, GA: University of Georgia, College of Agriculture Experiment Stations.

Parton, W. J., Coughenour, M. B., Scurlock, J. M. O., et al. (1996). Global grassland ecosystem modeling: Development and test of ecosystem models for grassland systems. In *Global Change: Effects on Coniferous Forests and Grasslands*, ed. A. I. Breymeyer, D. M. Hall, J. M. Melillo, and G. I. Agren. SCOPE 56. New York: John Wiley and Sons.

Parton, W. J., Schimel, D. S., Cole, C. V., and Ojima, D. S. (1987). Analysis of factors controlling soil organic matter levels in Great Plains Grasslands. *Soil Science Society of America Journal*, **51**, 1173–9.

Paul, E. A., ed. (2014). *Soil Microbiology, Ecology, and Biochemistry*, 4th edn. San Diego, CA: Elsevier, Academic Press.

Paustian, K. (2014). Carbon sequestration in soil and vegetation and greenhouse gas emissions reduction. In *Global Environmental Change*, ed. B. Freedman. Dordrecht, Heidelberg, New York, London: Springer Reference, Springer, 399–406.

Pielke, R. A., Cotton, W. R., Walko, R. L., et al. (1992). A comprehensive meteorological modeling system: RAMS. *Meteorology and Atmospheric Physics*, **49**, 69–91.

Pielke, R. A., Dalu, G., Snook, J. S., Lee, T. J., and Kittel, T. G. F. (1991). Nonlinear influence of mesoscale landuse on weather and climate. *Journal of Climate*, **4**, 1053–69.

Pielke, R. A., Schimel, D. S., Lee, T. J., Kittel, T. G. F., and Zeng, X. (1993). Atmosphere-terrestrial ecosystem interactions: Implications for coupled modeling. *Ecological Modelling*, **67**, 5–18.

Pielke, R. A., Walko, R. L., Steyaert, L. T., et al. (1999). The influence of anthropogenic landscape changes on weather in south Florida. *Monthly Weather Review*, **127**, 1663–73.

Pinder, R. W., Davidson, E. A., Goodale, C. L., et al. (2012). Climate change impacts of US reactive nitrogen. *Proceedings of the National Academy of Sciences*, **109**(20), 7671–5.

Pitman, A. J. (2003). The evolution of, and revolution in, land surface schemes designed for climate models. *International Journal of Climatology*, **23**, 479–510.

Preston, E. M., O'Guinn, D. W., and Wilson, R. A., eds. (1981). The bioenvironmental impact of a coal-fired power plant. Sixth interim report, Colstrip, Montana, August 1980. Corvallis Environmental Research Laboratory Office of Research and Development, US Environmental Protection Agency, Corvallis, Oregon. EPA 600/3–81–007.

Qi, Y., Bai, S., Gao, W., and Heisler, G. M. (2003). Intra- and inter-specific comparisons of leaf UV-B absorbing-compound concentration of southern broadleaf tree in the United States. Proceedings of SPIE, Ultraviolet Ground- and Space-based Measurements, Models, and Effects II, 4896. http://doi:10.1117/12.466231.

Reddy, K. R., Kakani, V. G., Zhao, D., Koti, S., and Gao, W. (2004). Interactive effects of ultraviolet-B radiation and temperature on cotton physiology, growth, development and hyperspectral reflectance. *Photochemistry and Photobiology*, **79**(5), 416–27.

Reddy, K. R., Kakani, V. G., Zhao, D., Mohammed, A. R., and Gao, W. (2003). Cotton responses to ultraviolet-B radiation: Experimentation and algorithm development. *Agricultural and Forest Meteorology*, **120**, 249–65.

Reddy, K. R., Patro, H., Lokhande, S., Bellaloui, N., and Gao, W. (2016). Ultraviolet-B radiation alters soybean growth and seed quality. *Food and Nutrition Sciences*, **7**, 55–66.

Reddy, K. R., Singh, S. K., Koti, S., et al. (2013). Quantifying the effects of corn growth and physiological responses to ultraviolet-B radiation for modeling. *Agronomy Journal*, **105**(5), 1367–77.

Rigby, M., Park, S., Saito, T., et al. (2019). Increase in CFC-11 emissions from eastern China based on atmospheric observations. *Nature*, **569**, 546–50.

Rueth, H. M., Baron, J. S., and Allstott, E. J. (2003). Responses of Engelmann spruce forests to nitrogen fertilization in the Colorado Rocky Mountains. *Ecological Applications*, **13**(3), 664–73.

Sala, O. E., Lauenroth, W. K., and Parton, W. J. (1992). Long-term soil-water dynamics in the shortgrass steppe. *Ecology* **73**, 1175–81.

Schimel, D. S. (1986). Carbon and nitrogen turnover in adjacent grassland and cropland ecosystems. *Biogeochemistry*, **2**(4), 345–57.

Schimel, D. S., Kittel, T. G. F., and Parton, W. J. (1991). Terrestrial biogeochemical cycles: global interactions with the atmosphere and hydrology. *Tellus A: Dynamic Meteorology and Oceanography*, **43**, 188–203.

Schimel, D. S., Parton, W. J., Adamsen, F. J., et al. (1986). Role of cattle in the volatile loss of nitrogen from a shortgrass steppe. *Biogeochemistry*, **2**, 39–52.

Schimel, D. S., Stillwell, M. A., and Woodmansee, R. G. (1985). Biogeochemistry of C, N, and P in a soil catena of the shortgrass steppe. *Ecology*, **66**(1), 276–82.

Senft, R. L., Coughenour, M. B., Bailey, D. W., et al. (1987). Large herbivore foraging and ecological hierarchies. *BioScience*, **37**, 789–99.

Shindell, D. T., Rind, D., and Lonergan, P. (1998). Increased polar stratospheric ozone losses and delayed eventual recover owing to increasing greenhouse-gas concentrations. *Nature*, **392**, 589–92.

Simkin, S. M., Allen, E. B., Bowman, W. D., et al. (2016). Conditional vulnerability of plant diversity to atmospheric nitrogen deposition across the United States. *Proceedings of the National Academy of Sciences*, **113**(15), 4086–91.

Singh, B., Norvell, E., Wijewardana, C., Wallace, T., Chastain, D., and Reddy, K. R. (2018). Assessing morpho-physiological characteristics of elite cotton lines from different breeding programs for low temperature and drought tolerance. *Journal of Agronomy and Crop Science*, 1–10. http://doi:10.1111/jac.12276.

Solomon, S., Ivy, D. J., Kinnison, D., Mills, M. J., Neely, R. R., and Schmidt, A. (2016). Emergence of healing the Antarctic ozone layer. *Science*, **353**(6296), 269–74.

Sun, Z., Davis, J., and Gao, W. (2015). Combined UV irradiance from TOMS-OMI satellite and UVMRP ground measurements across the continental US. *Proceedings of SPIE, Remote Sensing and Modeling of Ecosystems for Sustainability XII*, 9610, 961004. http://doi:10.1117/12.2188760.

Sutton, M. A., Oenema, O., Erisman, J. W., et al. (2011). Too much of a good thing. *Nature*, **472**(7342), 159.

Vitousek, P. M., Aber, J. D., Howarth, R. W., et al. (1997). Human alteration of the global nitrogen cycle: Sources and consequences. *Ecological Applications*, **7**(3), 737–50.

Von der Gathen, P., Rex, M., Harris, N. R. P., et al. (1995). Observation evidence for chemical ozone depletion over the Arctic in winter 1991–92. *Nature*, **375**, 131–4.

Walko, R. L., Band, L. E., Baron, J., et al. (2000), Coupled atmosphere-biophysics-hydrology models for environmental modeling. *Journal of Applied Meteorology*, **39**, 931–44.

Wallenstein, M. D., and Hall, E. K. (2012). A trait-based framework for predicting when and where microbial adaptation to climate change will affect ecosystem functioning. *Bioegeochemistry*, **109**, 35–47.

Westhoek, H., Lesschen, J. P., Rood, T., et al. (2014). Food choices, health and environment: effects of cutting Europe's meat and dairy intake. *Global Environmental Change*, **26**, 196–205.

Wijewardana, C., Reddy, K. R., Shankle, M. W., Meyers, S., and Gao, W. (2018). Low and high-temperature effects on sweetpotato storage root initiation and early transplant establishment. *Scientia Horticulturae*, **240**, 38–48.

Williams III, G. J., and Kemp, P. R. (1978). Simultaneous measurement of leaf and root gas exchange of shortgrass prairie species. *International Journal of Plant Sciences*, **139**, 150–7.

Woodmansee, R. G. (1975). Sulfur in grassland ecosystems. *Sulfur in the Environment*. In W. M. Klein, J. G. Severson, Jr., and H. S. Parker. St. Louis: Missouri Botanical Garden, 134–40.

(1978). Additions and losses of nitrogen in grassland ecosystems. *Bioscience*, **28**(7), 448–53.

Woodmansee, R. G., Dodd, J. L., Bowman, R. A., Clark, F. E., and Dickinson, C. E. (1978). Nitrogen budget of a shortgrass prairie ecosystem. *Oecologia*, **34**(3), 363–76.

Wu, Y., Liang, X., and Gao, W. (2015). Climate change impacts on the U.S. agricultural economy. *Proceedings of SPIE, Remote Sensing and Modeling* of Ecosystems for Sustainability XII, 9610, 96100J. http://doi:10.1117/12 .2192469.

Xu, M., Liang, X.-Z., Gao, W., and Krotkov, N. (2010). Comparison of TOMS retrievals and UVMRP measurements of surface spectral UV radiation in the United States. *Atmospheric Chemistry and Physics*, **10**, 8669–83.

Xu, M., Liang, X.-Z., Gao, W., Reddy, K. R., Slusser, J., and Kunkel, K. (2005). Preliminary results of the coupled CWRF-GOSSYM system. Proceedings of SPIE, Remote Sensing and Modeling of Ecosystems for Sustainability II, 5884, 588409. http://doi:10.1117/12.621017.

Zhang, H., Wang, J., Garcia, L. C., et al. (2019). Surface erythemal UV irradiance in the continental United States derived from ground-based and OMI observations: Quality assessment, trend analysis and sampling issues. *Atmospheric Chemistry and Physics*, **19**(4), 2165–81.

9 · *Humans in Ecosystems*

DAVID M. SWIFT, RANDALL B. BOONE,
MICHAEL B. COUGHENOUR, AND
GREGORY NEWMAN

9.1 Introduction

When ecology began as a discipline, its practitioners concentrated on systems that were natural in the sense that humans were normally not present or had limited impact. The same was true for the initial phases of ecosystem ecology. The least "natural" organisms considered in the US International Biological Program (IBP) were cattle, which were included in the Grassland Biome study. Initially, if humans were considered at all it was as an outside, perturbing force. This was probably a good idea at the time because the systems being studied were complex enough even without considering the people to present daunting challenges to the new discipline. However, as time progressed it became increasingly clear that most ecosystems actually had humans in them and that we might expect that there would be effects in both directions – from the human to the nonhuman part and vice versa. Further, if ecosystem ecology was going to have a significant societal impact, we would have to start looking at ecosystems that included humans and include these humans as components of the system. This chapter traces the development of the idea of "humans in ecosystems" from its beginning to the present highlighting important milestones in that development.

Figure 9.1 attempts to show how this development occurred. First, we moved from the study of "natural" systems to the study of human-dominated systems which then led to two new developments for ecosystem ecologists. The first development was a foray into agroecosystems: according to Keith Paustian of the NREL, it was now "acceptable for an ecologist to be found in a barley field" (personal communication). The other direction was to study ecosystems that contained people and to consider them as part of the system rather than as an outside force.

As we studied more and more ecosystems with people in them and talked with the people about their use of the systems they inhabited and their ideas about how they functioned, we developed an increasing

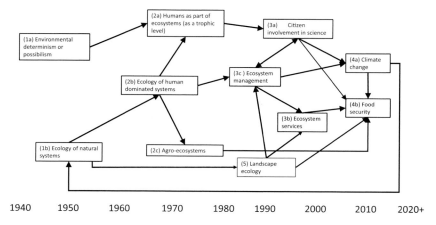

Figure 9.1 Relationships among various aspects of the development of humans in ecosystems over time.

interest in involving local people in the scientific process, from the development of research questions to co-generation of knowledge. This also led to an increasing interest in understanding the ecosystem services that local people found important.

In the 1980s, increasing use of geographic information system (GIS) technology and advances in computing power allowed ecologists to escape from their traditional meter square prison and begin to look at systems across space. Landscape ecology was born. Recently, the ideas of landscape ecology have been applied to the study of ecosystem services allowing us to understand how the services of interest are produced across the landscape.

Meanwhile, climate change came center stage and our improving understanding of that phenomenon, combined with agroecosystem research, landscape ecology, citizen science, and an increased interest in sustainability, prompted an interest in food security analyses.

Box 3c in Figure 9.1 shows the relationship between ecosystem management and the other components dealt with in this chapter. This topic is not discussed explicitly in this chapter, but is included in Chapter 7. It is included in this figure simply to show its relationship to the other components dealt with in this chapter.

Box 4b is food security which became an important issue for investigation due to increasing concerns about climate change, the growth of citizen involvement in science, and an increased interest in understanding and managing agroecosystems. It is not discussed in this chapter, but rather in Chapter 13.

9.2 Including Humans As a Component of the Ecosystem: The South Turkana Ecosystem Project

The South Turkana Ecosystem Project began in 1981. Two important schools of thought led to its inception and informed the methods used to analyze and understand the ecology and society of the Turkana people of northwest Kenya. One of these was, of course, our experience in studying ecosystems in their entirety (ecosystem science and the ecosystem approach). The second was a concept from anthropology called variously ecological determinism, geographic determinism, or cultural determinism. While this concept appears in a variety of manifestations, some strongly criticized, the idea that appealed to us as ecologists was that the societies and cultures of people are strongly influenced by the ecosystems in which the people live and by the stresses and opportunities those systems impose and provide. Without exception, when we have suggested this idea to other ecologists, their immediate response has been, "Well, of course."

As in many scientific enterprises, serendipity played a role in the inception of this project. Before we began working on the proposal to study the South Turkana ecosystem, both Jim Ellis and Dave Swift were serving on the graduate committee of Kathleen Galvin, an MS student in anthropology at Colorado State University (CSU). She was interested in the society and ecology of East African pastoralism, and so all of us were reading everything we could find on the topic, and were developing plans to propose a study of an East African pastoral system. Prominent in the literature were papers by Neville Dyson-Hudson at the State University of New York in Binghamton. He had written extensively on the Karamojong of Uganda and had been involved in the South Turkana Expedition of the Royal Geographic Society of England which took place between 1968 and 1970. Having worked in the field in both of these places, Neville had come to believe very strongly that the characteristics he observed in the cultures and societies of these peoples had developed as adaptive responses to the vicissitudes of life as livestock keepers in dry and unpredictable environments. In 1979, Neville walked into the NREL and asked if anyone there would be interested in working with him to develop a proposal to study the South Turkana people and their ecosystem. We answered in the affirmative and began the development of a proposal to the National Science Foundation. In 1981, we were funded by both the ecosystems and anthropology programs for an initial period of two years. Funding continued through 1992.

During those 11 years, we traced the flow of energy and nitrogen through the system, from the plants through the livestock and into the human population, adding in the fairly small component of human foods arising from outside the system (Coughenour et al., 1985). We estimated animal and human energy and nitrogen balances and growth and reproduction (Coppock et al., 1986a; Galvin, 1992; Galvin and Little, 1999; Galvin et al., 1999). Surprisingly, perhaps the single most important pathway of energy flow into the human population was from the dwarf shrub *Indigofera spinosa* to camels to camel milk to humans. Quantitatively, camels were of greater importance to the people's diet than were cattle, but the Turkana generally thought of themselves as "cattle people."

The importance of the technique adopted by the Turkana for maintaining the widest variety of livestock possible became clear. The different diets of the five species kept by the Turkana (cattle, camels, sheep, goats, and donkeys) ensured a minimal competition among them by maximizing niche separation (Coppock et al., 1986a). This also meant that every herbivore niche was filled so that any plant that grew there could be a food resource for at least one species of livestock and thus contribute to the well-being of the pastoralists. The wide variety of livestock species also meant that a wide variety of labor opportunities exist. Fairly small children can and do herd sheep and goats, thus making their own contribution to the pastoral enterprise and freeing the older adolescents and adults to herd camels and cattle.

We were also able to demonstrate that two largely independent pathways of energy and nitrogen flow through the system existed, and that these two pathways had different temporal dynamics and contributed differentially to the well-being of the people. The pathway from grass to grazers to people is a fairly short-lived but highly productive pathway following the normally brief wet season (Coppock et al., 1986b). The shrub to browser to human pathway is active longer in most years and is less variable between years, but does not process as much energy per unit of time as does the grass–grazer pathway. The grass-based pathway is a growth or production pathway and the shrub-based one a survival pathway. We have referred to these two as the pulse maximization pathway and the pulse attenuation pathway because of the different ways they translate the rainfall pulse into human food. (Swift et al., 1996).

Perhaps the most important ecological insight to come out of this project was the idea of nonequilibrial systems (Ellis and Swift, 1988). The basic idea here is that in most systems with high year-to-year rainfall variability and frequent extended droughts, system dynamics are not well described by the traditional paradigm of systems that vary around some equilibrium state and that this configuration is maintained by a strong network of negative feedbacks among the system's components. Instead, we felt that the system was controlled almost exclusively by its abiotic drivers and their variability. Therefore, the negative feedbacks found in most other, less variable systems were either absent or rarely activated. It seemed to us that these two classes of ecosystems were qualitatively different from each other in their dynamics and demanded different approaches to their management.

We also, we believe, debunked the long-held and cherished belief that subsistence pastoralism is an inherently destructive system that inevitably leads to rangeland degradation and destruction as a result of the irrational "East African cattle complex" (Herskovits, 1926), and of the fact that the rangelands are used as a common resource. Instead, pastoralism proves to be a rational form of land use that employs mobility to cope with spatial-temporal variability in resource abundance across the landscape (Coughenour, 2012). Far from being a "free-for-all" commons, resource use is governed by norms of utilization involving grazing and watering rights for certain groups at certain times.

The other issue – the extent to which societies and cultures are influenced by the environments in which they develop – is less well settled, many anthropologists still being uncomfortable with this view. We do not intend to try to settle these differences here, but simply to point out the clear adaptive value of many of the traditions characteristic of East African pastoral societies.

Many East African pastoral societies share common cultural or social traits and traditions. These include attempts by herd owners to maximize their livestock holdings, the practice of polygamy, the requirement that "bride wealth" be paid to the father of a prospective wife to gain permission to marry, "reciprocal begging" of livestock or some other form of internal livestock redistribution, and a very high level of individual freedom among members of local groups of people. It may be mere coincidence that these practices are represented almost universally in East African pastoral societies, but all of them appear to have significant adaptive value. Thus, we must consider the possibility that this is the reason for their presence:

- *Accumulation of livestock.* Many East African pastoral systems are found in ecosystems which are nonequilibrial, and are thus subject to large density-independent losses of livestock. Others are found in systems that are potentially ecologically equilibrial, but fraught with the danger that many livestock might be lost to disease or to raiding by other people. The accumulation of large numbers of livestock acts as a hedge against these uncertainties, ensuring that if (or when) a livestock disaster occurs, the herd owner will still have enough animals to recover. In essence it is a risk-reducing approach – one of many that these pastoralists employ, such as herd-splitting and maintaining diverse herds.

- *Polygamy.* This practice permits the herd owner to increase the number of children he has. These children are the labor force he needs to ensure a successful livestock operation by acting as herders, water gatherers, and security agents. Having a large labor pool of this sort enables the herd owner to maximize his livestock holdings.

- *Bride wealth.* The requirement that a man use his livestock for payment of bride wealth to his future father-in-law confirms that he has been a wise livestock manager and is able to provide ongoing support for himself and his new acquisition. In Turkana, the traditional bride wealth payment is very large and is often met in part by borrowing livestock from friends and extended family. Such loans are easier to obtain if the prospective loaners have faith in the capabilities of the borrower. Incompetent pastoralists are frequently eliminated from pastoral society by the bride wealth requirement; being forced to migrate to agricultural or fishing communities often made up of others who have failed in the pastoral enterprise.

- *Reciprocal begging.* This is the term, with its slightly pejorative connotation, which has often been applied to the custom of pastoralists to request livestock as loans or gifts from friends and relatives. It is a form of risk reduction and social security in a very risky environment in which herd decimation is common and there is no institutionalized system of disaster relief such as we have in the US. Most pastoral herd owners develop intricate webs of obligation among their peers through this mechanism. The typical herd owner is in debt to many others for cattle, sheep, camels, or goats, and in the same manner others are in debt to him. When a man suffers a serious loss of livestock, he can call in his "loans" as a way of restocking and recovering. Among the Turkana, this habit of requesting livestock or goods has become a more generalized mode of action and is socially accepted. For example, one young Turkana lad approached Jim Ellis and said, "nakanai (give me) bicycle."

- *High level of individual freedom within local groups of friends and extended families.* Clearly, this represents our personal opinion about a characteristic of Turkana society. While there are rules in Turkana about access to water and forage, they are typically applied to people outside the local circle. Within that circle, every man is free to make his own decisions about what livestock to keep, where to take them, and what to do with them. As a result, there are many different strategies in play within the system at all times. This is helpful because if conditions cause one strategy to fail, someone else's may be successful. It is actually a form of risk-spreading and works in conjunction with the reciprocal begging discussed above. As with reciprocal begging, this characteristic has spread beyond the management of livestock to the point that it is very rare for one Turkana person to tell another what to do.

9.3 Work Subsequent to the South Turkana Ecosystem Project

9.3.1 Assessing Nutritional Status of Maasai Pastoralists under the Stress of Rapid Change

By the year 2000, the rate of change in East African pastoral systems was clearly accelerating. These changes included: (1) livelihood diversification, particularly increased dependence upon agriculture; (2) increased involvement in the market economy, both as sellers and consumers; (3) more access to both human and veterinary health care; and (4) increased landscape fragmentation and sedentarization. A study was undertaken to determine the effects of these rapid changes on the nutritional status of Maasai pastoralists in Kajiado County, Kenya (Galvin et al., 2015). Their estimates of nutritional state were compared to past studies of Maasai nutrition from 1930 to 2000. The results indicated that Maasai nutritional state was poor and had remained so despite better access to veterinary care and improved market integration. The potential benefits of these changes were apparently offset by increasing human population and decreased mobility.

9.3.2 Applying Knowledge about Pastoral Systems to Real-World Problems

9.3.2.1 IMAS and POLEYC Projects

A basic understanding of the dynamics of semi-arid East African pastoral systems, and of the social organization of the pastoralists themselves, were developed during the South Turkana Ecosystem Project. It remained to be seen if those understandings could be applied in a practical fashion to the solution of the problems facing pastoral societies in East Africa. Two projects funded by the Global Livestock Collaborative Research Support Program (GL-CRSP) of USAID allowed us the opportunity to address some of these issues. The first was the IMAS project (Integrated Modeling and Assessment System – 1997–2001, led by Mike Coughenour and Kathy Galvin). The second was the POLEYC project (*Policy Options for Livestock-based livelihoods, and EcosYstem Conservation* – 2001–2, led by Jim Ellis and Dave Swift).

The purpose of these projects was to assist managers and other stakeholders in East Africa with balancing food security, wildlife conservation, and ecosystem integrity in the wildlife-rich ecosystems inhabited by pastoralists. We conducted our research at two principle study sites – Kajiado District in Kenya, including Amboseli National Park, and the Ngorongoro Conservation Area (NCA) in Tanzania, which is adjacent to Serengeti National Park. Both of these areas have current or potential conflicts between pastoral land use and wildlife conservation. Both are included in the traditional territories of the Maasai, which straddle an area from southern Kenya into northern Tanzania, the Maasai Steppe. The NCA is a unique conservation area in that it was designated for multiple use, as a place where indigenous peoples could remain and coexist with wildlife as they had for centuries. Unfortunately, traditional patterns of pastoral land use had changed and human populations had increased, potentially coming into conflict with the wildlife. Kajiado is an area where traditional patterns of open land use were being modified by the development of group ranches that set up boundaries within the district. This resulted in fragmentation of the landscape and restricted the free movement of pastoralists and their livestock compared to traditional movement patterns. Restrictions on movement are particularly problematic for pastoralists because the freedom to move over large areas is critical to their survival during times of drought or when rainfall is spatially heterogeneous.

The SAVANNA Modeling System was used in these projects to address questions of concern in the two study areas. SAVANNA is a spatially explicit ecosystem model, first developed during the South Turkana Ecosystem Project. It simulates plant production, grazing off-take, livestock distributions, and livestock and wildlife conditions and productivity across the landscape (Coughenour, 1992, 2012; Weisberg et al., 2006). The SAVANNA Modeling System used for this project included the SAVANNA model itself (Boone et al., 2002, 2006), an animal disease model, and a pastoral household socioeconomic model (PHEWS) (Thornton et al., 2003; Galvin et al., 2004), all of which were dynamically interactive. See Chapters 4 and 6 of this book for detailed descriptions of the SAVANNA Modeling System.

We used the SAVANNA Modeling System at the NCA study site to evaluate the effects on wildlife and livestock of a series of possible changes in the system, such as a decrease in rainfall, improved veterinary care, permission or restriction of livestock grazing in key portions of the conservation area, renovation of nonfunctional water sources, human population growth, and increases in the amount of cultivation within the conservation area.

The most interesting predictions made include the following:

1. Improved veterinary care would increase the number of livestock available to Maasai for sale or slaughter.
2. Human population growth at its present rate of 3 percent per year would increase the population by 50 percent over a 15-year period and would also increase cultivation by approximately 50 percent.
3. Neither wildlife nor livestock populations were much affected, which is good for the wildlife but problematic for the Maasai as the number of livestock per person would continue to decline. An adequate ratio of livestock to humans must be maintained if the Maasai are to survive solely on their livestock. Since human numbers are expected to increase, a constant animal population will result in a decline in this ratio to unacceptable levels.
4. An increase of up to 5 percent in cultivation within the conservation area would result in minimal effects on livestock or wildlife populations, but could have significant positive impacts on the Maasai nutritional state. This could be particularly important as human populations increase and the ratio of livestock to humans declines.

At the Kajiado study site, we compared livestock numbers under traditional free access grazing over the entire area to their populations when movements were restricted to individual group ranches or other areas. In all cases, restrictions on movements had strong negative effects on livestock populations.

The results of these model experiments were relayed to Maasai pastoralists and all other stakeholders in the two areas to take into consideration when making policy or management decisions.

USAID requested a demand-driven approach, which required demonstrable support from stakeholders. As a result, numerous workshops were held and attended by a variety of stakeholders, ranging from pastoralists, wildlife management agencies (e.g., Kenya Wildlife Service, Tanzania

Division of Wildlife, Kenya National Parks, Tanzania National Park Authority), local university researchers, researchers from the International Livestock Research Institute, the tourism industry, agricultural agencies, and international conservation groups. We met with representatives from all of these agencies and groups to gain their assistance in determining appropriate model experiments to evaluate, and to assess and select, potential research sites where wildlife–livestock conflicts were important.

The IMAS project was based on the concept of integrated assessments, and the IMAS approach involved not only a whole systems model with ecosystem and human processes, but also the integration of knowledge from a wide variety of disciplines (e.g., soil and vegetation ecology, wildlife ecology, pastoral ecology, veterinary sciences, anthropology) and associated field research activities. This was truly a whole systems approach. The purpose of this approach was to integrate knowledge about the interactions among various parts of the system, either directly or indirectly, and then to find an optimal balance between the needs of the livestock versus the wildlife. This required analysis and process-based modeling of specific modes of interaction, such as through competition for grazing, disease transmission, wildlife damage, and depredation on livestock and crops. Furthermore, the benefits and costs of alternative policies and management practices could be identified through these types of whole-system integrated assessments.

9.3.2.2 Effects of Fragmentation of Rangelands on Wildlife, Livestock, and Humans

There has recently been a tendency to modify the traditional model of land tenure among pastoralists to an alternative form involving more private ownership. This has been driven by a concern that using land in common will result in its degradation (the tragedy of the commons) (Hardin, 1968). Often this has involved the formation of group ranches and then their subdivision in such a way that the mobility of the pastoralists involved is limited to a single subdivided unit. Free-ranging livestock are dependent upon access to a variety of resources across landscapes, including water sources, cover, and forage patches that vary in the amounts of food they provide. Landscapes composed of subdivided units put access by livestock at risk, which in turn can threaten pastoral well-being. The late NREL scientist James Ellis (Coughenour et al., 2004 reviews his contributions) organized a large team (later led by N. T. Hobbs) to propose a study of the effects of fragmentation on rangelands and their human inhabitants across four continents with

22 research sites. Several products flowed from this study. For example, Thornton et al. (2006) modeled the effects of such subdivision and land fragmentation on livestock numbers and food security in Kajiado, Kenya. Their results indicated that this subdivision resulted in a substantial reduction in livestock numbers, in part because pastoralists had to sell them to generate the cash needed to purchase nonpastoral foods. In the long run, this reduction in livestock numbers had deleterious effects on subsequent cash flow and food security. This coping strategy is nonsustainable, and has been termed a poverty spiral.

Boone et al. (2005) had previously shown that these subdivisions could lead to a reduction in the number of livestock a group ranch could support due to a loss of responsive mobility for pastoralists and their herds. They modeled the number of livestock that could be supported on various group ranches in Kajiado assuming different levels of subdivision. For one group ranch, the model indicated that fragmenting the ranch into 1 km square parcels would reduce the number of cattle that could be supported on the entire group ranch by 25 percent compared to the situation in which the ranch was not subdivided and pastoralists had free access to the entire ranch. Consequently, these subdivisions affected livestock numbers through the loss of mobility and then forced a further reduction in livestock numbers through sales to generate the cash needed to purchase nonpastoral foods.

Additional products resulting from this project include work on the effects of fragmentation on Australian rangelands (e.g., Stokes et al., 2006), insight into the severe weather effects in Mongolia (Begzsuren et al., 2004), and integrated modeling in East Africa (Galvin et al., 2006). The project culminated in two major products: a book that synthesizes results from the many studies (Galvin et al., 2008) and a summary of that synthesis (Hobbs et al., 2008).

9.4 Early Predictions of Growing Season Production for Great Plains Ranchers

NREL Senior Research Scientist William J. Parton and a team of collaborators are currently working on the development of a model-based system, Grass-Cast, which will allow springtime prediction of Great Plains grass production during the growing season.

This system is intended to assist ranchers in the region in adjusting stocking rates through the purchase or sale of livestock to match anticipated forage production. Grass-Cast predictions have been available to ranchers and others on the Colorado State University website beginning in May 2018. Recent precipitation data are incorporated into the system's predictions and then updated on the site every two weeks through the end of July. Ranchers and federal agencies involved in land management in the region have provided substantial input on the sort of information they would like to see on the website.

9.5 Ecosystem Services: Spatial Distribution in the Bale Mountains of Ethiopia

The inclusion of humans as part of the ecosystems they inhabit, and their involvement in the process of considering alternative management approaches to their lands, led to a more general interest in an evaluation of ecosystem services provided to the people. Scientists from NREL and elsewhere have been working in Ethiopia's Bale Mountains to better understand how provisioning services provided by the vegetation assemblage are spatially distributed and which services are most vulnerable as a result of climate change and increasing human pressure on the natural landscape (Luizza et al., 2013).

The vegetation of the area was characterized by placing modified Whittaker plots (Barnett and Stohlgren, 2003) in all nine of the identified vegetation types in the mountains. The services provided by the various plant species were determined through interviews with local Oromo agropastoral men and women. Interestingly, the understanding of the uses of the various species was enormously different between men and women, underscoring the importance of communicating with both men and women in cases where local knowledge or aspirations are important (Luizza et al., 2013). The two classes of data (uses and vegetation distribution) were combined in such a way that it was clear which vegetation zones were important for each of the services and which services were being provided uniquely by one plant species or redundantly by many (M. W. Luizza, Personal communication).

9.6 Landscape Ecology

9.6.1 Drought Susceptibility in Turkana District, Kenya

The work on the STEP project led to a contract with the Norwegian International Development Agency to evaluate the relative drought susceptibility of various regions within Turkana District and to elucidate the reasons for differential susceptibility among those regions. While the ongoing study in the southernmost region of Turkana (Ngisonyoka) had strong spatial aspects, this further study explicitly addressed the relationships among rainfall, topography, dominant livestock types, pastoral management strategies, and their impact on susceptibility to drought.

We combined field data collection with regional advanced very high resolution radiometer analysis to estimate primary production across the district under different rainfall conditions.

Chief among our findings was that topographic diversity, both at large and small spatial scales, enhanced the ability of pastoralists to withstand drought and reduce the tendency to proceed directly from drought to famine. Additional factors related to drought susceptibility included the dominant livestock type in each region (browser vs. grazer) and the spatial extent of the area available for pastoral exploitation (Ellis et al., 1987).

9.6.2 Examining the Wildland–Urban Interface

In 2007, Dave Theobald (former NREL research scientist) and Bill Romme (current research scientist) examined the location, extent, and trends in expansion of the wildland–urban interface (WUI) in the US – areas where urban development presses against private and public wildlands (Theobald and Romme, 2007; see Chapter 7). They reported that in 2000 the WUI covered over 719,000 km^2, and contained 39 percent of all housing units in the continental US. They also predicted that the area in the WUI would continue to expand as urban areas expanded. The WUI occurs disproportionately in the eastern US and primarily involves privately owned wildlands nationwide. One of the largest forest management issues within the WUI is forest fires; both in terms of firefighting and in terms of management interventions needed to reduce the likelihood and severity of fires.

Due to the dominance of private land ownership in the WUI, Theobald and Romme (2007) suggested a reevaluation of polices that might shift more of the costs of forest management and firefighting, now largely absorbed by the public, to private owners.

9.7 Citizen Involvement in Ecosystem Science

Citizen science and public engagement in ecosystem science at NREL evolved through a continually increasing realization of the importance of people in ecosystems and ecosystem science. Born through early projects at NREL, such as the South Turkana Ecosystem Project, was the idea that societies and cultures of people are strongly influenced by the ecosystems in which they live. Building upon this idea created an understanding that people also can (and do) participate in the scientific endeavor itself and, moreover, that such participation amplifies the impacts of science for society.

In the IMAS and POLEYC projects discussed earlier in this chapter, local inhabitants, among other stakeholders, were actively involved in determining which possible future scenarios could be addressed through our integrated modeling platform, and the results of the modeling exercises were explained to them when they were completed. These projects needed to be "demand-driven" to ensure the interests of both the pastoralist and wildlife stakeholder groups were being addressed, necessitating numerous workshops and outreach sessions for training and discussion. The stakeholder groups were sometimes not happy with what we predicted, but due to the rapport that was built during the developmental phases, and because they were given the opportunity to initially provide input into the analysis from the beginning, they generally, if sometimes begrudgingly, accepted them.

The Center for Sustainable Dryland Ecosystems and Societies was developed at the University of Nairobi through the joint efforts of scientists from CSU and the University of Nairobi. In late 2011, a Community Voices Workshop was held in Nairobi. Members of pastoral communities from throughout Kenya attended and participated. The objective of the workshop was to elicit input from people living in the dryland areas on what issues they felt were of greatest importance to be the subjects of research in these areas. In this case, citizens were prominently involved in setting research priorities.

Robin Reid was a PhD student on the STEP project. After earning her degree, she returned to Kenya to work for the International Livestock Research Institute, based in Nairobi. She worked there for many years, concentrating on pastoral livestock issues and continually drawing pastoral stakeholders into the research process from the development of research questions, to the collection of data, to application of results, to management of pastoral lands. One example among many was the work described in Reid et al. (2014). Here they described their efforts to develop a new model for community-based conservation in the Mara region of Kenya. This involved the development of research questions based on the concerns or observations of pastoralists, the co-production of knowledge, and the eventual management of the conservation efforts by local interests.

Before we began developing and implementing global citizen science support platforms and individual local and regional citizen science projects, Tom Stohlgren and a team of ecologists, research associates, and graduate students at NREL began tackling pressing issues related to invasive species and their impact on humans and ecosystems (Stohlgren et al., 1997, 1998, 1999; Young et al., 2012). However, while researching and modeling species invasions (with an aim to making predictions to inform decision makers), the team realized that there was a paucity of presence/absence data available for species distribution and habitat suitability modeling. It soon became clear that we had data near roads, porta-potties, and on accessible public lands, but we lacked important data on the whereabouts of invasive species on private lands and other under-sampled locations. How were we to obtain such critical data in these hard to sample locations? Thus began this story of serendipity.

While this team began its invasive species modeling journey, they discovered yet another daunting challenge — how to efficiently capture field presence/absence data (and later percentage cover and abundance data) for invasive species and how best to store these data for easy access and use in subsequent species distribution modeling. Thus the beginnings of field data capture apps were born, initially for the Palm operating system (e.g., EcoNab), but later for smartphone apps, as well as enterprise-level relational database systems for long-term data management, curation, storage, analysis, visualization, and use of data in analysis and modeling. Collectively, a cyberinfrastructure support system was developed to meet the needs of this invasive species research program (see Graham et al. 2007, 2008, 2010), a cyberinfrastructure that became the backbone of the US Geological Survey (USGS)-based National Institute of Invasive Species Science (NIISS, 2018) — an online portal through which field-based observations could be made by field crews to contribute to a growing database of invasive species occurrences valuable for modeling and research. This in turn led to the development of species-specific portals for occurrence data such as TamariskMap.org (commonly known as T-Map), regional portals such as the Great Lakes Early Detection and Monitoring Network, and global data repositories such as the Global Invasive Species Information Network (Jarnevich et al., 2015; GISIN, 2018). These efforts became the launching pad for the global citizen science platform CitSci.org (CitSci, 2018) — a platform that currently supports 463 projects and close to one million scientific measurements made by members of the general public to advance scientific research (Newman et al., 2011).

As our team evolved through our exploration of invasive species modeling, we became increasingly aware of the roles humans play in ecosystems and in particular the spread and distribution of invasive species. We also realized the importance of engaging people in science as essential members of the scientific endeavor who play a major role in scientific study, and in the active conservation of biodiversity and long-term monitoring of ecosystems. These themes emerged as we measured and predicted the biomass of Tamarix (Evangelista et al., 2007) and the spread and potential distributions of pythons under various climate predictions (Rodda et al., 2009). These mapping and modeling projects for specific invasive species forced our team to get outside and embed ourselves in those communities where we were conducting field-based ecosystem research. In doing so, we witnessed first hand the importance of people in ecosystems and in science itself. When we needed help, locals were always there to assist.

Thus began an arm of our work devoted to what is now seen as the burgeoning field of citizen science (Bonney et al., 2009, 2014). Our team contributed to the growth and advancement of this field by studying the degree to which trained volunteers can collect quality data on invasive species (Crall et al., 2010), and the extent to which participation in citizen science projects influences the attitudes, behaviors, scientific literacy, and self-efficacy of those involved (Crall et al., 2012). Team member Greg Newman later went on to serve as the inaugural board chair of what is now called the Citizen Science Association, and to author papers on the future of this growing research arena and community of practice (Newman et al. 2012), citizen cyberscience (Newman, 2014), and to web mapping user experience designs (Newman et al., 2010). Citizen science is now a phenomenon which is empowering scientists to study phenomena not otherwise possible by enlisting trained and willing volunteers to sample spatial and temporal scales that cannot be dealt with by traditional teams of graduate students (Cooper et al., 2007; Theobald et al., 2015), and making large data-interpretation tasks feasible (e.g., Galaxy Zoo's ability to comb through millions of Sloan Digital Sky Survey images of galaxies and classify them in weeks; Clery, 2011). Further examinations into the phenomenon of citizen science allows us to leverage our CitSci.org platform to examine and uncover a relationship between the use of place-based citizen science projects in their materials and the degree to which the data generated by them are used in conservation decision making (Newman et al., 2017). New projects emerging and evolving include investigations into harmful algal blooms in high alpine lakes in collaboration with Dr. Jill Baron, and the ability of remote-sensing techniques to detect and predict ephemeral stream flow through the StreamTracker citizen science project led by Drs. Stephanie Kampf, Michael Lefsky, and Greg Newman.

The data emerging from citizen science investigations into complex ecosystem science topics, and the recognition of the various roles humans play in these systems and in the scientific study of such systems, have emerged as a new paradigm for ecosystem science and the work of both NREL scientists and ecosystem scientists worldwide. New perspectives emerging from works such as Reinventing Discovery (Nielsen, 2012), the Fourth Paradigm (Hey et al., 2009), and The Origin of Science (Liebenberg, 1990) indicate that not only can anyone participate in science, but also that scientific reasoning may therefore be an innate ability of the human mind, with far-reaching implications for self-education, the sharing of indigenous knowledge, and citizen science – notably that anyone can perform rigorous science themselves, regardless of literacy or language spoken (Liebenberg, 2013).

9.8 Conclusions

When the South Turkana Ecosystem Project was funded in 1981, it was the first time that an ecosystem study that included its human component as a full actor in the system had been funded by NSF. Funding came from two NSF programs, Ecosystems Studies and Anthropology. Those two different programs, having never done such a thing before, had to work out how best to provide unified funding to the project. The NSF has since created the Dynamics of Coupled Natural and Human Systems (CNH) program, the sole purpose of which is to fund these types of projects. In 2016, CNH awarded $16.7 million in research grants, attesting to the substantial growth in the study of human-inhabited ecosystems and the interactions among the human and nonhuman components.

However, the human side of ecosystem ecology has grown in other directions as well. Chief among these are the important areas of agroecosystem ecology and understanding ecosystem services. Ongoing research in these areas has led to the realization that the human residents of the ecosystems under study can engage with research scientists to co-create knowledge about their systems and their operation.

Thus, in a relatively short period of time, we have witnessed the growth of ecology from a new science, whose principles needed to be worked out, to a mature science capable of providing guidance to the management of natural and human-dominated systems and the improvement of human welfare.

References

Barnett, D. T., and Stohlgren, T. J. (2003). A nested-intensity design for surveying plant diversity. *Biodiversity and Conservation*, 12, 255–78.

Begzsuren, S., Ellis, J. E., Ojima, D. S., Coughenour, M. B., and Chuluun, T. (2004). Livestock responses to droughts and severe weather in the Gobi Three Beauty National Park, Mongolia. *Journal of Arid Environments*, 59, 785–96.

Bonney, R., Ballard, H., Jordan, R., et al. (2009). *Public Participation in Scientific Research: Defining the Field and Assessing Its Potential for Informal Science Education.* A CAISE Inquiry Group Report. Washington, DC: Center for Advancement of Informal Science Education (CAISE).

Bonney, R., Shirk, J., Phillips, T., et al. (2014). Next Steps for Citizen Science. *Science*, 343, 1436–7.

Boone, R. B., BurnSilver, S. B., Thornton, P. K., Worden, J. S., and Galvin, K. A. (2005). Quantifying declines in livestock due to subdivision. *Rangeland Ecology & Management*, 58, 523–32.

Boone, R. B., Coughenour, M. B., Galvin, K. A., and Ellis, J. E. (2002). Addressing management questions for Ngorongoro Conservation Area, Tanzania, using the Savanna modeling system. *African Journal of Ecology*, 40, 138–58.

Boone, R. B., Galvin, K. A., Thornton, P. K., Swift, D. M., and Coughenour, M. B. (2006). Cultivation and conservation in Ngorongoro Conservation Area, Tanzania. *Human Ecology*, 34, 809–28.

CitSci. (2018). Global Citizen Science Platform. www.citsci.org (accessed August 13, 2020).

Clery, D. (2011). Galaxy Zoo volunteers share pain and glory of research. *Science*, 333, 173–5.

Cooper, C. B., Dickinson, J., Phillips, T., and Bonney, R. (2007). Citizen science as a tool for conservation in residential ecosystems. *Ecology and Society*, 12. www.ecologyandsociety.org/vol12/iss2/art11/ (accessed August 13, 2020).

Coppock, D. L., Swift, D. M., and Ellis, J. E. (1986a). Seasonal nutritional characteristics of livestock diets in a nomadic pastoral ecosystem. *Journal of Applied Ecology*, 23, 585–96.

Coppock, D. L., Swift, D. M., Ellis, J. E., and Galvin, K. A. (1986b). Seasonal patterns of energy allocation to basal metabolism, activity, and production for livestock in a nomadic pastoral ecosystem. *Journal of Agricultural Science – Cambridge*, 107, 357–65.

Coughenour, M. B. (1992). Spatial modeling and landscape characterization of an African pastoral ecosystem: A prototype model and its potential use for monitoring drought. In *Ecological Indicators*, vol. 1, ed. D. H. McKenzie, D. E. Hyatt, and V. J. McDonald. London and New York: Elsevier Applied Science, 787–810.

(2004). The Ellis paradigm: Humans, herbivores and rangeland systems. *African Journal of Range & Forage Science*, 21, 191–200.

(2012). The use of ecosystem simulation modeling to assess feed availabilities for large herbivores in heterogeneous landscapes. In *Conducting National Feed Assessments*, ed. M. B. Coughenour and P. S. Harinder. Animal Production and Health Manual 15. Rome: FAO, 155–63.

Coughenour, M. B., Ellis, J. E., Swift, D. M., et al. (1985). Energy extraction and use in a nomadic pastoral ecosystem. *Science*, 230, 619–24.

Crall, A. W., Holfelder, K., Waller, D. M., Newman, G. J., and Graham, J. (2012). The impacts of an invasive species citizen science training program on participant attitudes, behavior, and science literacy. *Public Understanding of Science*, 22(6), 745–64.

Crall, A. W., Newman, G. J., Jarnevich, C., et al. (2010). Improving and integrating data on invasive species collected by citizen scientists. *Biological Invasions*, 12, 3419–28.

Ellis, J. E., Galvin, K. A, McCabe, J. T., and Swift, D. M. (1987). *Pastoralism and Drought in Turkana District, Kenya*. A Report to NORAD. Nairobi, Kenya, Mimeo

Ellis, J. E., and Swift, D. M. (1988). Stability of African pastoral ecosystems: Alternate paradigms and implications for development. *Journal of Range Management*, 41, 450–9.

Evangelista, P., Kumar, S., Stohlgren, T. J., Crall, A., and Newman, G. (2007). Modeling aboveground biomass of *Tamarix ramosissima* in the Arkansas River Basin of Southeastern Colorado, USA. *Western North American Naturalist*, 67(4), 503–9.

Galvin, K. A. (1992). Nutritional ecology of pastoralists in dry tropical Africa. *American Journal of Human Biology*, 4(2), 209–21.

Galvin, K. A., Beeton, T., Boone, R., and BurnSilver, S. (2015). Nutritional status of Maasai pastoralists under change. *Human Ecology*, 43, 411–24.

Galvin, K. A., Coppock, D. L., and Leslie, P. W. (1999). Diet, nutrition and the pastoral strategy. In *Nutritional Anthropology: Biocultural Perspectives on Food and Nutrition*, ed. A. H. Goodman, D. L. Dufour, and G. H. Pelto. Mountain View, CA: Mayfield Publishing Company, 86–96.

Galvin, K. A., and Little, M. A. (1999). Dietary intake and nutritional status. In *Turkana Herders of the Dry Savanna: Ecology and Biobehavioral Response of Nomads to an Uncertain Environment*, ed. M. A. Little and P. W. Leslie. Oxford: Oxford University Press, 125–45.

Galvin, K. A., Reid, R. S., Behnke, Jr., R. H., and Hobbs, N. T., eds. (2008). *Fragmentation in semi-arid and arid landscapes*. Dordrecht: Springer.

Galvin, K. A., Thornton, P. K., Boone, R. B., and Sunderland, J. (2004). Climate variability and impacts on East African livestock herders. *African Journal of Range and Forage Science*, 21(3), 183–9.

Galvin, K., Thornton, P. K., Roque de Pinho, J., Sunderland, J., and Boone, R. B. (2006). Integrated modeling and its potential for resolving conflicts between conservation and people in the rangelands of East Africa. *Human Ecology*, 34, 155–83.

GISIN. (2018). Global Invasive Species Information Network. www.gisin.org.

Graham, J., Newman, G., Jarnevich, C., Shory, R., and Stohlgren, T. J. (2007). A global organism detection and monitoring system for non-native species. *Ecological Informatics*, 2, 177–83.

Graham, J., Newman, G., Kumar, S., et al. (2010). Bringing modeling to the masses: A web based system to predict potential species distributions. *Future Internet*, 2, 624–34.

Graham, J., Simpson, A., Crall, A., Jarnevich, C., Newman, G., and Stohlgren, T. J. (2008). Vision of a cyberinfrastructure for nonnative, invasive species management. *Bioscience*, 58, 263–8.

Hardin, G. (1968). The tragedy of the commons. *Science*, 162, 1243–8.

Herskovits, M. J. (1926). The cattle complex in East Africa. *American Anthropologist*, 28, 633–4.

Hey, T., Tansley, S., and Tolle, K. (2009). *The Fourth Paradigm: Data-Intensive Scientific Discovery*. Redmond, WA: Microsoft Research.

Hobbs, N. T., Galvin, K. A., Stokes, C. J., et al. (2008). Fragmentation of rangelands: Implications for humans, animals, and landscapes. *Global Environmental Change*, 18, 776–85.

Jarnevich, C. S., Simpson, A., Graham, J., Newman, G. J., and Bargeron, C. (2015). Running a network on a shoestring: The Global Invasive Species Information network. *Management of Biological Invasions*, 6, 137–46.

Liebenberg, L. (1990). *The Art of Tracking: The Origin of Science*. Claremont, South Africa: David Publishers. www.cybertracker.org/tracking/tracking-books/ 276-the-art-of-tracking-the-origin-of-science (accessed August 13, 2020).

(2013). *The Origin of Science*. Cape Town, South Africa: CyberTracker.

Luizza, M. W., Young, N., Kuroiwa, C., et al. (2013). Local knowledge of plants and their uses among women in the Bale Mountains, Ethiopia. *Ethnobotany Research and Applications*, 11, 315–39.

Newman, G. (2014). Citizen cyberscience: New directions and opportunities for human computation. *Human Computation*, 1, 103–9.

Newman, G., Chandler, M., Clyde, M., et al. (2017). Leveraging the power of place in citizen science for effective conservation decision making. *Biological Conservation*, 208, 55–64.

Newman, G., Graham, J., Crall, A., and Laituri, M. (2011). The art and science of multi-scale citizen science support. *Ecological Informatics*, 6, 217–27.

Newman, G., Wiggins, A., Crall, A., et al. (2012). The future of citizen science: Emerging technologies and shifting paradigms. *Frontiers in Ecology and the Environment*, 10, 298–304.

Newman, G., Zimmerman, D. E., Crall, A., et al. (2010). User friendly web mapping: Lessons from a citizen science website. *International Journal of Geographical Information Science*, 24, 1851–69.

Nielsen, M. (2012). *Reinventing Discovery: The New Era of Networked Science*. Princeton, NJ: Princeton University Press.

NIISS. (2018). USGS-based National Institute of Invasive Species Science. www .niiss.org (accessed August 13, 2020).

Reid, R. S., Kaelo, D., Nkedianye, D. K., et al. (2014). The Mara-Serengeti ecosystem and Greater Maasailand: Building the role of local leaders, institutions and communities. In *Conservation Catalysts*, ed. J. N. Leavitt. Danbury, CT: Westchester Publishing Services, 205–27.

Rodda, G. H., Jarnevich, C. S., and Reed, R. N. (2009). What parts of the US mainland are climatically suitable for invasive alien pythons spreading from Everglades National Park? *Biological Invasions*, 11, 241–52.

Stohlgren, T. J., Binkley, D., Chong, G. W., et al. (1999). Exotic plant species invade hot spots of native plant diversity. *Ecological Monographs*, 69, 25–46.

Stohlgren, T. J., Bull, K. A., and Otsuki, Y. (1998). Comparison of rangeland vegetation sampling techniques in the central grasslands. *Journal of Range Management*, 51, 164–72.

Stohlgren, T. J., Chong, G. W., Kalkhan, M. A., and Schell, L. D. (1997). Rapid assessment of plant diversity patterns: A methodology for landscapes. *Environmental Monitoring and Assessment*, 4, 25–43.

Stokes, C. J., McAllister, R. R. J., and Ash, A. J. (2006). Fragmentation of Australian rangelands: Processes, benefits and risks of changing patterns of land use. *Rangeland Journal*, 28, 83–96.

Swift, D. M., Coughenour, M. B., and Atsedu, M. (1996). Arid and semi-arid ecosystems. In *East African Ecosystems and their Conservation*, ed. T. R. McClanahan and T. P. Young. Oxford: Oxford University Press, 243–72.

Theobald, D. M., and Romme. W. H. (2007). Expansion of the US wildland–urban interface. *Landscape and Urban Planning*, 88, 340–54.

Theobald, E. J., Ettinger, A. K., Burgess, H. K., et al. (2015). Global change and local solutions: Tapping the unrealized potential of citizen science for biodiversity research. *Biological Conservation*, 181, 236–44.

Thornton, P. K., BurnSilver, S. B., Boone, R. B., and Galvin, K. A. (2006). Modelling the impacts of group ranch subdivision on agro-pastoral households in Kajiado, Kenya. *Agricultural Systems*, 87, 331–56.

Thornton, P. K., Galvin, K. A., and Boone, R. B. (2003). An agro-pastoral household model for the rangelands of East Africa. *Agricultural Systems*, 76, 601–22.

Weisberg, P., Coughenour, M., and Bugmann, H. (2006). Modelling of large herbivore–vegetation interactions in a landscape context. In *Large Herbivore Ecology and Ecosystem Dynamics*, ed. K. Danell, R. Bergstrom, P. Duncan, and J. Pastor. Cambridge: Cambridge University Press, 348–82.

Young, N., Stohlgren, T. J., Evangelista, P., et al. (2012). Regional data refine local predictions: Modeling the distribution of plant species abundance on a portion of the central plains. *Environmental Monitoring and Assessment*, 184(9), 5439–51.

10 · *A Systems Ecology Approach for Community-Based Decision Making*

The Structured Analysis Methodology

ROBERT G. WOODMANSEE AND
SARAH R. WOODMANSEE

> The problems of today cannot be solved by the level of thinking that caused them.
>
> Albert Einstein

10.1 Introduction

Many human communities, ranging from households and families to governments and their agencies, are grappling with management issues related to sustainable land use and best management of natural resources and the environment. This chapter gives details of an application of the systems ecology paradigm, the structured analysis methodology (SAM), as a starting place for those wishing to implement collaborative decision-making processes intended to promote resilient, sustainable, and desirable ecosystems. First, we lay out the background and philosophy for why methodologies such as SAM are needed to better manage the Earth's ecosystems. Second, we describe SAM, recognizing there are many similar ensuing protocols in existence. Third, we discuss essential needs for stakeholder involvement and collaboration. Finally, we offer an extensive set of questions and data needs as templates to effectively address complex environmental, natural resource, and societal issues.

Scientifically tested and validated concepts for sensible land-use and environmental management at many scales (see Chapter 1) are needed to achieve ecosystem health and sustainability and to ensure the needs of people and societies will be met both now and for future generations (Lubchenco et al., 1991; Hautaluoma and Woodmansee, 1994; Millennium Ecosystem Assessment Board, 2005; Future Earth, 2014;

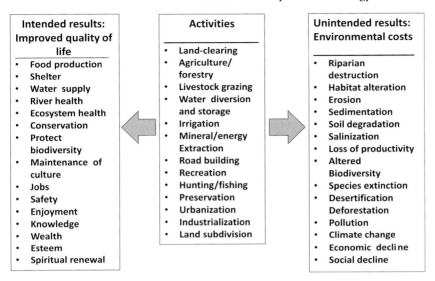

Intended results: Improved quality of life	Activities	Unintended results: Environmental costs
• Food production • Shelter • Water supply • River health • Ecosystem health • Conservation • Protect biodiversity • Maintenance of culture • Jobs • Safety • Enjoyment • Knowledge • Wealth • Esteem • Spiritual renewal	• Land-clearing • Agriculture/ forestry • Livestock grazing • Water diversion and storage • Irrigation • Mineral/energy Extraction • Road building • Recreation • Hunting/fishing • Preservation • Urbanization • Industrialization • Land subdivision	• Riparian destruction • Habitat alteration • Erosion • Sedimentation • Soil degradation • Salinization • Loss of productivity • Altered Biodiversity • Species extinction • Desertification Deforestation • Pollution • Climate change • Economic decline • Social decline

Figure 10.1 Examples of human activities that lead to both intended and unintended consequences.

UNSDG, 2015). Undesirable and unsustainable human–caused impacts on the environment and human well-being are obvious locally to globally to all but the most dogmatic denialists and ideologues (Achenbach, 2015). Prudent concepts and methodologies are needed to avert serious negative consequences on human activities. Successfully implemented, these concepts and methodologies will lead to improved economic conditions, enhanced human well-being, and sustainable local human populations, in addition to sustaining important and desirable ecosystems. But how can this be achieved?

As members of present and future societies, everyone has the right to conduct their lives in a way that will meet their basic human needs for food and water, shelter, safety, a sense of belonging, self–esteem, and spirituality. People should also live in a world that provides services for good health, sense of well–being, self-confidence, and safety (Figure 10.1). Such activities are intended to improve some aspect of the quality of life, but most often emphasis is placed on the positive aspects and much less often on the unintended consequences of the activities. Activities intended for positive goals may set up unforeseen negative impacts on the environment. Everyone has the responsibility to minimize the negative, unintended consequences of their activities.

Forecasting the consequences of human activities is a very complex and often difficult problem when there are environmental, economic, political, and social changes that occur in the same landscape or region, and/or time frame. Changes in climate that co-occur with changes in land-use management give rise to even more complexity. Such "perfect storms" or coexisting factors sometimes lead to epic disruptions, for example the 1930s drought in the North American Great Plains and southwest (Box 10.1). Other modern examples of co-occurring changes are: environmental natural resource and economic policies; human and animal population demographics; improved communications and travel; the globalization of markets; unprecedented organizational and political change; biotic redistribution of many species; increased vigilance and involvement of nontenant land users; and war. Further complications are a new awareness of the limits of ecosystem productivity, profitability, sustainability, and social equity. Determining the effects of these changes on specific problems requires: (1) careful definition of the area of concern geographically (locally to globally), temporally, and institutionally; (2) understanding precisely what the specific issues and problems are; (3) determining the goals for evaluation and solution; and (4) identifying who is involved. Rational and transparent methodologies for creating solutions and protocols for monitoring the progress of implemented solutions are also needed.

An example of a problem needing a collaborative decision-making framework is described in Box 10.1. The problem is, "How can a watershed and its included landscapes be restored to healthy functioning following drastic disturbance?"

Box 10.1 *Example of when things go wrong*

Examples of the lack of harmony between science, management, and policy are typically expressed when major stresses to the economy, shifts in land management practices, and climate extremes co-occur as with the droughts in the North American Great Plains and southwest in the 1930s and 1950s, in Africa in the 1980s, and recently (2014–18) in the Horn of Africa. The consequences of these co-occurrences were disastrous for human communities and their associated ecosystems. Human displacement and migration were common as local populations declined and communities were abandoned as whole families left in search of food, employment, or safety. A lack of appropriate management of land under drought conditions exacerbated by the lack of human institutional resources (social services, economic aid, and unemployment insurance) accelerated this migration.

Those droughts caused extensive ecological changes. Loss of surface cover by native vegetation in the uplands of watersheds has contributed to severe erosion of many agricultural and grazinglands. Loss and alteration of functioning riparian habitat, including gully down cutting, have disrupted the original dynamics of rivers and streams resulting in loss of available surface water and severe impairment of remaining waters due to heavy sedimentation. Reduced productivity of renewable resources, loss of biological diversity, and the introduction of exotic species are other examples of the biophysical effects of human intervention. During this same time frame dramatic fluctuations in climate have occurred often exacerbating human-induced effects.

Such ecological changes to ecosystems in countless watersheds have been influenced by and have impacted the economic and cultural well-being of its inhabitants. Many towns and villages, which once were productive agricultural communities, have been abandoned and people have moved to cities. Traditional natural resource-based lifestyles have been impaired or destroyed. Agricultural infrastructure including whole irrigation systems has been abandoned. Urban migration of younger inhabitants has occurred eroding local community infrastructure needed for transportation, education, health facilities, labor supply, etc. – the hallmarks of viable and sustainable communities.

Off-site impacts of progressive soil erosion within the many watersheds also has damaged the ecological and economic well-being of downstream communities through disruption of natural ecological processes and impairment of water quality by sediment, salts, trace metals, and in some cases radionuclides. A significant reduction in the water storage capacity and life expectancy of many dams and reservoir systems due to sedimentation has occurred. Chronic problems of irrigation system and stream and river channel maintenance occur throughout the world as do deposition of sediments and chemicals in estuaries and ocean margins.

Evaluating impacts and reversing the unintended consequences of human activities that have contributed to the decline of ecosystem health and community well-being are problems needing solutions. Some factors that complicate evaluation are geographical mosaics; mixed ownership

"WHAT YOU SEE DEPENDS ON WHERE YOU STAND"

Figure 10.2 Some of the many viewpoints involved in the analysis of an example watershed to answer the specific question, "how can a watershed (the Rio Puerco Watershed in New Mexico) and its included landscapes be restored to healthy functioning following drastic disturbance?" The quotation is originally from "What you see and what you hear depends a great deal on where you are standing. It also depends on what sort of person you are," in C. S. Lewis' (1955) *The Magicians Nephew*. Figure modified from Riebsame and Woodmansee (1995).

patterns of individual, community, and public land and waters, with their diverse and sometimes conflicting management objectives; time and institutional dimensions or scales associated with land use; and disturbance histories of ecosystems. Reversing unintended consequences are likewise daunting tasks.

Policy analysts, scientists, managers, and the public alike are imbued with their own visions of the landscape in question, bound by experience and training, often leading to overly simplified problem analysis and decisions (Figure 10.2). Each participant has his or her own way of managing, analyzing, and displaying the huge amounts of diverse data and information needed to make informed decisions about real and complex system problems. Overall management of the ecosystem within any region or landscape is a major challenge.

Historically, land and water management and regulation schemes have emphasized constrained (narrow) viewpoints of the environment and natural resources (WCED, 1987; Kessler et al., 1992; Grumbine, 1994; Christensen et al., 1996). These constrained viewpoints have focused on the economy and jobs, commodity production, disciplinary bias (academic and agency "silos"), isolated pollutant effects, single species, individual ecological services, and other narrowly conceived goals and problems (Walker and Salt, 2006). Consistent with these narrow viewpoints, many ecosystems are managed as a result of some form of institutional mandates implemented by legally appointed administrators from outside the problem location. These management structures are typically hierarchical, relatively uncomplicated, and allow decision making by fiat. Explicit and implicit policies and regulations derived and interpreted in myriad ways direct management decisions that are often not transparent.

Society is learning that achieving sustainability of significant and healthy ecosystems will ultimately depend upon how specific landscapes and regions are managed because natural biological and physical processes do not respect human–imposed boundaries or policies (Christensen et al., 1996). Farms, forests, grazinglands, riparian corridors, estuaries and coastal areas, rural and urban areas, wilderness preserves, and parks are all elements of a dynamic and interactive mosaic of ecosystems. These land uses affect each other as parts of the global system.

New and creative institutional and social arrangements combined with innovative new synthetic and original scientific research are required to reconcile competing stakeholder needs, land uses, and management goals (Riebsame and Woodmansee, 1995). Unfortunately, an analysis of influences and feedbacks in decision making are not ideal, as seen in Figure 10.3 (Hautaluoma and Woodmansee, 1994). Policy makers and rule setters are strongly influenced by special interest and paid lobbying groups. Policies strongly influence and inform management implementation and regulations. Often influence from scientists and implementors reported back to policy makers and regulators is weak, as indicated in Figure 10.3. In an ideal world, all feedback would be equally strong, especially those from science to policy makers and managers.

Greater public participation and cooperation among all groups, for example national, regional, local, interest groups, and citizens, are necessary to develop and implement sustainable land use and natural resource and environmental goals by integrating all the dimensions shown in Figure 10.4. Specific discussions of the spatial dimension are found in Chapters 1 and 6. Here we remind readers that spatial boundaries are defined by legal, biological, and physical features, or social/cultural uses, which can be plotted on maps. Attributes such as soil type, vegetation

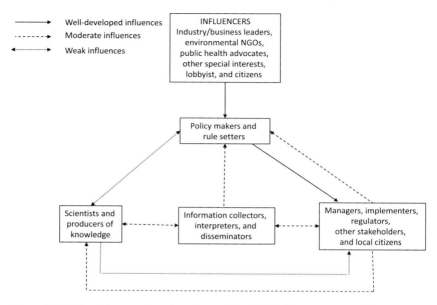

Figure 10.3 The influence functions in a policy feedback system. Modified from Hautaluoma and Woodmansee (1994).

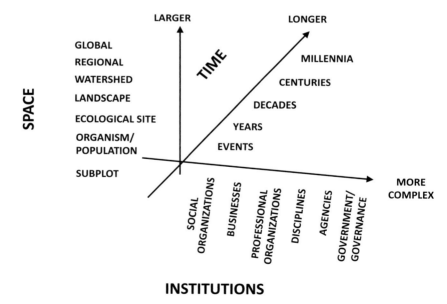

Figure 10.4 Some hierarchical dimensions needing specific attention when evaluating and managing ecological/social ecosystems.

communities, agricultural practices, administrative and political boundaries, physiographic characteristics, and geology further define spatial dimensions. The precise definition of appropriate boundaries is dependent on the problem of concern.

The time dimension requires differentiation between events, such as (1) floods, fires, tornados, and hurricanes; (2) phenomena represented by yearly time periods, for example insect outbreaks, short-term droughts, and toxic chemical spills; and (3) disturbances requiring decades for expression or recovery, for example forest fires, hurricanes, degradation of arable lands, and climate change, and their extension into centuries and even millennia.

Institutional dimensions could include social organizations such as households, families, clans, tribes, communities, cities and towns, states, and countries. Additionally, businesses, professional organizations, academics, the arts, labor, and other skills/disciplines and governmental and nongovernmental agencies could also be involved. Depending on the problem, issue, or question being addressed, consideration of any or many of these hierarchies may be critical for analysis and resolution.

Restoration of degraded ecosystem health, improved water quality, sequestered carbon, reduced pollution, protected biodiversity, and improved wildlife habitat are all collective benefits that require collaboration, cooperation, and coordination of activities by land and water managers. Decision-making processes used in the past by individual scientists, land owners, professional societies, funding agencies, regulatory and management agencies, and specific interest groups (Hautaluoma and Woodmansee, 1994; see Chapter 13) are no longer effective.

10.2 Collaborative Decision Making

New methods of decision making are needed to solve complex environmental and natural resource problems (see Chapter 7). These methods can be called community-based collaborative decision making, emphasizing stakeholder involvement. We refer readers to a few prominent references (Reed, 2008; Hicks et al., 2016; National Forest Foundation (NFF), 2016; Lavery, 2018), instead of reviewing the successes and failures of collaborative decision making here. The science and practice of these methodologies are still in their infancy (Lavery, 2018), but lacking better approaches these methodologies hold promise (see Box 10.2 and Chapter 13).

10.2.1 An Example Methodology

The protocol for managing ecosystems as described here is a formal application of the systems ecology approach. SAM, a science-based process, was developed to help communities of stakeholders evaluate and solve small, regional (such as watersheds, wildlife ranges, municipalities), environmental and natural resource problems (see Box 10.2). The basic structure of SAM can be used for problem solving at patch (ecological site) and landscape levels (farms, ranches, wetlands, etc.), at larger scales (river basins, nations and national borders, and the food, water, and energy nexus), and perhaps globally.

Box 10.2 *Origin of Structured Analysis Methodology*

People who influence and are influenced by local ecosystems need a collaborative, scientifically based management and policy decision-making and problem-solving methodology that accepts and accommodates complexity and complication because these are the norm (Woodmansee and Riebsame, 1993). The SAM is an ecosystem approach intended to help communities of stakeholders solve problems. Similar methodologies using the systems ecology approach have emerged throughout the world under various names and descriptions: adaptive management (Holling, 1978), ecosystem management (Kessler et al., 1992; Grumbine, 1994), and ecosystem sustainability (Woodmansee and Riebsame, 1993); rangeland health (National Research Council, 1994); and forest health (MPWG, 2015), ecological resilience (Resilience Alliance[1]), the ecosystem approach (Waltner-Toews et al., 2008), and collaborative restoration (Hautaluoma and Woodmansee, 1994; National Forest Foundation (NFF), 2016). Reed (2008) reviewed the successes and failures of many collaborative efforts.

SAM was developed in the Terrestrial Ecosystem Regional Research and Analysis Laboratory (TERRA), an intergovernmental and private industry collaborative project in the 1990s (Faber, et al. 1994). All of these methodologies, including SAM, require not being stifled by the demand for unrealistic simplification and expectations, nor should the process be expected to be quick and convenient. A collaborative ecosystem approach should not have to wait many years for new research results before decisions are made. And it must

---

[1] www.resalliance.org.

not be paralyzed by the inability of key stakeholders to communicate with one another. Forrester (1968) suggested that models should not be judged against some assumed perfection, instead they should be judged compared to other ways of describing a system of interest. Woodmansee (1978) expanded on this concept by suggesting that simulation models with well-documented and transparent assumptions should be compared to mental models, word models, photographs, or drawings as tools for describing systems. This concept is true for collaborative decision-making processes. At the very least it is better than the alternatives, at best it leads to enduring solutions to problems. Before continuing we present a cautionary note: the application of SAM and other similar community-based decision-making processes are very hard work for all participants and completion often takes a long time (Walker and Salt, 2006).

By using SAM, local people are accepted as partners and stakeholders in planning, policy, management decision making, and implementation. Local involvement is essential for successful implementation and management of ecosystems and natural resources. Management decisions that are not equitable and allow for stakeholders to demonstrate power, agency (Reed, 2008; Hicks et al., 2016), or decision making that is not supported by local communities are doomed to failure. It is very difficult to achieve ecosystem sustainability when social and political structures are not in place for equitable decision making and management.

SAM allows scientific analysis of complex problems for improved ecosystem health and human vitality. By using tools such as SAM, groups of stakeholders can focus on the interdependence of the ecological, economic, and social integrity of ecosystems. Issues of biological productivity, resilience, social equity, safety, and economic security are interwoven so that policy and management decisions can fully account for their interconnectedness. Through collaborative problem solving, identification, and implementation of management practices consistent with the ecological, cultural, sociological, and economic conditions in the region, many communities have solved perplexing environmental problems (National Forest Foundation (NFF), 2016; USFS, 2016; Bureau of Land Management, 2018).

SAM utilizes collaboration technologies such as geographic information systems (GIS), database management, simulation and mathematical models, and access to the internet with its wealth of valuable information in the ecosystem database. Traditional facilitation approaches are also incorporated to organize, integrate, synthesize, and communicate the knowledge and scientific understanding essential for policy makers, managers, and involved communities to effectively manage ecosystems for sustainability. These approaches will integrate along a variety of dimensions as shown in Figure 10.3.

There are new ways of dealing with the immense complexity associated with the integration of biological, physical, and social factors involved in ecosystem management and planning. Analyses of these interactions will require policy makers, managers, and the public at large to ensure decisions are open to scrutiny and transparency and are comprehendible. SAM guides a systems analysis approach to setting goals for managing ecosystems. It brings relevant actors (stakeholders) together in a collaborative process that resolves problems and conflicts through assessment of the ecological capability and community needs of a specified geographical area. Its ultimate aim is to establish scientifically sound management goals that are consistent with the ecological capacity and common human needs of the area in question, as well as building consensus through community agency (Hicks et al., 2016) before a group or individual resort to judicial action or violence. Such a consensual process that utilizes the best scientific knowledge available is an essential prerequisite for the success of ecosystem management. Ecosystem management must accommodate many viewpoints and stakeholders and involve long-range planning through space, time, and institution. We present the details of SAM to offer a starting place for those wishing to implement a collaborative process.

10.2.2 The Collaboration Framework

The SAM process described here is designed to move science, management, and policy debates beyond abstractions and rhetoric to a rigorous definition, analysis, and implementation of research, management, and policy making. Accomplishing the move from the "rhetoric of vision to the relentless pragmatism of application of science to decision making" (Ron Brown, secretary of commerce, deceased, in his address to the President's Council on Sustainable Development, October 18, 1993) requires a mutually agreed upon research analysis, integration, and synthesis framework. The science-driven process brings scientists, managers, policy makers, and stakeholders together to accomplish this synthesis and evaluation of issues, that is, causes and consequences of global changes,

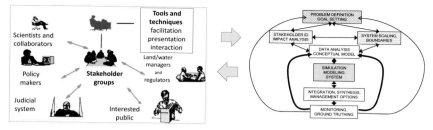

Figure 10.5 SAM represents a proven method of collaboration among scientists, managers, policy decision makers and the public. Focusing all stakeholders or subsets thereof on specific environmental, natural resource, and community issues and goals in open, collaborative settings is an essential step in developing enduring solutions. The right-hand side of this figure is from Figure 1.4.

changes in biological diversity, and factors and goals of ecological sustainability.

The activities illustrated on the right-hand side of Figure 10.5 and described below are steps necessary to define the information needs and solution options associated with environmental, natural resource, and community issues. The systems ecology approach represented in this diagram requires a clear and unambiguous statement of the specific problem and the goals that address it. During and following the initial problem statement, stakeholders (affected parties) are identified, recruited into an analysis team, and the impact of the specific problem for each stakeholder is articulated. SAM brings stakeholders into action forums as illustrated on the left-hand side of Figure 10.5. Traditional group-facilitation techniques and powerful computer-based collaboration and visualization technology serve as the interface between participants (Faber et al., 1994; Balram et al., 2009; Jankowski, 2009). The goals of these interactions are to define, describe, and understand the issues at hand and communicate that understanding to others who will use and be affected by the results of the analysis. Problem analyses raise some essential ecological, economic, social, and institutional considerations that must be included and clearly stated in any assessment process (Woodmansee and Riebsame, 1993; see Appendices 10.1–10.5).

Careful attention must be paid to the spatial, temporal, and institutional scales of the problem during this process (Figure 10.3). Data analysis and collaborative development of a conceptual model of the system will begin after the initial definition of the problem. Development of simulation models is needed to evaluate the systems of concern for many real-world dynamic and complex problems. Modeling efforts are needed to integrate knowledge, synthesize concepts, and develop management options. During the analysis and modeling phase and selection of preferred management options, it is essential to incorporate "ground truthing" (testing of probable outcomes on reality-based areas or treatments), and initiate monitoring programs to evaluate progress and suggest adaptations to changes in the system environment.

The SAM process is more time efficient when it is supported by computer technology; however, there is no substitute for honest human interactions. Healthy interactions develop from mutual trust and respect, especially when issues of stakeholder well-being, their values and sense of agency or empowerment, and feelings of equality or inequality are fully recognized (Hicks et al., 2016).

10.2.3 The Starting Place

The SAM process must be initiated by a governmental or informal authority that is able to identify a problem and then designate an initial group to form a collaboration. The authority could be selected from county commissioners, state governors, agency heads, citizen groups, nongovernmental organization boards, etc. Once selected, the process will begin for problem clarification and description, identification of the initial spatial, temporal, and institutional and dimensions of the problem, and ascertaining other stakeholders involved with the problem. These elements are likely to change as the group gathers facts and evidence, and identifies other stakeholders.

10.2.4 The Group Dynamics

To be successful, SAM requires members of the collaboration to trust and respect one another even if they have widely differing and conflicting viewpoints (Figure 10.2). Respect and trust can be developed if members follow the simple rules of civil discourse, start the process by establishing areas of agreement rather than disagreement, speak factually and honestly, and genuinely listen to each other. Each member must be able to distinguish between what is needed and what is wanted, and between ideology, myths, and facts. Stakeholders must move beyond ideology and accept factual and scientific evidence as drivers in the decision-making process (Hicks et al., 2016).

10.2.5 The Structured Analysis Methodology

SAM consists of sets of questions intended to prompt discussions and group generated, and hopefully agreed upon, answers in addition to generating new problem-specific questions. Appendix 10.1 consists of lists of questions that should be addressed. Similar questions are listed in Waltner-Toews et al. (2008). These questions may seem exhaustive but they are of significant importance. They are intended to serve as reminders or "mind prompts" for questions that often arise in discussions regarding natural resource management, the environment, and other types of land use. Often these questions are afterthoughts resulting from either a challenge created by dissenting individuals or groups, or they are simply ignored. Inattention to the answers of such questions can, and often do, lead to needless misunderstandings and delays.

Various methods of information, data management, and visualization are currently available. Others are in some form of development yet can help identify, organize, integrate, and display the vast amount of information necessary to adequately portray knowledge of ecological systems and answer questions raised by collaborators (Faber et al., 1994; Jankowski, 2009; Kaplan and Newman, 2013; Kaplan et al., 2014). The questions shown in Appendices 10.1–10.5 can be answered through GIS, GPS, and internet access to database and search engines such as Google.

10.2.5.1 Developing Problem and Goal Statements

Developing clear statements that describe the problems and goals of ecological issues remain the Achilles' heel of ecological, natural resource, and human community analysis. For example, we might all agree that loss of biodiversity, global warming, or changing timber and grazing management goals on public lands impact many people. As problem definitions, these general categories lack specificity and are of little help in guiding specific management analyses or ecological and social science research. Vague problem statements and definitions usually lead to endless debate, frustration, and poor communication. SAM emphasizes the need to create clear problems and goal statements through inclusive processes designed to reach agreement among people (stakeholders) with differing viewpoints (see Figure 10.2). The problem statement and goal-setting phase is the starting point for all other activities. Clear definition of the problem needing analysis is vital.

10.2.5.2 Stakeholder Identification and Impact Analysis

Along with the development of the initial problem statement and establishment of the geographic, time, and institutional dimensions of specific problems, the basic impact, or "cause and effect" assessment, and stakeholder identification phase of the analysis must be accomplished (Riebsame and Woodmansee, 1995). "Causes" include changes in management practices brought about by changes in goals; anticipated and unanticipated changes in other ecological or social/economic factors; or an "if left alone what will happen" analysis of the current status. This phase must be based on the strongest factual and theoretical foundations of the natural and social sciences, and the most complete information regarding specific ecological systems of interest using the best databases and expertise available.

Stakeholders (including those initiating the analysis, those who might dissent from an issue solution, or those who might be affected) must be identified and engaged in defining the problem. Participants need to agree on realistic goals for the analysis and also on the spatial, temporal, and institutional boundaries or dimensions of the problem.

Examples of issues addressed in the impact analysis phase are: (1) anticipated impacts of management goals on specific uses and users of ecosystems; (2) policy and management implications associated with the potential changes in global, regional, and local climate; (3) identification of key organizations or individuals responsible for defining policy and management goals and implementing management decisions; (4) identification of parties bearing the costs and realizing the benefits of ecosystem changes; and (5) descriptions of biological, physical, economic, and social constraints. Figure 10.1 shows examples of these types of causes (activities) and effects (intended and unintended results). Appendix 10.1 presents examples of stakeholder identification and assessing their perceived needs, desires, and aspirations. The process demands community involvement and participation.

A major goal of SAM is to link or bridge the best science and expert knowledge available from the biological, physical, economic, and social sectors through collaborative processes to bring about decisions. General categories examined in the Input Analysis include: physical and biological factors of sustainability, weather and climate, water, soil properties, assemblages of organisms, and energy. Social factors of sustainability include: viability within the economy, culture, communities, and organizations; individual behavior; politics; policy; laws; and regulation.

Appendix 10.2 shows greater detail for the factors related to biology, soils, and surface waters that have been considered in the SAM impact analysis. Appendix 10.3 lists the effects of change on climate, weather, energy, and economic factors of ecosystems and communities. Appendix 10.4 demonstrates the effects of change on the social and cultural factors of ecosystems and communities where Appendix 10.5 lists questions associated with geographic and timescales. Appendix 10.6 is an overview of a process for Rio Puerco Watershed stakeholder involvement in SAM.

10.2.5.3 System Geography, Time, and Institutional Dimensions

The space, time, and institutional scale attributes of ecological systems must be clearly characterized (Figure 10.4), even if they are ambiguous and arbitrary, so that stakeholders have a common understanding and agree on the underlying assumption about the system (Figure 10.5). Careful description of dimensional boundaries is also essential to avoid conflicts among scales, such as soil properties of a hilltop used to describe the soils of an entire landscape. These attributes must be described explicitly because generalizations and abstractions are of no more than heuristic value and are often the cause of needless (and endless) debate and misunderstanding. Accomplishing the goals of analysis and synthesis requires rigorous description of the current state of the specific ecosystems in question, their history, and the nature of proposed or continuing stresses and current and proposed management. Specific questions and problems will dictate how the systems of concern are bounded and characterized. The geographic (spatial) and time (temporal) dimensions of this ecosystem must reference problems and questions, such as how will biological invasions be expressed at the regional, landscape, or patch scales, and over what time period: seasons, years, decades, or centuries? Institutions that are affected or involved must also be determined.

Figures 10.6 and 10.7 represent a concept of past, current, and future ecosystems in addition to the types of information needed for thorough analysis. More detail is found in Appendix 10.5. As an ecosystem changes through time, its spatial expression may also change with respect to its biological, physical, economic, social, and political attributes. Important attributes must be described and quantified where possible, with careful attention given to the interrelationship between each.

The amount of information needed to complete the analysis shown in Figures 10.6 and 10.7 and in Appendix 10.5 is enormous and is simply not available except for a few ecosystems, yet even so we make assumptions about these attributes either consciously or unconsciously. Assumptions about important, but misunderstood, factors are an essential part of science, management, and daily living, yet they must be clearly stated. Clear descriptions

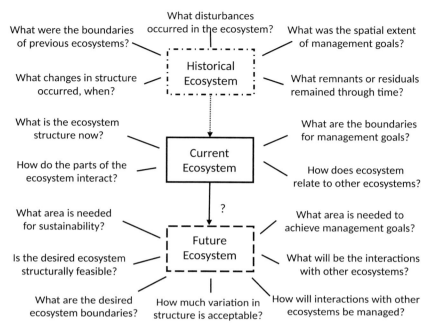

Figure 10.6 Representations of the spatial dimensions of historical, current, and future ecosystems and examples of questions needing answers to help understand how the ecosystem functions now, how it functioned in the past, and how it might function in the future.

of and assumptions about historical, current, and desired ecological systems are essential for evaluating issues ranging from the effects of global change, loss of biodiversity, or the resilience and sustainability of any ecosystem.

Figures similar to Figures 10.6 and 10.7 can be constructed and discussions presented for the institutional dimensions shown in Figure 10.3. Social organizations might include households, families, clans, communities, towns, and cities. Business hierarchies might include individual departments within a local retail franchise, a grouping of franchises within a city or state, and so on, up to multinational corporations. Professional organizations, disciplines, and agencies also have institutional hierarchies. As in all systems, each level is part of a larger system made up of smaller systems. Stakeholders involved in collaborative problem solving must recognize these concepts. Figure 12.2 illustrates this concept as it relates to the Natural Resource Ecology Laboratory and its role in the broader universe.

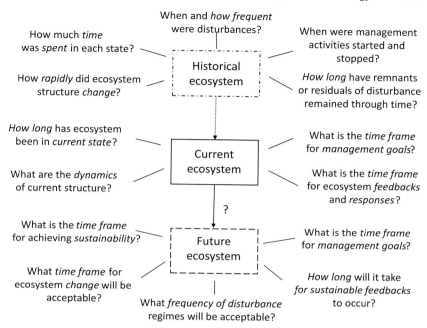

Figure 10.7 Representations of the temporal dimensions of historical, current, and future ecosystems and examples of questions needing answers to help understand how the ecosystem functions now, how it functioned in the past, and how it might function in the future.

10.2.5.4 Conceptual System Characterization and Modeling

A data analysis and conceptual modeling phase, based on clearly stated assumptions derived from integration of previous research findings, data analysis, expert opinion, traditional knowledge, and some SWAGs (scientific wild ass guesses), needs to follow the problem statement, scaling, and stakeholder identification/impact analysis phases of SAM. Technologies, such as GIS, remote sensing, advanced mapping systems, simulation modeling, and data archives of historical disturbance and management practices, contribute to the understanding of successional or developmental trajectories of ecosystems.

After diverse interest groups are identified and their viewpoints adequately represented, work can begin on resolving potential issues. The following are questions to be asked. What is the starting point of the "system"? Is the system being evaluated holistically? What are the characteristics of disturbance? What are the characteristics of the desired ecosystems? What are the likely effects of the stress or disturbance that places the desired ecosystem at risk? What are the indicators of disturbance or change? What are the indicators of sustainability of the desired ecosystem? Is the current ecosystem the desired ecosystem? Is some historical ecosystem the desired benchmark?

Stakeholders are helped by developing a conceptual system characterization or "box and arrow" model that emphasizes processes or linkages between various components (Forrester, 1968; Meadows, 2008). An agreement needs to be reached on how the parts work together (internal system dynamics) and how the ecosystem is influenced by factors outside of itself (driving forces). The conceptual model should explicitly account for the pertinent factors identified in the impact analysis and the stakeholder identification activity that can influence attainment of desired goals. These components are interactive and interdependent, none of which should be ignored without thoughtful consideration and documentation. Driving forces, such as climate, policies, and demographics, along with time and space characteristics, should be included. Following the description of the conceptual model, submodels that describe the dynamics within components can be developed if more detail is needed. Internal controls and feedbacks between components should be emphasized (i.e., how do the parts work together?). The conceptual modeling phase defines a system that is designed and diagramed showing the assumed essential components, processes, driving forces, and interactions within it.

10.2.5.5 Mathematical and Simulation Modeling

It may be necessary to build a mathematical simulation model that represents the dynamics of the system being studied to better understand its functioning and responses. Understanding the dynamics of complex systems such as these may be beyond the comprehension of almost anyone without the aid of tools such as simulation models. These simulation models can be of great value. Ecosystem problems may need complimentary field and laboratory research to delineate and test assumptions made during the model-building activity. Finally, field-monitoring programs may need to be designed to test model validity in a process call "ground truthing." A cautionary note is needed here. All these steps must be considered iterative, and if a problem solution demands it they will need to be repeated frequently as spelled out in the DayCent example in Chapter 4.

During the modeling phases, questions such as "What are the key constraints to achieving the desired goals?" can be addressed. Ecosystem analysis needs to evaluate natural change, the efficacy of implementing management practices and regulations, and inadvertent changes caused by people to ensure a reasonable chance to attain the desired goals. Questions on the components (human, natural, or biophysical) that might interfere with attaining ecosystem sustainability should be an explicit part of any analysis. This step requires exceptional attention to the process of system modeling (including physical, biological, economic, and social/cultural components) that can be used along with computer visualization and collaboration technology.

New methods of visualizing and evaluating modeling results, empirical studies, intuition, and common sense can aid analyses and integration of all the aforementioned steps. Finally, model results must allow scientists, managers, representatives of the public, and policy makers to interact, debate, discuss, and form as much consensus as possible in the evaluation of model results, especially if those results are to be used to develop management strategies for achieving goals such as sustainability, mitigating the factors causing global climate change, or maintaining or increasing biodiversity.

10.2.5.6 Planning Options, Plan Implementation, and Monitoring

The products of the collaborative analysis described above are usually one or more efficacious options for managing the ecosystem chosen by the group. Successful collaborations are achieved when group members reach a mutually agreed upon management plan resulting from shared analyses, discussions, and debates.

Following the choice of a preferred option, the plan can be implemented, assuming resources, labor, and appropriate authorizations are available. This phase is often the downfall of well-intended plans because individuals and institutions that are responsible for enabling the implementation fail to do so for reasons beyond the control of local participants (Hautaluoma and Woodmansee, 1994), resulting in acrimony. If the collaborative group remains cohesive, more political force is brought into place for plan enactment than when individuals act alone.

Assuming a plan is implemented, it becomes imperative that key system characteristics or indicators be monitored to determine whether or not the goals of the plan are succeeding (MPWG, 2015). Adjustments would become essential (adaptive management as described by Holling, 1978) if goals are not being met.

10.3 Summary: Linking Scientific Knowledge and Resource Management Needs, a Systems Ecology Approach

SAM was built to address regional and landscape-scale ecosystems and smaller-scale ecosystems, as well as their components and associated human communities. It is an example of the systems ecology paradigm. The goal is to demonstrate the value of basic science and analysis in the collaborative (participative) decision-making process for the purpose of meeting practical management needs. This approach can add value to ongoing governmental and community planning activities and stretch thinly spread budgets.

SAM or similar methodologies will hopefully contribute to a process for developing regional action plans to address pressing scientific, natural resource, and environmental issues at regional and landscape scales. Process goals include: (1) addressing critical science, resource management, and environmental issues in an integrated fashion on a regional scale; (2) strengthening the linkages among the sciences, management, and policy to address critical environmental issues; (3) facilitating participation by local and regional stakeholders for problem definition and the design and implementation of solutions; and (4) creating new institutional and collaborative arrangements among diverse partners.

These efforts will not only promote resilient and sustainable ecological systems and human communities but will also create a process that facilitates collaboration and partnerships between agencies, scientists, and local and regional stakeholders. This process is a model for focusing on scientific, natural resource management, and environmental issues in any geographic region.

Armed with the tools and philosophy of the systems ecology approach and SAM, the vast warehouse of knowledge from ecosystem science (broadly defined), sufficient resources for collaboration, analysis, and planning, and good will among collaborators, future ecological changes can be successful.

Appendix 10.1 Examples of Questions Guiding Problem Definition

What is the problem or issue confronting the collaborating group?

- What problems, policies or issues require analysis?
- What ecosystem(s) and human communities are impacted by the problems or issues?

Will the impacts be expressed at landscape or local watershed, regional, national, continental, or global geographic scales?

- What are the geographic dimensions of the largest area of concern for the analysis?
- What are the current conditions or states of the ecosystems within the larger area?
- Are the current ecosystems completely exotic as in croplands, pastures, converted forests, degraded native systems invaded by alien weeds, cities, etc.?
- Do the current ecosystems represent a major departure from "natural" conditions?
- Can specific ecosystems that are expected to be impacted by the problem or issue within the larger area be delineated?

Will the impacts be expressed over periods of seasons, years, decades, centuries, or millennia?

- What is the perceived time frame of impact or change?

What are the trends (ecosystem histories) in climate, land use, vegetation change, human habitation, and ecosystem structures (states)?

- What are the natural disturbance regimes in the ecosystems and what are their characteristics or indicators?
- What are the human-caused disturbance regimes and what are their characteristics or indicators?
- Has human intervention significantly altered the natural disturbance history of the ecosystems?
- Are the human-caused disturbance analogs for natural disturbances?

Who should be involved in the analysis?

- Who makes policy?
- Who defines the policy options?
- Who chooses the options?
- Who sets the management goals?
- Who implements the management practices intended to achieve the goals?
- Who pays and in what currency (money, services, values, or products)?
- Who benefits and in what ways?

What is the primary biophysical, social, economic, or policy-driven force (scenario) that is expected to cause change in a specified ecosystem? In other words, what is the key and urgently perceived problem needing analysis and solution?

- What are the expected changes within the ecosystem resulting from the key problem (first-order effects)?
- What ecosystem and human community attributes will be directly and significantly affected as a result of the key problem? For example, flooding may kill crop plants, which is a first-order effect.
- Assuming there are some significant direct effects of a key change, what are the second-order effects (factors affected by the first-order effects, not directly resulting from the primary driving force)? From the flooding example above, people depending on the crop plants go hungry, not as a direct result of the flood but because the plants were killed.
- Are there ancillary disturbances or other changes taking place in the ecosystem(s) that will influence the outcome of this analysis or the sustainability of ecosystems? If so, do they also need analysis?
- Are there indications that the climate is changing?
- Are chemical alterations taking place in the environment?
- Is land use changing due to recreation or commercial enterprises?

What are the goals for the ecosystem(s) of interest? What system attributes does the analysis group believe are necessary to ensure ecosystem sustainability? What is the desired ecosystem(s) and is it attainable given current and foreseen land uses?

- What do we want our desired ecosystems to provide for us and are these wants compatible with sustainability? (See discussion in Chapter 1.)
- What products are desired from the ecosystem(s)?
- What services are desired from the ecosystem(s)?
- What values are desired from the ecosystem(s)?
- What ecosystem characteristics (ecological endpoints) are desired now and for the future? How does the group want the ecosystem to look 10, 100, 1000 years from now?

What management practices, intensive or minimal, will be implemented to achieve these goals for desired ecosystems?

- What physical, biological, economic, and social characteristics (ecological endpoints) will indicate success or failure of the management practices?

Are there keystone (biological, physical, social/cultural, economic, or political) constraints to achieve the desired goals?

- Are there significant political, financial, or social realities that will block implementation of policies, regulations, or management goals?
- Are there significant natural or human-caused changes in biological factors (invasion of exotics, poaching, illegal harvesting, etc.) of the system that might interfere with achieving the desired outcome?
- Are there significant economic, social, or institutional factors that might interfere with achieving the desired outcome?

Appendix 10.2 Issues to Be Considered Regarding Biophysical Properties

Table 10.1 *Example issues to be addressed when analyzing the effects of change on biological, soils, and surface water factors of ecosystems and communities*

Biota	Soils	Streams and rivers	Lakes and reservoirs
Natural vegetation	Physical properties	Volume	Volume
Commercial plant crops	Organic matter	Discharge timing	Discharge timing
Self-maintaining vegetation	Nutrients	Nutrient status	Nutrient status
Game species	Pollutants	Contamination	Contamination
Nongame species	Soil organisms	Riparian condition	Shore condition
Biodiversity	Nutrient cycling	Temperature	Temperature
Weeds, pests, disease	Erosion	Channel configuration	Channel configuration
Aesthetic species	Sedimentation	Vegetation	Vegetation
	Management practice	Microorganisms	Microorganisms
		Meso-fauna	Meso-fauna
		Macro-fauna	Macro-fauna

Appendix 10.3 Climate, Weather, Energy, and Economic Factors

Table 10.2 *Example issues to be addressed when analyzing the effects of change on climate, weather, energy and economic factors of ecosystems and communities*

Weather and climate	Water development	Energy demands	Economics
Precipitation amounts	Agricultural requirements	Dependence on external markets	Subsistence requirement
Precipitation seasonality	Impoundments and diversions	Fossil fuel export	Cash products and services
Storm frequency and severity	River allocations	Fossil fuel generation	External income
Day/night temperatures	Surface water pollution	Fuel available for machines	Subsidies
Seasonal temperatures	Salinization	Fuel available for fertilizer	Water availability
Atmospheric chemistry	Sediments	By-products and disposal	Energy availability
Cloudiness	Aquifer utilization and retention	Air and water pollution	Raw material availability
	Recreation uses	Recreation uses, dependence	Fertilizer availability
			Machinery availability
			Services availability
			Labor availability
			Cost of operation
			Cost of conversion
			Jobs, jobs, jobs

Appendix 10.4 Social and Cultural Factors

Table 10.3 *Example issues to be addressed when analyzing the effects of change on social and cultural factors of ecosystems and communities*

Individual needs and behaviors*	Communities and culture (cultural norms)	Organizations	Politics and policies
Physiological needs	Group identity	Mission, mandates	Laws and regulations
Safety needs	Esteem needs	Goals, objectives	Mission, mandates
Love and sense of belonging needs	Traditional insular value	Human resource structure	Goals, objectives
Esteem needs	Contemporary external values	Culture, history	Human resource structure
Self-actualization	Future options	Receptivity to new ideas	Culture, history
Demographic trend	Feasibility of alternatives	Attitudes about change	Receptivity to new ideas
Essential social services	Issues of equity	Accommodation of surprises	Attitudes about change
Traditional insular values	Essential social services availability	Stability	Accommodation of surprises
Contemporary external values	Demographic trends	Vision of future	Stability
Future options	Social cost transformation		Vision of future
Feasibility of alternatives	Community well-being		Global perspective
Political strength	Political strength		
Social cost Transformation			

*After Maslow's hierarchy of needs.

- Physiological needs (food, water, air, sleep, touch, reproduction, sex, shelter, sanitation, etc.).
- Safety needs (protection, financial security, health, law and order, property, etc.).
- Love and sense of belonging needs (friendship, family, sexual intimacy, work group, etc.).

- Esteem needs (self-esteem, confidence, respect by others, respect of others, achievement, status, etc.).
- Self-actualization (personal growth and fulfillment, morality, creativity, spontaneity, problem solving, acceptance of facts, etc.).

Appendix 10.5 Questions Associated with Geographic and Time Scales

The following are example questions that need to be addressed relating to the geographic and time dimensions of ecosystems and their associated human communities.

Current Ecosystems

- Where are the physical and biological boundaries for each ecosystem within the landscape or region of concern? How long have they been there?
- Where are the boundaries for located management goals? How long have the management schemes been in place? How often have plans changed?
- Do the boundaries of the proposed management goals match the physical and biological boundaries? How frequently have the management boundaries changed?
- Is the structure of the ecosystem(s) known, that is, have the plants, animals (including people), soils, and geology been described? How long has the current structure been in place?
- Are the trends and dynamics of various parts of the ecosystem(s) known?
- What is the relationship of the ecosystem undergoing analysis to surrounding ecosystems?
- Are the natural changes (floods, fires, earthquakes, pest outbreaks, droughts, etc.) understood? Are their natural frequencies known?
- Are the human-caused disturbances (floods, fires, pest outbreaks, droughts, etc.) understood?
- How has the structure and functioning of former ecosystems influenced current ecosystems?

Historical Ecosystems

Where were the boundaries of ecosystems that previously occupied the site of the current ecosystems? How long did those former systems persist?

- What were the changes over time (natural or land use) in structure of the ecosystems occupying the local area?
- Are the former management goals and actions known for the geographic area of concern? What was the geographic extent (boundaries) of those goals and actions? Were the goals and actions successful? How long did each last?
- What were the historic disturbance patterns, frequencies, and durations in the area?
- How did the historical ecosystems relate to other systems?

Desired Ecosystems

- What are the hoped-for geographic boundaries of future ecosystems? How long will it take to get to the desired state? How long will those ecosystems be expected to be in place?
- Are the hoped-for ecosystems structurally feasible biologically and physically? Are the right parts present or will they ever be? Are the hoped-for ecosystems economically, socially, and politically feasible? If so, for how long?
- How large must the ecosystems be for feasibility and sustainability?
- How much variation in system structure will be acceptable?
- What disturbances will be allowed and to what degree will people attempt to control them?
- How large will the ecosystems need to be to effectively implement management goals?
- How will interactions with other systems be addressed or managed?

Some, if not most, of these questions are devilishly difficult to answer. But these types must be addressed even if the answers aren't known and assumptions are substituted. It is better to explicitly state and recognize assumptions than to implicitly ignore ignorance.

Appendix 10.6 Analysis of the Human Dimensions of the Rio Puerco Watershed

The following description is taken verbatim from a project initiated by staff of the Terrestrial Ecosystem Regional Research and Analysis Laboratory (TERRA) in the early 1990s (Fox et al., 1992). The TERRA protocol is similar to the community-based social marketing of McKenzie-Mohr (2011).

Introduction

Understanding and assessing the human resource component of the Rio Puerco Watershed is essential to the development of a land use plan for the area that will provide sustainable functioning of both human and natural ecological systems. Sustaining viable communities relies upon an interplay of natural environmental factors and the availability of human resources, such as health services, education, transportation and distance to trade centers, health of the local economy, public welfare resources, and beliefs and values held by those in communities. A human dimensions assessment of the Rio Puerco will: (1) inform land management and policy decision makers about human resource factors; (2) serve as a baseline of information about current conditions to be used later in evaluating the impacts of proposed management strategies; (3) develop a functional means of gaining input and cooperation from the private and community stakeholders who are most impacted by changes in the river and watershed; and (4) provide a first approximation for integrating human values and motivations in global change models.

Knowledge of the types and sizes of various economic institutions in the watershed can be used to determine the types and sizes of impacts various land management strategies would likely have on local communities. Availability of public resources and sources of funding, and their value within the community, adds to the likelihood of community stability and informs on the impacts from various land-use plans. Current patterns of use, cultural attitudes and beliefs, and values about community, land, and agencies are factors which play a large role in both the planning of land use and the best processes for obtaining public comment and cooperation.

Historical information about traditional patterns and attitudes towards prior planning, the type and quality of cooperation between agencies, and cultural values provide a background from which trends and developments can be measured. Individual and collective perceptions about historical and current trends in range and water management will be used to build conceptual models of the drainage and promote greater participation by the communities most interested in the planning efforts.

Census data for population size, amount of population change over past decades, age distribution, income sources and amounts, and occupations can be used to develop a picture of the local economic and age structures of communities. The number of people engaged in agriculture or occupations directly affected by the health and maintenance of the Rio Puerco ecosystems can also be determined.

Data obtained will inform the modeling process regarding: (1) economic viability of communities, subsidies, import and export of goods and services, trends and direction of changes to the economy; (2) community identity, history, culture, values, visions/options for the future, demographic trends, and perceptions of equity, community well-being, and political strength; (3) organizational dynamics, presence or absence of conflict, preferred means of participation; and (4) political structure and function.

Informing Land Managers and Decision Makers

Land managers and other decision makers often encounter local opposition to their plans, leading to lengthy hearings and changes in original planning efforts which are costly in both time and money. Development of a model that includes stakeholder attitudes, pressures, and long-term trends can save management energy and resources, and lead [to] more efficient planning. Information regarding jurisdictions and political, ethnic, and racial boundaries within the area will be obtained from land and water managers, the impacted public, and other political organizations, such as tribal leadership and city/county governments in each local area of the Rio Puerco Watershed.

Data obtained in this study will be integrated into a conceptual model that will formalize knowledge about the human systems in the Rio Puerco. Concerned populations will be organized into groups which can thoughtfully participate in a planning process with the agencies responsible for resource management. Using this information, resource managers will have a conceptualized method for developing plans and both long- and short-term goals.

Baseline Information, Current Conditions, and Measures for Future Evaluation

A survey will be used in each community to obtain the best and most complete information possible about the watershed. Historical information held in local populations can provide a clearer picture of the non-human ecology of the drainage. Census data, marketing information, and other economic data will provide a level of current conditions that can be independently measured and verified. Land and water managers, the impacted public, and other political organizations, such as tribal leadership and city/county governments in each local area of the Rio Puerco Watershed will be asked to participate in building an environmental data-base that will be incorporated into the conceptual model referred to in the TERRA proposal. Measures for program evaluation will be the result of a planning process jointly undertaken by land and resource managers, as well as the various political and social stakeholders who have elected to participate in this planning process. A feature of the modeling effort will be to identify goals and objectives that can be operationalized into measures of program strengths and weaknesses in future years.

A Functional Method for Gaining Input and Cooperation from Private and Community Stakeholders

An interactive procedure for involvement by the public as well as the land and resource managers of the Rio Puerco Watershed will contribute to the adoption of a cooperative management plan and also help define critical roles and effective agencies for resource management. Education and training in range and water management enhances cooperation and interest in jointly held goals and objectives. It also provides a unity that improves cost management over time. To obtain the best and most complete information regarding the watershed, surveys will be taken in each community. The procedures outlined below have integrated some principles of modern range ecology and management embedded within them.

All interested state and federal management personnel, community representatives, and other stakeholders will be invited to become a part of the information gathering process. Those contacted will be invited to: (1) develop a specific procedure for gaining information from their community or interest group; (2) provide contact with existing community organizations that currently work on watershed and range issues or identify persons from their community who might be willing to form a watershed committee; (3) provide interpretation as needed; and (4) develop local goals and objectives for their area of the watershed.

Meetings will be requested between the watershed organizations and their political representatives to determine the best method for obtaining public comment on the various factors listed below as part of the conceptual model-building process and the most effective method for conducting the survey. Depending upon local traditions and preferences, this survey may be given in a face-to-face interview with a subset of the general impacted population. Alternatively, it could be given to the population as a whole using TERRA technology as referred to in the TERRA proposal. After the survey is administered and results have been summarized, a new series of meetings with the watershed committees and local leadership will be held to share the survey results and for participation in the conceptual modeling process.

State and federal land and watershed managers will be asked to participate in both these local meetings as well as working separately on their own goal statements and surveys. Each community will then be asked to send representatives to a series of modeling workshops to complete the modeling process and develop an all-inclusive watershed plan. It is hoped that by including as many people as possible in the data collection and goal-setting process, a better management plan will be developed and there will be an increased level of cooperation and participation. If successful, this process may be used in the future to encourage cooperation from Rio Grande water users and others who have a secondary interest in the health of the Rio Puerco ecosystem.

Reconnaissance

Should be familiarized with existing community structures and boundaries, and able to identify sources of information and people who are interested in the issues of land and watershed management in the Rio Puerco.

Collect data from external sources such as political maps, census data, economic databases, and other informants (literature, personal contact, etc.).

Time: Two Months: One in New Mexico, one in literature and database research.

Engagement

Contact identified leadership, begin to explore the feasibility of conducting a survey in the area, facilitate and collaborate with community to obtain local information, begin development of problem statement. Assess community interest and involvement in water and land issues.

Time: Concurrent with step one in New Mexico, plus one week per month for three to four months.

Planning

Incorporate input from local committee and leadership (including federal, Indian, and state land managers) to determine the best questions, wording, and trial runs to include when creating the survey.

Help the committee to publicize its activities and the survey.

Time: Concurrent with end of step two, leading into winter months; two weeks per month until survey questionnaire is completed.

Implementation

Administer the survey to each local community, and then analyze the results using statistical methods suitable for a descriptive study.

Time: One week for each community (each stakeholder group is a community). One month for statistical analysis.

Share results with each committee, set new meetings for actual problem definitions and modeling activities (likely covered in more than one meeting), and begin consensus building. The process for these meetings will be decided upon by the committee.

Time: One week per community.

Convene a watershed-wide modeling group composed of representatives from each locality to begin problem definition, modeling, and planning for the watershed.
  Land managers develop final plan, which is shared with large group.

Time: To be determined, preferably before the Field Conference. The exact length of time and how that time will be used will be determined with the help of the group.

Land managers develop final plan, which is shared with large group.

Evaluation

Evaluate process and information developed through this method. Set process for continued involvement of committees in the watershed planning process.

Disengagement

Withdraw from activities.

References

Achenbach, J. (2015). The age of disbelief. *National Geographic*, 227, 30–47.

Balram, S., Dragicevic, S., and Feick, R. (2009). Collaborative GIS for spatial decision support and visualization. *Journal of Environmental Management*, 90(6), 1963–5.

Bureau of Land Management (BLM). (1989). *Little Snake Resource Management Plan and Record of Decision*. USDI Bureau of Land Management, Craig District, Little Snake Resource Area, urn:oclc:record:1048789307. https://archive.org/details/littlesnakeresou3740unit (accessed August 20, 2018).

Christensen, N. L., Bartuska, A. M., Brown, J. H., et al. (1996). The report of the Ecological Society of America committee on the scientific basis for ecosystem management. *Ecological Applications*, 6(3), 665–91.

Faber, B. G., Watts, R., Hautaluoma, J. E., et al. (1994). A groupware-enabled GIS. *GIS*, 94, 3–13.

Forrester, J. W. (1968). *Principles of Systems*. Cambridge, MA: Wright-Allen Press.

Fox, D. G., Faber, B. G., DeCoursey, D. G., et al. (1992). *The Terrestrial Ecosystems Regional Research and Analysis Laboratory: Regional Collaboration to Address Global Change Issues*. México: Montecillo, 41–6.

Future Earth. (2014). Future Earth 2025 Vision. http://old.futureearth.org/sites/default/files/future-earth_10-year-vision_web.pdf (accessed August 14, 2019).

Grumbine, R. E. (1994). What is ecosystem management? *Conservation Biology*, 8(1), 27–38.

Hautaluoma, J. E., and Woodmansee, R. G. (1994). New roles in ecological research and policy making. *Ecological International Bulletin*, 21(21), 1–10.

Hicks, C. C., Levine, A., Agrawal, A., et al. (2016). Engage key social concepts for sustainability. *Science*, 352, 38–40.

Holling, C. S. (1978). *Adaptive Environmental Assessment and Management*. New York: John Wiley and Sons.

Jankowski, P. (2009). Towards participatory geographic information systems for community-based environmental decision making. *Journal of Environmental Management*, 90(6), 1966–71.

Kaplan, N. E., Baker, K. S., Draper, D. C., and Swauger, S. (2014). *Packaging, Transforming and Migrating Data from a Scientific Research Project to an Institutional Repository: The SGS LTER Collection*. Digital Collections of Colorado. Fort Collins, CO: Colorado State University. http://hdl.handle.net/10217/87239 (accessed August 13, 2020).

Kaplan, N. E., and Newman, G. J. (2013). *Data Management for NREL and Beyond: A Roadmap and Recommendations*. Digital Collections of Colorado. Fort Collins, CO: Colorado State University. http://hdl.handle.net/10217/87381 (accessed August 13, 2020).

Kessler, W. B., Salwasser, H., Cartwright, Jr., C. W., and Caplan, J. A. (1992). New perspectives for sustainable natural resources management. *Ecological Applications*, 2, 221–5.

Lavery, J. V. (2018). Building an evidence base for stakeholder engagement. *Science*, 361, 554–6.

Lewis, C. S. (1955). *The Magician's Nephew*. New York: Harper Collins Children's Books.

Lubchenco, J., Olson, A. M., Brubaker, L. B., et al. (1991). The sustainable biosphere initiative: An ecological research agenda – A report from the Ecological Society of America. *Ecology*, 72(2), 371–412.

McKenzie-Mohr, D. (2011). *Fostering Sustainable Behavior: An Introduction to Community-Based Social Marketing*. Gabriola Island, BC: New Society Publishers.

Meadows, D. H. (2008). *Thinking in Systems: A Primer*. White River Junction, VT: Chelsea Green Publishing.

Millennium Ecosystem Assessment Board. (2005). Millennium Ecosystem Assessment, 2005. *Ecosystems and Human Well-being: Synthesis*. Washington, DC: Island Press. www.millenniumassessment.org/documents/document.356.aspx.pdf.

Montréal Process Working Group (MPWG). (2015). *The Montreal Process: Criteria and Indicators for the Conservation and Sustainable Management of Temperate and Boreal Forests*. www.montrealprocess.org/documents/publications/techreports/MontrealProcessSeptember2015.pdf (accessed August 17, 2018).

National Forest Foundation (NFF). (2016). Collaborative Restoration Workshop. The 2016 Collaborative Restoration Workshop, Denver Colorado. www.nationalforests.org/collaboration-resources/collaborative-restoration-workshop (accessed August 17, 2018).

National Research Council. (1994). *Rangeland Health: New Methods to Classify, Inventory, and Monitor Rangelands*. Washington, DC: The National Academies Press.

Reed, M. S. (2008). Stakeholder participation for environmental management: A literature review. *Biological Conservation*, 141, 2417–31.

Riebsame, W., and Woodmansee, R. (1995). Mapping common ground on public Rangelands. In *Let the People Judge*, ed. J. Echeverria and R. B. Eby. Washington, DC: Island Press, 69–81.

UN Sustainable Development Summit (UNSDG). (2015). *Sustainable Development Goals: 17 Goals to Transform Our World*. www.un.org/sustainabledevelopment/sustainable-development-goals/# (accessed June 18, 2018).

USDA Forest Service (USFS). (2016). *Northwest Forest Plan*. www.fs.fed.us/r6/reo/. (accessed August 17, 2018).

Walker, B., and Salt, D. (2006). *Resilience Thinking: Sustaining Ecosystems and People in a Changing World*. Washington, DC: Island Press.

Waltner-Toews, D., Kay, J., and Lister, N.-M., eds. (2008). *The Ecosystem Approach: Complexity, Uncertainty, and Managing for Sustainability*. New York: Columbia University Press.

Woodmansee, R. G. (1978). Critique and analyses of the grassland ecosystem model ELM. In *Grassland Simulation Model*, ed. G. S. Innis. New York: Springer Verlag.

Woodmansee, R. G., and Riebsame, W. (1993). Evaluating the effects of climate change on grasslands. In *Proceedings of the XVII International Grassland Congress*, ed. New Zealand Grassland Association, et al. Palmerston North, New Zealand: The Association. 1191–6.

World Commission on Environment and Development (WCED). (1987). *Our Common Future: Report of the World Commission on Environment and Development*. Oxford: Oxford University Press.

11 · *Environmental Literacy*

The Systems Ecology Paradigm

ROBERT G. WOODMANSEE,
JOHN C. MOORE, GREGORY NEWMAN,
PAUL H. EVANGELISTA, AND
KATHERINE S. WOODMANSEE

11.1 Emergence of Ecosystem Science and Systems Ecology Literacy

The Ecosystem Concept in Natural Resource Management, a book organized and edited by George Van Dyne (1969), was one of the first products of the immerging International Biological Program's (IBP) Grassland Biome. It introduced the notion of the "systems ecology approach" (see Chapters 1 and 7) to issues of natural resource management. Van Dyne used the term "ecosystem approach" in the book's introduction. Major topics included range management, forestry, fish and game management, and watershed management. It also included a chapter that introduced the ecosystem concept and systems ecology into academic training. The volume foreshadowed the systems ecology paradigm (SEP) and the integration of simulation modeling and field and laboratory research into applications for natural resource decision making and ecosystem management and education.

During the late 1960s and 1970s, Colorado State University (CSU) became known as a world leader in systems ecology, ecosystem science, and range management and education (Rykiel, 1999). The Range Science Department, an academic department under the leadership of C. Wayne Cook, established graduate and undergraduate curricula in rangeland ecosystem science. Many of the graduate students funded by the IBP Grassland Biome received their degrees from the department. Training programs (Ecosystem Management Short Courses) in the concepts of ecosystem structure and functioning (see Chapter 7) were developed jointly by the Natural Resource Ecology Laboratory (NREL) and the Range Science Department for federal land managers. These courses emphasized modules in primary production, decomposition, nutrient cycling, soils, secondary production, enterprise economics, statistics, and systems ecology and ecosystem modeling. Many prominent leaders in ecosystem science and land-use management were trained in these and subsequent programs (see Chapter 3 and 7). The stage was set for the infusion of basic ecosystem science into academic training as well as applied science and management (see Box 7.2).

The current holistic view of grazingland ecosystems emerged from the linkage between the IBP Grassland Biome, NREL, the Range Science Department, and the Agronomy Department at CSU, and with the USDA Agricultural Research Service in Fort Collins, Colorado (see Chapter 7). Whole ecological systems and their functioning, not just structure and production (see Chapter 6), were to become the focus of grazingland management in the United States and numerous other countries across the globe (Williams, 2005; see Chapter 7). During the early years, the term "whole-system functioning" meant understanding both above and belowground processes (above and belowground primary and secondary production, decomposition processes, nutrient cycling pathways, plant and animal interactions, ecological site scale and landscape hydrology, erosion, and sedimentation). Many of these processes are now considered "ecosystem services" (Christensen et al., 1996; MEA, 2005). Spatial and temporal scaling (ecological hierarchies) was identified as essential for both grazingland and agricultural ecosystem management (Anderson et al., 1983; Woodmansee, 1990). It would take until the late 1980s for humans to be recognized as integral components of ecosystems (see Chapters 1 and 9).

11.2 Systems Ecology and Simulation Modeling Training

Simulation models were essential for the development of the concepts that integrated the interactions of ecosystem components (see Chapter 4). The early focus and success of the NREL and the Range Science Department can be attributed to the discovery of how ecosystems function based on knowledge gained from field and laboratory research, data analysis and integration, and simulation modeling. Yet, systems ecology and simulation modeling education at CSU fell largely to the NREL staff who taught classes and short courses in various departments across campus. The early Grassland Biome "modelers" came to CSU from various institutions and disciplines (see Chapters 3 and 4). Two systems ecology/modeling courses were taught by NREL staff (Drs. George Van Dyne, Sam Bledsoe, and Freeman Smith) through the College of Forestry and Natural Resources and another by Dr. J. O. Reuss,

Agronomy Department and Dr. R. G. Woodmansee, NREL. Later in the 1980s, various versions of systems ecology/modeling courses were offered by Drs. W. J. Parton, W. K. Lauenroth, and H. W. Hunt. However, the courses were dropped due to low enrollment. Ironically, few formal ecosystem modeling courses have been taught at CSU after the 1980s, instead those modeling skills have been passed down to students and collaborators through hands-on learning under the mentorship of NREL-related scientists.

11.3 Emergence of Formal Academic Programs

From the inception of the Grassland Biome, the NREL maintained an impressive history of financially supporting graduate and postgraduate training, even though a formal academic program had not been established. In addition, many nontenured and tenure-track faculty supported graduate and undergraduate teaching at CSU. Involvement of NREL staff in formal graduate and undergraduate education was primarily offered through guest lectures or class instruction for absent faculty members on an "ad hoc basis." For those who had gained academic positions as regular faculty members, most courses taught using disciplinary department curricula. Few formal systems ecology or ecosystem science courses were offered.

Even though most NREL staff did not have academic appointments, they were instrumental in conceiving and developing the Graduate Degree Program in Ecology (GDPE) at CSU.[1] The GDPE is an interdepartmental program that allows students from academic departments to develop individualized coursework from a variety of departments. As a result, graduate students supported by NREL were provided with the opportunity to be based in a traditional department, as required by CSU, and yet obtain a degree from an academic program that supported their ecosystem science and systems ecology goals. Many students were thus not pigeonholed into traditional disciplinary silos but were rather able to obtain an "ecology" degree.

Another notable spinoff with close ties to the NREL was CSU's School of Global Environmental Sustainability (SoGES) with Dr. Diane Wall, former director of the NREL, as the inaugural director.[2]

---

[1] https://ecology.colostate.edu.   [2] https://sustainability.colostate.edu.

SoGES fosters collaborative cross-campus, cross-disciplinary partnerships in research, education, and engagement in environmental sustainability.

Formal academic status within the NREL changed in 2011 under the leadership of Dr. John C. Moore with the establishment of the Department of Ecosystem Science and Sustainability (ESS),[3] the fifth and newest department in the Warner College of Natural Resources. ESS was initially staffed with NREL researchers (Box 11.1).

The ESS offers graduate degrees in ecosystem sustainability, greenhouse gas management and accounting, and watershed science. Undergraduate degrees are offered in ecosystem science and sustainability and watershed sciences.

11.4 Nontraditional Education in the Digital Age

Systems ecologists and ecosystem scientists must take on the task of training new generations of citizens, both on and off campus, to make informed and responsible decisions about their planet. The development of formal, transdisciplinary education and engagement pathways for nontraditional undergraduate, graduate, and postgraduate learners[4] in remote locations is a new challenge facing today's academic institutions. Formal acknowledgment of training from academic departments is often required for job placement and promotion for working professionals. Nontraditional learners seeking career changes, interested citizens and thought leaders, and those wanting to upgrade their credentials can also benefit from formal, online academic training.

Online academic programs and courses offer twenty-first-century extensions of educational efforts (see Box 11.2). These efforts utilize the immense resources and capabilities of online learning management systems, webinars, blogs, videos, interactive virtual lectures, and field trips, in addition to resources offered by social media.

To fully engage students and other learners with fundamental information, instructors must offer interactive learning experiences. While the old modality of the "sage on a stage" lecturing to a group of "students" is effective for some, it does not encourage learners to interact with the information and certainly does not work with online learners. Educators

---

[3] https://warnercnr.colostate.edu/ess/.

[4] The term "learner" is used interchangeably with "student" in this discussion because many individuals and groups needing the ecosystem knowledge and systems approach described in this book are not formal students. All are learners, some are students.

Box 11.1 *Department of Ecosystem Science and Sustainability*

Ecosystems include the many processes of life that support and enrich humankind. These processes include interactions among organisms and species, the flow of energy and the cycling of matter, and the maintenance of diverse and complex communities of microbes, plants, and animals. Our responsibility is to understand the world's ecosystems and the effect of human societies on ecosystem processes and their long-term sustainability. Research and education are central to that understanding, enhancing our ability to manage for the sustainability of ecosystems, societies, and the biosphere. Students in the department will integrate the latest science into real-world decision-making and public policy, with the ultimate goal of managing our planet's natural resources – the air, water, land, and biological diversity upon which all life depends – sustainably into the future.

The mission of ESS is to understand ecosystem function and change across space and through time and to approach this understanding by examining interactions within and between natural and human systems. Through discovery and education, ESS contributes to understanding and sustaining ecosystems and their services. ESS examines these in the context of current stresses such as changing climate, species introductions, land-use change, and intensification. Our department uses state-of-the-art technologies and approaches to provide a quality education to future scientists, educators and decision makers, conducts cutting edge interdisciplinary research, and delivers culturally relevant outreach programs that empower our students and the general public locally, nationally, and internationally.

ESS is joined with a world premier Watershed Science Program, which was originally part of the Department of Forest and Rangeland Stewardship. Watershed Science is the study of the natural processes and human activities that affect fresh water resources. Water is a critical component of Earth's ecosystems and is used for human consumption, agriculture, energy production, transportation, and recreation. Management of fresh water resources is an increasingly important and complex challenge in Colorado and worldwide.[5]

---

[5] Text taken from https://warnercnr.colostate.edu/ess/.

Box 11.2 *Western Center for Integrated Resource Management (WCIRM)*

Today's agricultural managers are challenged to manage their land, animal, and natural resources in ways that ensure long-term profitability and sustainability of farms, ranches, and rural communities. Integrated resource management is a concept within agricultural production that examines economic and environmental variables with an orientation toward more sustainable production.

Colorado State University's online master's degree program in agriculture titled Integrated Resource Management is a multi-disciplinary program, blending animal science, business, range science, ecology, wildlife, policy, and human resources. This fusion of topics allows learners to understand how agricultural resource systems work together in a comprehensive way, and how to apply them in an agricultural management setting. The program is offered by the Western Center for Integrated Resource Management (WCIRM) and is supported by the: College of Agricultural Sciences; Warner College of Natural Resources; College of Veterinary Medicine and Biomedical Sciences; and the School of Global Environmental Sustainability (SoGES).

The online program has served students through the United States and many other countries throughout the world since 2009. Dr. R. G. Woodmansee offers a core, required course titled "Managing for Ecosystem Sustainability" in IRM program.[6]

know that it is vital to make meaningful connections between subject matter, information, and real-life applications. In a classroom setting, an online learning environment, or a blend of both, use of real-life case studies and research on local issues or current issues students face within their work or study environment, in addition to complex environmental issues, will encourage students to connect more fully with the important information they are receiving.

By creating opportunities for learners to engage with the subject matter content and apply it to real-life situations, educators allow students to convert information into actions that are meaningful to them. This engagement allows all learners, especially students, to not only do well on tests, but to carry that information with them into the real world.

---

[6] www.online.colostate.edu/degrees/irm/.

Taking a learner-centered approach to education allows students to convert knowledge into action and allows educators to dive more deeply into interaction and engagement.

At first this learner-centered approach may feel daunting to educators; however, by partnering with learning experts, instructional designers, and educational psychologists, experiential learning will create a more stimulating experience for the instructors and students alike. Lectures and multiple-choice tests are still useful tools, yet they should be tempered with discussions, hands-on projects, multimedia presentations, and opportunities for learners to not only regurgitate subject matter content, but also apply it to real-world situations. While this clearly improves the learner experience, it can also benefit educators; learners may bring up issues an instructor had no prior knowledge of or a new and different perspective from another field (true co-education).

The great diversity of learners' backgrounds is another challenge for ecosystem scientists and systems ecologists. It can often be difficult to assess the level of engagement in an online learning environment. In the past, this type of teaching often consisted of PowerPoint presentations (often not narrated), textbook readings, and simple quizzes or tests. Today's best practices call for a far more interactive educational experience (Hawtrey, 2007; Goh et al., 2019). Understanding that today's learners often have a relatively short attention span, but are also able to access innumerable resources, can help inform educators on how best to present information in an online setting. By mixing readings, short lectures, videos, self-directed learning projects, discussions, and a wide variety of interactive learning tools, educators can not only increase student engagement, but also increase student retention.

Teaching adults (andragogy), even young adults, is based on a wealth of experience that is brought into the learning environment (Knowles, 1977; Pappas, 2015). One of the principal ways adults learn and retain knowledge is by building on those experiences. A well-designed course will allow learners to make the connection between their past experiences and the new information received. Teaching children (pedagogy) who are not able to bring life experiences into the classroom is a very different process and should not be confused with teaching adults.

It is important to consider that adults often have life circumstances which can both aid and distract from the learning experience. Particularly with nontraditional students, especially online-only students, it is important to factor in barriers to learning such as family demands, work demands, and financial pressures. On the other hand, a supportive work environment, or the drive to improve the life of an individual and his/ her family, can be powerful motivators and stimulate the desire to continue their education.

Another major challenge facing systems ecology and ecosystem science education in remote areas is the unintended consequence that much of the knowledge and hard literature established prior to the digital age is either inaccessible, accessible only in libraries, or ignored because it is difficult to retrieve. Access to predigital scientific journals is improving, but access to books and book chapters is often difficult, if not impossible. During the development and evolution of ecosystem science and systems ecology many of the seminal papers were published as book chapters because they were based on concepts, ideas, and models drawn from the integration and synthesis of previous research and experience, rather than original data and data analysis. Scientific journal reviewers were loath to accept papers that were not data driven. Many of these ideas first appeared in proposals to the National Science Foundation (NSF) that requested funds to collect data and build models. At that time, the NSF and their review panels were receptive to bold, new ideas, and thus the birth of a new science.

One example for meeting the challenge of knowledge transfer is the evolving Data Observation Network for Earth (DataOne),[7] an NSF-funded program, that informs scientists, managers, decision makers, and citizens about this warehouse of knowledge. DataONE is the "foundation of new innovative environmental science through a distributed framework and sustainable cyberinfrastructure that meets the needs of science and society for open, persistent, robust, and secure access to well-described and easily discovered Earth observational data." Several of the NREL scientific staff have been involved with the development of DataOne (Kaplan and Newman, 2013; Kaplan et al., 2014; see Chapter 13).

Education for all learners and educators must continue to evolve and develop. Much like the science of ecosystems, education delivery must continually grow and evolve. In the very near future, both learners and formal students will have access to a vast amount of information (see Chapter 13), whereas students in 1985 had to seek out information in different ways and often relied solely upon the information presented in class or in textbooks. Creating learner engagement via the internet now and in the future will be critical to the success of environmental and ecosystem education.

---

[7] www.dataone.org.

11.5 Public Awareness and Engagement of Ecosystem Science in the Digital Age

Educating society about the value of sustaining healthy, resilient ecosystems is a profoundly important and challenging issue facing our research and educational systems. How do citizens, voters, decision makers, and land managers learn about ecosystems as societies become increasingly urbanized, demands on limited school system funding continues to increase, and natural resource managers and decision makers in rural communities' struggle to stay informed about a rapidly changing world?

A major challenge to ecosystem education is demystifying reliable methods of information acquisition and communication to achieve large-scale best management practices to support common beneficial goals (see Chapter 13). Ecosystem scientists and systems ecologists must continue to take advantage of the digital technology and social networking currently available as a vital link to information and communication (smartphones, social media, and internet resources). These technologies continue to emerge across the globe and are available to increasing numbers of stakeholders (see Figures 13.4 and 13.5). These tools can be used to inform citizens, land and water managers, decision makers, and indeed scientists and professionals in other disciplines about ecosystem science and the power of the systems approach. However, as McKenzie-Mohr (2011) pointed out, merely providing information is not enough. Information along with interaction, engagement, and co-education is required for true learning to take place. Many of the methods described in Section 11.4 apply to learners in the general public, yet information must be carefully tailored to specific audiences. An example of nonacademic online distance learning experience in which NREL staff are instrumental is described in Box 11.3.

Development of partnerships between information scientists, library scientists, learning and behavioral scientists, and marketing professionals will also promote the sharing of these resources vital to ecosystem sustainability. We must explore new ways of accessing knowledge and communicating it to diverse communities.

As with classroom and formal distance education, it is imperative to introduce the "human dimensions" of systems ecology to community stakeholders, for example critical thinking, civics, behavioral science, and marketing science. Systems ecologists must become more informed as to the learning styles of individual stakeholders from varied educational and professional backgrounds, for example farmers, homemakers, bankers, merchants, attorneys, engineers, ranchers, and ecologists.

Box 11.3 *Geospatial lessons and applications in natural resources*

The mission of this program, headed by Dr. Paul H. Evangelista, is to provide land managers, researchers, teachers and students with online training and an accessible source of information to facilitate the sustainable management and conservation of Ethiopia's natural resources. Simply stated, the goal is to build partnerships and increase information sharing among all those involved in conserving wildlife, forests, vegetation, and water resources throughout Ethiopia. The information compiled on this site has been compiled by scientists, resource managers, and academic professionals that come from an array of disciplines who share a common goal of building capacity through the sharing of knowledge.

The Geospatial Training and Applications website was created to provide training, resources and support in geospatial sciences for land managers, researchers, teachers and students in Ethiopia. As part of the Warner College of Natural Resources – Ethiopia Strategic Alliance, program's goal is to provide web-based training opportunities for independent and self-paced learning that will foster sustainable management and conservation of Ethiopia's natural resources.[8]

11.6 Citizen Science

The *Oxford English Dictionary* recently defined citizen science as "scientific work undertaken by members of the general public, often in collaboration with or under the direction of professional scientists and scientific institutions." In Section 11.5 we asked the question *how* best to convey scientific knowledge to nonscientist citizens. The citizen scientist concept is a powerful model fueling the notion expressed by McKenzie-Mohr (2011), who pointed out how information, along with engagement (interaction and experience), is required for true learning to take place. Significant effort is being expended on public engagement through citizen science activities. These extended programs are developing rapidly and are becoming models for implementation both nationally and internationally. Public participation in scientific research or citizen science engages diverse people and stakeholders through collaborative and transformative initiatives.

---

[8] Text taken from https://ethiopia-gis.nrel.colostate.edu.

An exemplary example of a citizen science framework is CitSci.org[9] supported through the NREL at CSU (Newman et al., 2017). It is an initiative to promote citizen involvement in scientific research. CitSci. org began as an online support system for monitoring and tracking observations. Leaders are moving to accommodate a wide range of citizen science projects including air and water quality, stream monitoring, and energy use. CitSci.org provides tools for the entire research process including creating and managing new projects, building custom data sheets, analyzing collected data, and gathering participant feedback.

CitSci.org partners with Citizen Science Central[10] to connect volunteer coordinators with resources to help them develop a citizen science program. They also collaborate with the citizen science data management working group of the DataONE[11] program to facilitate data sharing and stewardship.

11.7 Engaging Children and Teachers

In addition to university academic programs, a much greater emphasis is being placed in the development of public K-12 environmental education and outreach and engagement programs outside the CSU community. These critically important programs are developing rapidly and are becoming models for implementation in public institutions across the globe.

The NREL has spent many years working with K-12 students, science teachers, graduate students, and adult communities to provide high-quality immersion into the scientific practices through educational experiences under the leadership of Dr. John C. Moore. His recent work as the lead on a large NSF Mathematics and Science Partnership – culturally relevant ecology, learning progressions, and environmental literacy[12] – has led to key insights into the importance of systems thinking and the application of hierarchical reasoning to student understanding of environmental principles, teaching practices, and curriculum development.

Some current and past K-12 learning programs are described and linked in Table 11.1.

[9] www.citsci.org/CWIS438/Websites/CitSci/Home.php?WebSiteID=7.
[10] www.citizenscience.org.   [11] www.dataone.org.
[12] http://lter.mspnet.org/index.cfm/profile.

Table 11.1 *Examples of projects devised by NREL systems ecologists and ecosystem scientists and collaborators to enhance environmental literacy in K-12 students and teachers*

Program/website	Description	Participants/locations	Funding source
Comp Hydro, http://ibis-live1 .nrel.colostate.edu/ CompHydro/	Comp Hydro fosters water and computational science literacy by integrating authentic, place- and data-based learning as high school students build and use physical, mathematical and conceptual models	High school teachers, scientists in CO, AZ, MT, and MD	National Science Foundation
Bioenergy Alliance of the Northern Rockies (BANR), http://banr.nrel.colostate.edu/ projects/education-3/	The objective of the education team is to increase bioenergy literacy for students at all levels and build their capacity to engage in regional energy/climate/ economic debate as scientifically informed and knowledgeable citizens	K–12 teachers, graduate students, scientists, and science educators in CO, WY, ID, and MT	USDA – NIFA
Soil Ecology Science Enrichment, www.nrel .colostate.edu/education/k-12-development-current/	The overall goal of this project is to provide an engaging, hands-on science lesson on the ecology of soil systems	Elementary school students, teachers, scientists in Colorado	Fort Collins School System
WCNR Alliance Earth Systems, www.nrel.colostate.edu/ education/k-12-development-current/	Annual one-week high school enrichment course developed with additional WCNR departments to offer field and methods experiences in the geology, ecology, geography, biology, and cultural history of Colorado	Underrepresented, first-generation high school students in Colorado	Warner College of Natural Resources at CSU

Fire Ecology, www.nrel.colostate.edu/education/k-12-development-current/	A lightning-caused fire in 2012 burned 87,284 acres of forest just west of Fort Collins, Colorado. The event provided CSU scientists along with K-12 teachers and their students with an opportunity to study the recovery of an ecosystem after wildfire	Fort Collins School System	NASA, NSF
Environmental Literacy at the Natural Resource Ecology Laboratory, www2.nrel.colostate.edu/env-lit.html	A summary of earlier projects focusing on local systems ecology to teaching about the most pressing environmental issues	K-12 teachers and students at many locations	Many agencies

11.8 Institutes, Short Courses, and Workshops

The careers of NREL scientists have encompassed collaboration with numerous institutes, teaching of short courses, and participating in or managing workshops locally and internationally throughout its five decades of existence. These activities have been pursued by staff members for various reasons: learner demand; desire for teaching contact with students by nonacademic researchers; enthusiasm for expressing one's research passion; and importantly, income augmentation by nontenured researchers. Examples of current activities are shown in Table 11.2.

11.9 Conclusions

All topics covered in this book thus far should be translated into language understood by scientists and interested nonscientists alike. Reviewing data sets and research results and revisiting models for the purpose of translation to common language will provide "actionable learning" (Morrison, 2018), enlightenment, and engagement with students, the public, managers, and decision makers. Actionable learning, as with actionable science (see Chapters 2 and 13), is learning and research that has direct application to management and decision making related to environmental, natural resource, and ecological/societal problems. Until ecosystem science is integrated into practical and useful tools for everyday management and decision making, our society will continue to manage its resources and the environment based on ignorance, myths, political whim, and self-interest. Recognizing that science is essential, but insufficient alone, the required integration requires cross-discipline and outward-looking perspectives, systems thinking (see Chapter 1), and communication that effectively blend biophysical, social, cultural, economic, and political realities.

This chapter focuses heavily on the contributions to education by the NREL, a "soft money" research organization dependent on an entrepreneurial culture among staff members and collaborators. The NREL has been embedded within a land grant university (National Research Council, 1995) since its inception in 1967. The contributions to ecology, ecosystem science, and systems ecology education have been profound due to the creativity, flexibility, an outward-looking perspective, and the desire to succeed as a world-renowned research organization. The "take-home" message for other research organizations is that staff members who are willing to be flexible, take risks, and create opportunities for themselves and others can be successful in an "untenured" world.

Table 11.2 *Examples of workshops/institutes/short courses offered by NREL systems ecologists and ecosystem scientists and collaborators to enhance environmental literacy, systems thinking, and professional skills*

Workshops/institutes/short courses	Description	Participants/locations	Leaders
Century/DayCent model training workshops, www.nrel.colostate.edu/education/century-and-daycent-model-training-workshops/	The main goals are: to provide attendees with information about the ecological and biological theories associated with the Century series of models; and to provide training on how to use the monthly Century and DayCent (Daily Century) models. The ultimate goal is to familiarize students with the functionality of one or both models for use at their own research sites	Researchers, postdoctoral fellows, and graduate students in the United States, Australia, Costa Rica, China, Mongolia, and Uruguay	Dr. William J. Parton, Dr. Dennis S. Ojima, and others
Summer Soil Institute, www.nrel.colostate.edu/education/summer-soil-institute/	Participants gain hands-on experience in soil sampling, analytical techniques, and more importantly, a holistic understanding of soil systems formalized through model development. Field and laboratory experiences include soil core and gas efflux sampling, analyses of soil organic matter physical fractions, stable C and N isotope natural abundance, and microbial and fauna community traits, as well as use of simulation models	Graduate students, postdoctoral scientists, environmental professionals, faculty and K-12 teachers in across the United States – CSU campus-based	M. F. Cotrufo, S. Fonte, J. C. Moore, K. Paustian, J. von Fisher, M. Wallenstein

(cont.)

Table 11.2 (*cont.*)

Workshops/institutes/short courses	Description	Participants/locations	Leaders
Bayesian Modeling, www .nrel.colostate.edu/ education/bayesian-modeling/	This course provides a fundamental foundation in statistical principles required for use of the Bayesian approach for gaining insight into using data obtained from the models	Postdocs, university faculty, and agency scientists on the CSU campus	Dr. N. T. Hobbs
Skills for Undergraduate Participation in Ecological Research (SUPER), www.nrel .colostate.edu/projects/ super/	The SUPER program brings together teaching from ESS with research mentoring primarily performed by NREL scientists. SUPER provides students the opportunity for a two-semester, enhanced research experience that: (1) increases student scientific critical thinking skills; (2) expands scientific literacy; (3) increases the student's confidence in their ability to perform ecological research; and (4) enhances the student's qualifications for future research positions	CSU sophomores and juniors from all disciplines	Dr. S. Lynn

A cautionary note for excellent "soft money" research organizations seeking "hard money" support from academic institutions is needed here. Funding support for soft money researchers may be discontinuous but their livelihood, and that of their research team, depends on it. Given the difficulty in securing project support, the temptation is to "harden" one's support by seeking academic appointments or assistant faculty positions. The demands of teaching are often underestimated and can interfere with creative research activity, especially if those activities are in remote locations or demand intense personal involvement. A major consideration is that fear of uncertain funding may lead to creativity and entrepreneurial success, or alternatively may lead to numerous stress-related disorders (see Section 12.6).

References

Anderson, D., Heil, R. C., Cole, C. V., and Deutsch, P. (1983). Identification and characterization of ecosystems at different integrative levels. In *Nutrient Cycling in Agricultural Ecosystems*, ed. R. R. Lowrance, R. L. Todd, L. E. Asmussen, and R. A. Leonard. Special Publication No. 23. Athens, GA: University of Georgia, College of Agriculture Experiment Stations.

Christensen, N. L., Bartuska, A. M., Brown, J. H., et al. (1996). The report of the Ecological Society of America committee on the scientific basis for ecosystem management. *Ecological Applications*, 6(3), 665–91.

Goh, J., Truman, B., and Barber, D. (2019). Exploring individual differences as factors to maximize interactive learning environments for future learning. *Interactive Learning Environments*, 27(4), 497–507.

Hawtrey, K. (2007). Using experiential learning techniques. *The Journal of Economic Education*, 38(2), 143–52.

Kaplan, N. E., Baker, K. S., Draper, D. C., and Swauger, S. (2014). *Packaging, Transforming and Migrating Data from a Scientific Research Project to an Institutional Repository: The SGS LTER Collection*. Digital Collections of Colorado. Fort Collins, CO: Colorado State University. http://hdl.handle.net/10217/87239 (accessed August 13, 2020).

Kaplan, N. E., and Newman, G. J. (2013). *Data Management for NREL and Beyond: A Roadmap and Recommendations*. Digital Collections of Colorado. Fort Collins, CO: Colorado State University. http://hdl.handle.net/10217/87381 (accessed August 13, 2020).

Knowles, M. (1977). Adult learning processes: Pedagogy and andragogy. *Religious Education*, 72(2), 202–11.

McKenzie-Mohr, D. (2011). *Fostering Sustainable Behavior: An Introduction to Community-Based Social Marketing*. Gabriola Island, BC: New Society Publishers.

Millennium Ecosystem Assessment (MEA). (2005). *Ecosystems and Human Well-being: Synthesis*. Washington, DC: Island Press.

Morrison, T. (2018). *Actionable Learning: A Handbook for Capacity Building through Case-Based Learning.* Tokyo: Asian Development Bank Institute. www.adb.org/sites/default/files/publication/159394/adbi-actionable-learning-handbook-capacity-building-through-case-based-learning.pdf (accessed August 13, 2020).

National Research Council. (1995). *Colleges of Agriculture at the Land Grant Universities: A Profile.* Washington, DC: The National Academies Press. https://doi.org/10.17226/4980 (accessed August 13, 2020).

Newman, G., Chandler, M., Clyde, M., et al. (2017). Leveraging the power of place in citizen science for effective conservation decision making. *Biological Conservation,* 208(4), 55–64. http://dx.doi.org/10.1016/j.biocon.2016.07.019 (accessed August 13, 2020).

Pappas, C. (2015). Pedagogy vs., andragogy in eLearning: Can you tell the difference? *Instructional Design, eLearning Industry.* https://elearningindustry.com/pedagogy-vs-andragogy-in-elearning-can-you-tell-the-difference (accessed August 13, 2020).

Rykiel, E. (1999). Ecosystem science at the Natural Resource Ecology Laboratory. *BioScience,* 49(1), 69–70.

Van Dyne, G. (1969). *The Ecosystem Concept in Natural Resource Management.* New York: Academic Press.

Williams, G. W. (2005). *The USDA Forest Service: The First Century.* FS-650. Washington, DC: USDA Forest Service.

Woodmansee, R. (1990). Biogeochemical cycles and ecological hierarchies. In *Changing Landscapes: An Ecological Perspective,* ed. I. S. Zonneveld and R. T. T. Forman. New York: Springer, 57–71.

12 · *Organizational and Administrative Challenges and Innovations*

JACOB HAUTALUOMA, ROBERT G. WOODMANSEE, NICOLE E. KAPLAN, JOHN C. MOORE, AND CLARA J. WOODMANSEE

> Leaders stand on the shoulders of those who came before them.
> Paraphrased from Bernard of Chartres

12.1 Introduction

This chapter describes some of the attributes and influencers of the Natural Resource Ecology Laboratory (NREL) that have allowed it to exist and thrive for over half a century as an organization. One primary purpose of this chapter is to share lessons we learned to guide other institutions as they endeavor to establish or reinvigorate their own research organizations. It is our hope that ideas described within are gleaned in an effort to avoid some of the pitfalls that will inevitably arise in their development and take some of our successes and build upon those. However, readers should keep in mind that while many of the attributes of NREL's success were based on good, creative, and conscientious management practices, other attributes were opportune. Sometimes we didn't know the difference.

Another purpose of this chapter is to inform scientists, both young and old, that when performing collaborative ecosystem research they do not work in organizational isolation, but rather "stand on the shoulders of those who came before" (paraphrased from Bernard of Chartres) and they depend on those around them to hold them up so they can achieve their goals.

Also, this chapter briefly describes the measures of success needed to be competitive: (1) in gaining extramural funding support; (2) in obtaining collegiality, loyalty, and trust within the organization (e.g., NREL);

(3) in gaining institutional leadership support, for example Colorado State University (CSU); (4) in sharing administrative functions and; (5) in internal institution (CSU) détente. The chapter will conclude with a narrative by Dr. Jacob Hautaluoma, an organizational/industrial psychologist who over a span of more than 25 years consulted with NREL staff on matters ranging from strategic planning to interpersonal conflicts (see Appendix 12.1). This partnership was integral to NREL's success during many challenges and his observations are incorporated into the discussion that follows. For developing organizations and existing organizations needing reinvigoration, ignoring Dr. Hautaluoma's observations and insights about organizational behavior will be at their own peril.

Managing any organization for any length of time is a challenge. Leading and managing an organization as complex, ever changing, and unique as the NREL over five decades and projecting its legacy of scientific excellence and leadership into the future is certainly no exception. Preserving the legacy is important for several reasons: (1) promoting the philosophy embedded in the systems ecology paradigm (SEP); (2) history ignored cannot help guide the future; (3) access to the vast warehouse of knowledge generated by the NREL and collaborators and institutional support for development and maintenance of digital collections of information; and (4) curation of projects and information, especially long-term research and modeling efforts. Hopefully this book will help preserve the legacy of scientific excellence and leadership.

12.2 Administrative and Operational Support for Scientific Excellence

The function of organizational administration and operations is to support scientific excellence and productivity measured as successful grants and contracts, scientific publications, and national and international thought leadership. The administrative and operational functions of the NREL have been built to support the SEP, for example systems thinking, the role of modeling (see Chapter 4), long-term research, and societally relevant problems in a sustainable way (see Chapter 1). These functions have been shared within the organization to avoid inevitable conflicts of interest with other organizations. Successful administrative functions are dependent on both scientific leadership and competent, loyal, and self-confident support staff that feel empowered to contribute to collective success. Operational support staff functions include:

(1) administrative support professionals; (2) departmental financial management and accounting for grants and contracts; (3) information technology staff, including data management, deskside support, infrastructure, and analytics; (4) in-house proposal development and management support; (5) publication and proposal editing support; (6) travel assistance; and (7) laboratory and field technical support. These support functions have been and must be designed with the primary purpose of the organization in mind, and cannot be shared with other competing units with the risk of splitting loyalties. Mission alignment at all levels leads to a stronger, more innovative, highly functioning team.

12.3 Measures of Success

Measures of success include funding generated through grants and contracts, publications in widely recognized scientific journals, scientific leadership and peer recognition, and co-production of knowledge through collaboration. Since its inception, the NREL has been acknowledged for its leadership in scientific creativity and excellence (Rykiel, 1999). There were times following the end of the US International Biological Program (USIBP) when some people criticized the NREL and other IBP Biome programs for having spent millions of dollars with little scientific value to show for it, especially dollars for mathematical modeling (Golley, 1993; Coleman, 2010; see Chapter 3). Most of those criticisms came from ecologists who resented the amount of money being allocated to ecosystem science by the National Science Foundation. However, by the late 1970s and early 1980s those criticisms were proven baseless as the C, N, and P cycles and their interactions were resolved, plant and animal interactions were unraveled, belowground processes and interactions were quantified, landscape ecology became appreciated, long-term ecological research was initiated, and humans began recognizing for their own importance as ecosystem components. Critical to all of these advances was the role of systems analysis, SEP, simulation modeling, and the creation of enduring administrative and personnel structures supporting their application.

The NREL is unparalleled in its productivity as an ecological research organization. The raison d'être for its success and survival within a major American university is primarily the prodigious amount of funding generated by NREL's scientific staff, and secondarily the recognition the NREL has brought to CSU during the past 50 years. Until recently the NREL has been a dominantly self-supporting or "soft money" organization with salary support for scientific staff funded from grants and contracts. Most administrative support came from indirect cost recovery from those grants and contracts. With the development of the Department of Ecosystem Science and Sustainability, associated with the NREL, some new support has come from the academic functions of the university.

12.3.1 Funded Proposals

The development and evolution of the NREL can be viewed in four phases.

12.3.1.1 Phase One

In 1968, ecologists knew a lot about aboveground ecosystem structure, but little was known about how the components of ecosystems interacted or functioned, especially belowground. That year, the NSF awarded a six-year project for approximately $4 million US dollars (~$28 million today) to the NREL to initiate studies of the "Structure and Function of Ecosystems" in the Grassland Biome of USIBP and a new environmental science was being conceived, the SEP. Many of the early expenditures went to "cost of learning" or learning by doing, from mistakes, and other "inefficiencies," concepts well known in the military, business, and industry. Technologies needed to be adopted from other disciplines or invented. Systems concepts and computer-based methodologies needed to be borrowed from engineering. Belowground ecosystems and biogeochemistry were mere concepts, poorly if at all understood, and in need of development. All discoveries were expensive.

12.3.1.2 Phase Two

During Phase Two, NREL scientists helped define ecosystem science and established national and international research agendas. Following the USIBP studies, the NREL entered a period during the late 1970s and 1980s of investigator-initiated research, mostly supported by the NSF (see Section 12.2 and Chapter 6). Scientists were learning how ecosystems function with project awards large enough to financially support both scientists and staff. Funding during this period was spread across about eight projects, totaling about $35–$40 million in today's US dollars.

12.3.1.3 Phase Three

During the 1990s and 2000s, many funding agencies transitioned from investigator-initiated research to RFP-driven (request for proposals) research. Among the reasons for the shift was that federal support for research was not growing as in previous years. Funding agency philosophy was shifting toward internal control due largely to the influence of conservative politics. The size of grants and contracts generally decreased causing scientists to exist on smaller projects from multiple funding agencies. More new ecosystem scientists were graduating and competing for fewer dollars. Federal agency research agendas began shifting from investigator-initiated research to RFP driven by agency priorities. The investigator-initiated research funding model can be successful only if an organization's scientific thought leaders are members of funding agency advisory committees and review panels. The NREL received approximately $80 million of funding but it spread this between 30 funded projects during this period. The Shortgrass Steppe LTER program alone generated about $30 million in associated research funding.

12.3.1.4 Phase Four

From 2010 to 2019, the NREL funding portfolio included both large (see Chapters 7, 8, and 11) and small projects, in addition to the academic support from the academic Department of Ecosystem Science and Sustainability. Total funding during this period has reached more than $80 million in today's dollars.

Going forward administratively, establishing a balance between the large and small projects, basic vs. applied research, research vs. academic responsibilities, and ensuring excellent and relevant science is challenging. Fundamental questions need to be evaluated, such as: (1) Do future societal needs require more basic ecology and ecosystem research or do we already know enough? (2) Does the future demand application of the SEP to solve real-world, complex problems (wicked problems) using existing knowledge, the systems approach, mathematical modeling, and rapidly expanding technologies and instrumentation? (3) At what point can we no longer afford to commit resources to "hobbyhorse" science (see Hautaluoma narrative in Appendix 12.1, especially "kids in a sandbox")? (4) Who decides?

12.3.2 Publications

The NREL, as an organization, is unparalleled in its generation of peer-reviewed publications in major scientific journals, books, and invited book chapters.[1] These publications include research findings, concept papers, and integration and synthesis volumes. Multiauthored papers are

[1] https://scholar.google.com/citations?user=z43HJtsAAAAJ&hl=en.

the norm with many disciplines and institutions represented in authorship. References in this book lead readers to many of those publications.

As an example of forward thinking, NREL staff participated in the first effort at CSU to curate a series of research datasets for preservation and discovery through an institutional repository. Data produced by NREL sciencists are available online via search or browse interfaces as well as ecoinformatics data portals (DataONE, 2018). Within the CSU institutional repository, data are linked to other materials including publications, technical reports, image files, field and lab protocols, proposals, and presentations, all of which provide a richer context as to how and why data were collected, and how they were interpreted and used to support published scientific findings or ask new questions. NREL staff worked closely with experts in data management and services and archivists at CSU libraries on this pilot project. The broader university community benefited from the first collection of materials from a research organization on campus to include data. This partnership also influenced the design of effective information management services for the NREL (Kaplan and Newman, 2013; Kaplan et al., 2014), which has been used as an example for other research organizations both at CSU and across the globe.

12.3.3 Leadership and Peer Recognition

Another powerful measure of success is the scientific leadership provided to agencies, scientific organizations, and scientific review committees and panels by scientists from research organizations. NREL scientists have served in leadership positions in (1) federal agencies, for example NSF, USGS, USDA; (2) scientific societies as officers, editors, and thought leaders; (3) national and international organizations, such as Future Earth, the International Nitrogen Initiative, the International Nitrogen Management System, SCOPE, MAB, the IGBP, and the Intergovernmental Panel on Climate Change (IPCC); and (4) countless science review committees.

12.3.4 Internal Organization Collegiality and Institution Détente: Collaboration and Education

Successful ecosystem research organizations have championed a team-oriented, interdisciplinary research approach – *a we, us, and our mentality versus an I, me, and mine mentality* – both within and extending to external collaborations. These organizations have recognized the vital importance of integrating scientific and support staff talent, modeling, field studies, and laboratory research activities that demand cohesive teamwork and complex administration.

12.4 Organizational Leadership: Directors

Flexible leadership styles and the existence and support of top-level administrative leadership has allowed NREL leadership to adjust to external challenges. The leadership of NREL directors has always been visionary, assertive, flexible, and effective even though individual leadership styles varied. Each director faced and met new challenges, and some are ever-present within a major land grant university.

There are always tensions between the balance of basic vs. applied research, especially within agricultural- and natural resource-oriented institutions and politically at national policy-making levels. Additionally, many funding agencies require demonstration of applicability of research findings to societal needs. Both basic and applied perspectives are needed, and successful organizations will continually need to "scan the environment," be flexible, and creatively accomplish both.

The success of the organization has always been based on the scientific excellence of the research staff and collaborators, highly competent support staff, and outstanding graduate students and postdoctoral fellows. The priority of the NREL directors has always been to support scientific excellence and maintain supportive relationships with higher-level administrators.

Of special note is the essential role of administrative support and encouragement from the highest levels of an enabling institution. Many ecological research organizations have failed because higher-level administration has chosen different directions or simply lost interest. Figure 12.1 reflects the relationship of the NREL to other important collaborating agencies and organizations within CSU and beyond. All are important, as seen in Figure 12.2 (see Appendix 12.1).

Throughout its history, grants and contracts "soft money" supported salaries for scientists and staff in the NREL. But, in spite of the lack "hard money," institutional support for salaries the NREL enjoyed resolute support from the highest levels of CSU administrations. Administrative support included buildings, laboratories, office space, and facilitation of personnel appointments. Various forms of financial support have been used over the years, including indirect cost recovery from federal research grants to support office staff and occasionally senior staff. Another source

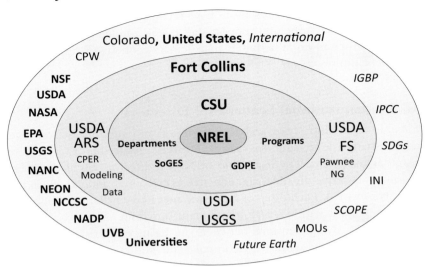

Figure 12.1 Diagram showing some of the relationships of the NREL with organizations within CSU; Fort Collins, Colorado; the State of Colorado; the United States; and internationally. A black and white version of this figure will appear in some formats. For the color version, please refer to the plate section.

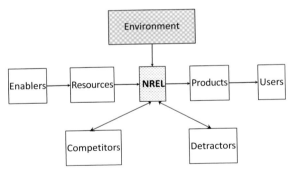

Figure 12.2 Diagram showing the influencers on and influences of the NREL (or any organization) within their environment.

would include "resolute" support, meaning effectively confronting detractors (Figure 12.2; see Appendix 12.1) who challenged the legitimacy of the NREL. As the success and reputation of the NREL grew, numerous administrative units within CSU viewed the NREL as an adversary receiving undue resources and recognition. The role of the higher administration in moderating these antagonisms has been critical.

Good relationships of NREL directors with CSU presidents has been essential for success for the NREL. From the beginning in 1967, when George Van Dyne convinced the then president of CSU to build an NREL building to house the infant USIBP Grassland Biome, each director has enjoyed top-level support. Administrative styles and scientific perspectives have varied but commitment to scientific excellence has not for more than 50 years.

12.4.1 George M. Van Dyne (1967–1974)

The original and enduring vision for the NREL was put forth by its founder George M. Van Dyne (Golley, 1993; Coleman et al., 2004; Coleman, 2010; Box 12.1; Chapters 3 and 7). Van Dyne had the unique ability to blend systems thinking with recognition and understanding of real-world land management experience, coming from a ranching background in rural southern Colorado and his formal training in animal science and range management (PhD, University of California, Berkeley). As one of the original systems ecologists along with Jerry Olsen, Bernard Patton, Howard Odum, Kenneth Watt, and C. S. Holling, Van Dyne was an incredibly hardworking polymath whose brilliance, charisma, and ability to articulate complex ideas was extraordinary. He was driven by a distinct and new vision of what systems ecology could become, what the ecosystem approach could do for the sciences, and what the ecosystem concept in natural resource management could mean for future generations. This vision was also driven by an understanding of the importance of systems ecology in education (Van Dyne ed., 1969; Breymeyer and Van Dyne, 1980).

Van Dyne moved to CSU from the Oak Ridge National Laboratory at the time when the USIBP was being formed and the NSF was

Box 12.1 *Legacy*

(1) One of the "fathers of systems ecology." (2) Brilliant, visionary, and innovative scientific leadership is necessary to achieve scientific excellence and build support infrastructure. (3) Establishment of a strong "pride of organization and collaboration" which became critical to long-term success and sustainability. (4) The attributes and skills needed to envision and create a successful organization may not be those needed to maintain and manage the organization.

initiating spending unparalleled amounts of money on "Big Biology" (Coleman, 2010). He was an aggressive and forceful program builder in establishing the Grassland Biome USIBP and he benefited from plentiful resources and an unprecedented new public awareness of environmental challenges. Many academic departments and colleges across the CSU campus were at best skeptical of the formation of a new, highly funded administrative structure and at worst deplored the formation of the new organization. Van Dyne ignored the existing insular or "silo" views of academia and disciplines, garnered the support of the university's top-level administration, and built the NREL as an unprecedented "soft money" research organization in a land grant academic institution.

Among the organizational innovations introduced by Van Dyne were a culture of egalitarianism where all perspectives regardless of rank, title, or education were valued, a "pride of organization," and a sense of "we," "us," and "our," rather than "I," "me," and "mine." Scientists, graduate students, technicians, and office staff alike went by first names rather than titles, and to Van Dyne all ideas were considered valid. Inherent in this philosophy was the idea that "those who party together, work together," regardless of employment status. The eclectic attitude also fostered an interdisciplinary collaborative model of behavior locally, nationally, and internationally. The driving concept underpinning this model was to work with the best scientists and minds regardless of institutional or disciplinary affiliation. Needless to say, the prevailing view in academia during the 1960s (still observed in some places) held this approach to be blasphemous.

Of special note was Van Dyne's insistence that the NREL must have a highly competent and loyal support staff of administrative professionals, human resource personnel, technical editors, travel assistants, bookkeepers, accountants, data managers, key punch operators, etc. Although the nature of support in the digital age has dramatically changed, those same organizational values have endured throughout the evolution of the NREL.

Van Dyne had an exceptional ability to hire talented young scientists (Coleman et al., 2004; Coleman, 2010; Chapter 3). He was able to do that because of funding provided by the USIBP Grassland Biome Program. Herein lies the paradox of Van Dyne the brilliant, egalitarian, charismatic, visionary scientist, and Van Dyne the alpha male, domineering, and authoritarian leader. He hired scientific staff as subordinates, but most also tended to be alpha males. Van Dyne's Achilles' heel was that "his way was *the* way," and others should follow: classic vertical or top-down leadership. The subordinates had different ideas about NREL's direction following completion and following USIBP. It doesn't take an animal behaviorist to predict the outcome. Van Dyne was removed as director in 1974. Sadly, he died suddenly from a heart attack in 1978 at age 48, leaving the legacy of systems ecology.

12.4.2 James H. Gibson (1974–1984)

James H. Gibson, a chemist (PhD, University of West Virginia), was hired by Van Dyne to be the business manager for the NREL and the Grassland Biome IBP project. Until then, no biologically based research program had been faced with the management of such a financially successful and complex organization. Gibson proved to be a creative, highly competent, and detail-oriented manager (Box 12.2).

Upon the dismissal of Van Dyne, Gibson became director after the consultation of CSU administrators with NSF leadership. Gibson had no illusions about being an ecosystem scientist, systems ecologist, or visionary. Rather, Gibson saw himself as an administrator/manager/facilitator of talent. He was a passive leader who deferred scientific leadership to the team (horizontal management) of scientists hired by Van Dyne and George Innis, who was the modeling leader for the Grassland Ecosystem Model (ELM) (see Chapter 4). The team consisted of former Grassland Biome senior scientists, ELM modeling team postdocs, and recent graduates of CSU systems ecology (Coleman, 2010; see Chapter 3). This signified a transition from vertical scientific leadership to horizontal or shared leadership.

Box 12.2 *Legacy*

(1) There is no substitute for scientific vision and excellence, and likewise there is no substitute for competent and creative management that is driven by the notion that the purpose of the administration is to support scientific excellence. (2) Very few scientists are competent operational managers. (3) When working across organizational and institutional boundaries, fair and transparent joint funding models must be established. (4) Promote shared leadership. (5) The "lifeblood" of a soft money research organization is the success of its entrepreneurial scientists.

Gibson was the administrative glue that held the NREL together during the completion of the USIBP, shrinking budgets, and the transition to new programs in ecosystem science. He facilitated the development of new "ecosystem science" projects by encouraging collaboration with the highly recognized/accomplished scientists, regardless of institutional affiliation. These new projects, combined with the scientific achievements of the Grassland Biome, were bringing the NREL and CSU recognition as one of the world's leading ecosystem research institutions. During Gibson's tenure, the NREL moved administratively from the College of Natural Sciences (CNS) to the College of Forestry and Natural Resources (CFNR). The CNS was a traditional academic college focused on basic sciences with faculty members operating as individuals managing their own laboratories with little or no incentive to collaborate. The CFNR focused on applied sciences, several of which were grounded in applied ecology. The CFNR had begun a transformation to collaboration largely through association with the Grassland Biome program. Following this move, strong relationships were established between the NREL and the Range Science Department, allowing CSU to emerge as an internationally recognized rangeland ecosystem research and education enterprise. The multidisciplinary enterprise included CSU's Department of Agronomy, the USDA Agricultural Research Service (ARS), and the USDA Forest Service. Their key to success was the development of jointly funded models that allowed fair distribution of money based on the affiliation with an individual's time and effort. By being truly focused on administration, operational support, and fairness of distribution of funding, Gibson was able to establish new funding models that helped lead to the breakdown of departmental and disciplinary "silos" within CSU and externally. The relationship was further strengthened when two NREL scientists, R. G. Woodmansee and W. K. Lauenroth, accepted academic appointments in the Range Science Department while retaining senior research scientist joint appointments in the NREL (Coleman, 2010; see Chapter 3). Other NREL scientists established partial teaching relationships with other academic departments. As a joint effort between the NREL and the Range Science Department, the first Shortgrass Steppe LTER proposal was funded with Woodmansee as principal investigator and Lauenroth and W. Laycock (ARS) as co-principal investigators.

While serving as director of the NREL, Jim Gibson was instrumental in the formation of the National Atmospheric Deposition Program (Cowling, 2008; see Chapter 8). He passed away from cancer in 2008 at the age of 76.

12.4.3 Robert G. Woodmansee (1984–1992)

James Gibson stepped down as NREL director in 1984. He was followed by Robert G. Woodmansee, a CSU-trained (PhD) systems ecologist, plant ecologist, range and soil scientist, and ecosystem scientist with a rural New Mexico and Colorado farming/ranching background. As with Van Dyne, his rural background greatly influenced his perspective of the blending of science and real-world management. Prior to assuming the role of director, Woodmansee served in a two-year appointment with the NSF as program director for Ecosystem Studies (Box 12.3).

Woodmansee inherited Van Dyne's vision of systems ecology and the potential of its role in environmental and natural resource science and management. He also inherited Gibson's well-organized and well-managed NREL organization.

Scientifically, Woodmansee had established himself in the ELM Grassland Ecosystem modeling team, biogeochemistry, N cycling, ecological hierarchies, landscape and regional scale ecology, and Long-Term Ecological Research (formation of the LTER network and founding principle investigator of the Shortgrass Steppe LTER). He was heavily involved with Scientific Committee for Problems on the Environment (SCOPE), Man and the Biosphere (MAB), the formation of the International Geosphere-Biosphere Program, and the founding of the Association of Ecosystem Research Centers (second president). One of his goals as director was to ensure both CSU and NREL collaborators were included in national and international scientific activities and

---

Box 12.3 *Legacy*

(1) Successful research organizations must have visionary leadership based on scientific creativity and excellence of research staff. (2) One of the key measures of a successful organization is recognition of excellence by national and international peer institutions. (3) Successful research organizations must have administrative and management structures whose functions are to support scientific excellence within the organization. (4) Strong and enduring support and leadership from higher administration is essential for success of a soft money research organization. (5) Within-organizational leadership style must match higher-level administrative styles. (6) Successful organizations learn as much from their losses as they do from their wins.

decision making. During this period, NREL and the CSU Range Science Department became established as one of the, if not the premier rangeland ecosystem research and education organizations in the world. This collaboration included USDA ARS and CSU's Crop and Soils Department. As quipped by C. Wayne Cook, department head of Range Science, "outside of CSU, we were all one."

As the scientific world began to accept that our climate was indeed changing, Woodmansee facilitated NREL involvement in what would become the IPCC. In 1989, NREL entered the NSF Science and Technology Centers competition, proposing a never-before-seen model of collaborative scientific leadership: Center for Analysis of the Dynamics of Regional Ecosystems (CADRE). If successful, CADRE would have integrated ecosystem, atmospheric, social, and organizational science into the study of the Great Plains region of North America. Coming in third, with only two awards given, this proposal was recognized by Roger Pielke as the most successful failed proposal he had even been involved with (personal communication). Though unsuccessful at the time, this model became the foundation of much of the research described in Chapter 8. Successful organizations learn as much from their losses as they do from their wins.

During Woodmansee's directorship the NREL was established as a CSU Center of Excellence and several half-time academic positions were created for NREL scientists. Other achievements during Woodmansee's leadership included the blending of ecosystem and social science, establishment of organizational science as a legitimate part of science management, aggressive promotion of women in ecosystem science (Baron and Galvin, 1990), and facilitation and promotion of the accomplishments of research staff and collaborators both nationally and internationally. These researchers had pioneered many breakthroughs in ecosystem science and indeed the SEP (see Chapters 4, 6–9). At the end of Woodmansee's tenure as director, he was heavily involved with the emerging concepts of "ecosystem management" and ecosystem services (Christensen et al., 1996).

12.4.4 Diana H. Wall (1993–2006)

Diana H. Wall (PhD in plant pathology from the University of Kentucky, Lexington) was selected as NREL director in 1993. She is a soil ecologist, nematologist, and ecosystem scientist. Her research contributions focus on belowground ecosystems, especially biodiversity (Wall

Box 12.4 *Legacy*

(1) Emphasis on making ecological knowledge more accessible to citizens and decision makers at all levels of government. (2) Competent vision and leadership by proficient scientific staff are essential for continued excellence of an organization. (3) Formal recognition by high-profile outside reviewers solidifies the stature of an organization both locally and nationally. (4) Maintenance of esprit de corps within an organization is vital. (5) Individual recognition of local leaders, nationally and internationally, enhances stature of an organization.

and Virginia, 1999), and how those systems relate to broader ecosystem functioning.

Wall's vision for NREL emphasized the importance of making ecological knowledge more accessible to citizens and decision makers at all levels of government (see Box 12.4). She emphasized that solving increasingly complex environmental problems requires integration of knowledge from the natural, physical, and social sciences, and experience of practitioners and local communities.

Wall is a contributor to international, national, and local collaborative projects such as the Millennium Ecosystem Assessment (MEA, 2005), Antarctic McMurdo Dry Valley LTER (MCMLTER, 2018), and CSU's School of Global Environmental Sustainability (SoGES, 2018). She was and is notably involved in leadership positions in many scientific organizations, as president, of the Ecological Society of America, chair of the SCOPE Committee on Soil and Sediment Biodiversity and Ecosystem Functioning, and science chair of the Global Soil Biodiversity Initiative. Her activities and leadership have brought visibility and recognition to CSU. She was elected to the National Academy of Sciences in 2018, was 2012 Tansley Lecturer, British Ecological Society, and received the 2015 Ulysses Medal, University College, Dublin. Within the NREL, Wall instituted External Review Committees and Distinguished Ecosystem Scientist Awards, and promoted in-house esprit de corps, diversity, and collaboration.

During Wall's tenure as director, she maintained the designation of NREL as a CSU Center of Excellence. She continued the expansion of funding from NSF to other US federal agencies, predominantly NSF, USDA, US Department of the Interior, National Oceanic and

Atmospheric Administration, NASA, USAID, and US Environmental Protection Agency, all led by senior scientific staff. However, the funding models for "soft money" research organizations were shifting due largely to shrinking federal dollars for research. The results were the size of grants trending downward and competition increasing due to less funding for research and to the influx of many new, young scientists. Scientists were forced to seek fewer and smaller grants to maintain their programs and salaries. Some of the scientists were able to build interdisciplinary programs and fund them from multiple sources. Others have retreated into more reductionist, disciplinary programs (silos). The trend was clearly moving away from large projects, with the exception of the LTER programs, with single-source funding as had been the case from the Grassland Biome days through the 1980s. Wall stepped down as NREL director in 2006. She became founding director of the School of Global Environmental Sustainability in 2008 (SoGES, 2018).

12.4.5 John C. Moore (2006–Present)

John C. Moore became director in 2006 following Diana Wall's tenure. Dr. Moore is a CSU-trained (PhD) zoologist, soil ecologist, theoretical ecologist, and ecosystem scientist. Moore has led the NREL into academic legitimacy by creating the Department of Ecosystem Science and Sustainability (ESS) which has created support for several permanent academic positions (see Chapter 11). The new department that now includes both undergraduate and graduate programs has exceeded all expectations for enrollment (ESS, 2018) (see Box 12.5).

Box 12.5 *Legacy*

(1) Recognition that funding environments change, requiring adaptation and redefinition of purpose. (2) Stabilization of funding for senior scientific staff is vital in an environment of reduced access to large-program resources. (3) The alternative is to attempt survival in reductionist research. (4) The danger of the latter is making the determination that research is no longer needed. (5) Access to large, outward-looking program resources requires innovation into new relationships with nontraditional partners using the SEP and power of mathematical modeling, for example food security, water and soil security, adaptation to climate change, and carbon management.

Moore's scientific interests center on soil ecology, the ecology of food webs, and theoretical ecology. His food web research has been carried out in Wind Cave National Park in South Dakota, the Toolik Lake Arctic Tundra LTER research site, the Shortgrass Steppe LTER site, and dryland agroecosystems in Colorado. He was principal investigator for the Shortgrass Steppe LTER site from 2010 to 2014.

His visionary leadership in science education and the study and advancement of environmental science literacy – the capacity for citizens to engage in evidence-based decision making about environmental issues – has resulted in numerous programs linking NREL scientists and graduate students to the K-12 public school systems, and programs to increase the engagement of students from diverse backgrounds (see Chapter 11). Moore advocated that addressing environmental challenges requires that science be available and accessible to all citizens, regardless of background (see Chapter 11). He has been recognized as a University Distinguished Teaching Scholar.

During Moore's directorship, several NREL scientists received Nobel Peace Prize recognition for their work on the IPCC. He has facilitated international institutional ties and official partnerships in Kenya, Mongolia, and China. He has expanded NREL's funding base with a diverse set of agencies and has maintained the role of NREL as a CSU Center of Excellence.

As of this writing, Moore's greatest challenge is maintaining the capability of the NREL to accomplish the vision of the SEP as required in order to meet the current and future challenges like food, water, and soil security, adaptation to climate change, and carbon management. Few other research organizations possess this capability, making the NREL truly unique at this time. The challenges are maintaining the research capability which could be diluted by the success of new academic programs that siphon off time and energy of top scientists, requirements to overextend research commitments to fewer and smaller grants and contracts, and of course federal policies that threaten availability of the research funds vital to the well-being of the environment, society, and the NREL.

Moore has enjoyed the strong support and advocacy of the CSU higher administration and the Warner College of Natural Resources.

12.4.6 Corps of Deputies

Since its inception, the NREL has prospered under the direction of several highly competent assistant, associate, and interim directors, all of whom have served to provide continuity to its scientific mission. These include Jim Gibson, Bob Woodmansee, Jim Ellis, Ted Elliot, Jim Detling, Dennis S. Ojima, and Stephen Ogle. This "bench strength" has often been essential for organizational success. NREL has also incubator for leadership. The USIBP and LTER were examples of young scientists taking on leadership roles for large, collaborative research programs. Throughout the generations of leadership has been the commitment to systems thinking, scientific excellence, ecosystem science, and what has become SEP.

12.5 Internal Organization Collegiality, Loyalty, Trust, and Within-Institution Détente: Collaboration and Education

Many lessons have been learned during the more than 50 years of NREL's existence. A few key lessons are listed here that may be helpful to others involved in joining, developing, participating in, and/or leading complex organizational structures:

- Co-production of knowledge and the sense of pride "pride of organization" integral to organizational culture at the NREL have been built on camaraderie; a sense of we, us, and our; the use of first names rather than titles; loyalty; and trust.
- Throughout its existence, the NREL has enjoyed administrative autonomy with most operational functions managed independently from the traditional college-level organizational functions.
- In spite of some inevitable institutional antagonisms, professional jealousies, and internal rivalries often found in academic institutions, the NREL was always able to build successful collaborations with many departments, colleges, agencies, and institutions.
- The pride of organization exists within the NREL while the spirit of collaboration and cooperation has allowed staff to forge innovative relationships by teaching courses in academic departments (Chapter 11), joint appointments in academic departments, cooperative agreements, and creative graduate-training opportunities.
- NREL staff have also been involved in creative graduate training with students housed in various academic departments, while working on research projects through the NREL.
- CSU graduates have attained leadership roles both at home and abroad, garnering the acclaim and recognition for themselves and for NREL and CSU.

This organizational model has led to long-term survival — as they say, "the proof of the pudding in the eating."

12.6 Summary: Advantages, Disadvantages, and Problems to Be Solved

NREL, like any similar organization, has faced and will continue to face both internal and external pressure from funding sources, organizational change, institutional leadership, and the personal development and interests of scientific staff. Enlisting individuals with expertise in organizational dynamics can greatly aid the functioning of an organization.

The long-term survival of organizations like the NREL has depended on the visionary and flexible leadership of directors, research staff, thought leaders, and the contribution of highly valued, highly competent support staff and university leadership. The value of having supportive funding entities is critical.

Balancing "soft money" against institutional "hard money" support will always present challenges. The NREL was created as a soft money organization, allowing researchers to be untethered from many academic responsibilities that required an "at home" presence. The price for that freedom and flexibility was financial uncertainty and stress for individual scientists.

Attracting and retaining top talent in a soft money organization is a persistent challenge, and the NREL is no exception. Part of the NREL's success has depended on the continuity of systems ecology thought leadership, accomplished by retaining top talent following graduation. This has occurred because of the soft money nature of the NREL. Recruiting systems ecologists is difficult because there are not many willing to come into a soft money position requiring an individual to bring their own funding without the guarantee of hard money support. The soft money model exacerbates this challenge.

Finally, preserving the legacy of the NREL is important for several reasons: (1) institutional history ignored cannot help guide the future; (2) the NREL is a repository for the philosophy embedded in the SEP; (3) it houses the vast knowledge base generated by the NREL and collaborators; and (4) provides institutional support for development and maintenance of digital collections of information including, long-term research and modeling efforts.

Appendix 12.1 Case Study: Observations of Consulting Organizational Psychologist Dr. Jacob Hautaluoma

Every organization has human management issues and challenges. Organizations must adapt to changing conditions and must improve to counteract entropy if they are to survive. Different Natural Resource Ecology Laboratory (NREL) (Lab) directors have used varying approaches to handle these challenges. One innovation tried by some of the directors, but not utilized by most labs elsewhere, was the retention of an organizational psychology consultant over a period of years to help the Lab get past difficult times and develop optimally. The consultant, Dr. Jacob (Jack) Hautaluoma, was first retained in 1978 by Dr. James Gibson, the director at the time the original USIBP Grassland Biome funding was coming to a close. Dr. Hautaluoma was a full-time faculty member in the Industrial/Organizational Psychology Program at CSU. He was active as a researcher, teacher, and graduate advisor. He served as a consultant within the university and to other organizations in the US and overseas. He had been a postdoctoral fellow at Yale University in organizational psychology. He later worked on an NSF RANN (Research Associated with National Needs) project to study interdisciplinary projects. It is also interesting that at this time, systems theory, which was a starting point for the NREL's identification, was making a mark on organizational psychology (Katz and Kahn, 1966). Dr. Hautaluoma was a strong proponent of its ideas.

A task of the NREL scientists at the conclusion of USIBP funding was to produce papers using integrated interdisciplinary ecosystem ideas to summarize the work of the Biome funding. The scientists were finding this difficult, because much of the research that had been done was mainly from a disciplinary (silo) perspective and synthesis from an interdisciplinary perspective was proving to be problematical. There were serious strains on the staff and Dr. Gibson was facing a quandary regarding how to fulfill what he saw as obligations of the Biome funding and how to procure future funding. He and others were even questioning whether the Lab should survive as a unit. Five years had been invested in the Biome work, but problems in completing the integrated assignments and yet not gaining a future organizational vision led to questions of the Lab's viability in its then present form. There was a great deal of personal and interpersonal stress among the scientists resulting in both physical and psychological strains.

Dr. Gibson asked for help in dealing with these situations. Dr. Hautaluoma initially made an "organizational diagnosis" by conducting interviews and group sessions with the Lab's staff. As is consistent with this work in his profession, especially when very capable organizational members are the clientele, he found resistance to the idea that the Lab would need such help. It is difficult for anyone inside an organization to acknowledge that such a great group of people would need the assistance of a stranger from a foreign profession. Most people think they are people experts, and they are up to a point. But the truth is that it is often quite difficult to be your own doctor, and there are times when it is not good practice. Fortunately for Dr. Hautaluoma, even though facing some expected resistance, many of the scientific staff supported his work, which continued for over 25 years. Dr. Gibson started the process, which with support from Drs. Vernon Cole, David C. Coleman, and Robert Heil made progress. In later years Dr. Robert G. Woodmansee was the most ardent advocate of Dr. Hautaluoma's services with Drs. Ted Elliot and William Lauenroth being highly engaged as well.

Dr. Hautaluoma initially dealt with individual cases involving the staff, which included fighting fires of disruption. Issues regarding "stealing ideas," "not getting appropriate credit," "feeling disrespected," or "feeling that their livelihood was threatened" were common. There were also splits along disciplinary lines and between younger and older scientists. The Lab became known as a "heart attack place."

Next, Dr. Hautaluoma developed some training and change plans for the Lab that involved interdisciplinary teamwork. He borrowed heavily from ideas he was using on an international water development project with the CSU Civil Engineering Department. The water project involved training people from different disciplines and cultures to produce effective results for the water resources, economy, farming, and soils of Egypt after a change in the Nile's flow due to the construction of the Aswan Dam. The water project staff included civil engineers, economists, soil scientists, sociologists, and others, including both Americans and Egyptians in all disciplines. To gain a complete picture of the effect of the changes in the river, all disciplines and cultural representatives needed to develop change information and effective remediation contributions for the project to be successful. The overall benefit of the project was to use the contributions of all the participants. These benefits could not have been accomplished if only an individual discipline or cultural group's efforts were considered. By analogy, the goal of the NREL was to produce interdisciplinary results, but they seemed unattainable at the end of the Biome studies.

Dr. Hautaluoma next developed training modules to change work processes at the Lab. As a first step in the training, the participants, primarily NREL's senior scientists, were asked to answer the following questions: "Why do we exist as an interdisciplinary Lab?" and "What is supposed to happen because we define ourselves so?" The participants were instructed to describe an imaginary but potentially real interdisciplinary project or program of research that they would be likely to do at the Lab. They then had to describe the desired results needed to ensure the Lab had accomplished its goals. This involved goal setting, yet unlike goals a single disciplinary researcher would describe. These goals would be derived from a team of scientists working on the same project, yet from different disciplinary perspectives. Each discipline was expected to make a contribution, but the goals were to come from the benefits of all the various disciplines contributing to them. It was important that this goal-setting process take place at the beginning of a project, and not after the fact, as had been the case in the Biome project.

An organization functioning as an interdisciplinary group has the potential to evolve into one of several stable states. The first state is called multidisciplinary group work, where the members work on occupational hobbies following their own interests and talents. In this situation, the participants are able to remain active on a project doing what they know best. They are somewhat like children playing in a sand box: they work closely and mostly get along, but they are working on their own sandcastles. This is a multidisciplinary stable state because although different disciplines are present, these participants are primarily producing products defined by their own discipline. This is not bad in itself, but the work products suffer from the unmet expectations of producing results that are informed and shaped by the knowledge of all the other disciplines working together. Multidisciplinary work resembles the Lab during its early, field research, Biome phase.

Another stable state of interdisciplinary or intercultural groups is where a dominant single discipline removes the ambiguity of the teamwork task by defining the goals and criteria of good processes in the dominant discipline's standpoint. This is called a "unidisciplinary groupwork" stable state. In some ways the civil engineers on the Egypt water project dominated the definition of the priorities and work practices of the project. This may be too strong a statement, but many of the water project staff felt underutilized and not very effective in their contribution to the project's goals. Questions arise in these situations about the need for different types of staff in the first place, and whether the project might have been more effective under a different organizational arrangement.

True interdisciplinary teamwork involves deciding, from a systems theory point of view, why different types of people are needed to accomplish a project's aims. Processes are followed to develop an understanding of the accomplishments and contributions required to meet them. Commitments are then procured from project participants to meet these goals. Participants come to learn the purpose of working together as a team and the end accomplishments that are to be realized. This involves front loading the setting of project goals that are then agreed upon. These goals might not look like those that would have been produced by the members individually. Each member is helped to determine how they can best contribute to the project's goals. Again, the temptation is to lapse into performing occupational hobbies or to accept the dominant discipline's ideas, but rather this is the time for systems thinking and devising goals that utilize the strengths of the many viewpoints of the team. In truth, the enablers of a project may have previously defined the goals of the work, with the team then deciding how to best accomplish the project aims. In any case, the project staff should set or accept team goals and then decide what each team member must do to accomplish them. This can often result in changing a team member's sense of what is their best contribution to the project.

The next phase of the training covered team communication. General rules about errors in communication caused by a lack of clarity were covered, but the primary topic focused on feedback as both an important reward mechanism and a corrective device. Accurate positive feedback about how someone else's behavior is effective is one of the most powerful reinforcements that can be given. On the other hand, it is almost impossible to correct a situation without negative feedback. It is relatively easy to give positive feedback, but negative feedback can produce adverse effects unless it is done correctly. As a result, much of the training focused on how to give negative feedback in an effective manner. The training emphasized that members of an effective interdisciplinary team should take the role of teaching one another, using positive feedback to improve good performance and negative feedback when corrections are necessary.

The following sessions emphasized conflict resolution. It has already been mentioned that conflicts were prominent in the team in earlier years. Dr. Hautaluoma stated that conflicts were inevitable; that is, they were going to happen no matter what was done to prevent them.

Nevertheless, good team practices can minimize their effects. The training focused on recognizing conflicts early, and then on the steps to be taken for resolution or remediation. During the time Dr. Hautaluoma was with the Lab, the frequency of conflicts lessened.

One important innovation for preventing conflicts was an offshoot of the work Dr. Hautaluoma did on strategic planning with the Lab. Participants were asked to define areas of research to be emphasized during the next year or so. Dr. Hautaluoma suggested that each scientist express their interests in working on the topics specified by the planning. Those who chose similar projects met to state their interests on future ventures and on the roles they would like to play. They were directed to share their desire to be a lead author, a supporting scientist, or another kind of role. If there were overlaps in the choices of projects or the roles, the scientists were instructed to talk out the competing commitments they were willing to make. This allowed for possible differentiation of possible overlaps before project work began. The purpose was to thwart any future statements, such as "you stole my ideas." Given the historical use of that phrase, which had caused interpersonal conflicts in the Lab, it was the goal of front loading a discussion of the desired commitments to specific types of work that future conflicts could be avoided.

The training on interdisciplinary teamwork was followed by additional training and practice on strategic planning. This was done to change the Lab from only responding to current opportunities to being more forward looking and deliberative in defining its own direction and identity. The strategic planning training again emanated from systems theory which thus altered the scientists' view of the Lab as a system, nested in an environment and other systems. A diagram representing this idea is shown in Figure 12.1.

Figure 12.2 places the physical Lab at the center of the diagram. The NREL relies on inputs for its existence, as described on the upstream side of figure. The Resources are inputs that can take many forms, including people, ideas, money, and social or political support, etc. by other persons or organizations. Enablers provide the Resources and are mainly people or other organizations who would like the Lab to continue to exist. The Products of the Lab and the Users of the products are shown on the downstream side of the figure. Products include papers, ideas, classes taught, innovations, and resource management recommendations, but could also include unintended or unwanted products such as waste or the creation of a bad image of the Lab. The Users are people or organizations who use the Lab's Products, such as other scientists and labs, resource managers, politicians, and students. A condition of systems theory is that the products should also be useful to other systems, otherwise the producing system tends to die out. If the Products are useful to the Users, the Users can also become Enablers. Two additional elements, Competitors and Detractors, are shown in the figure under the NREL. Competitors are other entities that perform similar types of work as the NREL. Detractors are entities that would like to see the Lab fail. Each of these sets of entities is described with double arrows to the Lab to signify the mutual influences on and from the Lab. The figure shows the Environment above the NREL. It includes the social, political, economic, scientific, historical, etc. forces that come from the environment that can influence the Lab's functioning. Defining as many of these forces as possible is useful. The strategic planning exercise requires that the participants discuss, in detail, the elements of the figure and then answer the questions that are implied. The effects of these answers on the NREL's future were then used in discussions about the best directions for the Lab to take.

Another exercise within the strategic planning was to describe the NREL's mission. The respondents answered these questions: "What is the Lab's main business?" and "How is it distinct from other organizations?" Participants were then asked to define a vision for the Lab. In that task participants were asked to answer the questions: "If the Lab were doing as well as it could be, what would it look like?" and "What should be changed to help attain that end?" Participants then used the large amount of material that had been generated to make choices about the direction of the NREL. It must be said that these exercises did not receive full participation from the Lab's members, nor was the process ever fully completed. Strategic planning is a long and tedious process and is difficult to accomplish with otherwise busy participants. The process is complicated and tiring and some scientists did not view the process as useful. The strategic planning process should be repeated periodically because an analysis once done has a finite shelf life. In defense of the process, Dr. Hautaluoma wanted the Lab's staff to choose their own direction, rather than merely being responsive to external direction imposed by requests for proposals (RFPs) on the Lab. Dr. Hautaluoma used the process to help the Lab write proposals for funding, with the most notable being a request for NSF funding to establish the Lab as an NSF Science Center. Elements of the process were primarily used during Dr. Woodmansee's directorship, Dr. Elliot's interim directorship, and during the Long-Term Ecological Research (LTER) grasslands project.

While Dr. Hautaluoma was working with the Lab he was also consulting with other colleges at CSU. As a result, he was often called upon to serve as a liaison in facilitating the Lab's commerce between colleges. He was especially active with the College of Natural Resources, where he had much experience, including a major strategic planning project that lasted more than a year. He spent a number of years working on the LTER grasslands project, alongside Drs. Bill Lauenroth and Indie Burke, in addition to Agricultural Research Service (ARS) representatives. He subsequently collaborated with the ARS on other projects. He completed a number of conflict and planning activities with the LTER, including one to institute a system-wide strategic planning activity for the entire LTER network. He attended national ecological science conferences with Lab members presenting a paper (Hautaluoma and Woodmansee, 1994) and poster presentation. Because of the interest generated by the paper, he was invited visit the Office of Technology Assistance in Washington DC to consult on the paper and work with them on a strategic planning project. Partly due to Dr. Hautaluoma's work with the Lab, he developed ties with the National Science Foundation, resulting in a tour as a rotating program officer in Washington DC from 1986 to 1988.

Dr. Hautaluoma worked with the Lab for over 25 years. He did conflict resolution cases, and his practice outside the Lab centered heavily on that topic. He was a member of the Lab's Executive Committee, contributing his perspectives on the organization. During his time with the Lab he was a full-time faculty member and in later years an associate dean of the College of Natural Sciences.

References

Baron, J., and Galvin, K. A. (1990). Future directions of ecosystem science. *BioScience*, 40, 640–2.

Breymeyer, A. I., and Van Dyne, G. M. (1980). *Grasslands, System Analysis and Man.* Cambridge: Cambridge University Press.

Christensen, N. L., Bartuska, A. M., Brown, J. H., et al. (1996). The report of the Ecological Society of America committee on the scientific basis for ecosystem management. *Ecological Applications*, 6(3), 665–91.

Coleman, D. C. (2010). *Big Ecology: The Emergence of Ecosystem Science.* Oakland: University of California Press.

Coleman, D. C., Swift, D. M., and Mitchell, J. E. (2004). From the frontier to the biosphere: A brief history of the USIBP Grasslands Biome program and its impacts on scientific research in North America. *Rangelands*, 26, 8–15.

Cowling, E. B. (2008). *Thirty Years Down and a Century to Go: A Narrative History of the Origins and Early Development of the National Atmospheric Deposition Program.* Madison, WI: National Atmospheric Deposition Program. http://nadp.slh .wisc.edu/NADP/cowlinghistory.pdf (accessed August 29, 2018).

DataONE (2018). DataONE: Data Observation Network for Earth. University of New Mexico. www.dataone.org (accessed August 29, 2018).

ESS. (2018). Department of Ecosystem Science and Sustainability, Warner College of Natural Resources, Colorado State University. https://warnercnr.colostate .edu/ess/ (accessed September 2, 2019).

Golley, F. B. (1993). *History of the Ecosystem Concept in Ecology: More than the Sum of its Parts.* New Haven, CT: Yale University Press.

Hautaluoma, J. E., and Woodmansee, R. G. (1994). New roles in ecological research and policy making. *Ecology International Bulletin*, 21, 1–10.

Kaplan, N. E., Baker, K. S., Draper, D. C., and Swauger, S. (2014). *Packaging, Transforming and Migrating Data from a Scientific Research Project to an Institutional Repository: The SGS LTER Collection.* Digital Collections of Colorado. Fort Collins, CO: Colorado State University. http://hdl.handle.net/10217/87239.

Kaplan, N. E., and Newman, G. J. (2013). *Data Management for NREL and Beyond: A Roadmap and Recommendations.* Digital Collections of Colorado. Fort Collins, CO: Colorado State University. http://hdl.handle.net/10217/87381.

Katz, D., and Kahn, R. L. (1966). *The Social Psychology of Organizations.* New York: Wiley.

MCMLTER. (2018). McMurdo Dry Valleys LTER. National Science Foundation. https://lternet.edu/site/mcmurdo-dry-valleys-lter/ (accessed August 29, 2018).

MEA. (2005). Millennium Ecosystem Assessment. New York: United Nations. www.millenniumassessment.org/en/Synthesis.html (accessed August 29, 2018).

Rykiel, E. (1999). Ecosystem science at the Natural Resource Ecology Laboratory. *BioScience*, 49(1), 69–70.

SoGES (2018). School of Global Environmental Sustainability. Colorado State University, Fort Collins. https://sustainability.colostate.edu (accessed August 29, 2018).

Van Dyne, G. (1969). *The Ecosystem Concept in Natural Resource Management.* New York: Academic Press.

Wall, D. H., and Virginia, R. A. (1999). Control on soil biodiversity: Insights from extreme environments. *Applied Soil Ecology* 13, 137–50.

13 · *Where to From Here?*
Unraveling Wicked Problems

ROBERT G. WOODMANSEE,
DENNIS S. OJIMA, AND NICOLE E. KAPLAN

> No man is an island,
> Entire of itself.
> Each is a piece of the continent,
> A part of the main.
> If a clod be washed away by the sea,
> Europe is the less.
> As well as if a promontory were.
> As well as if a manor of thine own
> Or of thine friend's were.
> Each man's death diminishes me,
> For I am involved in mankind.
> Therefore, send not to know
> For whom the bell tolls,
> It tolls for thee.
>
> "For whom the bell tolls," John Donne, 1572–1631

13.1 Introduction

Some of the major challenges facing humanity and the Earth's ecosystems are outlined in Chapter 2. Among these vexing challenges are food security, soil security, land-use transformation and fragmentation, climate change and drought, water production and quality in river basins, and invasive species. All are real-world, complex or "wicked" problems (Rittel and Webber, 1973; APS, 2007; Balint et al., 2011; Berkowitz, 2017; Wikipedia, 2018a). Wicked problems are those that have multiple and interacting causes. Wicked problems have multiple driving forces or "drivers" that can interact to produce uncertain and unexpected environmental and societal challenges. They involve many poorly understood feedbacks within and among biological, physical, social, economic, and political subsystems. Their definitions are poorly articulated. Knowledge needed to address them is disbursed among many perspectives and disciplines if that knowledge exists at all. Wicked problems are socially complex and complicated and require collaboration among many disciplines and organizations for evaluation and resolution. Resolving them may require changing the behaviors of individuals and groups of individuals. These principles are used here to demonstrate the need for the systems ecology paradigm (SEP) to confront environmental and natural resource problems throughout the world.

The sciences alone, especially traditional natural sciences and ecology, are not enough to resolve problems such as increasing temperatures influencing water availability and economies in arid regions; chemical and nutrient loading from industry, urbanization, agriculture, and transportation polluting the atmosphere, waters, soils, and sediments; ecosystem structural alteration and fragmentation on rural land and wildlife; and political turmoil, even war, on food, water, and energy resources and reliability. Resolution will require the incorporation of policy and management realities of large-scale problems such as the those described in the "water–energy–food nexus" (FAO, 2018; UNWater, 2018). Maybe the most challenging problem of all will be convincing people and groups of people to collectively change behaviors related to the use and management of Earth's lands, waters, and natural resources.

The SEP can be the "go-to" methodology for integrating knowledge and resolving many real-world, complex (wicked) problems. The SEP, defined in Chapters 1 and 10, has two major components: (1) the *systems ecology approach* (Van Dyne, 1969; Montague, 2016), and (2) the use of *ecosystem science*. The systems ecology approach is the holistic, systems perspective and methodology developed for the rigorous and methodical study of ecosystems (Figure 13.1) and is crucial for systematically unraveling, understanding, and resolving important environmental, natural resource, and societal/ecological challenges. Ecosystem science is a vast body of scientific data and knowledge, much of which has been assembled using the "ecosystem approach," for example the Millennium Ecosystem Assessment (UNMEA, 2005). The ecosystem approach is discussed throughout this book and in the vast scientific literature related to the environment and natural resources. This body of knowledge includes data, literature, and experiences (including traditional experience) reported over the past century and earlier. Care must be taken to include literature produced before the digital age to make this body of knowledge findable, accessible, interoperable, and usable (Wilkinson et al., 2016; Easterday et al., 2018). Michael Usher (personal communication) stated "One of the problems of this electronic age is that almost everything published prior to 2000, in printed format, is forgotten."

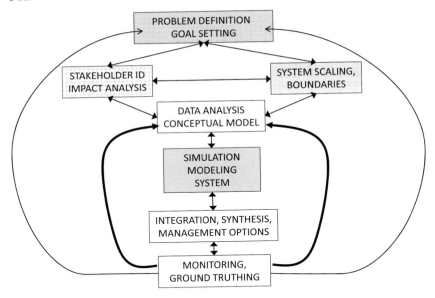

Figure 13.1 Generalized steps in the SEP.

This chapter addresses the need to overcome sociatal barriers to the adoption of beneficial management practices and technologies in addition to addressing multiscaled science associated with the problems introduced in Chapter 2. Major challenges are overcoming communication, knowledge, and innovation barriers; detrimental cultural norms; science skepticism; and political ideologies that are harmful to advancements toward sustainable ecosystems including the Earth. Other challenges are using the systems ecology approach to interact with the social, behavioral, and institutional perspectives encountered while attempting to resolve problems.

Throughout this book we have demonstrated the usefulness of the SEP for addressing many problems at lower levels of the ecological hierarchies shown in Figure 13.2. Now is the time to demonstrate the usefulness of the SEP for large-scale wicked problems involving people (Figure 13.3).

13.2 Getting to the Future

The greatest challenge for land and natural resource management going forward in the twenty-first century may not be more research and data collection in the biophysical and applied (agriculture, rangeland, forest,

Figure 13.2 Important "scales" needing consideration in decision making. Some hierarchical dimensions need specific attention when evaluating and managing ecological/social ecosystems.

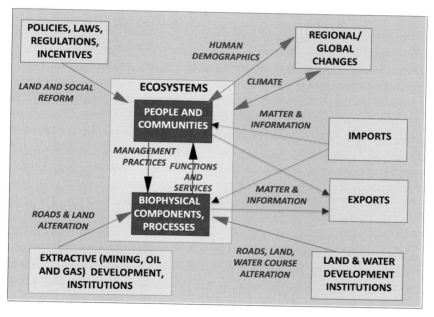

Figure 13.3 Ecosystems: the relationship of people and communities (societies) to the biophysical components and interactions (land, water, and air) in an ecosystem context. A black and white version of this figure will appear in some formats. For the color version, please refer to Figure 1.1 in the plate section.

aquatic) sciences and technology. That research has been successful and will continue to be supported through traditional funding structures.

More research is needed now in the social, behavioral, learning, economic, and marketing sciences related to acceptance of beneficial innovations in agriculture, forestry, and natural resource management by policy makers and private and public land and water managers. *This is especially true at the landscape and regional scales where collective actions are required for meaningful impact (scales larger than individual properties or jurisdictions).* Examples of large-scale problems requiring collective action are: water management, conservation, and quality in river basins (Grafton et al., 2013); carbon sequestration; nitrogen emissions and losses from agricultural practices; reduction of use of harmful pesticides; reduction of habitat fragmentation; and restoration of disturbed landscapes and regions. As challenges get larger in scale, it becomes vital for those involved in the problems (stakeholders) to engage in collaborative problem resolutions.

13.2.1 Conceptual Model Development

The problem statement and goals setting, boundary setting and scaling, and stakeholder identification steps in the SEP (Figure 13.1) occur concurrently, are iterative, and require good communication skills such as active listening and honest feedback. These skills are needed because problem resolutions are often contentious due to varying perceptions and viewpoints among stakeholders (Figure 13.4). Good communication skills form the basis of relationships and trust among stakeholders needed to do the upcoming work of analyzing information and data and developing conceptual models and strategies for resolving agreed-upon problems. This phase of the SEP seen in Figure 13.1 is where the true interactions of biological, physical, and social sciences merge. Humans are included as subjects of analysis, and they are the analysts.

Communication, trust, and interpretation issues encountered during analysis must be satisfactorily resolved by stakeholders attempting to understand and resolve wicked problems. Co-designing the conceptual model is the phase in which stakeholder interactions must lead to acceptable representations (conceptual models) of ecosystem behavior. Conceptual models associated with dynamic problems will probably require development of simulation models for reasons described in Chapters 1 and 4.

Basic requirements for accomplishing the collaborative conceptual modeling phase of wicked problems are:

- All stakeholders must understand, trust, and embrace the SEP.
- Stakeholders must understand the sources and limitations of available concepts, data, information, and models.

"WHAT YOU SEE DEPENDS ON WHERE YOU STAND"

Figure 13.4 Some of the many viewpoints involved in the analysis of an example watershed to answer the specific question "how can a watershed (the Rio Puerco Watershed in New Mexico) and its included landscapes be restored to healthy functioning following drastic disturbance?" The quote "What you see depends on where you stand" is variously attributed to Albert Einstein, C. S. Lewis (1955) in *The Magicians Nephew*, and many others. Figure modified from Riebsame and Woodmansee (1995).

• Stakeholders must learn about the basic technologies used to extract and interpret reliable knowledge or learn to trust others with those skills.
• Stakeholders must be willing and able to critically evaluate information and knowledge and be disposed to adopting new ideas and technology.

Willingness to adopt new concepts, knowledge, technology, and management practices is important for both stakeholder analysts and users of the management options proposed by the modeling efforts of the stakeholders (see Section 13.3.2).

13.2.2 Demystifying the SEP
Many tools that underpin the SEP are available but not well understood by stakeholders. Most people in the developed world are familiar with common simulation models, for example weather forecasts, traffic flows and signaling, cancer treatments, and provisioning of aircraft and naval carriers. Models of ranches, farms, haying operations, river basin water flows and allocations, and precision agriculture are well known in some sectors of

agriculture (see Chapters 4, 7, and 8). Demonstrating in clear and transparent language that SEP and simulation models can be used for analysis of both intended and unintended consequences of human activities, and that they can be "predictive" tools, is essential but difficult (see Chapter 4).

A major challenge for systems ecologists is demystifying the systems approach and the modeling process, as well as demonstrating its usefulness to all stakeholders. We need new learning modalities to describe systems thinking (Meadows, 2008), the SEP, and the value of modeling to various user and adoption groups (Diederen et al., 2003; Rogers, 2003; Moore, 2014). These user groups include policy makers, land and water managers, thought leaders, and citizens. Research from behavioral, learning, and marketing science is needed to help legitimize systems ecology and mathematical modeling by demonstrating its methodology, transparency of assumptions, and fact- and evidence-based analysis, and demonstrating that peer review is capable of addressing real-world, complex issues. Expert opinion in the modeling process needs to be relegitimized as described by Nichols (2017) in his book *The Death of Expertise: The Campaign against Established Knowledge and Why it Matters.* Engaging policy decision makers in rational dialogue is essential for bridging the gap between good science, special interest power centers, the public, stakeholders, and on-the-ground managers (Balint et al., 2011; see Chapter 7).

Using the SEP, systems ecologists have been able to analyze known interactive controlling forces (drivers) and linkages for determining healthy functioning ecosystems, and their intended and unintended consequences in the biophysical realm of ecosystems. Systems ecologists have begun the development of linked biophysical and social systems, but this area is still in its infancy. More collaboration and integration across disciplines, as well as development of interactive models of society and the environment (see Chapter 4 and Figure 13.3) are needed. Systems ecologists need to continue upgrading and developing conceptual and mathematical models. More new systems ecologists who can think beyond "pure" science and technology need to be trained. Collaboration among many individuals, disparate disciplines, and stakeholders of various viewpoints is essential (Figure 13.4).

13.2.3 Data Mining, Analysis, Integration, Synthesis, and Interpretation

Access to reliable data and knowledge, and standards for judging their validity, are critical for maintaining and restoring healthy, resilient, and sustainable ecosystems. In the last few decades land and water scientists and managers have been confronted with an explosion of access to information, only some of which is reliable knowledge. Information generated by "thought leaders," "big money," political influencers, scientists, and media outlets is overwhelming (Nichols, 2017). Good and bad information is available to agricultural and natural resource policy makers, managers, and citizens almost anywhere in the world.

Judging the validity of the available information requires evaluating facts and evidence, critical thinking, and rationality (Thaler and Sunstine, 2009; Nichols, 2017). Critical thinking is the objective analysis and evaluation of an issue in order to form a judgment. Rationality is the quality of being based on, or in accordance with reason or logic (Wikipedia, 2019). Decisions based on facts and evidence rather than unsupported ideology, family and cultural traditions, group think, or political persuasion are essential for differentiating between the needs, wants, desires, wishes, and aspirations. Facts and evidence are required in modern management (Sohrabi and Zarghi, 2015). Table 13.1 lists some of the information sources available to land managers and stakeholders. The table is arranged with the relatively reliable sources of information near the top and the less reliable toward the bottom. However, all sources require vetting, fact checking, cross-checking, and verification because, unfortunately, some of the sources, especially in the lower portion of the table, are known to be unreliable and some of those at the top may appear to be reliable but may be subject to manipulation by special interests.

To support application of the SEP, evidence from field and laboratory studies, simulated values from reliable modeling exercises, and transparent processes that form expert opinion are essential to support contemporary expectations of access to data in science. The US National Resource Council addresses the potential open data as a resource that can be mined, integrated, and synthesized through various open access activities (National Research Council, 1995). Major challenges still exist in archiving and mining data and information from the vast warehouse of ecological knowledge (Waide et al., 2017; *Environmental Science*, 2018; Wikipedia, 2018b). Stakeholders need to be able to discover, retrieve, and determine how to use data and information in ways that can apply it to generating new knowledge, and which support decision making (Gewin, 2016). New repositories which treat data and information as digital assets and design technologies for gaining the most potential from

Table 13.1 *Some of the sources of information flooding private and public land managers with notes about oversight and review processes of the sources and their reliability*

Sources	Oversight and review	Reliability
Scientific research and models	Peer review in reputable journals, predigital literature must be included, must reveal sources of information	High reliability, requires critical thinking and rationality, tends to be myopic (silos), should reveal sources of funding
Expertise, expert opinion	Based on reputation and proven record of achievement, integrity, and transparency	Reliable, requires critical thinking and rationality, requires transparency of sources of funding
University classroom courses, workshops, short courses	Based on reputation and proven record of achievement and integrity, subject to institutional review	High reliability, requires critical thinking and rationality
University online learning – adult education, professional continuing education	Based on reputation and proven record of achievement and integrity, institutional review	High reliability, requires critical thinking and rationality
Extension seminars, forums, webinars	Oversight by agency review processes	Reliable, dependent on good science and expertise, requires critical thinking
Traditional or local knowledge, experience	Based on observations and cultural norms – "What you see depends on where you stand"	Can be invaluable but frequently biased, requires extreme vetting and cross-checking
Government and intergovernmental reports, webinars	Oversight by agency review process	Reliable, dependent on good science, requires critical thinking, subject to political intervention
Nongovernmental agencies	Oversight by agency review process, subject bias	Reliable if well vetted and based on science and expertise but may be biased
Globalization and international market reports	Oversight by financial and international organization review processes	Reliable if well vetted and based on expertise

Table 13.1 (*cont.*)

Sources	Oversight and review	Reliability
Commodity market reports	Oversight by financial organization review processes	Reliable if well vetted and based on expertise
Advertising, messaging, and marketing★	Oversight by corporate leadership	Always biased, requires extreme vetting and cross-checking
Big banks and "local" banks	Oversight by corporate leadership, government regulations, and review	Reliable if well vetted and based on facts and expertise
Investors, developers	No oversight	Requires extreme vetting, focus on intended results and little or no unintended consequences, subject to fraud and corruption
Print media	Oversight by corporate leadership and journalism code of ethics, depends on reliability of sources, subject to false equivalencies and "fake news"	Requires extreme vetting of sources – some reliable, others are propaganda machines for political and religious ideologies
Talk radio and TV	Oversight by corporate leadership and journalism code of ethics, depends on reliability of sources, subject to false equivalencies	Requires extreme vetting of sources – some reliable, others are propaganda machines for political and religious ideologies
Internet	No oversight but huge source of information, both good and bad, depends on reliability of sources	Assume unreliable – access to all other categories, requires extreme vetting, cross-checking, fact checking, and verification
Social media, YouTube	No oversight, potential for great good and bad	Assume unreliable – requires extreme vetting, cross-checking, and verification

(cont.)

Table 13.1 (*cont.*)

Sources	Oversight and review	Reliability
Word of mouth – family, friends, neighbors, ministers, bars	No oversight	Assume unreliable – requires extreme vetting, cross-checking, and verification
Local agriculture merchants	Based on reputation and local record of reliability and integrity	Assume reliable but biased – requires critical thinking, vetting, cross-checking, and verification
Advocacy groups	Oversight by group leadership	Requires extreme vetting, focus on intended results, and little or no unintended consequences
Political agendas – e.g., Trump, Pruett, Zinke, et al.	Currently lacking ethics, critical thinking, and rationality	Assume unreliable until proven otherwise – requires extreme vetting of sources – some reliable, others are propaganda machines for political and religious ideologies

*Oil and gas lobby, corporate agricultural lobby, corporate sales (seeds and genes, equipment, big chemistry, etc.).

them require a change in thinking to strategically plan for value-added features that support novel research activities such as data mining, integration, and synthesis (Peer and Green, 2012). Critical challenges in dealing with "mined" data include methods to interpret the data once it is found and displayed. We need to continue fostering tight linkages between data management and modeling, field, laboratory, and monitoring work to promote more openness of data and science in ecology (Hampton et al., 2015). Sharing data and information in reliable and sustainable infrastructure can enable powerful synergies from our broader knowledge backdrop, allowing for applications of legacy data to new approaches, eliminating redundancy, and contributing to new data-intensive science (Cheruvelil and Soranno, 2018).

13.2.4 Transfer of Information and Knowledge

Explaining methods of information acquisition and communication to achieve management practices supporting common beneficial goals is a major challenge facing stakeholder groups and society as a whole. Many people throughout the world have entered the digital age using digital technology and social networking as a vital link to information and communication (smartphones, social media, and the internet). These technologies are emerging in modern developed and developing world agriculture (Figures 13.5 and 13.6).

Access to information is not necessarily access to reliable knowledge. Many rural and older citizens are reluctant to or can't engage in new methods of communication for numerous reasons (see Section 13.2.5). Some people are dubious about participating in new models of cooperation, collaboration, and especially collaboration technology (see Chapter 10; Ojima and Corell, 2009; Balint et al., 2011). Significant numbers of people are reluctant to abandon established ways of thinking (i.e., beliefs, values, and cultural norms) even when scientifically based

Figure 13.5 Illustration of digital technology in farming. Photo courtesy of USDA Natural Resource Conservation Service. A black and white version of this figure will appear in some formats. For the color version, please refer to the plate section.

Figure 13.6 Maasai herder using cell phone for entertainment, herd management tips, and marketing information. Photo origin unknown – used on many African websites. A black and white version of this figure will appear in some formats. For the color version, please refer to the plate section.

facts and experienced experts have established evidence to improve individual welfare and that of others. Research focusing on overcoming these barriers is critically needed to better manage landscapes, small regions (e.g., watersheds), regions, and larger ecosystems.

13.2.5 Ability and Willingness to Evaluate Information and Knowledge

Information gathered from sources in Table 13.1 can be used to consider the adoption of new and valuable concepts, methods, or technology. Adoption depends on the ability and willingness of individual stakeholders to learn and the motivation to explore new innovations and behaviors, and incentives to make transitions to new practices (McKenzie-Mohr, 2011).

Tackling the sensitive issue of the ability and willingness to learn requires openly and transparently addressing the impacts of true ignorance, consensual or willful ignorance, and an inability to learn or lack of good sense on the learning process itself (Cipolla, 1987; Pomeroy, 2016, 2019). True ignorance is the lack of knowledge or understanding. Ignorant people lack education or knowledge and they may be unaware and uninformed. They may not have access to knowledge, or they may not have the mental capacity to learn. It can be overcome with the study of factual and reliable information if one is intellectually capable of learning and has access to that information. Even modern experts and geniuses are ignorant about many things – we don't have many da Vincis. Most truly ignorant people are good candidates for adopting new ideas because they are willing to learn. Consensual or willful ignorance is a choice not to study and accept factual knowledge that may differ with one's own, or one's group cultural, political, or religious ideology. It may be rooted in the inability to reconcile science and faith, dogmatic adherence to certain interpretations of political documents like constitutions, or religious writings such as the Bible, Torah, or the Quran. Consensually, ignorant people may be capable of learning but choose not to; they consensually may be reluctant candidates for adopting new ideas. Some people are unable to learn. Some simply lack good sense, which may be caused by lack of rationality or judgment leading to irrational and unintelligent decisions or acts (Cipolla, 1987). For some people, lack of good sense is a choice as in consensual ignorance, for others it is not. People lacking good sense may not be able to successfully adopt new ideas, and they may be disruptive in collaborative decision-making efforts, even if their disruption causes harm to others and/or themselves.

13.2.6 Recognizing Differences in Adoption Groups within Communities

Individuals and groups seem to fall along a scale of willingness to assimilate new knowledge and adopt new ideas and pragmatic innovations (Rogers, 2003; Tetard and Collan, 2007; Moore, 2014). Rogers (2003) categorizes willingness to adopt into five basic groups:

- Innovators (2.5 percent of potential users) – willing to take risks; open to scientific information; likely financially sound; excellent candidates for innovation adoption.

- Early adopters (13.5 percent of potential users) – community leaders; thought leaders; display gravitas; are better educated; careful about choosing innovations.
- Early majority (34 percent of potential users) – slower to adopt innovations; not known for thought leadership; followers; slow to adopt innovations.
- Late majority (34 percent of potential users) – skeptical about adoption of innovations; eventually may adopt; little thought leadership.
- Laggards (16 percent of potential users) – no thought leadership; averse to changes; likely focused on cultural constraints.

Rogers did not consider inventors (scientists, practitioners, and researchers) as a group but they generate new ideas, concepts, and technology. In general, rural landowners and managers follow the categories of adoption willingness proposed by Rogers (2003), Pannell et al. (2006), and Vanclay (2004). A summary of willingness to adopt new concepts and technology is given in Digital Marketing (2018).

A critical SEP research need is to discover approaches to bring scientifically valid concepts, data, and technologies to individuals and communities in each adoption group. Depending on the problems confronting land managers, different approaches will be required for each group. The location, cultural setting, and degree of community cooperation needed to address the problem will determine the approach. The collaboration of systems ecologists, and sociological, behavioral, learning, and marketing scientists, is needed to learn the best approaches to influencing various adoption and stakeholder groups (Mckenzie-Mohr, 2011).

13.2.7 Factors Influencing the Adoption of New Ideas and Technology

The willingness of all stakeholders to learn and accept new technology is critical. The concepts of adoption groups in accepting innovations in land management and policy making are likewise critical. They represent one of the biggest challenges facing systems ecology (Rogers, 2003; McKenzie-Mohr, 2011). The intertwined nature of the interactions of information availability, capability, willingness to learn, the propensity to adopt new ideas, the roles of rural values, and cultural norms in managing the land are addressed in the context of complex problem resolution. Suggestions addressing the critical need to overcome the barriers impeding the adoption of management practices that will benefit individuals,

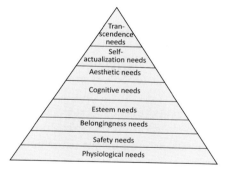

Figure 13.7 Version of Maslow's hierarchy. McLeod (2018).

communities, and society as a whole are presented below. As stated in the quote at the beginning of the chapter, "no man is an island."

Recognizing the needs, wants, desires, and aspirations of individual farmers, ranchers, public land managers, and policy makers at the individual farm, ranch, administrative unit, and community scales is essential when considering the adoption of new ideas and technology. Many people are familiar with the concept of the hierarchy of human needs proposed by Abraham Maslow and others to be intuitively reasonable (Figure 13.7; Values, 2010; McLeod, 2018). Some psychologists and social scientists criticize aspects of Maslow's ideas, just as some biologists criticize aspects of Darwin's theories. However, most generally agree that his concepts are sound. Some people view Maslow's hierarchy in a linear fashion moving from bottom to top. Another view is that individuals reside in different places (often more than one) at any one time in the hierarchy, depending on their needs and motivations at the time. A set of fundamental requirements for land managers is that they must be successful at managing their land to meet their needs wherever they are in Maslow's hierarchy. To meet their needs, rural farmers, ranchers, public land managers, and policy makers require many complex sources of information; most of all acquiring useful knowledge from the vast amount on information available today.

Pragmatic realities confronting individuals and groups who are potential users and adopters of new ideas and technology are the needs to access reliable knowledge and be willing to use it. The goal of adoption of new ideas and technologies must be clearly defined (see Chapter 10). What are the intended and unintended consequences of newly adopted practices and technologies? What is the "relative advantage" of the new innovation (Vanclay, 2004; Pannell et al., 2006). Microeconomic factors of actual cost of conversion or adoption and availability of financial resources are paramount in decision making. Where collective management changes are envisioned, community funding sources need to be developed collaboratively. Opportunity costs or the loss of potential gain from other alternatives when one alternative is chosen should be considered and justified. Labor availability, cost, and manager time and effort must be evaluated. A clear understanding of the risks involved must be transparent. All of the pragmatic considerations must be evaluated before new management practices are adopted.

13.3 Formulating Management Options and Adopting Best Management Practices

Known problems at different spatial scales from nanometers to global in scope were addressed in Chapter 2. At the ecological site and smaller scales, the warehouse of ecological data and knowledge is extensive and many solutions to problems exist. Major challenges are (1) recognizing when enough original research is enough and (2) knowing how to apply the existing data and information for evaluating and formulating management options for important landscape and regional-scale problems.

13.3.1 The Global Challenge

Integrating existing knowledge and synthesizing new management strategies to achieve sustainability at all levels in the hierarchies shown in Figure 13.2 are major current and future management challenges (Boxes 2.1–2.3) for societies worldwide. Simulation modeling and associated decision support systems are concepts and methodologies that set the SEP apart from the broader field of empirically based ecosystem science (see Figure 13.1 and Chapters 4 and 7). They are tools that need continued development to help evaluate the interactions of factors influencing greater scientific understanding and adoption of new management practices.

The systems-based methodology utilized for over 50 years at the NREL allows stakeholders and scientists to examine ecosystem behavior dynamically. Models are tools that allow the integration of vast amounts of diverse information; they promote the synthesis of new ideas. The modeling process forces assumptions to be made transparent. Many models are becoming so reliable that they can be considered predictive.

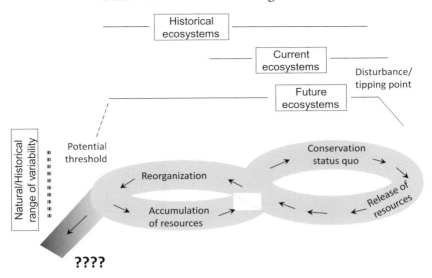

Figure 13.8 Modified adaptive cycle from Walker and Salt (2006). Tipping points can send the adaptive cycle into a cycle of reorganization whose outcome is similar to the existing system. If the disturbance is severe the system is at risk of being shunted past a threshold and into a new state.

Finally, they allow scenarios to be developed that inform management options and lead to the adoption of new management practices (see Chapters 6–8).

The utility of the SEP is to help achieve positive management outcomes and avoid undesirable outcomes such as those described in managing adaptive cycles for resilience (Figure 13.8; Walker and Salt, 2006; Mitchell, 2014; Resilience Alliance, 2018).

All ecosystems experience adaptive cycles in response to disturbances large or small. Historical ecosystems and their legacies have gone through unknown numbers of full cycles in the past. Current managed ecosystems tend to range from exploitation (annual crops and tillage agriculture) to conservation (grasslands, scrublands, and forests) phases in Figure 13.8. Most productive perennial ecosystems tend to be in early conservation phases; the goal of most management practices is to keep them there or direct them to more desirable states.

Disturbances such as fires, floods, volcanoes, surface mining, and infrastructure development, for example roads and oil and gas exploration, can introduce a "tipping point." If a disturbance triggers a tipping point, the goal of management is to keep the amplitude of the release phase constrained to manageable limits so that recovery is predictable and desirable (ecosystem resilience).

Achieving and maintaining healthy, resilient, and sustainable ecosystems demands adapting our management practices, lifestyles, and behaviors to achieve resilience when confronting multiple, interacting, and changing system stressors and drivers. Management practices must seek to avoid reaching extreme tipping points that will initiate unwanted resets of the whole adaptive cycle or worse, cross a "threshold" that will shunt the ecosystem into new unpredicted and undesirable states. Examples of crossed thresholds are desertification in sub-Saharan Africa, gulley cutting in the Rio Puerco Watershed, New Mexico (see Chapter 10), and eroded forestlands and soil fertility losses throughout the world. Managing ecosystems to achieve desirable adaptive cycles, avoiding unwanted thresholds (see Figure 13.8), and mitigating or adapting to changes are examples of "wicked problems" and demand the application of the SEP, the collaboration of many land managers, citizen stakeholders, and policy makers, and political will for evaluation and resolution.

13.3.2 Overcoming Barriers to Adopting Beneficial Management Practices

Basic and applied science (field, laboratory, and modeling) and modern management practices of some croplands, rangelands, and forestlands have advanced remarkably during the past five decades. These advances have been supported through federal land, water, and agricultural policies and funding in the United States, for example the USDA Farm Bills of 2010, 2014, and 2018 (USDA Farm Bill, 2018) and US Environmental Protection Agency programs and National Science Foundation (NSF) basic research funding. Similar measures have taken place in many other countries, for example Australia (Kanowski and McKenzie, 2011), Canada,[1] the United Kingdom,[2] the European Union,[3] and in some developing countries.[4] These policies have included education programs and incentives targeting individual landowners for soil conservation to reduce erosion and pollution and improving water quality. Recent Farm Bills in the US have included

[1] www.agr.gc.ca/eng/science-and-innovation/agricultural-practices/?id=1360876327795.
[2] https://en.wikipedia.org/wiki/Agriculture_in_the_United_Kingdom.
[3] www.eea.europa.eu/themes/landuse/intro.
[4] www.fao.org/about/who-we-are/departments/climate-biodiversity-land-water/en/.

funding for carbon sequestration and greenhouse gas mitigation research. However, the acceptance and implementation of new and modern management practices and the science supporting them has been slow among many individual landowners and managers. *Widespread acceptance of best management practices by many neighboring land managers is needed to solve landscape, regional, and some global problems.*

One major challenge confronting ecosystem scientists is getting reliable knowledge about the "best management practices," or at least "better management practices," to the people who are actually managing the land. Information alone is not enough (McKenzie-Mohr, 2011), because the second challenge is getting individual managers to adopt new management practices based on that reliable knowledge. Land managers must be encouraged to collaborate on solutions for larger-scale problems within watersheds, river basins, and regions. Resolving large-scale problems requires individual land managers to look beyond their own fences for the good of the broader community and society. How can that be accomplished?

All stakeholders including scientists, policy makers, and land managers need to learn how to overcome significant barriers to the transfer and adoption of new and existing ideas, innovations, established knowledge, technology, and management practices discussed in Section 13.2. Many considerations are needed when evaluating new concepts, methods, or technology during adoption decision making (Vanclay, 2004; Pannell et al., 2006). Rational criteria are needed to consider the adoption of beneficial management practices for individuals, groups, and society. Specific research about developing those criteria is needed.

When the steps described in the SEP have been completed, management options can be evaluated and plans adopted by affected stakeholders. Implementation will depend on the actual managers of the land. While the SEP and associated empirical basic and applied science have made great leaps forward in the analysis and understanding of ecosystem behavior, there remain significant barriers to the adoption and implementation of the best management practices suggested by scientific research and understanding. A major challenge is persuading policy makers and land managers to adopt new attitudes, concepts, behaviors, and technologies that will benefit their own, their communities', and society's physical, mental, economic, and environmental well-being. This challenge confronts scientists, outreach and extension communities, educational institutions, and management agencies alike throughout the world (see Chapter 2).

The SEP, including its emphases on stakeholder and community involvement, data mining and synthesis, dynamic simulation modeling, and collaborative learning is the best practical approach to evaluating and resolving wicked problems. Solving wicked problems may not be possible but resolving and adapting to them by finding and implementing better management practices will benefit all. Forrester (1968) suggested that models should not be judged against some assumed perfection, instead they should be judged compared to other ways of describing a system of interest. Woodmansee (1978) expanded on this concept by suggesting that simulation models with well-documented and transparent assumptions should be compared to mental models, word models, photographs, or drawings as tools for describing systems. Similarly, the SEP should not be compared to some idea of imaginary perfection, but rather should be judged for clarity of structure and transparency of assumptions compared to other means of resolving wicked problems, for example political debates, public forums, focus groups, papers written by individual special interest experts, documentaries, committee discussions, mental models, pictures, drawings, and old belief systems. Application of the SEP may include information from some of these sources, but only after careful evaluation (see Table 13.1). The paradigm truly represents "new frontiers" within ecosystem science (Weathers et al., 2016). The SEP goes beyond science and addresses the need for science implementation.

New research from fields, such as common pool resource theory (Sarker et al., 2008), community-based social marketing (McKenzie-Mohr, 2011), collaboration science and technology (see Chapter 10), actionable science (Weichselgartner and Kasperson, 2010), and coupling human information and knowledge systems (Tabara and Chabay, 2013; Moser, 2016) are needed to help solve many of these challenges. Meeting these challenges will require access to reliable data and knowledge (see Table 13.1) and the ability and willingness of all stakeholders to learn, adopt, and adapt. Research addressing the ability and willingness to learn is in the realm of the social, behavioral, marketing, and learning sciences. Breakthroughs are critically needed in order to persuade a sufficient number of land managers to adopt management practices to mitigate and adapt to issues such as climate change, soil degradation, nitrogen loading, pollution, and loss of biodiversity (see Chapter 2). Among the great challenges facing land and water managers throughout the world are the needs to overcome selfishness, greed, and apathy by learning how to introduce spiritual and cultural transformations, and environmental scientists don't know how to do that according to J. G. Spath as quoted in Woo (2010).

13.3.3 Monitoring and Adaptive Management

Assuming a management plan based on best management practices is implemented by vested stakeholders, key system characteristics or indicators must be monitored to determine if the plan is succeeding (see Chapter 10). If the goals are not being met, adjustments need to be made (adaptive management as described by Holling, 1978). In extreme cases the SEP process shown in Figure 13.1 may need to be reiterated. Working backward through the steps in Figure 13.1, the basic simulation model(s) needs to be evaluated for reliability of the assumptions and coding therein. Concurrently, the original agreed-upon conceptual model may need to be reexamined for its logic and whether or not new research is needed to fill knowledge gaps. The model examination may cause reflection on whether the spatial, temporal, or organizational scales represented in the models were correct and whether the members of the analysis team (stakeholders) adequately represented the expertise needed to model the system. Finally, and often painfully, the analysis group may discover they have been trying to solve the wrong problem. For example, attempting to improve forest health by suppressing fire and extensive logging. In the worst-case scenario, the SEP offers a guided and transparent pathway for reevaluation.

13.4 Critical Scientific Needs Going Forward

13.4.1 Establish the SEP as the "Go-To" Methodology for Resolving Wicked Problems

Science and trusted scientific research are critically needed to solve real-world complex problems. Some of those problems are relatively simple and have been the driving force in successful ecosystem science for over five decades as described in this book. Resolution of large-scale wicked problems discussed in this chapter and Chapter 2 using the SEP is developing. Successful application will require the collective action of scientists in collaboration with land managers, policy makers, and myriad stakeholder citizens, using new techniques of knowledge acquisition, transfer, and application. SEP offers a pathway forward.

13.4.2 Demystifying the SEP

Demystifying the SEP and explaining its utility to a broad array of stakeholders is crucial (see Box 13.1). The development of scientists to become holistic integrators of knowledge is essential for solving complex problems. Likewise, recognizing that some people are integrators and that others think more narrowly in a reductionist mode is also essential. Systems ecologists and modelers who are good listeners and who can communicate with a diverse array of stakeholders in understandable language and accomplish true collaboration are needed. This will require specific new methods of training. Visionaries are also needed; how are they recognized, developed, and recruited from professional environments that tend toward disciplinary segregation is an administrative challenge.

13.4.3 Funding Supporting SEP

Developing mechanisms to fund transdisciplinary, long-term, and expensive research programs and train new generations of scientists capable of studying large-scale ecosystems is critically needed. None of the wicked problems addressed in this book can be resolved with the traditional funding models employed by funding agencies. A major reason for the success of the NREL has been the continuity of modeling programs over five decades (see Chapter 4).

13.4.4 Continued Empirical Ecosystem Research to Fill Gaps in Knowledge

Continued research is needed about specific aspects of the structure and functioning of large-scale ecosystems. Among the critical gaps in the knowledge base are: the interactions of subunits within landscape and larger-scale ecosystems; interactions of climate driving variables (e.g., temperature, water, nutrient loading, and pollution); and interactions between biophysical, social, economic, and governance systems. Research establishments throughout the world are structured to accommodate empirical research needs within disciplines, but less frequently between disciplines. Thus, the emphasis of Chapter 13 and Chapter 2 has been on large-scale, complex or wicked problems requiring transdisciplinary collaboration.

Box 13.1 *Educational approaches for demystifying the SEP*

Demystifying the SEP requires innovations in education and knowledge transfer to inform land and water managers, policy makers, and citizens of its utility. What follows are examples of concepts and technologies needing large-scale knowledge transfer, education, and ultimately adoption of beneficial management practices:

- Berkowitz (2017) organized a symposium called Wicked Problems in Ecology Teaching and Learning that dealt with education itself as a wicked problem. Demystifying the SEP is such a problem.
- Online learning including adult education, professional continuing education, webinars, YouTube "how tos," seminars, and forums have become commonplace in society. These methods have great potential for informing stakeholders. But presentation of information alone is not sufficient. Interaction among stakeholders is necessary for comprehension and practice (McKenzie-Mohr, 2011).
- New presentation techniques for faculty, researchers, the public, extension agents, outreach managers, and policy decision makers must become part of professional training. The assumption here is that most scientists are poorly equipped to listen to and directly communicate with land managers. This model is based on "train the trainers."
- New methods for faculty, researchers, and extension personnel to actively promote critical thinking, rationality, and fact-based decision making to openly and transparently address problems are needed. Identifying where reliable knowledge comes from and how to use it is part of this need.
- Humanizing faculty, researchers, and extension agents is critical. Some are ranchers and farmers and professionally have strong ties to agriculture, forestry, and ranching – they aren't them; they are us. Concentrating on expertise and actual experience can reinforce this understanding.
- The public needs to be informed that most bureaucrats in agency headquarters are people who have been transferred from the field to regional centers or governmental centers such as the Washington DC area. Agency personnel have been chosen as the "best and brightest" based on their qualifications and records of achievements. They are, with few exceptions, well trained, experienced, dedicated, and trustworthy.

- Scientists need to continue upgrading and developing conceptual and mathematical models and training more systems ecologists who can go beyond the science and technology and address the needs for science implementation.

13.4.5 Collaboration with Social, Behavioral, Learning, and Marketing Sciences

Gaining acceptance of good ecosystem and social science in developing beneficial management innovations needed by private and public land managers and policy makers is critical. To accomplish acceptance, collaboration and mutual learning among systems ecologists, social, behavioral, learning, and marketing scientists and professionals will be required. Collaborative research is needed to learn how to bring these disparate professions together to solve problems and facilitate acceptance of science and beneficial management innovations (see Section 13.3.2). All collaborators must learn to listen and provide feedback to one another.

13.4.6 Data and Knowledge Archiving, Mining, and Interpretation

Anyone exploring wicked environmental/societal problems learns immediately that the amount of data and information available is overwhelming. Finding, sorting, organizing, and interpreting data sets, publications, and modeling results is a "hit or miss" effort at best. Concepts and technologies that manage massive amounts of data which tie systems ecology and knowledge acquisition to wicked problems are needed now. Examples of the need are collaborations described in this chapter, Chapter 10, and *Environmental Science* (2018).

Big data is referred to by Hampton et al. (2013) as large amounts of data not readily handled by the usual data tools. Big data require new kinds of data infrastructures that tie together partners and their data in ways which creates new avenues for data discovery, data management, and interoperability including machine-to-machine services. It is expected that all data, code, and other research products are findable, accessible, interoperable, and reusable (Wilkinson et al., 2016). Data sharing makes research data and findings more freely accessible for long-term archiving and mining in the future. If data access and reuse are to be successful, science must pioneer the development of infrastructures that support the work of researchers and data managers with data. Data infrastructures that are strategic and not ad hoc, coherent and interoperable across organizations, and reliable and sustainable, hold the potential to make available not only freely accessible data, but additional digital capabilities such as data visualization and analytics to a wide range of research participants and stakeholders. Data infrastructure can tie together the multiple venues of scientific activities from individuals and laboratories to research centers, and will allow the addition of new projects as needed. Such benefits are especially needed to answer integrative research questions about the patterns that exist and the processes that operate at more than one scale across space, time, and organizations, which can be done by integrating smaller data sets into larger, heterogeneous ones (Peters et al., 2014). Significant funding and innovations will be required to address these data and knowledge needs.

13.4.7 Innovations in Land Management

Adoption of beneficial innovations in cooperative land management and policy making may be the most critical needs confronting twenty-first-century environmental and natural resource challenges. The problems discussed in this chapter and throughout the book require good policies, good governance, and many landowners and managers working together for resolution. Accomplishing this need means applying the best science available, gaining the trust of stakeholders, sharing knowledge, and assuming that all stakeholders are smart people even though some barriers interfere with solutions. New methods to persuade obstinate landowners and managers to adopt new beneficial management practices are needed.

13.5 Summary

Many environmental and natural resource challenges have either been resolved or made more tractable through traditional empirical research and relatively well-known modeling approaches. These challenges include basic understanding of biogeochemical cycles, hydrologic cycles, mechanics of erosion and sedimentation, and population dynamics. Gaps need to be filled, but the basic science addressing these challenges is available. The real-world, large-scale, long-term, complex challenges (wicked problems) involving institutional interactions and many stakeholders are in the realm of the SEP that is based on resolving problems (Figure 13.9). The role of the SEP in forecasting and acting on future

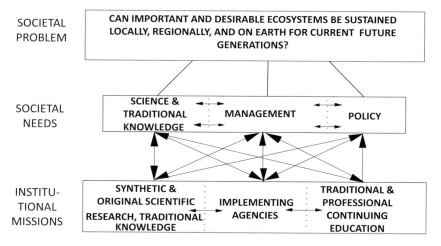

SOCIETAL PROBLEM

SOCIETAL NEEDS

INSTITUTIONAL MISSIONS

Figure 13.9 Ideal relationship of science and traditional knowledge, based on facts and evidence, management, and policy sectors in addressing societal problems, issues, and goals. In a perfect world, the arrows representing knowledge sharing between the science, management, and policy sectors would be transparent and interactive. To accomplish the ideal state, many research, outreach, and education institutions must contribute reliable knowledge to policy makers and management agencies.

management alternatives is critical for achieving sustainability of important and desirable ecosystems.

Confronting future challenges using the SEP requires "breakthroughs" in co-design of research (Moser, 2016); scientific discovery; knowledge acquisition and transfer; co-design of science education and engagement; and the adoption of "beneficial management practices" by land managers and practitioners.

Public and private rangelands, forests, and agricultural lands occupy the vast majority of the Earth's land surface. These lands are managed by farmers, ranchers, foresters, and rangeland managers. Rural private land managers (farmers and ranchers) and public lands managers are a focus of this chapter because rural lands throughout the world are the keys to resolving many of the Earth's wicked problems. These problems require collective actions by many individuals for resolution and they require access to reliable information, capability and willingness to learn, and propensity to adopt new ideas. These requirements are greatly influenced by values, beliefs, and cultural norms among land managers.

Individual or personal values often attributed to ranchers and farmers include: rural lifestyle choice, a strong work ethic, honesty, independence, self-reliance, religion, environmental awareness and land stewardship, willingness to help neighbors, and tolerance (see Appendix 13.1). Vanclay (2004) lists some 26 values of importance to farmers and ranchers.

Cultural norms are collections of personal values, beliefs, and attitudes adopted by communities. Common cultural norms include adherence to traditions (We've always done it this way) as a means of framing traditional values with modern knowledge, technology, and societal aspirations and benefits. Cultural norms encompass the degree of willingness to *look beyond one's fence line or personal sphere of influence* and attitudes about *collaboration for greater community good*. The willingness to look beyond one's current community and generation and consider the impacts of today's management activities and cultural norms on neighboring or distant communities and future generations is vital.

Some individual values, beliefs, and cultural norms represent barriers to achieving the resolution of many environmental/societal challenges (see Appendix 13.1). Overcoming the barriers to adoption of beneficial innovations caused by adherence to dogmatic cultural norms and ideologies by managers is essential when dealing with large-scale challenges such as carbon sequestration, water allocation, water quality, habitat fragmentation, and endangered species. These challenges require collaborative and coordinated management of public and private lands by many individuals within landscapes, watersheds, regions, and globally. Overcoming these barriers is a wicked problem that must be solved. "No man is an island."

Appendix 13.1 Individual Values, Beliefs, and Cultural Norms as Barriers to Ecosystem Resilience and Sustainability – A Rant

The focus of this discussion is on some rural farmers and ranchers in the western United States who embrace values, beliefs, and cultural norms detrimental to wider local-to-global communities and, indeed, often their own well-being. However, similar thoughts can be developed for other groups throughout the world who embrace similar views (see Box 13.2).

Lifestyle Choices

A core value expressed by rural peoples, whether ranchers and farmers in developed countries, indigenous persons such as Native Americans, Turkana herders in Africa, or nomads in Mongolia is the desire to maintain

Box 13.2 *Personal observations*

The ideas presented in Appendix 13.1 are those of the senior editor (Robert G. Woodmansee) who is not in any way shape or form an expert in social, behavioral, learning, or marketing sciences. However, as a farmer, an ecosystem scientist and educator, and observer of rural lifestyles for almost eight decades of living, I recognize the need for changing landowner and manager attitudes about adopting new management practices for the benefit not only for themselves but for society as a whole.

My experience with rural lifestyles began during my youth growing up on a farm in central New Mexico in the 1940s and 1950s. The Great American Drought of the 1950s dominated the environment. My family's farm was within poor farming and ranching cultures where the dominant culture was Hispanic descending from Spanish colonization in the sixteenth and seventeenth centuries. The Hispanic culture was superimposed on the Native American Pueblo culture dating back to thirteenth and fourteenth centuries. These Pueblo people were probably climate refugees who migrated to the Rio Grande River following the drought-induced collapse of the Anasazi cultures in western America. The next migration came in the late nineteenth century following the American Civil War when "white" people of Northern and Western European descent moved into the American West following the conquest of hostile tribes of Native Americans. Our concepts of the "western" or "cowboy" lifestyle originated among these people. The final migration into central New Mexico that influenced my upbringing were the "white" people who were environmental refugees from drought-stricken areas of the United States during the Great American "Dust Bowl" in the 1930s. Many of these people adopted the western lifestyle. Friends from all these cultures were classmates.

Inherent in all these cultures was a sense of self-sufficiency, self-reliance, and culturally proclaimed expertise in land and water management. Every group knew that weather, water, and fertilizer somehow made plants and animals grow and reproduce. The Pueblo and Hispanic peoples were successful, by their standards, for centuries because they knew how to manage their land and water based on traditional knowledge or "that's how they have always done it." The later white settlers had no traditional knowledge base for managing lands in arid western America. They generally made a mess of their management of the newly colonized lands. Had it not been for programs funded by the federal government, most would have failed as many did.

After leaving the farm and discovering "ecology" as an undergraduate in biology and master's degree student in plant ecology, I started learning about primary and secondary production in ecological systems and integrating how and why plants and animals interact. Ecology is a wonderful way to explain how the natural world works. I also began to learn how mismanagement of ecosystems can lead to disastrous consequences. Only after entering my PhD program in 1969 in systems ecology and soils at Colorado State University and joining NREL's Grassland Ecosystem Model (ELM) modeling team as a postdoc did I learn that knowledge and expertise about the natural world, while essential, it is not enough to explain ecosystem functioning, especially when humans are introduced as components of those systems. Those discoveries as an ecosystem scientist and systems ecologist 50 years later have led me to the world view expressed in this book. The book, co-edited with John C. Moore, Dennis S. Ojima, and Laurie Richards, is intended to lead to better understanding of local-to-global ecosystems and how to develop better ways of dealing with our uncertain ecological future.

I have borrowed liberally from the work of others and attempted to integrate their insights with my experience to synthesize ideas about overcoming the barriers impeding the transfer of knowledge and adoption of beneficial management practices. Yes, I am also guilty of "cognitive bias."[5] As with other ignorant people (see Section 13.2.5), I can identify problems and even scope out what might to be done to address them, but I struggle with how to solve or resolve wicked problems involving individual and group values, beliefs, cultural norms, and other barriers to cooperative actions. Hence, I call for more integration of systems ecology and ecosystem science with the social, behavioral, organizational, learning, and marketing sciences to confront the barriers.

The speculations in this appendix are based on my life experience as a farmer, rancher, systems ecologist, researcher, academician in the Range Science Department and College of Natural Resources, outdoorsman, husband, father, and ordinary retired person dealing with real human issues in rural communities of the American West.

---

[5] https://en.wikipedia.org/wiki/Cognitive_bias.

their current lifestyle or "way of life." Many people struggle with recon-
ciling their lifestyle choices and the reality of encroachment of external
cultures, technologies, and other modern influences on their way of life.
They are confronted with unprecedented changes in their environments
brought about by television, access to the internet and digital technology,
expanding transportation networks, changes in land ownership and governance, access to social services and medical care, and perceptions of
better lives and education for their children. A key fear shared by many
is losing their culture, livelihoods, communities, and indeed their values.
Some responses to these fears may be expressed as the stages of grief
(denial, anger, bargaining, depression, acceptance) when confronting loss,
as described by Kubler-Ross (1969) and Wegscheider-Cruse (1987).

Lifestyles and perceived roles in society are often expressed in physical
appearance. In the American West for example, some men and boys
view themselves as heros and icons of a wholesome American society and
dress with big "cowboy" hats (outside and often inside buildings), boots,
big belt buckles, western-cut clothing, and snuff can ware-marks on their
hip pockets. Their clothing represents them as icons in their popular
culture but people outside the culture have a less heroic view based on
appearance. People outside the culture often view them as exhibits in the
"Museum of the American West" leading pack trains of "city slickers" on
"dude ranches." Others view them as hillbillys, hicks, country bumpkins,
and backward. Similar descriptions can be built about rural peoples and
other people identifying with specific stereotypic groups throughout the
world, for example environmentalists, gang members, and tourists.

A major challenge facing the environment and natural resources is
recognizing that many of the problems outlined in Chapters 2 and 13 are
dependent on rural land (ecosystem) managers and their lifestyle choices
for resolution. Adoption of the best possible management practices by
collaborating land managers will be vital for resolving many of the real-
world, complex problems. Communication and cooperation among all
stakeholders will be required. Unfortunately, communication is often
hindered by dress, appearance, use of language, and preexisting stereo-
types. The gap between communities must be bridged to accomplish
vital individual and societal goals.

Strong Work Ethic

Hard work is part of the rural way of life. Demonstration of this ethic can
often be seen as calluses on hands, suntans, soiled hats, etc., all parts of the

uniform of the rural way of life. This value is laudable except when used to judge the worth of other people with different lifestyles or softer occupations, for example those bureaucrats and academicians "who don't know what work is," environmentalists, tourists, and lawyers.

Honesty

Honesty is an expressed value within most rural cultures. Most individuals try to be honest, at least within their communities where social feedbacks curb negative behaviors. However, hypocrisy intervenes with acceptance of lying and distortions of facts and truth by politicians and other thought leaders.

Independence and Self-Reliance

Many rural people express independence as a value yet in practice they are "herd followers" (McKenzie-Mohr, 2011). According to the theory of concept and technology adoption cycles, inventors, innovators, and early adopters may be relatively independent but the majority within a community are followers, especially regarding beliefs and ideologies.

Rural dwellers must be relatively self-reliant. It is in their own self-interest to be so. Many in the rural United States are ardent believers in property rights and dismiss the concept of the rights of broader communities. Yet farmers and ranchers are dependent on agro-business and industrial support, government financial and infrastructure support for roads and electricity, price supports for crops, schools, social services, Medicare and Medicaid, and political and policy support. In addition, many ranchers also get government support for fencing, water development, irrigation, water management, and below cost pricing, grazing allotment management, lower than market grazing fees, and now communication services. Often, they ascribe to the concept of pay me (incentives) to do the right thing but they don't acknowledge that the cost of adoption of new beneficial management practices may cost taxpayers via government incentive programs.

Religion

Lofty religious traditions, beliefs, and practices are common in rural communities. However, these communities also face the challenges of mental health issues, teen pregnancy rates, venereal disease rates, opioid use and abuse, alcohol abuse, and other illicit drug use that are as high or higher in rural America than in urban and suburban sectors of society (CDC, 2018). Hypocrisy and bigotry are also common among some rural people and communities.

Land Stewardship

A prominent value listed by rural people is an acute awareness of the environment and land stewardship. This may be true for individual land managers and perceptions of their personal impacts on the land, but maybe not for the broader environment. Comparing the mission statements of federal and state agencies, nongovernmental organizations (NGOs), and professional scientific societies with commodity producer groups reveals key distinctions (see Box 13.3). The mission statements of federal land management agencies, professional scientific societies, and NGOs emphasize conservation of resources, ecosystems, biodiversity, and environmental sustainability in addition to production, profit (economics), and lifestyle. Mission statements of ranching and farming organizations emphasize production, profit, lifestyle, and political advocacy.

Speaking as individuals, farmers and ranchers may argue that their core values of are the same as federal land management agencies, NGOs, and professional scientific organizations. All are looking for a means of taking care of the environment and the land. Rural land managers are focused on their local experience and properties, while federal and state managers, NGOs, and scientists are focused on longer timelines, larger areas, and broader communities. Why don't the producer groups recognize the environment or the broader citizenry in their mission statements? Rural groups may not appreciate any value in supporting activities that help outside of their local focus, even when incentives are offered by government agencies (see Box 13.4).

Willingness to Help Neighbors

Willingness to help neighbors is another prominent value among rural communities. This value has definite survival advantages as resources and services are often limited in rural areas. The scope of interest may be limited to the people in a community who know each other, and the area used and shared by that particular community. Their perspectives may not extend to a broader universe. Collaboration for the greater social good may be less valued. For example, collective community actions

Box 13.3 *Key elements of mission and vision statements of selected scientific societies, NGOs, governmental agencies, and farmer/rancher groups*

In what follows, note the lack of reference to environment, conservation, sustainability, public health, or safety in rancher/farmer groups.

Scientific Societies
Society for Range Management[6]

- Study, conserve, manage, and sustain resources of rangelands.
- Provide leadership for stewardship based on ecological principles.

Society of American Foresters[7]

- Advance sustainable management of forest resources through science, education, and technology.
- Use knowledge, skills, and conservation ethic to ensure the continued health, integrity of forests.
- Manage forests to benefit society in perpetuity.

The Wildlife Society[8]

- Sustain wildlife populations and habitats through science-based management and conservation.
- Represent wildlife conservation and management and ensure sustainable wildlife populations in healthy ecosystems.

Nongovernmental Organizations
The Nature Conservancy[9]

- Protect nature, for people today and future generations.
- Conserve the lands and waters on which all life depends.
- Conserve biodiversity.

---

[6] https://rangelands.org/about/.
[7] www.eforester.org/Main/About/History/Main/About/History.aspx?hkey=f112ee86-0f07-4cca-b342-b9d4bca0f535.
[8] https://wildlife.org/history-and-mission/.
[9] www.nature.org/en-us/about-us/who-we-are/our-mission-vision-and-values/.

Sierra Club[10]

- Protect the wild places of the earth.
- Promote the responsible use of the Earth's ecosystems and resources.
- Protect and restore the quality of the natural and human environment.

Governmental Agencies

USDA Natural Resource Conservation Service[11]

- Provide resources to farmers and landowners to aid them with conservation.
- Ensure productive lands in harmony with a healthy environment.

USDA Forest Service[12]

- Sustain the health, diversity, and productivity of the nation's forests and grasslands.
- Meet the needs of present and future generations.

USDI Bureau of Land Management[13]

- Sustain the health, diversity, and productivity of public lands.
- Manage public lands for the use and enjoyment of present and future generations.

Ranchers and Farmers

Colorado Cattlemen's Association[14]

- Serves as the principal voice and advocate for Colorado beef production.
- Advance the legacy and viability of beef production.
- Ensure a dynamic and profitable industry that promotes growth and opportunity for future generations.

Colorado Wool Growers Association[15]

- Protect the Colorado sheep industry through the management of legislative, regulatory, and policy issues.

---

[10] www.sierraclub.org/policy.
[11] www.nrcs.usda.gov/wps/portal/nrcs/main/national/people/.
[12] www.fs.fed.us/about-agency.   [13] www.blm.gov/about/our-mission.
[14] www.coloradocattle.org/about.
[15] www.coloradosheep.org/colo–wool–growers–.html.

American Farm Bureau Federation[16]

- Enhance and strengthen the lives of rural Americans.
- Build strong, prosperous agricultural communities.

Box 13.4 *USDA NRCS uses Landscape Conservation Initiatives*

The NRCS uses Landscape Conservation Initiatives to accelerate the benefits of voluntary conservation programs, such as cleaner water and air, healthier soil, and enhanced wildlife habitat.[17] NRCS conservation programs help agricultural producers improve the environment while maintaining a vibrant agricultural sector.

These initiatives are intended to enhance locally driven process to better address nationally and regionally important conservation goals that transcend localities. They build on locally led efforts and partnerships and they're based on science. Through the initiatives, the NRCS and its partners coordinate the delivery of assistance where it can have the most impact. Where applicable, the NRCS works with regulators to help producers get predictability for their use of voluntary conservation systems or practices, giving them peace of mind and allowing them to sustain agricultural production in the future.

These landscape-level efforts have seen success across the country. From the removal of streams from the federal impaired streams list to the determination not to list the greater sage-grouse and New England cottontail, the NRCS's work with producers benefits wildlife, natural resources, and agricultural operations across the country.

---

needed to mitigate and adapt to climate change, improve water quality in stream or river basins, protect endangered species, and biodiversity may not be viewed as important.

Accepting of Other Viewpoints and Tolerance

Many rural inhabitants list tolerance as an important value. This is an interesting outcome because personal experience suggests that some

---

[16] www.fb.org/about/overview.

[17] www.nrcs.usda.gov/wps/portal/nrcs/main/national/programs/initiatives/.

individuals in rural communities express excessive bigotry such as negative labeling of other people and groups: greenies, environmentalists, ecologists, liberal ilk, leftists, scientists, academics, tree-huggers, various racial slurs, and "them and those." Other intolerant notions are science skepticism and denial; anti-intellectualism; anti-elitism; and anti-government, anti-regulation, and anti-tax ideology. Unfortunately, truly tolerant individuals in the same communities are often too polite to challenge those expressing intolerant views. A very interesting insight to this issue is found in Guilbeault et al. (2018).

Science skepticism and denial. Something that is often heard are statements like "I don't trust scientists and academics who don't know anything about real life – they just sit in their ivory towers and think." The subtexts of this idea might be, "science might yield knowledge I don't want to hear about my management practices or life style" or "science may question issues of beliefs, faith and ideology," or put another way religious fundamentalism asserts "science is against the teachings of God, Jesus, and the Bible." Katharine Hayhoe, a devout Christian and climate change believer, argues that the religious argument may be a shill for underlying conservative political ideology (Hayhoe, 2017). Furthermore, she argues that this position may be unique to the United States. One other very important subtext might be, "I don't understand the science and technology associated with new ideas and I am too embarrassed to admit it."

Anti-intellectualism, elitism, and expertise. Many faculty members, research scientists, agency land managers, and extension agents are professionally tied to farming and ranching and are or have been ranchers and farmers themselves. Many came from rural backgrounds and have gained professional credentials as experts through learning, hard work, and achievement. They happen to be employed by universities, federal or state research agencies, or other organizations dedicated to learning. They have earned elite status! *Elitism is not a dirty word.* No one would question the elite status of Seal Team 6, the Marine Corp Band, Tom Brady, LeBron James, Albert Einstein, Yogi Berra, Baxter Black, or Dolly Parton. They are elite because of their achievements not because of inheritance. So it is with most professional scientists and academicians who have become experts and are among the elite.

Unfortunately, many ranchers and farmers have declared themselves "experts" because they (1) have farmed or ranched one or a few pieces of property for a long period of time and feel they know the best way to manage it, and (2) have access to enormous amounts of information, both good and bad, as described in Section 13.2. The self-appointment of oneself as an expert rather than consulting with and learning from persons who have established credentials is discussed in *The Death of Expertise: The Campaign Against Established Knowledge and Why it Matters* (Nichols, 2017). Certainly, some ranchers and farmers have knowledge that can be helpful in scientific deliberations, but declaration of oneself as an "expert" based on local experience can be a fool's folly.

Anti-government, anti-regulation, anti-tax ideology. Among the most anti-social and counterproductive "values" held by some rural peoples is the notion that the government and its regulations and taxes are abhorrent. It matters not that most regulations and taxes exist for good and beneficial reasons. How often have we heard "don't care, don't like the government, and I want them out of my life." In the "Theory of Stupid" discussed by Cipolla (1987), the most absurd state of stupid is when one commits an action (or inaction) that brings harm to someone else and harms or brings no benefit to oneself. "No man is an island."

References

APS. (2007). *Tackling Wicked Problems: A Policy Perspective*. The Australian Public Service Commission. www.enablingchange.com.au/wickedproblems.pdf (accessed August 13, 2020).

Australia Land Management. (2011). Land use and management. https://soe .environment.gov.au/theme/land/topic/land-use-and-management (accessed August 13, 2020).

Balint, P. J., Stewart, R. E., Desai, A., and Walters, L. C. (2011). *Wicked Environmental Problems*. Washington, DC: Island Press.

Berkowitz, A. R. (2017). *Wicked Problems in Ecology Teaching and Learning: Biodiversity, Material Cycling, Ecosystem Services and Climate Change*. Ecological Society of America. https://eco.confex.com/eco/2017/webprogram/ Session12907.html (accessed August 13, 2020).

CDC. (2018). Center for Disease Control and Prevention. www.cdc.gov.

Cheruvelil, K. S., and Soranno, P. A. (2018). Data-intensive ecological research is catalyzed by open science and team science. *BioScience*, 68(10), 813–22.

Cipolla, C. M. (1987). The basic laws of human stupidity. *Whole Earth Review* (Spring), 2–7. http://harmful.cat-v.org/people/basic-laws-of-human-stupidity/.

Diederen P., van Meijl, H., Wolters, A., and Bijak, K. (2003). Innovation adoption in agriculture: Innovators, early adopters and laggards. *Cahiers d'économie et sociologie rurales*, 67, 29–50. http://ageconsearch.umn.edu/bitstream/205937/ 2/67–29–50.pdf.

Digital Marketing. (2018). The 5 customer segments of technology adoption. Digital Marketing. https://ondigitalmarketing.com/learn/odm/foundations/5-cus tomer-segments-technology-adoption/

Easterday, K., Paulson, T., DasMohapatra, P., Alagona, P., Feirer, S., and Kelly, M. (2018). From the field to the cloud: A review of three approaches to sharing historical data from field stations using principles from data science. *Frontiers of Environmemental Science*, 6, 88. https://pdfs.semanticscholar.org/fecb/ ef6cba5198836bfa80f38af843c3ffe0a5b1.pdf.

Environmental Science. (2018). Big data: Explaining its uses to environmental sciences. *Environmental Science*. www.environmentalscience.org/data-science-big-dataFAO. (2018). Water-energy-food-nexus. The Food and Agriculture Organization of the United Nations. www.fao.org/energy/water-food-energy-nexus/en/.

Forrester, J. W. (1968). *Principles of Systems*. Cambridge, MA: Wright-Allen Press.

Gewin, V. (2016). An open mind on open data. *Nature*, 529, 117–19.

Grafton, R. Q., Pittock, J., and Davis, R. (2013). Global insights into water resources, climate change and governance. *Nature Climate Change*, 3, 315–21.

Guilbeaulta, D., Beckera, J., and Centola, D. (2018). Social learning and partisan bias in the interpretation of climate trends. *Proceedings of the National Academy of Science USA*, 115(39), 9714–19.

Hampton, S. E., Anderson, S. S., Bagby, S. C., et al. (2015). The Tao of open science for ecology. *Ecosphere*, 6(7), 1–13.

Hampton, S. E., Strasser, C. A., Tewksbury, J. J., et al. (2013). Big data and the future of ecology. *Frontiers in Ecology and the Environment*, 11(3), 156–62.

Hayhoe, K. (2017). Bridging the faith-science divide. Got Science podcast. Episode 8: Union of Concerned Scientists. www.ucsusa.org/bridging-faith-science-divide#.W7PCnS-ZNTY.

Holling, C. S. (1978). *Adaptive Environmental Assessment and Management*. New York: John Wiley & Sons.

Kanowski, P., and McKenzie, N. (2011). Land: Land use and management. In *Australia State of the Environment 2011*, ed. Australian Government Department of the Environment and Energy, Canberra. https://soe .environment.gov.au/theme/land/topic/land-use-and-management.

Kubler-Ross, H. (1969). *On Death and Dying*. New York: Scribner.

Lewis, C. S. (1955). *The Magician's Nephew*. New York: Harper Collins Children's Books.

McKenzie-Mohr, D. (2011). *Fostering Sustainable Behavior: An Introduction to Community-Based Social Marketing*. Gabriola Island, BC: New Society Publishers.

McLeod, S. (2018). Maslow's hierarchy of needs. *SimplePsychology* www .simplypsychology.org/maslow.html.

Meadows, D. H. (2008). *Thinking in Systems: A Primer*. White River Junction, VT: Chelsea Green Publishing.

Mitchell, M., Griffith, R., Ryan, P., et al. (2014). Applying resilience thinking to natural resource management through a "planning-by-doing" framework. *Society and Natural Resources*, 27, 299–314.

Montague, C. L. (2016). Systems ecology. *Oxford Bibliographies*. www.oxford bibliographies.com/view/document/obo-9780199830060/obo-9780199830060–0078.xml.

Moore, G. A. (2014). *Crossing the Chasm: Marketing and Selling Disruptive Products to Mainstream Customers*, 3rd edn. New York: Harper-Collins.

Moser, S. (2016). Can science on transformation transform science? Lessons from co-design. *Current Opinion in Environmental Sustainability*, 20, 106–15.

National Research Council. (1995). *On the Full and Open Exchange of Scientific Data.* Washington, DC: The National Academies Press. https://doi.org/10.17226/18769.

Nichols, T. M. (2017). *The Death of Expertise: The Campaign against Established Knowledge and Why it Matters.* Oxford: Oxford University Press.

Ojima, D. S., and Corell, R. W. (2009). Managing grassland ecosystems under global environmental change: Developing strategies to meet challenges and opportunities of global change. In *Farming with Grass: Achieving Sustainable Mixed Agricultural Landscapes*, ed. A. J. Franzluebbers. Ankeny, IA: Soil and Water Conservation Society, 146–55

Pannell, D. J., Marshall, G. R., Barr, N., Curtis, A., Vanclay, F., and Wilkinson, R. (2006). Understanding and promoting adoption of conservation practices by rural landholders. *Australian Journal of Experimental Agriculture*, 46(11), 1407–24.

Peer, L., and Green, A. (2012). Building an open data repository for a specialized research community: Process, challenges and lessons. *International Journal of Digital Curation*, 7(1), 151–62.

Peters, D. P., Loescher, H. W., SanClements, M. D., and Havstad, K. M. (2014). Taking the pulse of a continent: Expanding site-based research infrastructure for regional-to continental-scale ecology. *Ecosphere*, 5(3), 1–23.

Pomeroy, R. (2016). The basic laws of human stupidity. RealClearScience. www.realclearscience.com/blog/2016/09/the_basic_laws_of_human_stupidity.html.

(2019). What is stupidity? RealClearScience. www.realclearscience.com/blog/2019/03/02/what_is_stupidity.html.

Resilience Alliance. (2018). Resilience Alliance. www.resalliance.org (accessed June 18, 2018).

Riebsame, W., and Woodmansee, R. (1995). Mapping common ground on public Rangelands. In *Let the People Judge*, ed. J. Echeverria and R. B. Eby. Washington, DC: Island Press, 69–81.

Rittel, H. W., and Webber, M. M. (1973). Dilemmas in a general theory of planning. *Policy Sciences*, 4(2), 155–69. www.cc.gatech.edu/fac/ellendo/rittel/rittel-dilemma.pdf.

Rogers, E. M. (2003). *Diffusion of Innovations*, 5th edn. New York: Simon and Schuster.

Sohrabi, Z., and Zarghi, N. (2015). Evidence-based management: An overview. *Creative Education*, 6, 1776–81.

Tabara, J. and Chabay, I. (2013). Coupling human information and knowledge systems with social–ecological systems change: Reframing research, education, and policy for sustainability. *Environmental Science and Policy*, 28, 71–81.

Tetard, F., and Collan, M. (2007). Lazy user theory: A dynamic model to understand user selection of products and services. Proceedings of the 42nd Hawaii International Conference on System Sciences. IEEE Computer Society. www.computer.org/csdl/proceedings/hicss/2009/3450/00/09–13–01.pdf.

Thaler, R., and Sunstine, C. R. (2009). *Nudge: Improving Decisions About Health, Wealth, and Happiness.* New York: Penguin Books.

UNMEA. (2005). Millennium Ecosystem Assessment, United Nations. www
.millenniumassessment.org/en/index.html.

UNWater. (2018). Water, food, and energy. UN-Water, the United Nations. www
.unwater.org/water-facts/water-food-and-energy/.

USDA Farm Bill. (2018). Agriculture Improvement Act of 2018. Washington, DC:
US Department of Agriculture. www.ers.usda.gov/agriculture-improvement-
act-of-2018-highlights-and-implications/.

Values. (2010). Values. Philosophy of Nature. https://physicalspace.wordpress.com/
2010/10/.

Van Dyne, G. (1969). *The Ecosystem Concept in Natural Resource Management*. New
York: Academic Press.

Vanclay, F (2004). Social principles for agricultural extension to assist in the promotion of natural resource management. *Australian Journal of Experimental
Agriculture*, 44(3), 213–22 www.researchgate.net/profile/Frank_Vanclay/publi
cation/228555077.

Waide, R. B., Brunt, J. W., and Servilla, M. S. (2017). Demystifying the landscape
of ecological data repositories in the United States. *BioScience*, 67(12), 1044–51.

Walker, B., and Salt, D. (2006). *Resilience Thinking: Sustaining Ecosystems and People in
a Changing World*. Washington, DC: Island Press.

Weathers, K. C., Groffman, P. M., Van Dolah, E., et al. (2016). Frontiers in
ecosystem ecology from a community perspective: The future is boundless
and bright. *Ecosystems*, 19, 753.

Wegscheider-Cruse, S. (1987). *Choice Making*. Deerfield Beach, FL: Health
Communications, Inc.

Weichselgartner, J., and Kasperson, R. (2010). Barriers in the science–policy–
practice interface: Toward a knowledge-action-system in global environmental
change research. *Global Environmental Change*, 20, 266–77.

Wikipedia. (2018a). Wicked problems. https://en.wikipedia.org/wiki/Wicked_
problem.

(2018b). Big data. https://en.wikipedia.org/wiki/Big_data.

(2019). Critical thinking. https://en.wikipedia.org/wiki/Critical_thinking.

Wilkinson, M. D., Dumontier, M., Aalbersberg, I. J., et al. (2016). The FAIR
Guiding Principles for scientific data management and stewardship. *Scientific
Data*, 3, 160018.

Woo, C. (2010). Religion rejuvenates environmentalism. *The Miami Herald*. http://
fore.yale.edu/news/item/religion-rejuvenates-environmentalism/.

Woodmansee, R. G. (1978). Critique and analyses of the grassland ecosystem model
ELM. In *Grassland Simulation Model*, ed. G. S. Innis. New York: Springer-
Verlag.

Index